Henry Parkes

Speeches on Various Occasions

Connected With the Public Affairs of New South Wales, 1848-1874

Henry Parkes

Speeches on Various Occasions
Connected With the Public Affairs of New South Wales, 1848-1874

ISBN/EAN: 9783337323448

Printed in Europe, USA, Canada, Australia, Japan

Cover: Foto ©ninafisch / pixelio.de

More available books at **www.hansebooks.com**

SPEECHES

ON VARIOUS OCCASIONS CONNECTED WITH THE PUBLIC
AFFAIRS OF NEW SOUTH WALES
1848—1874

BY

HENRY PARKES

WITH AN INTRODUCTION
BY DAVID BLAIR

Melbourne
GEORGE ROBERTSON, LITTLE COLLINS STREET WEST
SYDNEY 125 NEW PITT STREET
LONDON: LONGMANS, GREEN, AND CO
MDCCCLXXVI

PREFATORY NOTE.

THE substance of the speeches here collected has been gathered from various sources, but chiefly from printed reports in the local newspapers; the earlier ones from the *Empire*, and most of the later ones from the *Sydney Morning Herald*. In two instances special reports were taken. All the reports have undergone more or less of verbal revision.

It is to be added that the introduction was written without any co-operation with Mr. Parkes. It is an entirely independent composition. As the volume was being printed in Melbourne, Mr. Parkes requested me, as a friend, to see the sheets through the Press, and to write an introduction. On the ground of having had some personal acquaintance with that gentleman five-and-twenty years ago, I complied with this request; but of Mr. Parkes personally, or of New South Wales politics, during all that time, I knew nothing directly. The introduction is based wholly on the speeches.

D. B.

TABLE OF CONTENTS.

PAGE

I. ELECTIVE FRANCHISE—
Speech at Public Meeting in Sydney, Jan. 22nd 1849 ... 1
,, ,, ,, Sept. 1st 1857 ... 76
,, on Self-registration of Voters, in Legislative Assembly, March 5th 1873 370

II. TRANSPORTATION QUESTION—
Prefatory Note 3
Speech at Public Meeting in Sydney, June 11th 1849 ... 4
,, ,, ,, June 18th 1849 ... 5
,, ,, ,, Sept. 16th 1850 ... 7
,, ,, ,, April 3rd 1851 ... 9
,, ,, ,, April 6th 1852 ... 10
,, ,, ,, June 30th 1852 ... 14

III. CONSTITUTION ACT—
Prefatory Note 17
Speech at Public Meeting in Sydney, Aug. 15th 1853 ... 18
,, ,, ,, Sept. 5th 1853 ... 25

IV. ELECTION SPEECHES—
Election for Sydney, May 1st 1854 38

V. AGRICULTURE—
Speech in Legislative Council, July 3rd 1855 43

VI. TAXATION AND FREE TRADE—
Prefatory Note... 49
Speech in Legislative Council, July 5th 1855 ... 50
,, ,, ,, July 25th 1855 ... 51
,, on *Ad Valorem* Duties, in Legislative Assembly, Dec. 20th 1865 197
,, on Border Duties, at Albury, May 15th 1866 ... 202
,, at Public Dinner at Albury, May 15th 1866 ... 206
,, on Border Customs Duties, in Legislative Assembly, June 19th 1872 339
Speech on Policy of Protection, in Legislative Assembly, Oct. 29th 1873 384

VII. EIGHT-HOURS MOVEMENT—
Speech at Meeting of Trades, at Sydney, Nov. 17th 1856 ... 70

VIII. PACIFIC MAIL ROUTE—
Speech in Legislative Assembly, Aug. 6th 1858 86

IX. DEFENCE OF THE COLONIES—
Speech in Legislative Assembly, Dec. 20th 1859 97
,, ,, ,, in reply 109

iv Table of Contents.

X. STATE OF POLITICS— PAGE
Speech at Meeting of E. Sydney Electors, Nov. 29th 1860 ... 112
,, at Meeting of Electors at Kiama, Aug. 10th 1865 ... 181
,, at Public Dinner at Mudgee, July 3rd 1866 ... 209
,, to Working Classes at Mudgee, Aug. 4th 1866 ... 212
,, in defence of Martin Government, in Legislative Assembly, Jan. 10th 1868 259
,, on Coalition of Sir James Martin and Mr. Robertson, at E. Sydney, Feb. 10th 1872 324

XI. LAND QUESTION—
Speech on Price of Land, in Legislative Assembly, March 6th 1861 136

XII. NEW SOUTH WALES AS A FIELD FOR EMIGRATION—
Speech in Town Hall, Derby, Oct. 7th 1861 141
,, Town Hall, Birmingham, Oct. 22nd 1861 ... 148
,, Working Men's College, London, May 17th 1862 ... 154

XIII. FRIENDLESS CHILDREN—
Speech at Annual Meeting of Sydney Ragged School, July 1st 1863 168

XIV. RESPONSIBLE GOVERNMENT—
Speech at Public Dinner, at Braidwood, March 31st 1864 ... 171
,, ,, at Kiama, Aug. 15th 1865 ... 191
,, on Evils of a Weak Government, in Legislative Assembly, April 27th 1870 305
,, on Reform of Legislative Council, in Legislative Assembly, Feb. 13th 1873 351

XV. PUBLIC EDUCATION—
Speech on Public Schools Bill, in Legislative Assembly, Sept. 12th 1866 217
,, on Administration of Public Schools Act, at Dundas, Sept. 4th 1869 276
,, on Progress of Education System, at Liverpool, June 4th 1871 316
,, on State of Public School System in 1873, at West Maitland, Aug. 5th 1873 374

XVI. FEDERATION OF THE COLONIES—
Speech at Melbourne, March 16th 1867 252

XVII. CASE OF THE PRISONER GARDINER—
Speech in the Legislative Assembly, June 3rd 1874 ... 404
A Chapter of History [Appendix A] 438

XVIII. APPOINTMENTS TO MAGISTRACY—
Appendix B 460

XIX. APPOINTMENTS TO CIVIL SERVICE—
Appendix C 462

INTRODUCTION.

THE publication in Australia of a volume of speeches delivered, for the most part, in the Legislature of an Australian colony is an incident that marks the political growth of these communities. It is the first contribution of the kind made to our local literature, although single speeches have been frequently printed for general circulation. The single speech, however, seldom or never forms an addition to the permanent literature of a country: it is at best a fugitive pamphlet, designed to serve a special and transient purpose. But the collected speeches of a statesman who has also established his reputation as a public orator are always a substantial and valuable contribution to the materials for national history. Regarded in that light alone, the present volume may claim the merit of forming an excellent precedent which, it is to be hoped, will lead in time to the publication of many similar volumes. For there can be no reason why political oratory should not be as sedulously cultivated, and held in as high estimation, by the citizens of these young Australian republics as it was amongst the citizens of ancient Greece and Rome, and as it still is in all civilised countries enjoying the blessings of free institutions. In merely literary value it stands high amongst the agencies of civilisation. For what factors would express the worth to the world's heritage of intellectual wealth of the printed speeches of Demosthenes and Cicero, of Burke, Grattan, and Canning? But a still higher value must be assigned to political oratory considered as an agency of popular education. What tests and standards could measure, for example, the direct effect in the diffusion of popular enlightenment on all the manifold topics of national interest of the reported debates in the British House of Commons? Or of the speeches, whether delivered in Parliament or from the public platform, of statesmen such as Mr. Gladstone or Mr. Bright? And, highest of all, the function of political oratory considered as the public exposition of the principles of wise and just and liberal legislation, as the open defence of the true principles of political freedom, and as the fearless advocacy of all that aids in making a nation prosperous and exalted—this function of an intrinsically noble art is of simply inestimable worth, not only to the community for whose benefit it is primarily exercised, but to mankind at large. Its influence for good in this respect is limitless and imperishable. "To do justice to that immortal person"—said Grattan, in his own grand style, of Charles James Fox—" you must not limit your view to his country. His genius was not confined to England: it was seen 3000 miles off, in communicating freedom to the Americans; it was visible, I know not how far off, in ameliorating the condition of the Indian; it was discernible on the coast of Africa, in accomplishing the abolition of the Slave Trade. You are to measure the magnitude of his mind by parallels of latitude."

The period has hardly yet arrived in the growth of the Australian republics when due weight will be given to these considerations. The sentiment of nationality has still to be created amongst us. Or if there be some first faint stirrings of any such sentiment, they are confined to a few individual minds of superior stamp. There never, perhaps, was an English " plantation"—to use the fine old Baconian phrase—which, having a magnificent future before it, certain, and not remote, possessed so dim a forecasting of that future. There is probably less of those ennobling anticipations amongst us than there was amongst the American colonists long prior to their earliest movements towards independence. Nor, let it be observed, is there in the language I am here using any intentional latent reference to the British connexion. The future of the Australian colonies is now, in fact, quite independent of their continued allegiance to the Crown of England. They are separate, independent, and self-governing republics, to the full extent that they would be such if their common connexion with Great Britain were entirely severed. No such immediate and marvellous expansion in population, trade, commerce, and general enterprise, would result from the severance as followed upon the achievement of independence in the American colonies. The simple truth is that the British supremacy here—in so far as it affects the internal development of the several colonies, the growth of a sentiment of Australian nationality, or the republican freedom and simplicity of our institutions—has ceased to be anything more than nominal. The fact reflects glory on the mother-country. When she gave us our freedom, she gave it in amplest measure, and with no grudging hand. May the silken bond that unites the venerated parent and her children in the sunny South prove of asbestine strength and durability! But, although an Australian Colonial Governor keeps constantly a dutiful watch over the interests of the distant Power whose delegate he is, the change to the colony he governs would be quite imperceptible if, to-morrow, his patent of office were to be exchanged for that of first President of an independent Australian Republic.

The absence of the sentiment of nationality, then, is in no degree owing to the presence of the British connexion. It is due, indeed, to far different causes—to the intensity with which individual and purely local interests are regarded, to lurking mutual jealousies amongst the various colonies, and to the littleness of mind and narrowness of view which these engender. A haunting conviction of this littleness and narrowness makes itself felt in every department of our social and political life. It pervades both the common conversation of the marts of business and the debates in the Legislature. It shows itself alike in journalism, literature, and politics. Allusions to such subjects as the federation of the colonies, the creation of an Australian national sentiment, the splendid future awaiting these colonies, or the desirableness of cultivating commercial relations with the populations inhabiting the vast world lying to the northward of our continent, usually evoke no worthier comment than a derisive smile or a whispered remark of "talking to Buncombe." For so far, the mind of the youthful Australian is still left wholly unoccupied by any feeling either of traditionary or of anticipated national greatness.

It is the crowning quality of the speeches contained in the present volume that they are each and all instinct with this feeling in both relations. The speaker glories in being an Englishman, and he equally glories in being an Australian colonist. Genuine home-born loyalty to the land of his birth does not in the least dim his clear perception of the grandeur of the destiny in store for the land of his adoption. In this respect the speeches are not alone superior to, but they hold a place apart from, those of any other Australian politician which I have ever read. There is in all of them that underlying, instinctive sense of national greatness which is so characteristic of the speeches of leading English statesmen, notably of Mr. Gladstone. The immediate subject under discussion may be of the very smallest importance, but the elevating sentiment is always present. It may be the Compound Householder, the Cattle Plague, the dues of the River Weaver, or the Budget for the year : but always the speaker is an English statesman.

The second leading quality of the speeches is the consistent assertion of the genuine principles of republican freedom. From the first speech to the last, alike in 1849 as in 1874, the speaker clearly discerns and lucidly expounds the right relations of the people to the free institutions they

Introduction. ix

now enjoy. What he claimed for them before those institutions came into existence, he vindicated and confirmed by his action when he himself became a popular representative and a responsible Minister of the Crown under the better system. The beginnings of freedom in New South Wales were not favourable to its vigorous growth. The people required educating up to it, and the course of their education is legibly traced out in these speeches. Both courage and ability were required to fulfil the self-imposed mission of the teacher. The small and rigidly exclusive class that, in the earlier days, had monopolised all the political power and social privilege in the colony were indignant at the bare idea of any man from among the people "coming between the wind and their (sham) nobility." Their fixed idea of the only political institutions suitable for the mass of their fellow-colonists was what, in one of the speeches, is caustically but truthfully described as a "Norfolk-Island Government." The Constitution, as they originally framed it, was merely an elaborate machinery for perpetuating the odious monopoly which they held. They dreaded the people and distrusted their capacity for political freedom. A truer, higher, manlier sentiment—"an ampler ether, a diviner air" —breathes through these speeches. The "Norfolk-Island Government" conception is here witheringly exposed and scornfully rejected. Time and the progress of events have abundantly confirmed the correctness, as well as the innate nobleness, of the views herein enforced. Nothing less than the unconditional simplicity of republican equality would have stood for a single month in a community where all men are of the same political rank. But nevertheless it was a hard and strenuous fight for liberty. The leaders in the struggle had to endure much opposition and persecution of a meanly unworthy kind. The old monopolist class— many of them men destitute alike of good birth, breeding, and intellectual culture—were loud in their parrot-cries of "demagogue," "socialist," "revolutionist," and similar cant phrases. The class has passed away, and the cant phrases have dropped out of use; but the enduring victory remains with the faithful friends of popular freedom and social justice. As a record of the main points in the bygone struggle, these speeches may claim to have lasting importance for the people of New South Wales. As a sustained pleading for freedom, they should be held by the colonists invaluable. "The speeches of great orators," says Lieber, "are a fund of wealth for a free people, from which the schoolboy begins to draw when he declaims from his Reader, and which enriches, elevates, and nourishes the souls of the old."

The distinctive quality of statesmanship becomes evident in such speeches as those on Taxation and Free-trade, on the Federation of the Colonies, and especially on Public Education. Measures of this high class embody principles of Political Economy and of Civil Government which, like the axioms of geometry, are of permanent and universal application. A clear apprehension of such principles does not, of itself, demand the statesman's faculty; but that faculty is certainly required for their practical application under given conditions of place, time, and social circumstance. The highest and most difficult function of Legislation lies, not in the large and comprehensive grasp of principles, but in the wise discernment of needful limitations. This truth is beautifully wrought-out in one of Tennyson's earlier poems, unnamed, but evidently addressed to some rising young statesman amongst the Laureate's friends, whom he counsels to "watch what main-currents draw the years"—

"Not clinging to some ancient saw;
Not mastered by some modern term;
Not swift nor slow to change, but firm;
And in its season bring THE LAW."

The familiar stanzas of this finely thoughtful poem were frequently suggested by the perusal of the present volume.

Introduction. xi

The speeches on Taxation and Free-trade in 1855 exhibit a most careful and conscientious study of the writings of John Stuart Mill, and of recent Parliamentary deliverances from leading English statesmen—certainly the very best text-books that a colonial legislator could have chosen for the purpose of forming his own code of principles in relation to Taxation and Public Finance. For several years subsequently those principles were set aside,* and a system of *ad valorem* duties was imposed by Ministries to which Mr. Parkes was hostile; and on his assumption of office, in 1873, one of the first acts of his Government was to repeal the duties, and to simplify the tariff as nearly to the limits of free-trade as existing circumstances would permit. This is an example of true statesmanship. There is, first, the comprehensive grasp of sound principles, gained by patient study, and next there is the prompt embodiment of the same principles in practical legislation when the opportunity arrives. Such sustained consistency of public conduct is, unhappily, not frequently displayed by Australian politicians. The temptation of winning a brief and uncertain term of office is quite sufficient, in most cases, to induce an open recantation of the avowed principles and cherished convictions of a lifetime.

On the cardinal question of the Federal Union of these colonies the right key-note is struck in the speech delivered in Melbourne in 1867. But the Australian politician who holds the views set forth in that speech is in advance of his age by at least a generation. Even upon the incidental subject of Border Customs Duties, it is still found impossible to induce neighbouring colonies to come to a mutual understanding based on a common interest. In practice, the present state of things is exactly what would exist in England if every two counties separated by a river had different tariffs; and, in fact, the boundary between neighbouring colonies is sometimes not any definite natural feature at all, but only an imaginary line. Federation, an Australian Zollverein, and the abolition of all the practical absurdities involved in jarring tariffs, will only become possible for us when our local statesmen shall all be imbued with that spirit of generous local patriotism, combined with those sound views upon political economy and the enlarged sentiment of Australian nationality, which are the pervading characteristics of these speeches.

But it is as the author of the system of Public Education now firmly established, and working so beneficially, in New South Wales, that the author of the speeches makes good his claim to be ranked high on the roll of Australian statesmen. A nobler monument for himself and heritage for his country could not be bequeathed to posterity by any man. On this question, also, a striking example was given of sustained consistency. From the outset of his public career —as these speeches testify—Mr. Parkes had clearly before his mind the paramount necessity of a broadly popular and thoroughly liberal scheme of Education. Upon every fitting occasion he gave expression to this conviction; and almost his first act upon gaining office was the framing and carrying of the Public Schools Bill. So far as I am aware, the speech delivered on the second reading of that Bill has not been excelled by any Parliamentary deliverance on the same great question, either in this or the mother-country, for comprehensive grasp of principles, lucidness of detail, and adaptation to the special circumstances of time and place. It is at once exhaustive and unanswerable. It forms a manual of the question to which, on all future occasions when discussions arise either on the principles or the details of the Act of 1866, ultimate reference will be made. And, without repeating any of the well-worn truisms on this subject, a word of warm congratulation must here be given to those Australian statesmen who, in the various colonies, have fulfilled the highest of all their duties to their fellow-citizens by pro-

Introduction. xiii

viding them freely with ample and efficient means of elementary education. To "make knowledge circle with the winds," as the Laureate counsels, is in a democratic community the truest conservatism. For, an ignorant democracy is self-destructive; and it surely is the first duty of every State—as Paley defines it to be of every Government—to make provision for its own preservation. Nor even upon this open field of public advantage was success won without a hard and prolonged struggle. The opposing foe of the friends of enlightenment was, not popular ignorance, but Sectarianism. To wrest the sacred function of public education from the iron grasp of Sectarianism was an achievement of itself sufficient to found a lasting reputation for any Australian statesman. It is a fact of the largest significance and the brightest promise, that the legal recognition of Sectarianism is now erased from the Statute-book of every one of the colonies. The religious freedom of the citizens is thus made commensurate with their civil liberty. It may be hoped that the beneficent operation of our systems of free and universal education upon the young Australians will, in the course of a generation or two, completely extinguish in their minds even the traditionary recollections of sectarian hatred.

The absence of any speeches on the Land Question strikes me as a peculiarity in the volume. Mr. Parkes, no doubt, has had his full share in the successive struggles that have taken place in New South Wales for the institution of a liberal Land system; and the omission mentioned may be solely due to the fact that Land-question speeches are never very readable, however important they may be when delivered. But the omission is the more marked for me, because that, in Victoria, the Land question is the key to all the political discussions, Parliamentary embroilments, and Ministerial changes, that have taken place since free institutions were first established. The history of the Land question, largely written, would really be the entire political history of the colony from its foundation. To gain possession of the territory has been the inflexible purpose of one powerful party from the first. That purpose has always dominated, and still dominates, every political movement and every legislative measure. Up till the present moment, the one question that ultimately determines both the personal composition and the tenure of existence of any Victorian Ministry is its attitude in relation to the Land question. If this be not so in New South Wales—as the absence of any speeches in this volume on the one supreme topic would imply—then is that colony in a much sounder condition politically than her neighbour Victoria.

There are in the volume two speeches in which the personal element is unusually conspicuous. These are the speech on the coalition of Sir James Martin and Mr. John Robertson, and Mr. Parkes's defence of his conduct in the case of the prisoner Gardiner. Now, in deliverances of this character, the point to be specially noted is the serious impeachment conveyed against other persons. A politician cannot successfully defend himself from grave accusations of inconsistency, amounting to a deliberate violation of all honour and principle, without sheeting home to his accusers charges equally grave. In the two instances in question this retributive action of plain truth seems to me to be exhibited with really crushing effect. Accepting the facts as they are set forth in the speeches, what does an impartial reader of them find? He finds that Sir James Martin and Mr. John Robertson, having been for twelve years flatly opposed to each other on every cardinal point in politics, and having carried this opposition to the extreme length of declared personal dislike, suddenly join together to form a Cabinet. Upon what grounds? From what motives? For what ends? Certainly upon grounds that include the recantation by

Introduction.

both of all the political principles they had ever avowed. It was a virtual declaration that never for a moment had either of them been sincere in his professions, in his speeches, or even in his votes. For if up till the time of their coalition they had never had any, even the least, common ground of action as politicians, what common ground could they find or frame to render such coalition possible? There is none conceivable in the case but that of mutual apostasy; and such apostasy must have been a foregone purpose with both. The opportunity for consummating it alone was wanting, and it came at length. Well might Mr. Parkes challenge any person to find an analogous instance in recent English political history; and he was thoroughly justified in speaking of the "infamy" of the combination. Coalitions in English history there have been, but they were grounded on compromises that fell far short of wholesale abandonment of all principles and summary sacrifices of all political honour and honesty. One conspicuous instance of a hurried and unhappy combination between two open political enemies stands recorded in the parliamentary history of the last century. It was that between Lord North and Fox; and it is immortalised in the famous epigram which tells how the Premier of George the Third's early days, having exhausted his vocabulary of abusive terms on his remorseless enemy—

"In spite of his real or fancied alarms,
Took the 'fool' to his councils, the 'beast' to his arms."

But shameless political profligacy of this character has long been impossible in English politics. There are, unhappily, too many indications that it is becoming the rule rather than the exception in Australian politics.

The case relating to the prisoner Gardiner is of a still darker complexion. Here was a case in which certain leading politicians used all their influence as private citizens to induce the Governor to exercise the prerogative of pardon in the summary release of a notorious malefactor, and subsequently fomented a popular outcry against both the Governor and his chief adviser for the serious crime of having acted upon their own recommendation ! A movement grounded on so glaring an act of injustice could only be sustained by persistent falsehood. It was alleged, for instance, that the Chief Secretary had advised the Governor to release Gardiner—an allegation which the official documents show to be wholly without foundation. The Chief Secretary was condemned for releasing Gardiner, when in fact he had not alone not done so, but had even refused to put his name to a petition for the man's release. The Governor was accused of complying with the prayer of a memorial signed by the very men who condemned him, when in fact he had postponed compliance, and had only registered a conditional promise, which he felt himself bound as a gentleman to fulfil. Further, the conditional promise was fulfilled three years after the presentation of the memorial that prayed for a summary release. There is something absolutely incredible in the inversion of all truth, honesty, and fair dealing, that marks this memorable case throughout Yet the political ruse was, for the time, successful—just as Wrong, and Falsehood, and Injustice have been successful many a time before.

The two cases, nevertheless, are terrible impeachments and the printing of the present volume consigns them to the perpetual keeping of History.

Mr. Parkes's oratory is of the same stamp as the late Richard Cobden's—"unadorned eloquence," as Sir Robert Peel characterised it. Yet there are not wanting passages which show that the speaker might have risen, had he chosen, to much loftier heights than he essayed. He eschewed rhetoric, however, for plain, straightforward, business-like speaking. Of this kind of Parliamentary oratory some of the speeches are true models ; and it may be safely asserted that no other model will ever be followed by leading Australian politicians.

Introduction. xvii

Taken as a whole, they are the utterances of a public man who has realised to himself with singular vividness the present duties and future destinies of Australian colonists, and of one who forecasts, with the Laureate, that—

> " A slow-developed strength awaits
> Completion in a painful school;
> Phantoms of other forms of rule,
> New Majesties of mighty States."

D. B.

Melbourne, February 10th, 1876.

SPEECHES.

THE ELECTIVE FRANCHISE.

SPEECH

Delivered at a public meeting of the citizens of Sydney, convened for the purpose of petitioning the Queen and Parliament for an extension of the Elective Franchise, January 22nd, 1849.*

MR. PARKES said he had been requested to second the resolution which had just been moved, asserting the right of universal suffrage. It was thought advisable to lay down this broad principle, though it was not intended in their petitions to ask for more than political equality with the people of England. To universal suffrage they must come at last; any measure short of that would be defective, and would fail to satisfy the public mind. The Anglo-Saxon communities of America had obtained this full measure of liberty; and what other people grew so rapidly and securely in national prosperity? The time would come, more quickly than some dark prophets could foresee, when it would be in the possession of the Australian people. Those who were opposed to universal suffrage directed their attention to France and other Continental nations, and said that there it caused the hands of the

---

*At this time the elective franchise in the colony was, by the Act 6 Vic. 76, confined to £20 householders, and freeholders possessing estates worth £200. But a bill to confer a new and extended Constitution on the colony was then in contemplation by the British Government. The petitions to the Imperial Parliament, adopted at the meeting of Jan. 22, 1849, in favour of a reduction of the qualification, were transmitted by Mr. Parkes, the one for presentation to the Lords, to Lord Monteagle; and the other for presentation to the Commons, to the late W. Scholefield, Esq. In due course they were presented, and while the new bill was under consideration in the House of Lords, an amendment was moved by Lord Lyttelton, and adopted by the Secretary of State (Earl Grey), who had charge of the measure, reducing the qualification to £10 household, and £100 freehold.

B

people to be imbrued with blood. It might be so; but if the people had been sooner enfranchised, they would not have abused a power which they already had learnt to use. It was even within the range of probability that Louis Philippe might still have been upon the throne of France if the people had sooner received the concession of universal suffrage. By the exercise of their rights the people would have become enlightened, and might have enforced by moral means such reforms as would have saved the Government from disruption. They need only look at their own country to find reasons for a more extended suffrage. Who had returned the best men to the Legislative Council? Were not the best men returned where the franchise was most popularly exercised, where the force of public opinion could be brought to bear most effectually on the election? Sydney had returned Messrs. Wentworth and Lowe, who were both of them men of superior education and ability, while the worst men were sent in by the remote country constituencies. The present meeting had been opposed by some persons on the ground that before political rights were granted to the people, the people should be educated. But who was to educate them?—the present legislators? With the exception of three or four members, the whole body of their present Legislature ridiculed all sympathy with the popular feeling. Were they the men to provide the means of education for the people? They must not expect it. Place political power in the hands of the people, and the people would see to their own interests.*

---

* One of the resolutions of this meeting was moved by the Right Hon. Robert Lowe, late Chancellor of the Exchequer, who was then one of the members for Sydney.

THE TRANSPORTATION QUESTION.

[IN the latter part of 1848 the English Government proposed the resumption of transportation, in a modified form, to the Australian colonies. The proposal was communicated by a dispatch from Earl Grey, dated the 8th September, and created immediately a perfect storm of dissatisfaction and indignant feeling. An agitation sprung up in New South Wales in the following year, which continued with increasing vitality through 1850, culminating in the formation of a League of all the colonies against what was regarded as a common calamity. Mr. Parkes took an active part throughout this agitation, writing in the papers and speaking at public meetings, until the cause was completely triumphant by the final revocation in 1852 of the Order-in-Council which made the colonies places to which British convicts might be transported. The first convict vessel that arrived in Port Jackson under the new system (for the Secretary of State did not wait to see how his proposal would be received in the colonies) was the "Hashmey," which came in June 8th, 1849, on which day two ships, with immigrants, entered the Heads from England. On the following day three other immigrant ships arrived, so that the convicts lay at anchor amidst 1400 to 1500 newly-arrived immigrants. These circumstances gave intensity to the feeling of resentment which agitated the popular mind. Three days after the arrival of the "Hashmey" an open-air meeting of the citizens of Sydney was held near the Circular Quay, under the presidency of the late Mr. Robert Campbell, which was long talked of as "The Great Protest Meeting." The "protest" which was adopted by this great gathering was written by Mr. Parkes. It was moved by the late Mr. John Lamb, and seconded by Mr. Lowe (now the Right Honourable Robert Lowe). A second great meeting was held on the same spot seven days afterwards; other similar demonstrations followed in Sydney and in most of the country towns. The following is a copy of the protest :—

We, the free and loyal subjects of Her Most Gracious Majesty, inhabitants of the city of Sydney and its immediate neighbourhood, in public meeting assembled, do hereby enter our most deliberate and solemn protest against the transportation of British criminals to the colony of New South Wales.

Firstly.—Because it is in violation of the will of the majority of the colonists, as is clearly evidenced by their expressed opinions on the question at all times.

Secondly.—Because numbers among us have emigrated on the faith of the British Government, that transportation to this colony had ceased for ever.

Thirdly.—Because it is incompatible with our existence as a free colony, desiring self-government, to be made the receptacle of another country's felons.

Fourthly.—Because it is in the highest degree unjust to sacrifice the great social and political interests of the colony at large to the pecuniary profit of a fraction of its inhabitants.

Fifthly.—Because, being firmly and devoutly attached to the British Crown, we greatly fear that the perpetuation of so stupendous an act of injustice by Her Majesty's Government will go far towards alienating the affections of the people of this colony from the mother country.

For these and for many kindred reasons—in the exercise of our duty to our country, for the love of our families, in the strength of our loyalty to Great Britain, and from the depth of our reverence for Almighty God—we protest against the landing again of British convicts on these shores.]

SUBSTANCE OF SPEECH

At the Great Protest Meeting, June 11, 1849, on seconding the following resolution—" That it is the urgent request of this meeting that the Local Government do send the prisoners arrived in the ' Hashmey ' immediately back to England, if necessary at the expense of the colony."

MR. PARKES said : After the speeches they had already heard it would be unwise in him to detain them, save for one word on behalf of a class to whom as yet no allusion had been made, but who were most unjustly dealt with in this matter. Let him ask that meeting did the fourteen hundred emigrants now afloat on the waters of Port Jackson suspect when they left Great Britain that they would find a convict ship in the midst of the vessels that brought them hither? Would they, had they dreamt of such a thing, have sacrificed all home ties and volunteered to degrade themselves? In the colony the whole question had been discussed over and over again, but these emigrants when they embarked could know nothing of the injustice to which they were about to be subjected. To place the situation of these people in a true light, let them suppose the Immigration Agent to go on board the ships, and after congratulating the passengers on their safe arrival in health and comfort, tell them how much they had for which to be grateful—let them suppose him to exhort the young men to emulate these convict labourers in the race of industry in their new home, and to assure the young women that the Home

Government had not only provided for them a free passage to this land flowing with milk and honey, but had been so exceedingly paternal in their consideration of them as to send out a ship-load of convicts to be their future husbands. He could but express his deep feeling of indignation at the deception that had been practised on these unsuspecting strangers and the insult that had been offered to the community at large, and the only remedy he could see— the only course consistent with justice to the colonists—was that the convict ship and cargo should be sent back as the resolution proposed. It was necessary to express our willingness to be at the expense of sending these prisoners back, to evince our abhorrence of the importation.

SUBSTANCE OF SPEECH

At a meeting of the citizens of Sydney held at the Circular Quay, June 18, 1849.

[THE following resolution was moved by Mr. Archibald Michie —" That it is indispensable to the well-being of the colony, and to the satisfactory conduct of its affairs, that its Government should no longer be administered by the remote, ill-informed, and irresponsible Colonial Office, but by Ministers chosen from and responsible to the colonists themselves, in accordance with the principles of the British Constitution."]

MR. PARKES seconded the resolution. They had met on that spot a week ago to raise their voice against a grievous act of injustice, with the very heavens weeping for their calamity; they were assembled there again to assert the spirit of British freemen, in demanding those rights to which they were entitled by birth, and the same Australian heavens smiled and rejoiced. He did not suppose there was a man in the country so careless of his repute for common sense and independence, as to express his disagreement with that resolution. It was not in the nature of things that a Minister, placed as far distant from us as this earth could place him—even if he devoted an entire life to the study of our history and condition, our geographical relations, our social progress, our political wants, and our natural capabilities—could do administrative justice to this colony; still less that a nobleman who never bestowed a thought on New South Wales in his life, till some political chance or accident gave him his ministerial position, should be qualified to govern us. We wanted men practically acquainted with every impulse, effort, transition, and phase of our existence as a people. To show the enormous amount of ignorance concerning New South Wales which prevailed among men of the highest education and possessing the best means of information, he would mention one or two instances. One of our favourite modern poets, the author of the *Pleasures of Hope*, in that celebrated poem speaks of the extensive islands of Sydney Cove. We were assembled on its shores. Could anyone see

Where the long isles of Sydney Cove extend?

And the poet Southey—a man of most varied and extensive information—represents Botany Bay prisoners as going to their huts after nightfall, trembling at every step lest they should be devoured by wild beasts. Within the last year or two he had seen it put forth in English papers, as an important announcement, that regular communication was likely to be established between Sydney and New Zealand! If such was the state of British ignorance with men who spent their lives in acquiring knowledge, it was not surprising that Ministers who often were raised to power or precipitated from office by the accumulative force of a series of accidents, should prove incapable of governing the distant colonies of England. And was it right that such a state of things should continue? No; we had a perfect right, and it was our duty, to demand a change—to adopt every legal and constitutional means to effect it. We sought not to do this from disaffection or disloyalty, but in the spirit of the truest and best of all loyalty. We had been charged with rebelliousness and disaffection; but where was the foundation for such charges? We were all warmly and sincerely attached to the institutions of the mother country. He would yield to no man in feelings of loyalty to the British Crown; but his loyalty did not teach him to shut his eyes to the faults of Government; it rather constrained him— and the stronger it grew the more it constrained him—to seek a reform of public abuses, that the Government might be established firmly and permanently in the affections of a free people. Certain weak gentlemen told us that we had brought about a "reign of terror." Where was it to be seen? The alarm was all moonshine. There was not a sane man in the community who could believe there was anything like intimidation exercised. He denied the statement. He did not agree with the allusions which had been made to America. He did not see what good would come from such allusions. We were not at a state of advancement to be benefited by separation from the mother country, even if we had cause to desire separation. As a community we possessed little of the stern and sturdy spirit of the old American colonists. If oppressive duties were levied on our imports, he did not think our Sydney merchants would passively resist by entering into a non-importation compact. If our Crown lawyers were called upon to enforce obnoxious laws, he feared none would be found like the young and lofty-spirited George Otis, to resign office and join cause with the people. And he was afraid it would be long before many men would be found on the benches of our senate house like the earnest and impassioned Patrick Henry. It would be wise and well to cherish a feeling of true loyalty towards Great Britain. But that was no reason why we should not peaceably and constitutionally contend for our rights—no reason why we should not insist upon being entrusted with the management of our own affairs.

SUBSTANCE OF SPEECH

At a meeting of the citizens of Sydney held in the Barrack Square,*
Sept. 16, 1850.

[MR. T. S. MORT moved—" That with a view to ensure the united exertion of every individual in this colony interested in this great question, an association be now formed under the designation of 'The New South Wales Association for preventing the Revival of Transportation.' And that such an association be not dissolved until the Transportation Question be satisfactorily and finally determined. That the gentlemen who have convened the present meeting be the first committee for managing the association, with power to add to their number, and that an annual contribution of one shilling be sufficient to constitute a member of the association."]

MR. PARKES supported the resolution. At that late hour of the day it would be more becoming in him to give place to the gentlemen who in the order of the business had to follow him; but he would beg

*This meeting was held where Wynyard Square is now laid out, and was attended by 8000 or 10,000 persons.

to say a few words in support of the resolution. The mover and seconder, in their able arguments on the transportation question, had forgotten the more immediate consideration of the proposition now before the meeting—that a popular association be formed to oppose the renewal of transportation. This resolution certainly opened up a wide field for remark, if time permitted. The principle of association for the achievement of great objects was now universally acted upon by the British people; union of public efforts was one of the most remarkable effects produced by the progress of enlightenment. It was a new and noble feature in the national character of modern Englishmen. At the close of the last disastrous war, the English people, as they settled down into rational feeling again, began to consider for what good they had been contending and overburdening their country with taxes. They looked into the political condition of the country, and a demand for parliamentary reform was at once enkindled. Year by year this spirit grew stronger and stronger, till at last it embodied itself in the form of popular associations. The Political Unions were organised, and the great Reform Bill became the law of the land as a consequence. Thus a revolution was brought about, greater and more glorious in its benefits than was ever effected before by the people of any State in their internal policy, without the desolation of any man's home, or the shedding of a single drop of blood. From the passing of the Reform Bill to the present time, every great public movement had been prosecuted by the English people by the means of such peaceful and lawful associations as was contemplated in the present resolution. He must allude to one other signal triumph of this unity of purpose in the people—the abolition of slavery in our West Indian possessions. It was by the union of the people that that great glory had been added to the diadem of England—the emancipation of her slaves. The struggle they were now engaged in was of the first importance, and demanded the most vigorous co-operation. The men they had to contend against were equally as unprincipled and unscrupulous as the former slaveholders of the West Indies. As far as they could ascertain men's motives by the exercise of reason, the motives of the great employers now clamouring for convict labour were precisely the motives of the slaveholders. It was said that they were anxious to assist the Government in a wise

Transportation Question. 9

solution of that great problem—the proper disposal of England's criminals so as to protect society, and at the same time to correct its offenders. But he did not believe that such considerations entered into the philosophy of the squatters of New South Wales. It mattered not to them how men fell into their hands, so that they were completely subservient to the master's will, so that they were in reality his slaves. The people of the colony must therefore unite to ward off the threatened infamy and degradation. He cordially supported the resolution.

SPEECH

At the Anti-Transportation Conference Banquet held in Sydney, April 3rd, 1851, in acknowledgment of the toast, "The Ladies of Australasia, and particularly those who signed the Anti-Transportation Petitions."

MR. PARKES said he considered it a heavy misfortune that the honourable member for Durham* was not in their ranks that night ; for who could respond so happily and well to the toast which had just been proposed by their worthy friend, and which had been drunk by them all with such unbounded and becoming enthusiasm ? It was not till a late hour that afternoon that he became aware of the distinction which had been conferred on him ; and he confessed that when he first saw his name affixed as respondent to that important toast, he felt almost startled from his propriety. His first feeling was, how should he escape ? Under what enchantment had his friends made so singular a selection as to choose him for that pleasing duty ? Why had he been singled out to return thanks for the ladies of that great colony on an occasion like the present ? For what reason had the duty been allotted to him, a plain and plodding citizen, who was an utter stranger to those gaieties and splendours in which it was supposed that woman had her world, the very honeymoon of whose life was far away behind in the dim vista of the past ? But when, in a little, he recollected that he had had the honour to originate a petition against transportation which was signed by 12,000 of the daughters, wives, and mothers of that noble city, including the second

---

* The late Sir Stuart Alexander Donaldson.

highest lady in the land, he thought he could understand the kindness which had operated with their friends in setting apart for him the present distinction. With that feeling he accepted the honourable duty with all his heart; and he pined at that moment for some power of eloquence, some word of electric might and influence, to speak out the fervour of his admiration and the depth of his reverence for the lofty and angelic character of a virtuous woman. The greatest poets, the purest patriots, the noblest Christians, had ascribed their brilliant successes in life, all the more valuable and enduring of their enjoyments, to the teachings and influence of pure-hearted and exemplary mothers. Let Australia once become a land of virtuous and Christian-minded mothers, and it would be a land of patriots and heroes. But how would the advocates of transportation bring about this happy and glorious condition of society? Would it be by surrounding the female portion of their kindred by systems of industry and of commerce based on the very element of crime? He trusted a time would soon arrive when no man would dare to raise his voice to advocate transportation in the presence of a daughter of Australia. On behalf of the ladies of Australasia, he begged very sincerely to thank that meeting—as a father, as a husband, as a citizen, he tendered his thanks—for the enthusiastic manner in which the toast had been received.

SPEECH

Delivered at a meeting of the citizens of Sydney convened by the Australasian Anti-Transportation League in Malcolm's Circus, April 6, 1852, "To take into consideration Earl Grey's determination to continue transportation to Van Diemen's Land."

MR. PARKES said it was a great advantage for any man having to speak toward the close of the proceedings on an occasion like the present, that he had the old staple of all bad speakers to fall back upon—the many excellent speeches already delivered. And certainly few in such a situation could compliment previous speakers with more truth than he might. But that was no time for compliments; it was one of those occasions which ought to make the plainest and the most ungifted men find some sort of utterance for their indignant feelings. After all the pain and toil of the protracted agitation of this question—after an agitation, conducted with the fullest enquiry and the deepest earnestness, which had stirred the heart of the country to its very core—after these communities, having been polled almost to a man, had declared with one voice against receiving English criminals as an evil which all believed was in the highest degree disastrous to their moral and social interests—a canker eating into their very souls,—after all this, they were forced back to its renewed agitation by the perverseness of one obstinate man who happened to hold a seat in the British Government. He agreed with previous speakers that the time for deliberation and argument was past. Why, they had deliberated for years—they had exhausted all arguments. The matter now resolved itself into a simple question of natural right, and they had only to consider how best to vindicate that right. No man or body of men could have a right to force upon a community a thing from without which they unanimously refused to receive; which they abhorred and believed would be ruinous to them. Argument and discussion had been of no service to them; their remonstrances and petitions had fallen upon deaf ears. They had done all in this way which men could do, and they could pursue this course no longer. It was a singular and striking feature of this agitation that a very large amount of talent had been exhibited in it. The last debate in the Legislative Council the year before last was one so ably sustained that it would have done honour to the British Parliament. Their petitions from all parts of the country had been able and argumentative documents, and such was their unanimity of sentiment, that when the question was last under discussion in this colony the numbers were 36,000 against, and only 500 in favour of the system. But in the face of all this—notwithstanding their repeated protests and petitions—notwithstanding the intelligence which they had brought to bear in the discussion of the question, and their unanimity in the decision which they had arrived at—the tyrannical Minister persisted in thrusting upon them the evil which they were determined not to receive. Well, then, what was to be done? As a free people, as men, they could not retreat from their position, they could no longer go through the farce of remonstrating against an injustice which was persevered in with an utter disregard of their wishes and their interests; they must do something else. He was well pleased to hear their president, Mr. Cowper, talk of fighting. Knowing the mild, affable, and benignant character of that gentleman, he was at first half-afraid that he was hardly stern enough for the duties which he might be called upon to perform in his mission to Van Diemen's Land. They had been told that night of the serious consequences which might ensue. Now, he had no desire to bring before them rebellious examples, or he might most properly point to the example of the American colonists: for in the progress of events which led to the loss of those colonies, there was a remarkable analogy between some stages and their own case. He would pass over this, because he believed the meeting did not need to be reminded of the glorious and successful struggle of men who were treated with contumely and oppressed in a manner similar to themselves. There was, however, a suggestive passage in a speech of one of those early patriots which he would with their permission repeat to the meeting. When young Patrick Henry, in the General Assembly of Virginia, was moving his resolutions in reference to the odious Stamp Act, he exclaimed, "Cæsar had his Brutus, Charles the First his Cromwell, and George the Third—" "Treason!" cried the Speaker. The young patriot, standing up more proudly than ever, and fixing his eyes on the alarmed Speaker, concluded the sentence—"George the Third may profit by their example; if that be treason, make the most of it!" He would point to the successful resistance of the American colonists, and in the name of that meeting tell the British Government to profit by that example. He had no treason to promulgate; on the contrary, the man did not breathe whose heart beat with a truer loyalty to the gracious and glorious lady who presides over the destinies of the British Empire. But as was said by their chairman, there was a higher loyalty than that to any earthly monarch—our loyalty to our own nature and to the all-wise God, who has planted in us pure and holy sentiments, and warmed our being with the love of justice and truth. To fall away from this loyalty would be to debase ourselves before our Creator—to deface the divine impress of humanity which had been printed on our hearts. They must go right onward in their course. There could be no mistake in the matter. If Earl Grey had indeed been deceived and misled, the last elections throughout the colonies would surely undeceive him. Even under a Constitution concocted by his own Government, the people of Van Diemen's Land had in every instance elected anti-transportationists to their representative seats. In that unfortunate island—that very sinkhole of English iniquity, where the prison population was so alarming in numbers, and where it could not be doubted many of that class possessed the elective franchise—no representative favourable to the continuance of transportation had been chosen. It was fair to assume that many of the emancipist class in that island had recorded their votes on the side of the anti-transportationists. How could it be otherwise? How could men wish to continue to their children the curse of their own lives? What was it, this desire to get rid of the infamy and degradation of which they had themselves been victims, but the triumph of all that was good and virtuous and lofty and aspiring in the human breast? They were about to send Mr. Cowper as a delegate to the conference of the League at Hobart Town. When he approached the shores of the island-home of those sturdy and stout-hearted patriots, it was to be hoped that the bracing influences of their climate would make him even bolder than he had been in his speech that evening; and that if the Tasmanian colonists should determine to resist the landing of any more convicts, he would solemnly assure them that the inhabitants of New South Wales were ready to assemble again in some place under heaven, where all the people could be gathered to ratify all the acts so done and to share in all the consequences. The example of the Cape colonists was before them. The time was come when their only course was to follow that example; and whenever a prison-ship should arrive in the Derwent, or in any other port, to resist at all hazards the landing of the prisoners thus tyrannically forced upon us. He most sincerely hoped they would not be driven to the catastrophe hinted at by their respected member, Mr. Campbell, that of tumbling the prisoners into the sea; but whatever sufferings might ensue, at whatever sacrifices, they were now bound to stand by each other in the protection of their own liberties. There were times when men had no right to look round for consequences, when they were bound by all that was dear and sacred to advance. He believed this was a time for such conduct. When he was asked by his colleagues in the council of the League to take part in the business of that meeting, he consented, because he considered he had no right to refuse any duty in the cause; had they asked him to fight, his consent for the reasons he had stated would have been as freely and as quietly given. He had come to the meeting determined to put it to them whether the time had not arrived for the Van Diemen's Land colonists to resist the landing of the convicts. He could see no other way to get rid of this cruel and desolating agitation. He therefore solemnly asked that meeting, if they agreed with him that the time for this decisive action had arrived, to hold up their right hands in the affirmative. [Here the speaker held up his hand, and was responded to by the hands of nearly all in the body of the meeting.] This he accepted as a pledge of their honest and serious determination in the matter. In the name of that meeting, their respected delegate might tell the colonists of Van Diemen's Land that the people of New South Wales were prepared to stand by them in resisting any further landing of convicts on their shores. He would now most cordially move the resolution which had been intrusted to his hands :—" That the previous resolutions be embodied in an address, and that such address be presented by the president, in the name of this meeting, to the Tasmanian delegates at the Hobart Town conference."

SPEECH

Delivered at a meeting of the citizens of Sydney convened by the Australasian Anti-Transportation League, in Malcolm's Circus, June 30, 1852.

MR. PARKES : The resolution which had been intrusted to him to move was an important one. If not a declaration of war, it was a definition of the limits within which men could adhere to peace. Before offering the few remarks which he had to make, he would read the resolution :—" That this meeting, while solemnly denouncing the continuance of transportation to any of these colonies as incompatible with the permanence of British rule in Australasia, earnestly protests against their language being represented as that of wanton defiance or of anti-British feeling; prompted as it is by a deep consciousness that in their case the sense of oppression is increased in the very proportion in which those feelings which are a Briton's noblest heritage gain strength among the colonists ; and that if the fatal alternative should continue to be thrust upon them of choosing between British connection in name and an unsullied British character in fact, the dictates of principle and the onward course of events must before long lead to the preference of the latter at any sacrifice." It would be admitted that the substance of the resolution was deeply important, that the topics to which it referred were sufficient to carry the mind away to more eventful times, to the bright issues of what was now dark and gloomy and discouraging around them. That discussion would open up a field of vast speculation into which, even if he had the ability, he had not the time to enter. On a resolution possessing so much importance he would, however, make one or two remarks. In the first place it called upon them to denounce the continuance of transportation. Man, woman, and child, throughout the breadth and length of the colony, with very few exceptions, had a hundred times over denounced transportation, but that resolution called upon them to denounce it as incompatible with their present relation to the mother country. They were all unanimous in joining in that feeling if he were to judge by the speeches which had been delivered, and the manner in which they had been received. They were unanimous in their determination that these colonies should no longer continue to be the cesspool of the British Empire, or of any portion of it. Again, the resolution vindicated them from the slanderous charges of native turbulence and anti-British feeling, which had most unmeritedly been made against them. It showed that they had a true British resolve to eradicate those seeds of dissension which would speedily lead to separation, that they were the not unworthy children of their British forefathers. They were the inheritors of no common patrimony. They were a people whose ancestors had planted a tree of liberty so universal in its growth that its offshoots, transplanted to savage shores, had sprung up and borne abundant fruit for the advancing nations of more than one world. Their language and the spirit of their institutions had spread throughout the vast American continent from the Atlantic to the Pacific, and were now carrying civilisation over the rich and glorious land of which these struggling colonies were the embryo peoples. They inherited a glory which belonged to no other race, and their highest duty and their truest loyalty to the British name consisted in preserving that inheritance unimpaired for their posterity. If they were loyal to themselves as true-born Britons they would assert, in the language of the resolution before them, that the continuance of this monstrous system of convictism was incompatible with the preservation of their rights; and that, if it were forced upon them, resistance would become a duty, so as to vindicate their character at any price and at any sacrifice. On a former occasion in that building he had stated his belief that the time had arrived in Van Diemen's Land for the colonists to resist. But in the unparalleled circumstances of that unfortunate colony she had no strength to resist. The same event—the discovery of gold—which had caused new streams of population to flow into these communities, had the effect of draining her of all social life. Society, as at present existing in Van Diemen's Land, was a thing stripped of its natural energies. There was nothing left there now but the convict Government and its subordinate interests, which in the language of the honourable member for Melbourne bound down the colony in a network of degradation: none other except the convicts themselves, and a few middle men, who were anchored in the colony by their property, and could not escape. If convict ships were again to arrive here, it would be their duty to resist any such attempt at oppression. And in this spirit they had denounced the continuance of the system. Therefore the distinct terms of the resolution were necessary when speaking of such a fatal alternative.

THE CONSTITUTION ACT.

[IN the year 1853 a Select Committee of the old Legislative Council was appointed, on the motion of Mr. Wentworth, to prepare a Constitution for the Colony of New South Wales. The Committee consisted of Mr. Wentworth, Mr. James Macarthur, Mr. James Martin, Mr. Charles Cowper, Mr. T. A. Murray, Mr. George Macleay, Mr. E. Deas Thomson, Mr. J. H. Plunket, Dr. Douglas, and Mr. William Thurlow. The first meeting of the Committee was held on the 27th May, and fifteen meetings altogether were summoned. Half of the members did not attend one half the meetings. The result of the Committee's deliberations was "A Bill to confer a Constitution on New South Wales, and to grant a Civil List to Her Majesty." This Bill was reported on the 28th July, and with important modifications, all of a popular character, is now the law of the colony. On the first publication of the Bill an instantaneous feeling of indignation spread throughout the colony. The whole newspaper press, with the single exception of the *Sydney Morning Herald*, denounced its more unpopular provisions, which were forcibly summarised in the advertisement convening the first meeting to oppose it, which was held on August 15th. The notice of meeting (which ought to be regarded as historical) reads as follows: —"A Committee of the Legislative Council has framed a new Constitution for the colony by which it is proposed—1. To create a colonial nobility with hereditary privileges. 2. To construct an Upper House of Legislature in which the people will have no voice. 3. To add eighteen new seats to the Lower House, only one of which is to be allotted to Sydney, while the other seventeen are to be distributed among the country and squatting districts. 4. To squander the public revenue by pensioning off the officers of Government on their full salaries; thus implanting in our institutions a principle of jobbery and corruption. 5. To fix this oligarchy in the name of free institutions on the people irrevocably, so that no future Legislature can reform it, even by an absolute majority. The Legislative Council has the hardihood to propose passing this unconstitutional and anti-British measure, with only a few days' notice, and before it can possibly be considered by the colonists at large." Though this meeting was called after only two days' notice, and held in the middle of the day, the attendance was so large that many hundreds could not obtain admittance within the theatre. The gentlemen who took part in the proceedings were Mr. John Gilchrist, Mr. W. R. Piddington, Mr. J. B. Darvall, Mr. Robert Johnson, Mr. J. L. Montefiore, Mr. J. W. Bligh, Mr. D. H. Deniehy, Mr. T. S. Mort, Mr. J. R. Wilshire, Mr. Adam Bogue, Mr. Edward Flood, and Mr. John Brown. Meetings for the same object were subsequently held in all parts of the colony. The result was that a longer time was given for the second reading of the Bill, and the hereditary peerage scheme was abandoned. Most of the other objectionable provisions were retained, including the iniquitous pension scheme by which Sir Edward Deas Thomson, K.C.M.G. (who accepted the office of Colonial Secretary at £1500 a year, and received, before he retired, an increase of £500 to his salary, with a retrospective effect for six years), has now received in the shape of pension £40,000 of the people's money.]

SPEECH

Delivered at a public meeting in the Victoria Theatre, Sydney, August 15th, 1853, to "resist the flagrant attack upon the public liberty" contained in the provisions of Mr. Wentworth's Constitution Bill.

Mr. PARKES rose to move the following resolution :—

"That this meeting earnestly protests against any attempt, in the hasty manner now proposed in the Legislative Council, to impose a Constitution on the colony which is passed in direct opposition to the wishes of the people."

The people were called upon by the terms of this resolution to enter their deliberate and solemn protest against the constituted legislative authorities of the country, and this was a course which they ought not to adopt lightly, or without good and sufficient reason ; for the legislature of any country depended for its power and stability on the confidence and respect of the people. And even if he possessed the power, he should shrink from inducing any one present to affirm such a resolution as this upon frivolous or trifling grounds. We forget one of our first duties as citizens when we forget the respect due to those authorities which even here, to some extent, we have brought into existence by our own voice. But it did appear that there was an overpowering weight of evidence to lead that meeting to one only course, which was that pointed out in the resolution he had to propose. The meeting would see that this resolution referred more particularly to the manner in which this Constitution business had been conducted by the Select Committee of the Legislative Council. It would be well to advert to the origin of the Committee, and he was the more inclined to go back to the origin of that Committee, inasmuch as he could not concur in the respect for the motives by which it had been actuated that had been avowed by previous speakers. He did not believe that the Committee deliberated with the best possible intentions. He, as a citizen, felt called upon to express his disbelief in their purity of intention. He believed that no one who carefully regarded the manner in which it was first formed could avoid the impression that it was glaringly packed. When Mr. Wentworth first named his Committee, the name of Mr. Cowper, who really appeared to have been the only troublesome presence in this cabal against the public liberty, was omitted; but he (Mr. Parkes) remembered that the name of Mr. Morris, for one, was included. He had no desire to express any disrespect towards the young gentleman, but he would ask whether that juvenile statesman had been placed on the Committee for his experience in making Constitutions ? It was evident that there was another and more forcible reason for the selection. It was pretty well understood that the honourable gentleman was Mr. Wentworth's echo. Now, when he (Mr. Parkes) saw Mr. Wentworth (whose great abilities and perfect knowledge of the momentous business in hand he fully admitted) take one of the most inexperienced members in the Council to assist him in framing a Constitution, he was forced to believe that this young gentleman was selected for other reasons than that he might most effectually serve the country. The Committee was, however, eventually elected by ballot; and, as one result of that ballot, the name of Mr. Cowper was substituted for that of Mr. Morris. Two other names were also introduced by that result, and he thought that with the introduction of those two names a principle was admitted into its composition, utterly unsound and unconstitutional—there were added the Colonial Secretary and the Attorney-General.* Now, there was no one who entertained a higher respect for this latter officer of the Crown, as a public man, than he (Mr. Parkes) did; but he altogether denied the right of any nominee member of that House

---

* Mr. E. Deas Thomson and Mr. J. H. Plunket, the two leading official nominees of the old form of Government, which was to be abolished by the new Constitution.

to assist in framing a Constitution for the colony. This objection was taken by Mr. Wentworth himself, and it was no doubt a sound and constitutional one. For what was the principle admitted in this appointment? It was nothing short of allowing men who had not been chosen by them—who had in no way been authorised by the voice of the people—not simply to carry on the ordinary legislation of the country—that was bad enough at present—but to uproot the whole existing order of things, to set up a new Constitution which was to be saddled upon us and our children. He denied the right of these two gentlemen to act upon that Committee; and he denied, on the same ground, the moral competence of the nominees, as a body, to vote on this question at all. It was simply a matter of absolute right that a Constitution for the country should be framed by persons who had the consent of the people for whom it was to become law. Such a position appeared to him unanswerable, and he must therefore deny the moral competency of the Legislative Council itself, as at present constituted, to frame a Constitution for the colony. A work of so grand and fundamental a nature should be delegated to the hands of men elected especially for that task, and for that task alone. The work was one of immeasurable importance, and lay beyond the reach of any such mongrel body as we had in existence here. If any illustration were needed of the truth of this assertion, he would point to the monstrous production which was now before the public—a production to which, if we submitted, we should deserve to lose our status as free subjects of the greatest nation in the world. To return to this select committee : he had carefully examined the abstract of their proceedings, published under their own supervision, and he was struck with the spirit of levity which seemed to have characterised their conduct. They were found doing and undoing, saying and unsaying, in such an extraordinary manner, that one would suppose from their actions they were a parcel of children—what he recollected once hearing Daniel O'Connell describe as "pickled youths." It was impossible to read the proceedings of that Committee without being strongly impressed with the extreme slovenliness and inconsistency displayed throughout. He found, for example, that at an early meeting of the Committee, when there were six members present besides the chairman, it was decided that the constituency of Cook and Westmoreland should not have an additional member, there being one (Mr. Martin) for the proposition of two members and five against it; this was the solemnly-resolved decision of the Committee. But observe what followed: at the very next meeting they granted to the constituency in question, in the teeth of their own decision, an additional member. Now, he would appeal to the meeting whether men who could thus turn about, and thus jump about from one position to another, without regard to common decency or decorum, in conducting public business, were fit for the consideration of a measure of such grave importance. Would we, if we had our choice, select men of such unstable minds to frame a Constitution under which we and our children were to live? He would now proceed to show something further in opposition to the sentiment expressed by a previous speaker, that this measure had been constructed with a fervent desire for the public welfare. He could assure the meeting that in the draft report of this Committee there was a clause,—which, however, was afterwards expunged,—recommending an Act of Council to send one of their body to England, as their envoy, with plenary powers, to take charge of this Bill and urge its enactment by the Imperial legislature. Could there be a moment's doubt who would have been the envoy? This clause contained internal evidence that it was written by Mr. Wentworth, who doubtless anticipated that the Council would vote a comfortable sum of £2000 or £4000 towards his expenses in London and on the Continent. Now, did this look like a studious regard for the public interest? The matter was so completely cut and dried, that it was impossible not to see the design to take the public by surprise. The Committee thought the household were all asleep, and that they might break in and steal our liberties without being observed. The resolution now submitted to the meeting also alleged that the new Constitution had been framed in direct opposition to the wishes of the people; and no better evidence of the truth of this statement could be adduced than the presence of such enthusiastic numbers on this occasion. And how could it be hoped that a Constitution would find acceptance with the community, which proposed the creation of an order of things that sensible men were now anxious to get rid of all over the world—a Constitution that proposed to appoint a House of Legislature in which the people were to have no voice whatever; a Constitution that proposed to squander the public money in pensioning off, at full salaries, men still in the prime of life, who were as well able to work as he or any other man in that meeting; a Constitution which proposed to do this and many other monstrous things in direct opposition to the people. One of the speakers had been careful to inform the meeting that he was no Radical. He (Mr. Parkes) could not blame him for this delicacy of feeling on being found in strange company; but he felt it to be his duty fearlessly to assert that one of the greatest evils in the colony was the present unjust distribution of the representation. He had found an explanation of the wonderful change in the opinions of the Committee as to whether Cook and Westmoreland should have another member—the new-born liberality was to repay the present member for that district for his readiness in proposing that the city of Sydney should have only one additional member. On the same day it was decided that four of the pastoral districts should have four additional members, while Sydney was to have but one. He would not be understood as denying, or wishing to deny, the right of the persons engaged in pastoral pursuits to representation, as he fully recognised that right; but he maintained that we were not to go beyond the ordinary limits of the Constitution to create new-fangled and un-English constituencies to meet the peculiar circumstances of their case. In granting the elective franchise to the squatters, it was never intended that these pocket constituencies should be created for their special and exclusive advantage. Such was the condition of these constituencies, that it was next to impossible for any vital action of the elective principle to be felt in them. In none of these constituencies had there been an election at all. Some three or four pastoral princes held a meeting in a comfortable log-cabin, and decided on their delegate; and then, riding over to the place of nomination, they chose him in the presence of a handful of their own shepherds and two or three gum trees. With this rough sort of constitutional brand upon him, the squatting member came down to the Council, where his vote was of course as good as that of a representative of the city of Sydney. Why, this state of things was worse than that of the old rotten boroughs in England before the passing of the Reform Bill. It was worse in this respect: those boroughs, if they were seats of patronage, were yet in the hands of highly-educated gentlemen, who almost invariably nominated men of

Constitution Act.

parliamentary talent; but here we always found that the most useless men in the Council were sent down from the squatting districts. In some instances members were returned whose occupations prevented them from attending to their parliamentary duties. It was even now stated in the Legislative Council that certain squatting members could not wait to attend the second reading of the new Constitution Bill if it were postponed, because they were obliged to return to their stations. These gentlemen would doubtless think it unreasonable that so trifling a matter as the construction of a political Constitution should hinder them from looking after their sheep. Look at the district of New England. In the first session of Council the member for that constituency never presented himself at all. The fact that the existing member stopped away one whole session presented no strong argument, certainly, why that district should have another. Yet such practically was the logic of the Select Committee in the course they had adopted. They had allotted additional members to districts, the representatives of which did not think it worth their while to attend to their duties. He would now advert to the manifest impatience with which it had been endeavoured to hurry this Bill through the House. When the honourable and learned author of the Bill first introduced the matter, he deprecated any discussion on the occasion, intimating that the principles of his measure would be fully discussed on its first reading. When it came on to be read a first time, the honourable member still deprecated all discussion, hoping that this might be deferred to its second reading as the more proper time; and he (Mr. Parkes) firmly believed, and those who had closely watched the proceedings must also believe, that the design was to put off as long as possible all discussion— to stifle all consideration of the question till the last moment, and then to precipitate the measure through the House, and fasten it upon the country. Nor could he see, in candour, how such manifestations of conduct in the authors of the scheme entitled them to much consideration at the hands of the people for the purity of their intentions. We were told that great points would be conceded; that the peerage would be given up; that Sydney should be allowed three additional members instead of one; that the pastoral districts should not have the lion's share in the representation. He (Mr. Parkes) did not, of course, know whether these announcements were authorised; but, if so, it appeared to him only heaping insult upon injury. If this was the purity of motive that was manifested, it was like the purity of motive to be detected in the man who asked you five pounds for what he intended to sell for two pounds; or who attempted to rob you of your watch and purse, and on finding he could not get it said that you were welcome to keep it. Why, if it was now right that Sydney should have six members, it was equally so when the Committee was sitting. They seemed to hope that, in consideration of such concessions as these, we should spare our denunciations of the other objectionable portions of the measure: that, if they relinquished their plunder, we should not set the police upon them. For his part, he would advise the people to place no trust whatever in the present Legislative Council; but, at the same time, to insist loudly on the necessity of having a new Constitution at once formed, and its consideration delayed no longer. It had been urged that the question should be postponed for further consideration. But was it right, when so gross and flagrant an attempt upon our liberty had been made, that we should postpone for a single day this important work of self-preservation, with such manifest proofs before us of the viciousness of the body with which the country was saddled? Whatever decision might be arrived at that day, the people must meet again and again, and insist upon a Constitution being formed with or without the concurrence of the Legislative Council. So long as it was stamped with the concurrence and approval of the whole community, it would be treated with respect by the Imperial Parliament. He would again urge upon the meeting, not inconconsiderately to adopt a resolution which reflected so strongly upon the proceedings of the Legislature. He trusted they would only affirm it after bestowing their best attention upon the subject, as the embodiment of their determined will. But, familiar as all present must be with the noble examples of modern England, with the spirit-stirring associations of England's glorious past, kindling love of country in their souls; familiar as they must be with the high and eloquent teachings of her famous dead, whose life-words of patriotism pealed like trumpet tones from every period of her national history, and were echoed back from every shore where men were free, they would need no words from him to rouse their indignation, no arguments from him to convince their judgments, no appeal from him to strengthen their resolution, to resist the iniquitous measure which it was now threatened to inflict on this long-misgoverned country.

SPEECH

Delivered at an open-air meeting of the inhabitants of Sydney held on the Government grounds adjoining the Circular Quay, September 5, 1853, to petition the Queen and the Imperial Parliament against the new Consitution Bill.*

MR. PARKES said the gentleman who first addressed them had very properly called upon them to give three cheers for the Queen. In his turn he called upon them to give three cheers, three hearty cheers, for the eight patriotic men who formed the minority in the division in the Legislative Council against Mr. Wentworth's monstrous Bill. It was something, when they saw others falling away on every side from the principles they had espoused throughout their whole lives—it was something to find eight men so thoroughly staunch and determined, so alive to the true interests of the country, and so ready to stand by and defend their threatened liberties. He congratulated the meeting on having a gentleman who stood so high in the esteem of his fellow-citizens, occupying the chair that day. In addressing himself to the resolution that had been entrusted to him, he would endeavour to prove to their satisfaction that it was a just and proper one. It was :—

"That this meeting records its surprise and indignation at the unconstitutional doctrines advanced in the Legislative Council, during the discussion of the present measure, whereby the great maxim of just and enlightened government, that 'All power emanates from the people,' is sought to be denied; and that, viewing the inherent defects of nomineeism and class interest in the existing Legislature, this meeting publicly records its total want of confidence in that body in reference to this measure, which is fraught with the most momentous consequences to the whole people."

---

*Amongst the gentlemen who took part in this meeting (which was attended by 5000 persons) were Mr. John Gilchrist, Mr. T. W. Smart, Mr. John Richardson, Mr. J. B. Darvall, Mr. Robert Campbell, Mr. J. W. Bligh, Mr. (now Sir Charles) Cowper, Mr. Thomas Walker, Mr. G. K. Holden, Mr. J. L. Montefiore, Mr. John Campbell, Mr. R. A. A. Morehead, and Mr. W. R. Piddington.

It would be his duty, in the first place, to show that the doctrines which had been advanced in the Council were unconstitutional, and in the next, that they had just grounds to declare that they had lost all confidence in the Legislative Council with regard to this measure, from the inherent defects of nomineeism, and the prevalence of class interests in that body. He would then advert to the speeches that had been made in that House by the honourable member, Mr. Wentworth, and the honourable member for Cook and Westmoreland, Mr. Martin; and he should rely mainly on those two speeches, which had been received with so much applause, to prove his case. Mr. Wentworth in the course of his opening speech had informed them, doubtless much to their astonishment, that the mercantile and trading classes were altogether unnecessary and did not need representation. That gentleman could not see what there was to represent beyond the squatting interest. This was in strange taste as coming from the senior member for the city, to say nothing of its injustice and absurdity. The other honourable member, Mr. Martin, did not regard the "lower classes" at all. If he understood Mr. Martin's speech aright, he contended that the great body of the people had no right to be considered at all in questions of government. He told us plainly that man had no inherent right to representation; that it was for the Legislature to determine to whom should be granted this right; that the franchise was a mere matter of convenience, to be fixed by those who had the power to fix it. The Solicitor-General (Mr. Manning), who he was bound to say had met the question in a more fair and liberal manner than any of the other supporters of the Bill, had also talked about the people "as one of the estates of the realm." The learned gentleman repeatedly made use of that expression. Now, he would like to know, if that estate were taken away, where all the other estates would be. According to all the constitutional authorities he had ever read, the people were regarded as the basis of the realm itself. It certainly seemed strange to him to hear the people set down by a law officer of the Government as "one of the estates of the realm." If that estate were taken away, he should imagine that the honourable gentleman's salary would soon follow. Mr. Martin, in his speech, went on to state, "that he did not recognise the right of any meeting, or any body of men, to sit in revision of the acts of

Constitution Act.

that Council. The Council was elected for the purpose of legislation, and he (Mr. Martin) wanted to know what was the superior body that was to sit in review of their acts." This, let it be remembered, was the legislative body which was condemned by the very Constitution Bill which Mr. Martin himself was endeavouring to pass. Old-fashioned people thought that there was such a thing as the right of petition, as the right of free discussion,—to review in public meeting the conduct of Government, and the conduct of the people's representatives. It would be found that there was an ulterior right when their legislators were acting treason against the liberties of the people—the right to punish, the right to send them back into the obscurity from which they had emerged. These were some of the unconstitutional doctrines against which he for one protested, and against which the resolution was aimed. And considering how loudly they had been cheered, how cordially they had been responded to in the Legislative Council, he thought the reception they had met with was sufficient to destroy all faith in the Council's intelligence and sense of justice. But having some consideration for the large array of authorities which these members had brought to bear upon the question, he would beg permission to place before the meeting the opinions of men not less distinguished, in order to fortify his own opinions, which were of very little value in themselves. He would assure them that his authorities were not perverted as others had been in the Legislative Council, but that the sentiments expressed in the. extracts he was about to read were in accordance with the doctrines which these illustrious men had spent their lives in establishing. The first authority he would trouble them with was Jeremy Bentham, and he ventured to think that he was almost as great a philosopher as James Martin. Another of his authorities would be a statesman, who was now known in English history as the "Great Commoner;" he meant the illustrious Earl of Chatham. He ventured to think that he might be considered nearly as great as William Charles Wentworth. Bentham, then, said :—

"Property, it is continually said, is the only bond and pledge of attachment to country. Not it, indeed. Want of property is a much stronger one. He who has property can change the shape of it, and carry it away with him to another country whenever he pleases. He who has no property can do no such thing. In the eyes of those who live by the labour of others, the existence of those by whose labour they live is indeed of no value ; not so in the eyes of labourers themselves. Life is not worth more to yawners than to labourers; and their country is the only country in which they can so much as hope to live. Among a hundred of them not ten exceptions to this will you find."

He would now read, in connexion with this extract from Bentham, and to elucidate its full meaning, the opinion of one of the truest philanthropists—one of the purest and most elevated intellects of this or any other age—the great and good Dr. Channing :—

"Let us not disparage that nature which is common to all men, for no thought can measure its grandeur. It is the image of God—the image even of His infinity—for no limits can be set to its unfolding. He who possesses the divine powers of the soul is a great being, be his place what it may. You may clothe him with rags, may immure him in a dungeon, may chain him to slavish tasks, but he is still great. You may shut him out of your houses, but God opens to him heavenly mansions. He makes no show, indeed, in the streets of a splendid city ; but a clear thought, a pure affection, a resolute act of a virtuous will, have a dignity of quite another kind, and far higher than accumulations of brick and granite, of plaister and stucco, however cunningly put together, or though stretching far beyond our sight. Nor is this all. If we pass over this grandeur of our common nature, and turn our thoughts to that comparative greatness which draws chief attention, and which consists in the decided superiority of the individual to the general standard of power and character, we shall find this as free and frequent a growth among the obscure and unnoticed as in more conspicuous walks of life. The truly great are to be found everywhere ; nor is it easy to say in what condition they spring up most plentifully. Real greatness has nothing to do with a man's sphere. It does not lie in the magnitude of his outward agency, in the extent of the effects which he produces. The greatest men may do comparatively little abroad. Perhaps the greatest men in our city at this moment are buried in obscurity. Grandeur of character lies wholly in force of soul, that is in the force of thought, moral principle, and love, and this may be found in the humblest condition of life. A man brought up to an obscure trade, and hemmed in by the wants of a growing family, may in his narrow sphere perceive more clearly, discriminate more keenly, weigh evidence more wisely, seize on the right means more decisively, and have more presence of mind in difficulty, than another who has accumulated vast stores of knowledge by laborious study ; and he has more of intellectual greatness. Many a man who has gone but a few miles from home understands human nature better, detects motives and weighs character more sagaciously, than another who has travelled over the known world and made a name by his reports of different countries. It is force of thought which measures intellectual, and so it is force of principle which measures moral, greatness—that highest of human endowments, that brightest manifestation of the Divinity. The greatest man is he who chooses the right with invincible resolution, who resists the sorest temptations from within and without, who bears the heaviest burdens cheerfully, who is calmest in storms, and most fearless under menace and frowns, whose reliance on truth, on virtue, on God, is most unfaltering; and is this a greatness which is apt to make a show, or which is most likely to abound in conspicuous stations? Perhaps in our presence the most heroic deed on earth is done in some silent spirit, the loftiest purpose cherished, the most generous sacrifice made, and we do not suspect it. I believe this greatness to be most common among the multitude whose names are never heard. Among common people will be found more of hardship borne manfully, more of unvarnished truth, more of religious trust, more of that generosity which gives what the giver needs himself, and more of a wise estimate of life and death, than among the more prosperous. And even in regard to influence over other beings, which is thought the peculiar prerogative of distinguished station, I believe that the difference between the conspicuous and the obscure does not amount to much. Influence is to be measured, not by the extent of surface it covers, but by its kind. A man may spread his mind, his feelings and opinions through a great extent; but if his mind be a low one, he manifests no greatness. A wretched artist may fill a city with daubs, and by a false showy style achieve reputation; but the man of genius, who leaves behind him one grand picture, in which immortal beauty is embodied, and which is silently to spread a true taste in his art, exerts an incomparably higher influence."

He had felt some hesitation in taking up their time with this long extract, which was somewhat out of place at a public meeting, but it became necessary to expose the pernicious and wicked attempts which had been made in the Legislative Council to disparage the intelligence of the great body of the people. There was the Postmaster-General—who told them that he had visited many foreign countries. That gentleman appeared a fair illustration of Dr. Channing's remark, that many persons did not profit by their travels. They had been told by Mr. Martin that they were not able to form a serious opinion, or one of any value on important questions; but he would rather take the judgment of Dr. Channing. Let them now hear what Lord Chatham had said upon the subject, speaking in the House of Peers :—

"I myself am one of the people. I esteem that security and independence which is the original birthright of an Englishman, far beyond the privileges, however splendid, which are annexed to the Peerage."

He hoped these authorities would be sufficient to prove that the people of this colony had been treated with a contumely and arrogant disregard which were foreign to the feelings of Englishmen of whatever rank, and that the course pursued in the recent debate did not entitle the Council to their confidence and respect. What was the doctrine that had been advanced in the Council but, in effect, that the people were unworthy of the free expression of opinion or the exercise of political influence ? He would now address himself to the other part of the resolution, which declared that, from the inherent defects of nomineeism and the existence of class interests in the Council, that body was not deserving of the confidence of the people. And on this subject he must trouble them with one more quotation. It was from a gentleman born in the colony, one who was now living an active life in their midst, one who was universally regarded as one of the most powerful intellects that this country had produced. He was about to read the opinions of no less a personage than Mr. Wentworth himself on the subject of nomineeism. Some twelve years ago, many of them would remember, there was an investigation made into the subject of certain land claims in New Zealand. This investigation was conducted by that most able man, Governor Sir George Gipps; and they would remember with what masterly ease he turned Mr. Wentworth—great as he was now among the pigmies of Macquarie-street—completely round his finger. It would appear that, shortly before that investigation, Sir George Gipps had sent home the name of Mr. Wentworth, whom he recommended for apppointment to the next vacancy in the old Nominee Council. But in consequence, as it would seem, of facts which discovered themselves to the mind of the late Governor in the progress of this investigation, Sir George felt himself compelled to send another despatch to the Secretary of State, advising that his recommendation in favour of Mr. Wentworth should not be carried out. In course of time the first despatch and the counter-despatch arrived in this colony and were printed. Mr Wentworth immediately wrote a furious letter to a Sydney newspaper, defending himself from what he considered an injustice done to his public character. And what paper did he select for his manifesto ? He did not go to the *Sydney Morning Herald* then, but to the *Free Press*, the most democratic paper in the colony, conducted by Mr. James M'Eachern, who certainly could not be considered as a very high Conservative. This was the paper which was then his political organ ; and the fact had some significance, considering that Mr. Wentworth had so vehemently declared that he never was a democrat. His letter appeared in the *Free Press* of January 6th, 1842. He wished the meeting to notice how highly Mr. Wentworth spoke then of nominee members. This was what he said :—

Constitution Act. 31

" If the Governor, before he made his recommendation, had condescended to explain his gracious intentions to me, I would have told him, in reply, what all my more intimate friends can vouch for, that even under the government of Sir Richard Bourke, and notwithstanding my reverence for his public character, when it was generally understood that I was to be offered the vacant seat in the Legislative Council which was ultimately given to Sir John Jamison, that I had made up my mind, after the fullest consideration, not to accept the office, if it had been tendered to me, even by *him*. If my repugnance was invincible *then* to become a *mere nominee*, and to *lose caste* by suffering myself to be enrolled among a body of official and unofficial members, the former of whom are given to understand, notwithstanding their oaths, that it is a condition of their tenure of office that they are to support all measures of the Government, whether good or bad ; and the latter of whom, for the most part, seem only to have been selected from their utter incompetency to offer any effectual resistance to such measures ; or from their known or expected obsequiousness to the powers that be ;—I ask whether it is probable that I would have submitted, under the rule of Sir George Gipps, to lose my time in struggling against the hopeless majorities of such colleagues, or to sacrifice my independence by becoming one of his puppets, and succumbing to the contumelious treatment which he ever and anon indulges in towards those of his creatures whose sycophancy does not keep pace with his rabid appetite for adulation."

Now, these " creatures," as he called them, whose portraits he had painted so faithfully, for whom he had expressed such bitter contempt—these were the very men whom he now sought to elevate into the region of perpetual nomineeism. No wonder those gentlemen, seeing his vivid powers of description, were now delighted to get him on their side. This was Mr. Wentworth's opinion in 1842; no doubt, if they could penetrate the inmost recesses of that gentleman's heart, they would find that he had the same opinion still of his new allies. But, without any such supernatural scrutiny, they might arrive at what was Mr. Wentworth's opinion now, or at least what it was only a few months ago. He would give them an extract from Mr. Wentworth's speech, on moving for a Committee to draw up this very Bill that they were now discussing :—

" In excluding from the list of the Committee which he proposed the name of any nominee, more especially any official nominee, he was actuated by a consideration of delicacy towards these gentlemen. To place them on such a Committee as this would be to place them in a false position—false to themselves and the office they held—and a position in which they ought not to be placed. This was the sole reason why, in the composition of the Committee, he had confined it to the elective members of that House, and to infuse any other element into the constitution of the Committee would be to prevent the sense of the House from being properly arrived at. These were his views in reference to the composition of the Committee. He trusted that if any opposition to such a course manifested itself, the elective element in that House was strong enough to put it down."

This was an extract from Mr. Wentworth's speech in the Legislative Council on June 16th, 1852, and he thought it contained pretty strong language in condemnation of nominee legislators. He would ask, if the nominees were unfit to deal with the Constitution question twelve months ago, how much better fitted were they on Friday night last, when Mr. Wentworth implored these very men to give him their votes. There remained one more point in the resolution, and that was the assertion of the existence of a class ascendancy in the House. Since he had been on the hustings that afternoon, he had been told by a member of the House that there were no less than 33 members of that body closely connected with the squatting interest. That was a very significant fact, especially when they took it in connexion with Mr. Wentworth's assertion of the right of fifty or sixty families to erect themselves into an aristocracy, and to form eventually, as he proposed, an Upper House of Legislature. This right on the part of an arrogant few was assumed in Mr. Wentworth's first speech, and in his second speech we were told that he had devised his notable scheme of hereditary titles with a view to the peculiar qualifications of the "shepherd kings" of the country, who already possessed splendid acquisitions of land, and were on the high road to fortunes which would maintain them in a state of nobility. The squatters were, in fact, the only class in the country who could support the dignity and splendour of a title. If they duly weighed all this, and then looked at the last clauses of the Bill they would see, by the provisions Mr. Wentworth had made to secure the possession of their lands in the hands of the squatting interest, that a deep design to exalt and aggrandise a class by the spoliation of the people was at the bottom of the present measure. Unless two-thirds of the Legislature, a large proportion of whom they might clearly see would be connected with the squatting interest, gave their assent to any alteration in the Constitution, the lands would be theirs in perpetuity. He thought this was most conclusive evidence that there was this class ascendancy in that body which was denounced in the resolution as dangerous to the liberties of the people. If the members of the Legislature were so daring, so deeply infected with treason—he could use no milder term—

Constitution Act. 33

towards the liberties of the people, as to deny their right to meet and express their opinions; and if they treated their petitions with contumely and disregard, he must say that it was idle to petition that body any longer, and that it was indeed time to express a public want of confidence in its deliberations and its acts. When they remembered that one-third of the members of that House were there without the concurrence of the people at all, and the majority of the elective members—elected, it was true, but by a system which was a perfect mockery of representation—were opposed to the wishes and the interests of the people, surely, in the name of everything that was just and true, in the name of everything that was thoroughly British, it was time to express our total want of confidence in that body. He would now call their attention to the aspersion of the mercantile interest that had been indulged in by Mr. Wentworth; and he thought he could not do better than contrast his opinions with those of the great Earl of Chatham. Mr. Wentworth boldly declared that the merchants of Sydney were of no use, that the colony could do very well without them. The Earl of Chatham had said, in speaking of the same class—

"I hope, my lords, that nothing I have said will be understood to extend to the honest, industrious tradesman, who holds the middle rank, and has given repeated proofs that he prefers law and liberty to gold. I love that class of men. Much less would I be thought to reflect upon the fair merchant, whose liberal commerce is the prime source of national wealth. I esteem his occupation, and respect his character."

Though no arguments were required to expose the absurdity of Mr. Wentworth's notions, he could not help quoting the estimate formed of the value of the tradesman and the merchant by the great English commoner. According to Mr. Wentworth, these great classes—whose intelligence and enterprise were of such immense importance to every civilised community, and who were themselves generally the most enlightened promoters of the well-being of the State—were perfectly useless, and disentitled to any consideration in the working of representative Government. (Here the speaker was interrupted by much cheering and repeated cries of "Bob Nichols."*) Well, he had been frequently reminded

---

*The late George Robert Nichols who, though carried away on the Constitution question by his admiration for his fellow countryman, Mr. Wentworth, had been identified with most of the liberal movements in the colony, and was the author of many useful measures.

D

of that honourable member, but he had not much to say about him. He would tell them what a witty friend of his had said respecting that gentleman a few days ago. On being told that Mr. Nichols had recanted and joined the nominees, he replied, "poor Robert! he has been canting all his life, and it is now high time that he recanted." It might be truly said that Mr. Nichols had been canting in more senses than one—canting like a ship without ballast, as well as dealing in all the discarded cant of political quackery. But with respect to Mr. Nichols, who was now so conservative in his ideas, they would all remember that that gentleman not long ago had talked very loudly about 100,000 American sympathisers coming over to enable the colony to obtain its independence. This was said at a public dinner in this city presided over by Mr. Nichols; and who did they think was the person who on that occasion took exception to the anti-British language of Mr. Nichols? Why, it was Mr. Wentworth's arch-anarchist, the humble person now speaking, who in that room protested against the disloyal language of the honourable gentleman. And now with regard to the aspersions so freely cast upon himself. Mr. Wentworth had honoured him with the title of the "arch-anarchist." He supposed he was regarded as the leader of the imaginary "ruffians" who were to go down to Vaucluse and pillage it.* He would tell that honourable gentleman that he had no such power, no such influence, as was attributed to him. The part he had taken in the present movement was a very humble one; he had done no more than any other member of this Committee; and with regard to his being an anarchist, he most indignantly denied that he was in any respect a worse citizen than Mr. Wentworth himself. In the opposition he had felt it his duty to give to the measure now under discussion, he was actuated by the same singleness of purpose which he believed actuated all the gentlemen with whom he was associated. Mr. Wentworth had said that if certain persons—the "arch-anarchist," he supposed, among them—got the upper hand, they would trample on the country with an iron heel. But the truth was that they were seeking to rescue the country from the "iron heel" of others. He had himself been charged with want of loyalty to his fatherland. It would be more pardonable in Mr. Wentworth than in

---

* Language of the character indicated was frequently applied to the opponents of the Constitution Bill by Mr. Wentworth and his friends.

Constitution Act.

him to be deficient in patriotic feeling and in loyalty. He, at all events, had right good reason to be proud of his fatherland, and there was no pulse of his life that beat with truer warmth than that which responded to the title of a loyal Englishman. He was born in the heart of Old England, within a few hours' walk of the spot where Shakspeare was born, where some of the noblest associations of English history were fresh in the hearts of even the rural population; and he had been reared in one of the greatest and most prosperous and public-spirited towns in Great Britain. He spurned the attempt to fix upon him any advocacy of republican government. He was sincerely attached to his native country and her institutions. It was his heartfelt desire that that flag (pointing to the British ensign over the hustings) might wave in peace and security over his grave, and over the graves of his children; and in ages to come might float the banner of a great and glorious people here, affiliated by all the bonds of affection and justice to that dear old land from which they were all descended. In his judgment it would be a great and fatal mistake to attempt in Australia any mere imitation of the noble form of Government under which the great American people had risen to such colossal power. Nor did he imagine that, with the progress of events, the character of any known nation would be slavishly reproduced here. He thought this country was destined to show the spectacle of a great nation perfectly free, profoundly prosperous, and glowing with distinctive national aspirations, and yet united in the bonds of affection and political interests to the mother country. He did not want a "Yankee Constitution" any more than Mr. Wentworth. But by all that was sacred, by the God who had given them a great and fruitful country to dwell in, he for one would never consent to have a Norfolk Island Constitution. He objected—and the gentlemen with whom he was proud to act on this occasion objected—to Mr. Wentworth's scheme, because it was a scheme in violation of the true principles of the British Constitution. He had thought it right thus publicly and explicitly to defend himself and those who were associated with him against the charges which had been so recklessly made; he flung back those charges with unutterable scorn; he desired nothing beyond that which he was entitled to ask as a loyal and patriotic subject of the Queen of England. Before he sat down he would briefly advert to some of the misrepresentations of matters of history which had been put forward in the Council. A gentleman for whose public character he had a high respect, he meant the Attorney-General (Mr. Plunket) had told them, with an air of triumph, that the great men who framed the American Constitution had sat for months and years in discussion on the measure with closed doors, and that when their plan was matured they promulgated it by authority. But the historical fact was that, in the eleventh year of the Confederation, it was found that the Articles of Confederation were so defective for affording adequate power for national purposes—and this conviction had been forcing itself upon the minds of statesmen for several years—that it was determined to form a Convention for the revision of the form of government. Delegates for this purpose were appointed by twelve out of thirteen States, who met in Philadelphia on the 14th of May, 1787, to form a Constitution; and so far from sitting for years, he found that on the 17th of September in the same year they presented their report to Congress, which on the 28th of the same month remitted it to the several States for approval. To a certain extent it might be true that the delegates sat with closed doors, for as it was cold in America they probably did not leave them open. But so far from the Constitution being promulgated by authority, he found that one State, Rhode Island, refused to accept it, and stood out from the Union for two years and eight months. Virginia, stirred up by the great eloquence of Patrick Henry, one of the most remarkable men of the Revolution, also opposed it, and refused to accept it for many months. These were the facts of the case, and they showed the false basis of knowledge upon which gentlemen in the Council proceeded when they could listen to such distorted statements, and at the same time brand the people out of doors with ignorance and meddling with matters they did not understand. The Attorney-General had also told them that the Senate of the United States was elected by the Sovereign States, and therefore was appointed by a process analogous to the appointment of nominees by the Queen's representative; this, at all events, was what he understood from the speech of that learned gentleman. But Mr. Plunket must have been greatly misled, for it was known to most of them that the senators were elected by a majority of the votes of the State Legislatures. He was somewhat at a loss to understand why the

Attorney-General had pronounced such a high eulogium on the speech of Mr. Martin. He was ready to admit that that speech in many respects was an able one, but still he was surprised to hear the Attorney-General speak of it in terms of rapture. But he found, on referring to the conclusion of that speech, a very satisfactory reason for Mr. Plunket's admiration. Mr. Martin concluded with a very patriotic avowal that he would pension off the officers of the Crown at their full salaries, and doubtless such an idea of constitutional government was very delightful to the worthy Attorney-General. In conclusion, he urged them to consider whether they had not just reason to assent to the resolution he had read to them. After the contumely that had been heaped on them and their petitions,—after the unconstitutional doctrines which had been propounded by the Legislative Council—he for one would never send another petition to that body on this question. He denied the right of that House to force this Constitution on the people of the colony; and it was the bounden duty of all classes to appeal to a higher power—a more impartial tribunal. He had no doubt as to what the result of that appeal would be. Despite the overwhelming majority in the Council, the reasonableness and justice of their petitions would prevail, and the youthful energies of this fair country would be freed from the infliction of this most detestable and un-British measure.

ELECTION FOR SYDNEY IN 1854.

[MR. WENTWORTH had resigned his seat as member for the city of Sydney in the old Legislative Council, and had departed for England. The late Mr. Charles Kemp was a candidate for the vacancy, and Mr. Parkes was proposed in opposition. The suffrage was then held on a property-qualification, with open voting. The result of the poll was—Parkes, 1427 ; Kemp, 779.]

SPEECH .

Delivered at the nomination of candidates for the seat in the representation of Sydney vacated by the resignation of Mr. Wentworth, May 1, 1854.

Mr. PARKES said : I shall endeavour in addressing you to avoid the personalities which have supplied the chief staple of these proceedings. This meeting impresses me too deeply, not with any paltry expectation of triumph, but with a sense of my own unimportance and want of merit, to indulge in those feelings which the extent and warmth of the support I have met with hitherto are calculated to inspire. I am not one of those who look out for persons of leisure to fill important public offices, for I believe that every one created in God's image must do what he conceives to be his duty, whether he have leisure or not; and whatever the sacrifices he may be called upon to make, a man must not shrink from discharging that duty. It is with this feeling, and remembering that my own duties are already numerous and heavy, that I affirm that I would rather support any other candidate whose principles were in accordance, not with those of levellers and seditionists, but with those avowed by the present Government of Queen Victoria. If any man stood before you whose political views were as far advanced as those maintained by Her Majesty's Ministers, I would retire now at the eleventh hour and support that candidate. But I cannot, with this determination, support the election of Mr.

Election for Sydney in 1854. 39

Kemp, who is emphatically the stagnant man of New South Wales. Indeed, he is stagnation personified, and if you take him for your member you will be thrown back a century in your political history. I do not say this without having seriously considered what Mr. Kemp's principles are, as expounded by himself during this contest. I believe we can only advance in prosperity and security by adopting those principles of political progress which have, on more occasions than one, saved the mother country from perdition. I believe that had it not been for the repeated reforms in the institutions of England, she would have been shaken to her foundations by the anarchy which has overwhelmed other European states. Believing all this, and seeing that in England at the present day the parliamentary representation of the people comes more closely home to every man than it does here, what on earth is there seditious, disloyal, or un-English, in extending to every man in this country the right to which every British subject is entitled ? Yet this is regarded as the head and front of my offending with the "Plutocracy" of New South Wales. I shall now enter at some little length into an explanation of the principles which will guide me, if elected to the Legislative Council. I will not express that extravagant confidence of success which Mr. Kemp has expressed. If I am not constituted your representative, I shall not be very sorry for it, but if you do commit your interests to me, it is only right that you should know how I shall seek to discharge my duty. I believe that the danger here will be in limiting, not in extending, the power of the people ; for, as was justly remarked by my friend Mr. Darvall the other evening when supporting me as a fit candidate, there are very few persons amongst us who do not possess some stake in the country, or who have not the power to acquire that stake. Seeing, then, that the means of obtaining property are within the reach of every man of industrious habits ; seeing that every man here can pursue a course which must lead to competence or, at least, a position of comfort, I believe that the only danger which can accrue to the country will and must result from withholding that political power and those full privileges to which the people are entitled as free-born Britons. I should therefore use all my efforts, progressively—for I am fond of beginning with little and improving by degrees—to extend to every free-born man in this country, of unstained character and mature age, those rights which I myself possess. With regard to the great question of education, I have already declared myself, as systems at present stand, in favour of the national system. But so much importance do I attach to the work of mental training as the foundation of every social virtue, that I should be prepared to support any modification or alteration of that system which would more adapt it to the peculiar wants of the remote, thinly-populated and scattered districts of the colony. Some questions have been asked of me as to my views on the construction of railways. I, with every other man of common sense, believe that railways on a gigantic scale should be at once commenced, whatever the present cost, or whatever debt, within reasonable bounds, may result to posterity. We must, however, see first that the work is based upon sound principles, which if carried out will render the railways permanently useful. In connection with the construction of better roads, I desire to explain that if I go into the Legislature now or at any other time, I shall constantly bear in mind the vast importance to the country of public works of all descriptions. I shall give particular attention to the condition of our harbours along the whole sea coast, to get the bars and other natural obstructions removed, and thus to render their waters navigable. I am informed that even in our own harbour many of the bays are fast filling up, through want of efficient means of protection. There is one thing in the political reforms of the Constitution to which I promise, if elected, to give my best attention : I shall steadily exert myself to give this city a larger share in the general representation than it at present possesses. The bare idea that possibly I may, at four o'clock to-morrow afternoon, be your representative, instead of stimulating me to feelings of idle vanity, afflicts me with a deep sense of responsibility, and of the difficult task which will be thrown upon me so to shape my course as to be able to advance our infant liberties, and to be—without the prospect of which I would not continue to hold my seat—a valued member of the Legislature. If it should be my fortune to be elected, and I should find myself an uninfluential member of the House, my pride would not allow me to remain, whether you asked me to resign or not. That pride would compel me to retreat from a position for which I found myself unqualified, as much for my own sake as for the character of the constituency. Having thus briefly stated the reasons that have induced me to appear before you, and

Election for Sydney in 1854.

the principles by which I shall be guided, I have nothing more to do than to impress upon you that if you desire to see a free and prosperous country, to see a happy and virtuous population spread over the length and breadth of the land, to see households flourishing in places where now there is nothing but sterility and barrenness, you will not vote for Charles Kemp. This reminds me of some remarks made by Mr. Mort as to the value which the present squatting system has been to the country. He told us, somewhat irrelevantly, of cases of extreme hardship and even of absolute ruin endured by some of those enterprising pioneers who have penetrated the bush and been unsuccessful. Of all such great enterprises, no doubt, painful circumstances in special cases might be detailed; but what has that to do with the system itself? As to the squatters suffering from the want of labour, if, instead of taking in past years from parsimonious motives unsettled roving men who had no home, and therefore no inducement to remain on their stations, they had planted families there, and encouraged the system which nature clearly ordered in the beginning, they would have had a colonial-born population by this time, and their servants would have been too deeply anchored amongst them by domestic attachments to be tempted away, even by the inducements of the goldfields. I am far from being an enemy to the production of wool; I am as sensible as my friend Mr. Mort is—though I do not derive from it the splendid profits he does—of the vast importance our wool staple is to the country. But if the growth of wool were dispersed amongst more hands the production would be increased, and the staple be finer and more valuable, and it would take a higher relative standing in the markets of the world. I indignantly deny that I desire to injure any class in the community. I would contend for the rights of one man as soon as I would for another. I would support the rights of the richest amongst you, but at the same time with the same vigour, the same determination, the same energy, I would support the rights of the humblest and poorest. So far from being an instigator of class dissensions, I have ever set myself against class legislation of every kind. I would no more truckle to the working classes than to the highest; and at the same time, I believe that among the lowest classes there is often to be found the largest amount of virtue, the largest share of those energies which are most valuable to a young country, and on which every institution of the country must depend. It has been alleged that I am mainly supported in this election by the labouring and shop-keeping classes. I am proud of having the support of these classes, but if we are to place the rank and file of our supporters in array against each other, certainly I have on my side an immeasurably greater amount of education, social standing, and property than my opponent, for I have had the representatives of some of the oldest and most respectable families in the colony, members of the Legislature who are really ornaments of that House, supporting my election, whereas my opponent has gentlemen clinging round him with whom, only a week or two ago, he would have been ashamed to associate. Depend upon it, if Mr. Kemp remains in the country, his qualifications for one particular side of the House are such that he will not remain long without obtaining a seat in it. He is sure to be offered the first nominee seat that becomes vacant. Gentlemen, I thank you for the patience you have given me; I have declined to solicit a single vote, and if any man thinks in his conscience that I am an unfit man, then, in the name of heaven, let him vote against me. I ask for no such vote. I only say to you, exercise your right of suffrage faithfully, holding it, as you do, for the general good of the country. Elect the man whom calmly, deliberately, and apart from all personal considerations, you believe to be best fitted to promote the liberty and true interests of this young and beautiful country. As to the result, I may be left in a minority to-morrow. If that should be the case, my judgment will be deceived without my feelings being wronged. If I know this constituency after some years of experience, I shall be returned by a triumphant majority.

STATE OF AGRICULTURE BEFORE RESPONSIBLE GOVERNMENT.*

SPEECH

Delivered in the Legislative Council, July 3rd, 1855, on moving for appointment of "A Select Committee, to inquire into and report upon the state of agriculture in the colony, with special reference to the raising of wheaten grain, and to the causes of hindrance or failure in that great industrial pursuit, whether arising from the social condition of the people, the policy of the Government, or the physical character of the country."

MR. PARKES said—In submitting to the House the resolution standing in his name, it was not his intention to occupy the public time beyond what was necessary to state the reasons which, as it appeared to him, should induce the House to grant the Committee now asked for. He had, for some few years past, been much surprised that no motion relative to the agricultural condition of the colony had been made in that House; during last session especially he had entertained this feeling, and expressed it to several honourable members. It appeared to him to be, if not a great neglect, at all events a strange oversight on the part of those who directed the public affairs of the country, that no attempt had been made to collect, in some accessible and authoritative shape, such information as might be obtained relative to so important a branch of our industrial life, so intimately connected with the welfare of the country. When we reflected that whatever might be the motives

---

* The experience of the last twenty years has abundantly proved that extensive districts of New South Wales are as favourable for the growth of wheat, and for general agricultural farming, as any part of the world. Seventy bushels per acre are often obtained from wheat lands. At the time when this speech was delivered it was, however, a common thing for members of the then-existing Legislature to declare that the interior of the colony was only fit for sheep farming.

to our private actions, whatever ends we might aim at in our public conduct, those motives and those ends could not possibly be separated from, and must depend upon, our relations with our fellow-creatures, it appeared exceedingly strange that the great question as to what provision we possessed within ourselves for supplying the population with the principal article of food had been almost entirely left out of consideration. He thought it would not be disputed that to be in such a state as we now were, without some correct public statistics as to the supply of food from the soil, was to be in a condition not at all in accordance with the public safety. In the mother country the greatest possible attention was being paid to the question of obtaining accurate information as to the returns of wheat and grain, although even there the statistics obtained were anything but of the trustworthy character that could be hoped for. More recently, however, these had become more correct, owing to attention having been directed towards them by persons who considered these returns as of the utmost importance to the public economy of the State. It must be admitted that, whatever might be the circumstances of happiness in which we were placed individually, these circumstances would lose all their importance to us if it were not for the ministrations of the crowds round about us. However fertile and however beautiful the country might be, if it were barren of human life and activity beauty itself would become only another name for desolation, and the very light of heaven would be fearful to our eyes. This extensive city, so cheerful in the sunshine to-day, with its streets of palaces, its thousands of secure homes, its spacious marts and banks, would to-morrow, if population floated away from it, present the awful aspect of the tomb. Seeing then that our importance as individuals was in every respect just in proportion to the progress of the population as a whole, the Legislature and Government should pay every attention to supplying the people with that great staple of food, the extreme scarcity of which would be more severely felt in its consequences than the sword of an enemy. At a time when flour was being sold at from £55 to £60 per ton, when it was believed that there was a very inadequate supply of this article of food in the country, it seemed more than ever necessary that attention should be paid to the subject. It might be urged, in reply to his observations, in the usual set terms of one class of persons, that the land of this country was unfit for agriculture. But if, in reality, this country had been left deficient in this respect by the Creator; if the soil were proved to be incapable of producing sufficient food for the people—why, then, that fact admitted, it would be one of the strongest arguments for greater efforts to mitigate, as far as the dictates of wisdom could mitigate, the effect of so serious a barrier to the advancement of the country in wealth and power. At all events, no objection could reasonably be urged against an endeavour being made to ascertain the truth in the matter. If it were the case that the country was unsuited to the prosecution of those agricultural pursuits which, in all really prosperous countries, were of such magnitude and importance; and that grain could not, under any possible circumstances, be produced in quantity adequate to the wants of the population, it would be best that whatever information could be collected should be brought together and published in a shape accessible to those persons whose energies were likely to be turned in that direction. Individual instances might be given of the failure of persons who had settled on the lands of the country for agricultural purposes, but such cases of failure might be accounted for by the spirit of neglect and suppression which had been manifested towards this interest in the public policy of the country.' He was not disposed to take up the time of the House by entering upon any charges against other interests; but it struck him that towards the present destitution of the country a very great deal had been done, insidiously and unknown to the public, and to some extent unconsciously by the persons so acting, to depress the pursuit of agriculture on the one hand, and to encourage that of pastoral occupation on the other. He could give numerous instances to prove such had been the case in the course of legislation in that House, and in the conduct of the Government. One or two would be quite sufficient to put the case in a very clear light. In the first place, then, there had always been a greater facility and cheapness in obtaining lands for occupation as pastures than in obtaining lands for cultivation. We were all aware that, while pasture lands were held on a merely nominal rental, the other class of land was often bought up at £10 per acre. The system in which the Surveyor-General's department was managed tended largely to the same result. The surveyors were employed by contract to prosecute their surveys, and such was the want of proper organisation in the Survey department that these officers were frequently kept out of remuneration for their labour for several months ; and they were in many cases compelled to accept private engagements to support themselves. Instances had come to his knowledge of surveyors being obliged to undertake surveys of private properties because they could not obtain payment for their services to the Government. If this were the case, it would alone account for a great portion of the difficulty which industrious persons had experienced in securing lands for cultivation, because in such a state of things those who were best off would receive first attention. It was also found that laws had been passed by that House to facilitate the borrowing of money by persons engaged in pastoral occupations, while the pursuit of agriculture had obtained no such advantage. The Lien on Wool Act was really copied from an act passed for the West Indies, which was mainly intended to encourage the cultivation of the land. But here the principle was perverted to a species of class legislation for the exclusive advantage of the squatters. If the agriculturist possessed one or two hundred acres of wheat, worth from £1000 to £2000, he could not possibly obtain any similar assistance to provide for reaping and housing his produce, and conveying it to market; whereas, if the same amount of capital and industry were directed to pastoral pursuits, every possible facility would be afforded to the person so engaged, the capitalist assisting him having legally a preferent claim against other creditors on his property. When it was seen that our legislation had been directed to encourage the one pursuit and to place the other at a disadvantage, sufficient was presented to our view to account for persons being deterred from agricultural occupations. The bias he pointed out had been manifest throughout the legislation of this country, and the conduct of the Government had been marked by the same neglect of the agricultural interest. Even in the Impounding Act—which the honourable member (Mr. Nichols) proposed to remodel this session—the freeholder was placed at a disadvantage ; he sometimes paid £10 more on an acre for his farm land ; and if the squatter's cattle trespassed on his farm he could drive them to the pound and the squatter would be punished with one shilling per head damages. But if the freeholder's cattle were to stray upon the squatter's run, for which he paid only a mere peppercorn rent, besides the usual damages he could charge three shillings per head for driving them to the pound. Here was protection given in favor of those engaged in pastoral pursuits to four times the extent of what was allowed to the rest of the community. This was enough to show that the legislation of that Council had been aimed at protecting the interests of this particular party, fencing them round with special privileges, to the neglect of interests equally important to the community. One public benefit would certainly result from the labours of this Committee if it were appointed, namely—the initiation of a system of agricultural statistics. Such returns would be of great use to persons engaged in commerce, as it was absolutely necessary for merchants to be provided with correct information concerning the country's produce. He would, with the permission of the House, read a portion of a paper read before the Statistical Society of London in February of last year by Mr. Paull, a gentleman who had been all his life paying attention to the subject. After explaining very clearly and fully the two systems now adopted in the mother country, he proceeded to explain the plan he would recommend himself for collecting the agricultural statistics of Great Britain.

"In a statistical sense a nation is only an aggregate of parishes, as parishes are of farms ; so that we have a sound means of obtaining the corn statistics of all of them. Let us look at this in detail. We have a terrier or particulars of every parish, with or without maps, and there are in every parish some individuals distinguished for local knowledge in respect of the parish lands ; men who, on looking at the particulars, can recognise every field and its locality. Now, at given times of the year, that is to say when the lands are bearing their crops; a person so qualified could walk over the parish, map and terrier in hand, and mark every field with its visible crop ; and whilst this individual was so employed, the parish schoolmaster, or some other competent scribe, could prepare a copy of the parish terrier, giving columns for every sort of grain and vegetable crop. Then these two men, their mutual labour being so far advanced, should introduce into its proper column the area of each field, and obtain a correct total for every column. This done, I submit that they would have obtained safe parish statistics, in so far as acreage and produce are concerned. But here an important question arises as to the ability of the individuals whom I thus propose to furnish the requisite information. In answering this question, we must not allow ourselves to be prejudiced by the personal appearance of the agriculturist or agricultural labourer ; we must not allow the coarseness of his manners—if coarse they be—to blind us to his intelligence, to the faculty always in him of declaring the average produce per acre of his parish for any kind of grain or vegetable, and the consequences of unusually good or bad seasons, as they affect the average produce. After a life-long acquaintance with these men, I do not hesitate to assert that this instinctive knowledge of theirs would be justified by elaborate inquiries on the subject of parish produce. This fine faculty, then, being in every parish, we need not go beyond its limits to find men capable of declaring, at any point of the time that a particular crop takes to reach maturity, what the result will be in respect of production, both absolutely and with reference to the average produce; and were such men furnished by Government with skeleton-printed papers, comprising appropriate leading questions, with clear directions how to fill them up, I submit that, by these simple means, our Government would have, year by year, safe corn and vegetable statistics of produce from every parish."

Such persons might be found in those districts where it was known that the cultivation of grain was most pursued, who would readily perform this duty, and at a comparatively small cost to the State. At the same time he would admit that the information would be of no value whatever unless it were correct; and it certainly appeared that to employ such persons as were mostly engaged in agriculture would be the most correct mode of obtaining the information desired. If the House should see fit to grant this Committee, the eliciting of such particulars as might help to originate a satisfactory system would form one of the most important branches of the inquiry. Whatever might prove to be the position of the country as to the allegations so often made, that it was not able to supply sufficient food for its population, notwithstanding the immense extent of its territory, while bread was at so high a price that it caused a large amount of distress in this very metropolis— whatever might be the result of the inquiry, at all events let the truth be known. This Committee ought to be granted, for it was right that we should exactly know our condition. If the beggarly character of our agricultural produce arose from physical drawbacks, it was only right that the labouring population of this country and of the mother country, especially the smaller industrious capitalists, who form so valuable a class in all countries, should be made to understand that it would be of no avail to cultivate a soil which gave no guarantee from nature that their efforts would be successful, and where the laws of the country had been made with an utter forgetfulness of the objects of their industry.

TAXATION AND FREE TRADE.

[IN the last session of the mixed nominee and elective Legislature which existed before the introduction of Responsible Government, several measures were proposed under the auspices of the late Mr. Riddell and the present Sir William Manning, which were strongly opposed to the principles of Free-trade. On the 5th July, 1855, Sir William Manning—then Solicitor-General—moved the second reading of a Bill " to impose a tonnage duty on all vessels entering the port of Newcastle, the money so raised to be devoted to the purposes of constructing wharves and otherwise improving the harbour of Newcastle, and facilitating the navigation of the river Hunter to Morpeth and Maitland." The motion was opposed by the late Sir Stuart Alexander Donaldson, who moved that the Bill be read a second time that day six months. The original motion, however, was carried by 20 votes against 15. Mr. Parkes seconded and spoke in favour of the amendment, and his short speech on the occasion is included in this selection. The Bill was passed into law, and continued in force until the year 1873, when it was repealed by the Parkes Government. Among the members who advocated the principle of the Bill was Sir James Martin, to whose arguments reference is made by Mr. Parkes. While this Bill was under consideration, the Governor-General (Sir William Denison) sent to the Council a financial minute of unusual length and character, submitting the Estimates of expenditure and revenue, which were largely in excess of those of former years. As the amount reserved by the then existing Constitution Act for the civil departments was found, in consequence of the rise in prices caused by the discovery of gold and from other causes, to be insufficient by the large amount of £54,763, the Governor-General submitted the " reserved schedules," with the other Estimates, to the Council.* Other partial concessions were made, and at the same time large appropriations were proposed for public works. To meet the increased expenditure, new means of

---

*By the schedules of the Constitution Act of that day, the appropriations for the departments of the Government were placed beyond the control of the Legislature. The first election under the present Constitution took place in 1856.

taxation were required, and the three courses that suggested themselves to the Government were thus explained by Sir William Denison's minute :—" First, the imposition of an *ad valorem* duty upon all imports; second, an *ad valorem* duty upon articles of luxury, such as silks, &c.; third, a general increase in the rate of charge upon the articles in the present tariff, and the imposition of duties upon certain other articles of extensive consumption, where the charge could be determined according to the weight or bulk of the article without any direct reference to the value." The debate opened by the Colonial Treasurer's statement on the financial state of the colony, commenced July 12th, and occupied five nights. It was proposed by the Solicitor-General (now Sir William Manning) to refer the Estimates to the consideration of a Select Committee, and an amendment was moved by Mr. (now Sir James) Martin against entertaining the consideration of the schedules, as not being within the competent power of the Legislative Council. This amendment was negatived by 32 to 10. Mr. Parkes spoke on the fourth night of the debate, and the speech giving his opinions at some length on finance and taxation, and also exposing the wasteful character of the public expenditure twenty years ago, is here included.]

SPEECH

Delivered in the Legislative Council, July 5th, 1855.

MR. PARKES said he intended to vote for the amendment, and he thought every sincere advocate of free-trade must oppose the present measure. Notwithstanding what had been said by one honourable member (Mr. Martin), who had ever appeared as the champion of protection—and who, in fact, was in himself the protectionist party in that House—he regarded the Bill as adverse to the principles of free-trade. What was the object of that policy but to leave the commerce of the country as free as possible —not with reference to the particular classes engaged in trading pursuits, but for the promotion of the general trade by which all were equally benefited? Now, the measure before them sought to effect its object by placing a restriction on trade. And it was absurd to attempt to support this proposal in the manner of the honourable the Colonial Secretary, by saying it was carrying out a species of self-imposed taxation. Why, it was the House that was endeavouring to tax the people of Newcastle, if it could be considered as a tax on them at all. The only way to let them tax themselves was to give them corporate powers of taxation for

Taxation and Free Trade. 51

local purposes, not by a Bill like the present measure. But, in point of fact, this would be a tax, not on the people of Newcastle, but upon the owners of vessels trading to their port, and it would tend to cripple their trade; and if Newcastle suffered the colony at large would suffer in consequence. On the other hand, if Newcastle were benefited in her trade by the improvements contemplated, the benefits would not in their consequences be confined to Newcastle, but would extend to the whole colony; and therefore, the expense, as he thought, should be met from the general revenue. He agreed with the principles enunciated in this respect by the honourable and reverend member for Stanley (Dr. Lang), that works of a national character, like the improvements of our ports and navigable rivers, should be carried out at the expense of the country. If the revenue were not sufficient, then some new mode of taxation based on sound and comprehensive principles should be devised, which would fall with just equality on the general wealth and industry of the nation. The improvement of the navigation of the Hunter would not be for the sole advantage of the people of Newcastle; for, with the increasing trade of the Hunter, the commercial operations of the colony would also be increased. If they imposed a tonnage duty in the port of Newcastle, how long could they keep a similar duty from the port of Sydney? He regarded the present measure with suspicion, as one that was the forerunner of other measures opposed to those principles of free-trade which had been laid down by the House. He gave the honourable member for Cook and Westmoreland every credit for consistency in the course which he had pursued that night, as it was in accordance with the views he had always entertained. But he was surprised to see the Bill supported by the enlightened member of the Government who had introduced it to the House.

SPEECH

Delivered in the Legislative Council, July 25th, 1855.

Mr. PARKES: In the course of the debate that night the honourable member for Durham* had remarked that, if there should be a

---
*Sir Charles Cowper, K.C.M.G.

division upon the amendment before the House, it would be the most singular division that had ever taken place. Certainly he should for his part divide against the honourable member in this instance, much as he desired on all occasions to be on the same side with him; for, if the amendment were assented to by the House, they would in his humble judgment be led into an error —an error of grave consequence to the whole country, as far as its legislation was concerned. In addressing himself to the important subject brought before them by the motion of the honourable the Colonial Treasurer, he admitted at once that the time had now arrived when this country ought to be prepared— when it was the duty of that House to prepare the people—to submit to an increased taxation. The interests of the country demanded that a much larger revenue should be raised, in order to carry out those important works which were so necessary to the development of the resources of the country; and it was impossible to execute those works without, to some extent, throwing a burden upon posterity. But while he was of opinion that it was the duty of the people to submit to a much larger expenditure, he disapproved altogether of the manner in which the Governor-General proposed to raise the additional revenue. Before proceeding to a full consideration of this topic he would, in support of his view of the advantages of an adequate revenue from taxation, so long as it was strictly and intelligently limited by the actual necessities of the public, read a short passage from the well-known work of Mr. John Stuart Mill, whose words he thought were closely applicable to the present case :—

"That part of the public expenditure which is devoted to the maintenance of civil and military establishments is still, in many cases, unnecessarily profuse ; but though many of the items will bear great reduction, others certainly require increase. There is hardly any public reform or improvement of the first rank proposed of late years, and still remaining to be effected, which would not probably require, at least for a time, an increased instead of a diminished appropriation of public money. Whether the object be popular education ; emigration and colonisation ; a more efficient and accessible administration of justice ; a more judicious treatment of criminals ; improvements in the condition of soldiers and sailors ; a more effective police ; reforms of any kind which, like the slave emancipation, require compensation to individual interests ; or, finally, what is as important as any of these—the establishment of a sufficient staff of able and highly-educated public servants, to conduct in a better than the present awkward manner the business of legislation and administration. Every

Taxation and Free Trade. 53

one of these things implies considerable expense ; and many of them have again and again been prevented by the reluctance which exists to apply to Parliament for an increased grant of public money, though the cost would be repaid—often a hundredfold—in more pecuniary advantages to the community generally. I fear that we should have to wait long for most of these things, if taxation were as odious as it probably would be if it were exclusively direct."

This eminent writer was here speaking in favour of a system of mixed taxation, but he thought that his remarks applied to the present circumstances of the colony, in the view which he took of the duty of the Legislature to prepare the people to submit to a larger taxation in order that they might advance in public improvement. But with respect to the manner in which it was proposed to increase the revenue of the country, he entirely objected to it. He thought that the proposals of His Excellency the Governor-General were to all intents and purposes of a distinctly protectionist character; that, in fact, they were in every respect opposed to the principles of free-trade. They were in some instances so unwisely in opposition to free-trade principles that he believed that, even if they were sanctioned by the House, they would defeat their own ends for all purposes of revenue. As examples of this, he would mention the proposed taxes upon soap and candles ; the tax of 4s. per cwt. upon soap and that of 18s. 8d. per cwt. upon candles would prove, in effect, a large protectionist duty in favour of the home manufacturers. These taxes, if imposed, would entirely fail in their purpose, and no revenue would be derived from them, as the importation of the taxed articles would for the most part cease. Then as to the proposed tax upon salt, he had been informed on good authority that the colony exported in 1854 no less than 180,000 raw hides, or 89,562 cwt. Now in the preparation of those hides 14 lbs. of salt were required to each, and thus it would be seen that a tax upon salt would actually be an export duty of 3d. per hide on our own produce. It was easy to perceive the evil effects which a tax of this description would have upon the public generally, and it seemed strange to him that such a duty—a duty in fact upon one of the commonest necessaries—should have been thought of at all. He believed that the intentions of His Excellency the present Governor-General were of the purest and best; from the time of his arrival he had always given him credit for an earnest desire to govern the country well ; and he therefore the more deeply regretted that

His Excellency had now taken a course which must bring him into some degree of disfavour, and was not unlikely to embroil him with the House. He thought the time had arrived—and in this respect he could not altogether agree with the opinion put forth by the honourable member for the Sydney Hamlets (Mr. Donaldson), to the effect that the tariff of 1852 should be considered a finality; although he fully admitted that that tariff was a great step in the right direction—he thought, he said, that the time had arrived when the broad principles of free-trade which had been so successful in the mother-country, and which were rapidly gaining ground in all countries of a commercial standing, should be adopted in this colony to the fullest extent. The tariff of 1852 was however in some degree protectionist; he found, for instance, that there was a duty imposed upon wine, which it was hard to reconcile with the principle that taxes should be imposed only for the purposes of revenue. He was so far from thinking that the mode of raising revenue was unexceptionable, that he believed the time had now arrived when they should follow the example of England, and as far as possible raise their additional revenue by new modes of taxation. Until that good time arrived, which was looked forward to by many, when the enlightenment of men and the improved condition of society would admit of the abolition of customs duties altogether, the idea which had entered the minds of the financiers of England was, that every step further should be taken in the path that led towards direct taxation. Even in the recent war budget of Sir George Cornewall Lewis this was the characteristic; and though the new Chancellor of the Exchequer had resorted to the customs for an increase on several commodities of consumption, yet it was observable in the proceedings of Parliament that the members of highest financial reputation strongly protested against this feature of the Government scheme. He (Mr. Parkes) would confess he had to a considerable extent fallen in with the views of the honourable member for Cumberland with regard to the imposition of a stamp duty. He believed that at the present juncture such a duty would be the most politic and statesmanlike mode of taxation that could be resorted to. How was it that the Government had not suggested the expediency of an income tax ? He ventured to express a hope that on a future day when there should be in the country a Legislature

Taxation and Free Trade.

capable of entertaining such a proposal, the propriety of adopting a land tax would be considered. Such a tax he had no doubt would work as beneficially in this colony as a similar tax had worked in the United States of America. Apart from the question of revenue this kind of direct taxation would prove most beneficial to the colony, by preventing that system of speculation in land which had been well described by Earl Grey as a system most disastrous to the settlement of young countries. A land tax would prove most beneficial by forcing land into cultivation and general use, and so stimulating improvement that would react in enhancing the value of all classes of property. Such had been the result of a land tax in the United States, and he did not see why a similar result should not follow here. With regard to what had been said by some of the speakers who addressed the House on former evenings, as to the wisdom of imposing a duty on those articles which were deemed articles of luxury, he noticed that tobacco and ardent spirits were alluded to in a manner indicating that these articles ought to be selected for an increased duty. In reply to the arguments which had been adduced in support of those views, he would simply quote a passage from the eminent economist whom he had previously cited as an authority. Mr. Stuart Mill said :—

"There is, however, a frequent plea in support of indirect taxation which must be altogether rejected as grounded on a fallacy. We are often told that taxes on commodities are less burdensome than other taxes, because the contributor can escape from them by ceasing to use the taxed commodity. He certainly can, if that be his object, deprive the Government of the money ; but he does so by a sacrifice of his own indulgences, which, if he chose to undergo it, would equally make up to him for the same amount taken from him by direct taxation. Suppose a tax be laid on wine sufficient to add £5 to the price of the quantity of wine which he consumes in a year ; he has only, we are told, to diminish his consumption of wine by £5, and he escapes the burden. True ; but if the £5, instead of being laid on wine, had been taken from him by an income-tax, he could, by expending £5 less on wine, equally save the amount of the tax, so that the difference between the two cases is really illusory. If the Government takes from the contributor £5 a year—whether in one way or another—exactly that amount must be retrenched from his consumption to leave him as well off as before ; and, in either way, the same amount of sacrifice—neither more nor less—is imposed on him."

In addition to this argument it seemed to him to be an extraordinary policy to raise the revenue of the country from commodities which, at the same time, it was sought to drive out of consumption. No one would deny that it was opposed to the advancement of the public morals and detrimental to the increase of our national wealth that spirits and tobacco should be extensively used, and it therefore seemed to him to be an extraordinary line of argument to urge that on these articles especially should depend the revenue of the the country. If morality advanced, the very elements from which the revenue was derived would be correspondingly impaired. If on the other hand the revenue prospered, it was evident that it would be at the cost of the public morality. Again, if the revenue prospered, the public expenditure would necessarily increase by reason of the spread of vice and crime which must be the consequence of increased consumption. The honourable the Chairman of Committees (Mr. Parker)* had laid before the House the true principles on which all taxation should be based—the principle that taxes should be imposed so as to press proportionately on all classes according to their means to bear the burden; and that, in the second place, they should be collected in such a way as that they would be least sensibly felt. These were the principles which had of late years guided legislation in England, and these were the principles which had been carried into effect, so far as the intelligence of the times and the circumstances of the country would permit, under the guidance of Sir Robert Peel. With regard to the proposed assessment on stock, he confessed that his mind was not clearly decided as to this means of raising revenue. He admitted that there was considerable force in the objections of the honourable member for the Sydney Hamlets, that such a proposal savoured of class-legislation. On the other hand, however, the squatters held a different position from all other classes of the people. They were tenants of the Crown—in no respect holding the position of freeholders or ordinary leaseholders—but occupying immense tracts of land which belonged to the whole body of the people. Now if those lands were held at a price altogether disproportionate to their value—and that such was the fact had been admitted by honourable members known to be the organs of the squatters in that House—by the honourable member for the Murrumbidgee, and by one or two honourable members known to be extensively connected with

---

* Now Sir Henry Watson Parker.

the squatting interests—if, he said, it were admitted that the squatters were thus deriving advantages from the occupation of the public lands altogether disproportionate to the amount they paid towards the general revenue, then he thought the proposal for an assessment on stock might very reasonably be entertained.

Mr. G. MACLEAY rose to explain : What he said was, that the amount paid by the squatters was somewhat disproportionate, not that their contributions to the revenue were altogether disproportionate.

Mr. PARKES resumed : At all events he understood that it was admitted on all hands that the squatters should bear a larger share of the public burdens ; and if no other means of increasing their contributions to the State, and no other mode of raising the required revenue presented itself, he should give his assent to the levying of the proposed assessment, although on other grounds he might object to it as opposed to correct principles. With regard to the future mode of dealing with the Estimates—towards which the amendment before the House was directed—he took a different view from the honourable member for Durham as to the manner in which the proposal of the Governor-General, to submit the reserved schedules to the consideration of the House, should be received. He was inclined to adopt the ruling of the honourable and learned Attorney-General* on the point that there was sufficient power given by the 18th section of the Constitution Act in regard to this matter. He could by no means submit to the doctrine of the honourable member for Cook and Westmoreland (Mr. Martin), that a despatch from the Colonial Office could override an Act of Parliament. If this were a correct view, they would not be safe even under their new Constitution Act itself. If a despatch could define away the provisions of an Act of Parliament, they might possibly have a despatch sent out hereafter declaring that their miniature House of Lords should —in spite of the Constitution—be elected by democratic constituencies. But whatever might be the nature and effect of any despatch from the Secretary of State, it was certain that the Governor-General, who was in constant communication with the Colonial Office, was in a better position to put a proper construction on the terms of any such despatch than any member of the House.

* The late Mr. John Hubert Plunket.

If His Excellency thought he was justified in submitting to the Council, to be dealt with in good faith, those portions of the public expenditure which had hitherto been reserved under the schedules, he for one was prepared in equally good faith to meet the proposal; and he thought the House would be guilty of a great dereliction of duty if they threw any impediment in the way of the proposal. So far from assenting to the amendment before the House, he should be more inclined to assent to a resolution of which the following was a draft :—

"That this House, in resolving itself into a committee of the whole, for the consideration of the Estimates, desires to express its acknowledgment of the constitutional principles which His Excellency the Governor-General has acted upon, in submitting unreservedly to the disposal of the Council the sums reserved by the schedules of the Constitution Act 1, 2, 3. In meeting this concession on the part of His Excellency with the same feeling of good faith in which it has been made, this House pledges itself that, while it will make proper provision for the efficiency of the public service, it will use its utmost efforts to enforce that strict economy which it believes His Excellency anxiously desires."

He would be much more inclined to go into committee on the Estimates, with some such clear exposition of the spirit in which the House received the schedules as that contained in the draft resolution he had read, than with the adoption of the amendment before the House. He believed it would be advantageous to the country to raise an increased revenue, provided such revenue were limited to the amounts actually required for the necessary expenditure in carrying out great public improvements, and for rendering the Government more efficient. But under all the circumstances of the time, and looking to the unsatisfactory state in which they found several of the subordinate departments of the Government, he thought it would have been well had the Governor-General* applied a larger amount of his zeal and energy to discovering those departments where a greater economy might readily be enforced. There were several branches of the public service which might readily be pared down ; and others wherein efficient and useful men might be substituted for men who were notoriously inefficient and useless. He thought it would have been more creditable to His

---

* Before the introduction of Responsible Government the Governor was in reality the sole Executive Administrator, and the heads of Departments appointed by the Imperial Government were his officers rather than his Ministers.

Excellency had he devoted a larger amount of attention than he appeared to have bestowed in discovering how the public revenue had heretofore been misapplied. Had such an investigation taken place, much cause for complaint would have been brought to light. In support of these assertions he would call the attention of the House to a few items which he had chosen at random, and in connexion with which he had been at some trouble to inform himself. In the first place, he would refer to the expenditure on account of the anchors, chain-cable, hawsers, and other things required for the port of Newcastle, for which he found a total sum of £1363 18s. 7d. asked for in the Supplementary Estimates. Of the anchors which had been sent to Newcastle he had ascertained that five had been lying on the wharf at the Cove for a number of years, and by previous use and natural decay they were worn so as to be now not more than two-thirds of their original weight; so useless were they for the purpose for which they were intended that in the process of bending one of the flukes, which was necessary for the purpose of sinking, one of them gave way at the crown. He understood from authority derived from several sources that the market value of five of these six anchors was about £11 5s. each; the remaining one being worth about £40. The cost of the chain-cable, anchors, buoys, hawsers, &c., was £853 18s. 9d. Now this chain-cable was a very formidable affair, fitted for a 74-gun line-of-battle ship. It was 140 fathoms in length; its weight was $2\frac{1}{2}$ cwt. per fathom; and altogether it was so monstrously disproportioned to the anchors and buoys that it would sink the buoys, and so render the whole apparatus useless for the purposes for which it was designed. Besides, it was laid down in such an extraordinary manner that it endangered the vessels trading to the Hunter, and was thus calculated to be of enormous injury instead of advantage. It being laid across the channel, vessels arriving at the port were in danger of hooking it with their anchors and thus losing them. Among these items he found £160 for a life-boat. Now he believed that any possible life-boat on the best and most improved principle—that by which the vessel, if she filled with water, could empty and right herself—would be built by any boat-builder in Sydney for £100. Then there was a patent winch, for which he found the sum of £800 set down. He would ask any member of the House, he would ask any gentleman who had any knowledge of the subject, whether he thought a patent winch could possibly cost £300. The winch had not yet gone, he believed, nor had the life-boat; but there were sums set down for them which seemed to him preposterously high. In the works to which he had referred double the money necessary had been expended; and the work had been done so badly that it would have been far better left undone. There was another item which to him seemed preposterous—£100 for the conveyance of a boat's crew of six men from Sydney to Port Curtis—a sum that would convey the same number of men to any part of the world. Another point to which he would direct attention was in reference to the celebrated gunboat "Spitfire." He found from a source of inquiry upon which he had every reason to rely that this gunboat cost the Government some £1500. Now there was at the present time lying off Balmain a boat that would answer the purposes required just as well as the "Spitfire," was nearly the size, and which he or any other person could buy for £300—a boat built in the best possible manner, coppered, sparred, and with everything in a state of completion, except rigging. Knowing this, and knowing that nearly £1500 had been paid for the "Spitfire," he could not possibly conceive otherwise than that there had been great neglect, if not something worse, in the manner in which the public money had been expended. There was another case to which he had paid some attention, that of the "Bramble" tender. Last year a sum of money had been voted for converting the "Bramble" into a lightship for Moreton Bay. This, however, was not carried into effect, but a vessel was purchased for the purpose. The sum of £1000 was paid to Mr. Want for the yacht called the "Pearl." Now it would strike any person at all conversant with the matter that the yacht "Pearl" was about the least suitable for the purpose of any vessel in the colony; yet £1000 was paid to Mr. Want for this vessel at the very time when, owing to the depression in the coasting trade and other causes, fifty vessels might have been purchased, any one of which would have been more suitable in every respect and would have cost far less.

The COLONIAL SECRETARY begged to correct the honourable member for Sydney. The "Pearl" was not bought for a lightship, she was bought for the purpose of being used to examine buoys, to take pilots out to sea, and other similar purposes.

Mr. PARKES: Perhaps he might be so far wrong; but the honourable the Colonial Secretary would admit, that £1000 was paid for the vessel; and even for the purposes the honourable the Colonial Secretary had mentioned, he had no doubt that a far more suitable vessel could have been bought for a much smaller sum. Another item was the provision of mooring chains and buoys for Kiama. He had never been to Kiama, but he believed it was a harbour where the sea broke in with great violence. Those chains and buoys were now lying at the Phœnix Wharf. He had walked down that morning to see them, and he believed that any person shod with a strong boot could kick in the ends of the buoys. They were very small—about two feet long only—a child might almost carry them away. Two or three gentlemen who were present—one of them a gentleman intimately known to the honourable and learned the Solicitor-General—had agreed with him in opinion that the money expended on these buoys might just as well have been thrown into the sea. He would give another instance, and it should be the last he would adduce, in which he thought he should be able to show clearly that there had been most unwarrantable and improvident expenditure of the public money. He referred to the establishment at Port Curtis. He would not unnecessarily detain the House, but would state briefly the facts of the case. On the 18th June 1853 a surveying party of twenty persons landed at Port Curtis, and for four months afterwards there was no other person at that place, and there was no station nearer than Mr. Little's station, distant about 60 miles. In November a party of twelve native police under the command of a lieutenant arrived; and a short time after that a Mr. Palmer arrived from Wide Bay and commenced a store. Thus, in the beginning of last year, as he was informed from various sources on which he could rely, there were at Port Curtis only the surveying party of twenty, twelve native police, and two storekeepers. In less than three months afterwards, however, on the 24th March, the Government Resident arrived in the "Tom Tough"; and to show the importance of the place, when Captain O'Connell arrived there with a salary of £675, including the temporary increase,—as it was called; but, as he called it, the permanent increase—he held in his hand a return signed by the chief constable on the 24th May, two months afterwards, which represented the population as follows :—Males, 21; females, 11; children, 25. These fifty-seven persons, nearly the whole of whom were in the employ of the Government, constituted the Utopia over which Captain O'Connell was appointed Government Resident. Now they were called upon to vote in salaries alone at this establishment, during the present year, upwards of £3300 (and he was not sure that he had got all the salaries), besides clothing, ammunition, and other items, and heavy sums for the public works. Then again, with respect to the "Tom Tough," there was something curious connected with the history of that vessel. She was chartered at an expense to the country of £350 per month besides passage and sustenance money. She arrived at Port Curtis with the Government Resident on the 24th March last year; and she lay there doing nothing till the 12th July—three months and a half. She was then sent back to Sydney, the settlement being in want of supplies, and again returned to Port Curtis, where she arrived on the 23rd August, after which she lay at anchor for another month. On the 23rd September, she was sent to Wide Bay; and for what purpose did honourable gentlemen suppose she was sent thither? To carry six or eight labourers to cut timber! And during the time they were cutting the timber the "Tom Tough" still lay waiting, at the cost of £350 per month. She eventually returned with the timber to Port Curtis, where it still lies, or at least did a month or two ago, just as it was landed and stacked on the beach. It seemed that this timber was wanted for no purpose whatsoever; and it appeared to him that it was a fair inference to conclude that the vessel was sent away on that occasion because the Government Resident was ashamed, even in the presence of the little community over which he presided, to allow her to lie at Port Curtis any longer. Among the sums they were asked to vote for that pet settlement was one of £676 10s 6d., besides rations, for a boat's crew; and this was the boat's crew for whose passage they were to pay £100. As far as he could learn the boat's crew had done nothing except collect oysters, catch fish, and now and then go out with a picnic party. They had never sounded a single inch of the waters there—never gone out to assist any vessel, notwithstanding that the steamer "William Miskin" had twice been ashore—never performed any duty whatever that might naturally be expected from them. A word or two with regard to the "William Miskin." This steamer was laid on for Port Curtis, on condition of the Government paying a subsidy of £150 or £200 per month. A steamer, with this heavy subsidy, trading to a place where there was no population! And the advantages to be derived from the steamer might be estimated from the fact that on her last trip she was about thirty days on the passage, whilst the passages of a number of sailing vessels, the particulars of which he had collected, showed that on the average they occupied scarcely more than half the time. In reference once more to the boat's crew he should have stated—and he had no doubt some member of the Government would correct him if he were wrong—he should have stated that this boat's crew, which was placed at the disposal of the Government Resident for the use of the establishment, had entered into an agreement while in Sydney by the terms of which they engaged to work on shore; and the way in which this clause was carried out was by the employment of the men in the erection of stockyards for the use of private persons. This brought him to another feature in this most shameful and unwarrantable waste of the public money. They were asked in the Supplementary Estimates to vote £3000 for constructing a dam for preserving fresh water at Port Curtis, in addition to another item of £757 18s. in the Estimates for 1856 for a similar purpose; making a total of nearly £4000 for the supply of fresh water to the settlement. And at the very time when the settlement was suffering from the want of water, there were kept there 300 horses, 150 head of cattle, and 1000 sheep belonging to private persons, which consumed more than a thousand buckets of water a-day. This exposure of what was going on led him to yet another feature in the character of transactions at Port Curtis. The sheep to which he had referred were sold to the clerk of the Bench, who kept a butcher's shop, and by whom they were regularly slaughtered and supplied to the Government people. When the settlement was first formed a person put up a store on Government land, and shortly afterwards he was made aware that on that account the building was legally forfeited; but it was politely intimated to him at the same time that he was at liberty to sell it, and it was ultimately purchased for the purpose of being converted into a kitchen and stable for the use of a private family. After a short time, however, it was found that the white ants had got into the wood of which the store was constructed ; it was then suddenly discovered that the store was admirably suited for a court-house, a court-house it was accordingly made, and had been used for the purposes of a court-house until very lately. Now when they were asked to vote the sum of £10,000 for this pet settlement—which there really seemed great reason to suppose was hit upon to find a comfortable situation for a gentleman who was, he admitted, the son of a meritorious officer and a respectable colonist—he thought there was an unanswerable charge against the Government of recklessness, if not of profligacy, in the expenditure of the public money. With such instances before them, they had a right to complain that greater care had not been exercised by the Government in reducing the expenditure before proceeding to tax their salt, their soap, and their means of light. As he had said before, he was disposed to take the schedules and to deal with them in all good faith to the country, and in a thoroughly just and candid spirit to make every proper provision for the public service ; the House exercising its judgment as to where retrenchment was required, and taking means to place the public service in a thoroughly sound and useful state. There was one special reason why he would accept the surrender of these schedules. They had at the present time three high administrative officers, whose tenure of office was a matter of colonial arrangement on the spot. The honourable gentleman at the head of the Government—Mr. Riddell—was an acting Colonial Secretary, and his temporary promotion gave them an acting Colonial Treasurer and an acting Auditor-General. He should be sorry to attempt a pun in the matter, but he could not help observing that they had in reality in the House three acting officials, and not one active officer. No merely Imperial authority would protect these officers in their present positions ; and the House would have an opportunity of correcting the mischief that was done by the shuffling of the official cards when Mr. Thomson left the colony on his visit to Europe. They might be able, possibly, to force back to the Audit Office the present acting Colonial Treasurer, and to restore to the Treasury its rightful occupant, leaving His Excellency the Governor-General to fill the temporary vacancy at the head as he might think fit. He could not leave the subject without adverting to a passage in the speech of the honourable member for Cook and Westmoreland, in relation to the

Taxation and Free Trade. 65

character of the late Sir Robert Peel. It was a privilege which Englishmen valued more than any other that they were all the protectors of the reputation of the common benefactors of their country, and he for one would not permit a wanton attack on the character of that great statesman to go forth to the world from an English Legislature without raising his voice against it. The honourable gentleman had characterised Sir Robert Peel's great service in the repeal of the Corn Laws as a mere yielding to the clamour of the people at the time, and had asserted that he continued until his death to hold the opinions which he had held in former years, before the avowed change in his policy. There could scarcely be a more serious charge made against the character of a public man. With the permission of the House he would read a short passage from one of the speeches of Sir Robert Peel, which would show with what earnestness and sincerity he acted. These words of Sir Robert Peel, in the most clear and unanswerable language, gave the sanction of that great statesman's authority to the principles which he (Mr. Parkes) had attempted to impress upon the House that night. Sir Robert Peel, on the second reading of his immortal measure (on the 27th March 1846), said in the course of his speech:—

I have not overlooked the circumstance that, respecting this Bill, it has been said to be a good political manœuvre on my part. Now I ask, what possible advantage can a Bill like this confer upon me as an individual? I know I have been taunted, and have more than once been told, that my days as a Minister are numbered. But I have introduced this measure, not for the purpose of prolonging my Ministerial existence, but for the purpose of averting a great national calamity, and for the purpose of sustaining a great public interest. I am quite aware of the fact that more than once I have been asked how long I can reckon upon the support of those honourable gentlemen opposite, without whose votes I could not hope to carry this Bill through the House—how long, in fact, I can reckon upon enjoying their support with respect to other subjects? I know, as well as those who taunt me, that I have not any right to the support or confidence of those honourable members. I acknowledge—and I admit that acknowledgment with perfect sincerity and plainness—that they have supported me in passing this measure, if it will pass into a law. I do not say this as a private man. I do not, on private grounds, attach importance to it; but I feel and acknowledge every proper obligation to them, as a public man, for the support which they have given to this measure, and for studiously avoiding everything calculated to create embarrassment to its progress; but then our differences remain the same. I have, sir, no right to claim their support, nor their protection; nor, I will fairly admit, shall I seek it by departing in the slightest degree from that course which my

F

public duty may urge me to adopt. If this measure pass, our temporary connexion is at an end; but I have not the slightest right to expect support or forbearance from them ; still less have I, after the declarations that have been made, a right to expect forbearance or support from this side of the House. Well, then, that being the case—it being the fact that there are but 112 members to support me—then I might be asked what great measures of national policy I can expect to pursue with these 112 members, constituting, as they do, but a little more than one-sixth of the House of Commons. I am not, I say, surprised to hear honourable members predict that my tenure of power is short. But let us pass this measure ; and, while it is in progress, let me request of you to suspend your indignation. This measure being once passed, you on this side, and you on that side of the House, may adopt whatever measures you think proper for the purpose of terminating my political existence. I assure you I deplore the loss of your confidence much more than I shall deplore the loss of political power. The accusations which you prefer against me are, on this account, harmless, because I feel that they are unjust. Every man has, within his own bosom and conscience, the scales which determine the real weight of reproach ; and if I had acted from any corrupt or unworthy motives, one-tenth part of the accusations you have levelled against me would have been fatal to my peace and my existence. When I do fall, I shall have the satisfaction of reflecting that I do not fall because I have shown subservience to a party. I shall not fall because I preferred the interests of party to the general interests of the community ; and I shall carry with me the satisfaction of reflecting that, during the course of my official career, my object has been to mitigate monopoly, to increase the demand for industry, to remove restrictions upon commerce, to equalise the burden of taxation, and to ameliorate the condition of those who labour."

He would ask whether that was the language of a man who could have any purpose in acting upon his opinions' excepting the single desire of discharging what he conscientiously felt to be a solemn duty? Was that the language of a man who could be suspected of hidden motives on that memorable occasion? The passage he had read in very forcible terms proclaimed the principles which he had endeavoured that night to maintain. Then, on the third reading of the Corn Law Repeal Bill on the 15th May 1846, Sir Robert Peel re-asserted these principles in still more clear and expressive language :—

" My earnest wish has been, during my tenure of power, to impress the people of this country with a belief that the Legislature was animated by a sincere desire to frame its legislation upon the principles of equity and justice. I have a strong belief that the greatest object which we or any other Government can contemplate should be to elevate the social condition of that class of the people with whom we are brought into no direct relationship, by the exercise of the elective franchise. I wish to convince them that our object has been to so apportion taxation, that we shall relieve industry and labour from any undue burden, and transfer it, so far as is consistent with the public good, to those who are better able to bear it. I look to the present peace of this country; I look to the absence of all disturbance, to the non-existence of any commitment for a seditious offence; I look to the calm that prevails in the public mind; I look to the absence of all disaffections; I look to the increased and growing public confidence on account of the course you have taken in relieving trade from restrictions, and industry from unjust burdens; and where there was disaffection I see contentment; where there was turbulence I see there is peace; where there was disloyalty I see there is loyalty; I see a disposition to confide in you, and not to agitate questions that are at the foundation of your institutions. Deprive me of power to-morrow: you can never deprive me of the consciousness that I have exercised the powers committed to me from no corrupt or interested motives; from no desire to gratify ambition, or attain any personal object; that I laboured to maintain peace abroad consistently with the national honour, and defending every public right; to increase the confidence of the great body of the people in the justice of your decisions, and by the means of equal law to dispense with all coercive powers to maintain loyalty to the Throne and attachment to the Constitution, from a conviction of the benefit that will accrue to the great body of the people."

These passages from the speeches of Sir Robert Peel would also show that that statesman was deeply impressed with a high reverence for the voice of the country—most unlike the spirit too frequently exhibited in the Legislature of this colony, which is a spirit of affected condemnation of any manifestation of public opinion out of doors. The close of the great Minister's term of office afforded occasion for the people of England to show how deeply they were actuated by gratitude and an unswerving love of justice, when on his resigning the reins of Government—which he did upon an adverse vote of the House of Commons immediately after the passing of his great measure—the multitude met him outside the House, not with noisy acclamations, but in silence and with bared heads, and accompanied him with those impressive demonstrations of respect to his home. Now that was an exhibition which showed that justice resides in the hearts of the people, who could at such a time appreciate the feelings and the conscientious views of the statesman who at the cost of office had taken away the tax from their daily bread. And yet in this colony the people were spoken of as undeserving of consideration in the work of legislation—as incapable of just feeling or thoughtful action. Adverting for a moment to the suggestion that had been thrown out in favour of a stamp duty, he might state that a calculation of its probable results had been placed in his hands by a gentleman engaged in commercial affairs, and which he had had tested by others, who concurred in its accuracy. According to this calculation, it appeared that by a stamp duty on notes in circulation, trust estates, bills current at the present time, bank cheques, instruments for the transfer of property, receipts, bills of lading, and policies of insurance, £150,000 might be raised. The only item in the list to which any objection could be raised was a stamp duty on bank cheques, which however would not yield more than £16,000 out of the £150,000. With regard to a stamp duty on ordinary receipts, he thought there was an argument of a moral nature which would go far to support such a mode of taxation. It would tend greatly to introduce into business a practice of regularity and precision, and a proper seriousness of action. Considering that a stamp duty would not oppress any class, and would fall equally on those engaged in large transactions connected with property, it was a most legitimate tax. That they should soon have to prepare to raise a larger revenue he was deeply convinced; and he did not see any just way of doing it unless they resorted to new means of taxation. It seemed to him that the amount of money which was annually drawn from the colony by absentees afforded a strong reason why the Government should do all in their power to promote such public improvements as would facilitate the settlement of the colony, and render it more agreeable for the residence of those possessed of large fortunes. He had a list in his hand by which it was shown that half-a-million of money was annually withdrawn from the colony by three or four institutions and some dozen wealthy individuals. Anything that could be done to make the colony more attractive as a place of residence to those who may retire from active life in circumstances of opulence should be an object of great anxiety to all of us. For these reasons the money expended in the erection of the University and other public institutions of a similar character had been well expended, because by such means they might induce those who would otherwise go where they could have the benefit of such institutions to remain in the colony. He thought the mode of taxation proposed by His Excellency was entirely wrong. It was utterly opposed to the principles which regulated English legislation, and also opposed to sound principles of political economy. He would therefore, when they went into committee, vote against many of the new items of expenditure, provision for which rested on the imposition of those taxes. At the same time he was disposed to take the schedules in good faith, and to deal with them with a desire to promote efficiency in the public service, combined with the maintenance of a wise economy.

THE EIGHT HOURS MOVEMENT.

SPEECH

Delivered at a meeting of the Trades of Sydney held in the new hall of the School of Arts, November 17th, 1856, to advocate the reduction of the hours of daily labour to eight. Mr. Parkes, by invitation, occupied the chair.

THE CHAIRMAN in opening the meeting said :—Gentlemen, if I were to say I do not feel gratified by being called upon to preside over this meeting I should do an injustice to my feelings. I am well aware that this meeting must contain, to a very large extent, the heart and soul, the true manly feeling, and the genuine self-cultivated intellect of the working classes of the metropolis. I am well aware that in the men assembled here this evening must be concentrated much of the strength, much of the intelligence, much of the constructive skill, much of that spirit of self-reliance, upon which society itself largely depends for everything that is valuable, serviceable or ornamental to its various grades and interests. I know that the trades which have been most conspicuous in this movement are trades remarkable for those qualities. I therefore felt particularly gratified that you should think of asking me to preside at a meeting of such a character in preference to many other much better men all around me, whose sympathies you may rest satisfied are with you. I feel gratified because I have worked as a journeyman tradesman, and so supported my family, for a number of years, and am well able to sympathise with you in all the disadvantages under which you labour, and in all the higher objects of recreation and instruction which the best and most intelligent amongst you seek to obtain. I come to this meeting believing it in no way partakes of a political character; I come to this meeting believing you have no purposes of combination against the just interests of your employers ; I come to this meeting because I think you assemble to exercise your reason to

Eight Hours Movement.

the best of your judgment, in rightly determining your capabilities and the responsibilities under which you lie in disposing of that greatest of all properties, the labour of your right arms. If I had thought that by coming here I could by any possibility create division between you and any other class of the community, I certainly should not have come; if I had thought that your object was to extract from your employers an unfair recompense for what you give, I should not have been amongst you. But I believe, so far as I understand your proceedings, that you maintain that you have a perfect right to exercise your reason as to how far it is proper for you to give your labour to meet the needs of society, and how far you require it for the preservation and cultivation of the faculties with which you are endowed, and for the performance of those varied duties and the fulfilment of those pressing responsibilities which have been cast upon you by an all-wise Creator. The only argument which I have heard against your having this reasonable limit set to your hours of labour is, that if you had the greater leisure you would not employ it well. I have heard it said repeatedly that if the hours of labour were shortened the time so granted to you would be ill-spent—spent in unfitting rather than in fitting you for the discharge of the duties and responsibilities to which I have alluded. I don't believe in these dark foreshadowings. Why should it be so? Does not the whole history of the world prove that among the working classes there is as much thought for the morrow, as much penetration into surrounding circumstances, as much anxiety and providence for the interests of those belonging to them, as among any other class? I affirm that the history of the world proves all this. I say, moreover, that the history of literature, the history of manufactures, and the history of science, also prove that we owe more—incomparably more—to the working classes for new and original thoughts in the various handicrafts of our industrial economy, in the various appliances by which social life is made more pleasant and agreeable to all, than to any other class whatsoever. I am one of those who believe that some of the holiest thoughts, some of the loftiest purposes, have birth and are cherished during hours of labour. And this very subject has been the theme of some of the holiest and most touching eloquence of gifted and cultivated men. Dr. Channing has dwelt upon the noble thoughts that are cherished by men amongst the working-classes until these pass into great and enduring actions, without even their relatives or fellow-workers suspecting that such sublime conceptions ever entered their minds. I could point to many illustrious names in proof of this; and when I think of the many striking instances of poets, philosophers, and contributors to the welfare of society in every way, who have sprung directly from the working classes, I cannot believe such a thing as that you more especially than others would make an ill use of the increased leisure you are seeking to obtain. When I think of the boy astronomer Ferguson who learned his first lessons by lying down in the open fields and measuring the distances of the stars with a string of rude wooden beads; when—

> I think of Chatterton, the marvellous boy,
> The sleepless soul that perished in his pride;
> Of Burns, who walked in glory and in joy,
> Following his plough upon the mountain side!

when I think of William Cobbett, one of the sturdiest and bravest of the political characters of the last generation; of Burritt, one of the greatest linguists of the present day,—the one a peasant boy, the other a working blacksmith; when I think of these, I cannot for a moment listen to such weak predictions of your misspending time. Only a very short time ago I read an account by Mr. William Howitt of his visit to a mechanic in a small two-roomed house in a back court in Birmingham, whom he found, while his wife was cooking his supper, engaged in the two-fold employment of nursing his baby and learning the German language. That is only one instance that comes to my mind now, only one out of thousands, of patient striving to perfect their faculties, of quiet endurance of sufferings and reproaches and neglects, of disinterested benevolence in those who, to quote Dr. Channing's words, often give what the giver needs himself; it is only one out of thousands of instances of the virtues which live, although they have no witness, among the humbler classes of society. But I shall be answered that the particular instances of individual distinction I have named are those of men of singular natural endowments. I confess it is so. They are, however, not the less a glory for the class to which you belong. But I would turn to the very numerous class of men who spring from the ranks of

Eight Hours Movement. 73

labour—the small farmers, the small tradesmen, the small manufacturers, the small contractors—the men who emerge all around you from the wages-receiving class, and who actually carry on the great mass of the business of society. In a debate in the Legislative Assembly a few nights ago relative to the construction of a bridge at Albury, it was stated that a sum of money was voted for building a punt there some years since, but the punt was never built until two mechanics saw that a means was there opened for them to raise themselves a little above the situation they had hitherto occupied, and by their joint labour and enterprise they built the punt which has served to connect the two colonies ever since. Numerous instances we have of men who were yesterday journeymen starting as shipwrights on our rivers, building small vessels for themselves which become of great value to our commerce, while the position and prospects of their owners are steadily improved. And similarly in the building trades, whilst in other callings we owe more than enters into our calculation to men who are impelled by the promptings of a humble ambition in obscure spheres of action. But how would these unseen strugglers for something better be sustained, if there were not penetrative force to see and seize opportunities, and wise reflection to turn them to best account, among the working classes themselves? Therefore the whole proof derived from the progress of society is against the calumny that if you had more time you would apply it to improper uses. I cannot see why such a subject as this should not be taken up in a calm, quiet, rational spirit, and thus debated between you and your employers. You can have no interest separate from theirs; they can have no interest separate from what is also yours. You, surely, if you think eight hours is sufficient for labour in this climate have a right to say so. Surely no men throughout the range of society have any right to express an opinion on any subject if you have not a right to express your opinion upon this subject. As to the necessity for the shorter time, I am one of those who think it absolutely necessary. I think it necessary, not so much for you as for society itself; in order that you may become better citizens, and that the community of which you are members may derive all the advantages from your various faculties it would then have a right to expect, and which to confer those very faculties have been implanted in your nature; and in order that you may be thinkers as well as workers, so that your thinking may bear fruit in the more genial services of social life and the finer creations of mind, as your labour is embodied in monuments of brick and stone. I think it necessary, because I believe that without it you cannot properly discharge all your duties—properly educate your children, or devote the time to the welfare of your families which you are bound to do. I for one would not willingly be the means of inspiring feelings of discontent with the condition of labour, for I think it the most glorious condition of all. But surely that condition in which you contribute to all durable advantages for other classes should not be one of cheerless toil, relieved only by cheerless rest. I believe that the condition of labour—the condition of the workman in the sense in which we use this phrase to-night—is capable of as much happiness as any condition this world offers. I have said that at one time I was a journeyman tradesman. I say now that I never felt happier, better, or prouder; and if a change were to come upon my life, so that it became my duty to go and work for daily wages again, I should do it as cheerfully and proudly as I ever performed any action throughout my life. You in that condition are at all events free from various anxieties, various cares, various losses, which engross the minds and frequently shorten the days of other men; and if you get a fair return for your labour, time to devote to your families, time to cultivate your own minds and to discharge the other various duties of life which are incumbent upon you, I cannot see but that you in your degree are as honourable, and may be as happy, as any other men, should cherish a feeling of as high pride, should walk abroad with a spirit of as true independence as the best in the land. While I say this I should not like to be misunderstood as discouraging any of you in your efforts to rise out of your class if you think you have the power. With respect to that, every man must judge as to his own capabilities and prospects. If any of you feels that he has the strength of mind to carry him into the highest position in the land, I for one see no reason why he should not set out in that career. All I desire to say is that with a limit set to your labour, and a just proportioning of your time for the cultivation of your moral and physical capabilities, you may be as happy in the workman's condition as in any other. I cannot see why a question of this kind should not be taken up as a great social problem equally by master and

Eight Hours Movement. 75

servant, by employer and workman, and brought to a satisfactory solution for the benefit of all. This is peculiarly a work, I think, in which anyone sharing may claim to be carrying out the maxim of our divine religion, of doing unto others as we would they should do unto us. I think it has become a question the right settlement of which involves the principle of love to our fellow-creatures. Some of you, perhaps, are acquainted with a beautiful poem by Leigh Hunt on a heathen's love for his fellow-creatures, and if you will allow me I will repeat it :—

> Abou Ben Adhem (may his tribe increase !)
> Awoke one night from a deep dream of peace,
> And saw, within the moonlight in his room,
> Making it rich, and like a lily in bloom,
> An angel writing in a book of gold.
> Exceeding peace had made Ben Adhem bold,
> And to the presence in the room he said,
> " What writest thou ?" The vision raised its head,
> And with a look made of all sweet accord,
> Answered, " The names of those who love the Lord !"
> " And is mine one ?" said Abou. " Nay, not so,"
> Replied the angel. Abou spoke more low,
> But cheerly still, and said, " I pray thee, then,
> Write me as one that loves his fellow-men."
> The angel wrote, and vanished. The next night
> It came again with a great wakening light,
> And showed the names whom love of God had blest ;
> And lo ! Ben Adhem's name led all the rest.

The CHAIRMAN then read the advertisement convening the meeting, and having called upon the mover of the first resolution, sat down amidst unanimous and reiterated applause.

ELECTORAL REFORM.

SPEECH

Delivered at a Public Meeting in the Prince of Wales' Theatre, Sydney, September 1st, 1857.

MR. PARKES said : Mr. Chairman and gentlemen, I think no apology will be required from me in appearing before you on an occasion of this kind, and under the present circumstances of the colony. It appears to me that your attendance here to-night in such an array of numbers, and with so strong a manifestation of earnest interest in this cause, is a sufficient justification for any man giving his opinion upon a question of such vast concern to the whole of the inhabitants of the country. A few days ago it might have been expected that there would scarcely arise occasion for this meeting at all, on account of the difficulties that threatened the existence of the present Government. As you are all aware, a day or two ago it was expected that the parents of the Bills now before Parliament would resign their offices and give place to other men. But even in that case I think the people would have done wrong not to enter on a discussion of the important question now engaging public attention— one of the very highest political concernment to us all, whosoever may be called upon to administer the affairs of the country. To me it makes very little difference whether Mr. Parker* remains at the head of the Government, or whether he is succeeded by any gentleman now sitting on the Opposition side of the House. I think it would be equally the duty of the country, under the auspices of any Minister whomsoever, to see that the general interests were cared for in carrying out a measure of this description. We meet to consider this fundamental alteration in the representation of the country, under circumstances calculated to awaken in the mind of every man the most serious anxiety for

---
* Sir Henry Watson Parker, now in England.

Electoral Reform. 77

the future prosperity of the land. We meet at a time when the financial policy of the Government, and the general state of the country, present questions for consideration intimately relating to the safety of our infant institutions and to the future progress of the various public works of the country. We meet at a time when, by the late visitations of Providence, the thoroughfares throughout many districts have been broken up, and the seed has been completely washed out of the land over large breadths of the country—misfortunes which must have an inevitable tendency to damp the energies and almost extinguish the hopes of the most industrious and valuable class of the people. If at any time in the history of a country a clear policy and a steady hand in administering its public affairs are required, it is assuredly at a time such as the present. But independently of these especial circumstances, the question itself is one that reasonable men might imagine a Government would deal with in the most impartial, the calmest, and the most comprehensive spirit. In the political arrangements upon which the institutions of the State are based, the people here, inhabiting a young country on terms of acknowledged equality, ought to have all grand fundamental principles so clearly defined and so fairly carried out that future contentions should be rendered almost impossible. The public mind in Australia ought not to be continually irritated by questions of a constitutional character. The principles of the laws which regulate the political liberty of the subject ought to assume forms of fixity and stability. If this were so, I contend, parties would much more wisely argue out their differences on questions of social improvement, questions of commercial policy, questions relating to our fiscal arrangements, questions having an economical bearing on industrial progress and on the natural resources of the country. There ought not be an endless struggle respecting the equality of classes, or the balancing of particular interests against a supposed or real preponderance in another direction. The political institutions of a young country like ours ought to be fixed upon so equable a basis that all classes of the community shall have reasonable cause to be satisfied. Now, the resolution entrusted to me declares that the Bill introduced by Mr. Parker, as the head of the Government, entirely fails to correct those inequalities which have been matter of loud complaint for many years past; that it not alone entirely fails to do this, but that it has a tendency to aggravate those inequalities, and as an inevitable consequence to breed public discontent and dissatisfaction. If it really be that the Bill is of this character, it becomes the duty of every man to oppose its passing into law. That great inequalities do exist in the present system I believe is generally admitted; and I believe the existence of such inequalities has been repeatedly admitted by the members of the present Government. Now so long as they do exist so long will discontent continue to agitate the public mind, and all measures calculated really to benefit the country will be imperfectly considered and retarded in their progress. Without going into the details of the measure—which would only be wearisome, and which you will, I doubt not, examine for yourselves—I find that, speaking generally, the pastoral interest, which most persons have hitherto felt has had an undue preponderance in the Legislature, has gained ground in the new arrangements. I find that whereas the members allotted to this interest in the present House of 54 are 12 to 42; now, notwithstanding that the total number of the proposed new Assembly is not quite double, the proportion of squatting representation is more than double. Instead of correcting inequalities this Bill tends to aggravate inequality in the most important particular. The Bill creates out of the whole country 70 electorates, and of these 70 electorates the pastoral constituencies with something over 3000 electors are to return 25 members to the Assembly, while the city of Sydney—numbering nearly 14,000 electors—will only be privileged to return 8 members. This, no doubt, is an extreme case, and I for one do not claim for the city of Sydney a numerical equality of representation with remote and scattered constituencies. I desire to be most clearly understood on this point; for while I accept the principle of a population basis as the only safe, the only really intelligible principle in the representation of the colony, I do not pretend to carry out that principle with rigid exactitude in the adjustment of different interests in our representative system. I say we must take it as our central light, because there is no other; and we must conform to it so far as the social anomalies of our condition will permit. Those who talk about the representation of special interests cannot give definite shape and form to any principle that will bring a certain and distinguishing light to bear upon

Electoral Reform. 79

the question. But while I admit that this principle in the details of any system cannot be carried out with arithmetical precision, I contend that there has been no attempt whatsoever to do justice to the masses of the people in the electoral arrangements proposed by Mr. Parker's Bill. I contend, moreover, that there has been no intelligible endeavour made to repair the causes of dissatisfaction felt throughout most of the rural districts. Excluding Sydney from consideration for the time, and turning our attention to the country districts, we find that one of the great causes of dissatisfaction has been the compulsory grouping together of remote and naturally separate communities. Thus, the town of Mudgee and the district of Orange have loudly complained of the incongruity of that arrangement by which a comparatively large town some 100 miles or so away has entirely swamped the other portion of the ill-assorted constituency. Now this state of things —as far as I can judge—will be aggravated in the new Bill. I believe that in one instance five small towns in one constituency are forcibly bound together against their will and consent and against their particular interests—each town being situated in a separate county. Nothing can be more incongruous than that— nothing more calculated to breed and perpetuate discontent in the public mind. The consequence of this arrangement would be, that some of these small towns would be practically disfranchised. It would be far better for them to be included in the county constituency, which would give them a far better opportunity of securing a voice in the election of representatives. Turning from the districts to which I have alluded, we find that the town of Newcastle—a town of rising importance and one which assuredly ought in any new electoral system to have a member to itself— is associated in the Ministerial plan with a number of small places, all of which would be completely swamped by the preponderating numbers of the town. Coming back to Sydney, we have the metropolis of the country divided into eight electorates under the respective names of the eight municipal wards. No men empowered for the time being to deal with our destinies, to put the stamp of their minds upon the character which the country is to assume in future years—if they were worthy of the high position they are permitted to occupy—would think of an arrangement in their plan of representation by which the metropolitan character of this city is, as it were, extinguished. In any arrangement the city of Sydney ought to remain politically intact. At least the central part of the city, embracing its commercial classes, should be retained in the electoral system under the name of the City of Sydney, so that the country would have—as it ought to have—its metropolitan constituency. Supposing that were done, it would of course be necessary to group around this central constituency other constituencies embracing the rest of that area of population which now returns the four members for the city. Then again, if we go to the county of Durham—perhaps the most important agricultural county—we shall find that under the present electoral law this county returns three members; and under the new Bill it is not proposed to alter this constituency in any particular. I don't know with what special favour this constituency is regarded that it should be the only one let alone. I don't know whether it is that the Government of the day are so extremely well satisfied with the gentlemen who represent the constituency, or whether it is some partiality arising from one of the Ministers having represented the constituency in former years; but whatever may be the cause this constituency is left untouched. Notwithstanding the members of the Assembly are to be nearly doubled in the aggregate, Durham will have no stronger voice in the new system than in the old. And it seems singular when other large counties returning several members are divided—such as Cumberland, Northumberland, and Camden—that Durham should be left untouched, to return by the whole body of its electors its three members as formerly. I mention this omission of interference in the Bill, only for the purpose of showing the entire absence of any rule of equality pervading the proposed new electoral arrangements. If the Bill were to pass in its present shape it would have the effect—which I fear is designed by its authors—of throwing the representation to a large extent into the hands of a particular party who seek to erect themselves into a governing class. I think, gentlemen, it would have the effect of throwing the affairs of the country for a time—for a time only—into the hands of men who in no sense would represent the intelligence, the industry, the enterprise, or the property of the country. But we may rest assured that the spirit of progress which is abroad will not allow the people to rest contented with exclusion from the

Electoral Reform. 81

representation. If in the mother country, where the wealthy classes are accustomed to look with kindly, almost parental concern upon the poorer classes around them—where among the higher ranks the culture of mind is generally accompanied by a spirit of enlightened philanthropy—if there a spirit is rising up to assert its equality and to demand an extension of political rights, and if the just claims of the people are recognised by the ablest and most distinguished statesmen of the day, can it be for a moment doubted that common sense, common justice, and common humanity will prevail in a land like this, where the members of the Legislature are nearly all sprung from the classes around and below them— where the interests of property are so much more widely diffused —where accumulated wealth is held for the most part by persons who came penniless to these shores—where the very lodestar of fortune to those who have come from other lands and to those who have been born in the country, is the open field which is afforded for every man to raise himself by his own exertions, and for the intelligent exercise of the mind and the physical energies, with a certain assurance of fitting reward? It will be utterly impossible for any Government to keep this spirit back. But if the men now in power really entertained a well-defined and well-grounded conservative policy—if they desired, in any enlightened sense, to conserve all that is good in the institutions of the country —if they were earnestly bent upon establishing a condition of peace and contentment and prosperity for all—they would of their own free will and accord extend upon the widest basis of equality the Constitution which they have voluntarily taken in hand to re-model. They would trust in future for the return of their own class to the virtues of their own class; they would trust to the abilities and services of their own class. It will always be found in the long run that the common mass of any free people — especially a people of British stock — will give their support, if they have fair play, to those candidates for their suffrages who offer for their service the largest amount of ability, of public virtue, and of character. This question, I am aware, has been encumbered by two or three fallacies which go far towards rendering the settlement of it difficult. It is said that if political power were extended generally to the great body of the people, the working classes would swamp every other interest. But experience based upon a correct knowledge of human nature shows that the working classes are more likely than any other class to record their votes, if the qualifications of candidates in other respects are equal, for some gentleman who moves in a sphere above them. Both in England and in this country and in the colonies around us, we know that a high example of straightforwardness in all the transactions of life, of ability fitted to grapple with the various questions engaging public attention, of private benevolence and personal virtue, has more weight with the labouring classes of the community than anything else that can be presented for their acceptance. Within my own experience I can give you one striking illustration of this. As I happen to know very intimately the circumstances connected with the election of Mr. Lowe, who is now as you are aware a member of the Privy Council and holds a distinguished place in the House of Commons, I can state as a positive fact that that gentleman was elected almost exclusively by the working men of Sydney. I believe Mr. Lowe had far fewer votes from persons of his own class, persons in his own rank of society, persons from whom he had a right to expect support, than any other candidate who was ever elected for this city. The history of elections both here and elsewhere would show that the votes of the labouring classes are at all times as equally divided according to the merits of candidates, irrespective of their condition in society, as those of any other class. I am inclined to think that so far from the labouring classes voting in a body in support of any one candidate, this charge might be fairly brought against the classes who move in spheres a little above them. I have seen instances of the mercantile body banding together to a man for some particular candidate of their own order. I have seen instances where the professions have similarly voted almost to a man for one of themselves; but I have seen no instance where the votes of the labouring population admitted to electoral rights have been given in a greatly preponderating degree to a particular candidate, and where the reason was at all intelligible, of their having been so given on account of his position in society. It is said also, as a reason why the city of Sydney should not have anything like a fair proportion of representation, that the members resident in Sydney may to a large extent be considered as virtually representing the city. This also I proclaim to be a fallacy. On the contrary, the argument might be turned against

Electoral Reform. 83

some of the remoter districts—that the members for Sydney have very frequently attended to these districts more than to the constituency which elected them. There is no force whatever in this so-called argument; and so far as many of the gentlemen are concerned whose names will readily suggest themselves to you as residing in Sydney, they are known to be remarkable for the tenacity with which they hang on to the interests of the country districts, against the supposed interests of the city. There is another fallacy—and I think a most complete fallacy—which is sought to be propagated far and near, and it is that there is a feeling of inveterate hostility in the minds of the inhabitants of Sydney against the occupants of the pastoral lands. I deny the existence of any such feeling. The people of Sydney have no feeling of hostility to the squatters as a body; any opposition to the squatters that has occasionally shown itself has been called into existence by the palpable aggressions of the squatters themselves —by their unfair and preposterous attempts to obtain an ascendancy in the affairs of the country. And this feeling, whatever it may be, has been fostered more by the friends of the pastoral occupants than it has by any persons connected with the metropolis or the other towns of the colony. The fact is that the interests of Sydney and of the other towns, and of the pastoral districts, have so much in common that their interests cannot be separated without injury to all. There would be no feeling of hostility to the pastoral occupants if the pastoral occupants had the wisdom to content themselves with pushing their legitimate pursuits, and to restrain themselves from efforts to obtain political power inconsistent with the rights of other classes. But that those gentlemen, many of them recent arrivals in the country, many of them intending to leave the country and spend their wealth in England or some other part of Europe, many of them with no particular claim to the gratitude or thanks of society, have not so contented themselves, has been sufficiently shown within the last few days. For we have had it proclaimed within the last few days that eight or ten squatters have set themselves up to decide who shall govern this country. It no longer rests upon any assertion of mine, or the assertions of any of you, but we have this incredible fact proclaimed in open daylight, that some eight or ten squatters are sufficiently powerful to determine in defiance of the whole community who shall be the Government.

And we have it proclaimed, moreover, that these squatters are not determining this question for the country upon the principles of any public measure, but they are determining it upon a question entirely affecting their own pockets. To me it is really alarming when the Government of this country can be kept in office or displaced by some half-dozen or dozen of gentlemen, who are displeased because some measure is introduced which affects their own pecuniary interests. These gentlemen stand in a very different relation to the country from that of other members of the Assembly. They carry their stock-in-trade, as it were, into the Assembly. They carry their business there, and while they are legislating ostensibly for the people they are really managing their own affairs. There is great reason to suspect—from the words they themselves have given utterance to and from the course of action they have adopted within the last few days —that the only object which brings some of these gentlemen into Parliament is to see that their own personal interests are taken care of, between themselves as tenants of the Crown and the Crown as trustee for the lands of the people. When we find it put on record that these gentlemen are disputing in Parliament about their own interests, and threatening to throw out the Government which they have hitherto supported—merely because the Government runs counter to their interests—we are brought face to face with a state of things which ought to awaken a feeling of alarm and anxiety throughout the country. We should forfeit our claim to the name of Englishmen if we were to allow these gentlemen thus to interfere with the course of public affairs, and to enforce compliance with their own interests at the expense of the rights and interests of the community at large. The resolution which has been put into my hands is as follows :—

"That this meeting, having considered the Bill submitted to the Legislative Assembly by the present Government for altering the representation of the colony, is of opinion that it is a measure calculated to aggravate rather than rectify the inequalities most complained of in the existing law and to create general and just dissatisfaction."

I have said sufficient to show that this measure is calculated to create a feeling of general and just dissatisfaction in the public mind. If it be so, it is the duty of every man, rich or poor, Conservative or Radical—whatever may be his condition in life or the colour of his political belief—to give it his most determined opposition; because it is for the general interest that this question should be dealt with in a manner that will afford contentment and satisfaction to all classes and all conditions. If the Bill should be carried into law, the very evils sought by such blind political artifice to be controlled will be extended and aggravated to a harassing, and I fear a dangerous degree; and no man amongst this multitude could answer for the consequences.

THE PACIFIC MAIL ROUTE.

[AT this period (1858), the railway across the American continent was looked upon as a dream of the future. Seven years after the passing of Mr. Parkes's resolutions a line of steamers between Sydney and Panama was established by an English company, under a joint subsidy from the Governments of New South Wales and New Zealand, but the company failed to carry out the contract, and the service was not continued long enough, even with its very imperfect management, to test its advantages. The arguments in the following speech are equally applicable to the mail service *viâ* San Francisco.]

SPEECH

Delivered in the Legislative Assembly on moving the following Resolutions, August 6th, 1858 :—

" 1. That the experience hitherto gained of steam communication between Australia and England *viâ* India has led to general disappointment and dissatisfaction in this colony.

" 2. That any new arrangement for the performance of the mail service by the India route, though it ensured postal regularity and speed, would confer no other considerable benefits on New South Wales, while it must necessarily place this community, as the last point of intercourse in the Australian system, at a permanent disadvantage in relation to the Southern colonies.

" 3. That it is in the highest degree necessary that immediate steps should be taken to prevent the public inconvenience and injury which would result from a total stoppage in the mail service, with which the colonies are at present threatened ; and that the interests of New South Wales would be best promoted in this emergency by opening communication with America and Europe, *viâ* the Isthmus of Panama.

" 4. That there are reasonable grounds for believing that a line of steamers of the requisite power and capacity, running between Sydney and Panama, in addition to the advantages of regular postal communication, would induce a spontaneous and valuable passenger traffic to these shores from the large numbers of persons constantly arriving on the Isthmus from the United States, British North America, and the West Indies, as well as from the countries of Europe and from the communities of Anglo-American origin on the Pacific.

"5. That in coming to a right determination on this subject the question of cost is not the first for consideration, but that the efficiency of the service to be performed should be secured beyond probability of failure, and that especial regard should be had to those social and commercial consequences which would tend most to the progress and prosperity of the colony of New South Wales.

"6. That an address, embodying the foregoing resolutions, be presented to the Governor-General, praying that His Excellency will be pleased to bring the subject under the early consideration of the Executive Government."

Mr. PARKES, in moving the resolutions standing in his name, said he hoped that however inefficiently he might treat them the importance of the subject would at least commend them to the attention of the House. He should endeavour to be as brief as he well could, and the decision to which the House was invited must have an effect one way or the other, for good or for evil, to determine not simply the relative prosperity of this colony but its position as a country in the new empire now in course of being founded in this hemisphere. He submitted these resolutions not alone as involving the question of postal communication with England; they might be supported upon different and far higher grounds affecting the future character and comparative greatness of the country. It had always seemed to him that the question of obtaining regular means of communication with the Isthmus of Panama included the question of a supply of that element without which the progress of this country would be slow and unsatisfactory—the element of fresh streams of industrious, enterprising population. Although desponding views might be taken at a time of temporary distress like the present, though loud might be the cry among some classes against immigration, it was only by means of a large amount of population that the colony could rise to its true place and its people enjoy permanent prosperity. He was one who thought that immigration to the country would be healthy just in proportion as it embodies in its volume a due proportion of capital and labour to carry on the operations of civilised society; and for that reason he thought a great advance would be made on all former systems if it were entirely voluntary and of a spontaneous character. In that case, if they could offer sufficient attraction, and if other circumstances combined to direct the great movement of population to these shores, they would receive the most enterprising and the most self-reliant class of persons, those who have made provision to assist themselves; but so long as immigration continued to be promoted chiefly by the funds derived from this side it would consist of persons to a large extent the least provident, the least energetic, the least qualified, and therefore the least capable of assisting in the advancement of the colony. In proceeding with his motion, he thought the best way would be to divide the subject into the various branches set out in the resolutions themselves. The first of the resolutions declared that their experience of steam communication by the Eastern route had produced nothing but disappointment and dissatisfaction in this country. He thought that he need not detain the House by any attempt at argument to prove the truth of this resolution, as the fact appeared self-evident and he apprehended it would scarcely be questioned. The second resolution affirmed that any new arrangement for the performance of the mail service by the India route, though it ensured postal regularity and speed, would confer no other considerable benefit on New South Wales, while it must necessarily place this community, as the last point of intercourse in the Australian system, at a permanent disadvantage in relation to the southern colonies. He thought that the truth of that resolution could be proved by reference to the dates of the arrivals and departures of the various steamers, since the present system had been established, at Melbourne and Sydney respectively. He found that the steamers in the present service had arrived at Melbourne and Sydney as follows :—The " Simla" left Southampton March 12th, arrived at Melbourne May 14th, and at Sydney on the 19th. The " European" left on the 12th April, arrived at Melbourne on June 6th, and at Sydney on the 10th. The "Columbian" left May 12th, arrived at Melbourne on July 6th, and at Sydney on the 9th. The " Emeu" left June 17th, arrived at Melbourne on the 15th August, and at Sydney on 18th. The " Simla" left July 12th, arrived at Melbourne on September 3rd, and Sydney on the 6th. The " European" left August 12th, arrived at Melbourne on October 14th, and Sydney on 18th. The "Columbian" left on the 12th of September, arrived at Melbourne on November 13th, and Sydney on the 17th. The " Emeu" did not arrive next trip, having grounded in the Red Sea. The "Simla" left November 12th, arrived in Melbourne January 7th, and Sydney the 11th. The " Victoria" left December 12th, and arrived at Melbourne February 21st and Sydney

Pacific Mail Route. 89

on the 25th. The " European" left on January 12th, arrived at Melbourne on March 11th, and arrived in Sydney on the 15th. The "Columbian" left on February 12th, arrived at Melbourne on April 24th, and in Sydney on the 29th. The " Australasian" left March 12th, and arrived at Melbourne on May 12th, and at Sydney on the 17th. The " Emeu " left on April 12th, and arrived at Melbourne on June 6th, and Sydney on the 9th. The "Victoria," with the May mails, arrived at Melbourne August 1st, and had arrived in Sydney on the 6th. Now they found on looking at the dates on which these steamers arrived at the two ports, that on nine different occasions the people of Sydney had been deprived of the advantage of availing themselves of the return post, whilst the people of Melbourne had only lost the post on three occasions—namely, in February, April, and August. Thus it would be seen that by this arrangement they had not alone been disappointed in the ends of postal communication and placed at a disadvantage each month, as compared with the sister colony of Victoria, but it was sufficiently obvious that they were giving a portion of the subsidy for the express purpose of affording the people of Melbourne an opportunity of communicating with their friends and commercial relations in Europe in a month's less time than that allowed to the people of Sydney. From the geographical position of their colony, something like this, though probably not in the same degree, must be the case by any line of steamers which went by the Eastern route ; but this was by no means the only ground upon which he thought it could be shown that they would be placed at a disadvantage by continuing the communication by way of India. This country had little in common with the inhabitants of the Asiatic countries. Beyond taking from them supplies of tea, sugar, and spices, they had scarcely any commerce with those countries ; they had very little of social affinity with any of the populations of the East ; their only connexion with the Eastern world was one of Imperial policy. But these objections would not apply to the trans-Pacific route. It would be found that there were many reasons, which he would touch upon presently, why they should desire that the route he proposed should be opened. To a very large extent it appeared to him that the establishment of steam communication with India was an Imperial question. It was to the interest of the British Government, to keep up rapid communication with India for political reasons, but those reasons did not affect this colony. It was most desirable that rapid and frequent communication should exist between England and the East, and of course any branch steam service that would tend in any degree to support the lines of communication between London and India would be of very great service to the mother country; but he contended that the Australian colonies had scarcely any interest in maintaining a line of steam communication *viâ* India, except so far as it might be made an efficient and rapid means of postal communication, and at the same time to some small extent a convenience for the purposes of their Indian commerce. But a great objection, in addition to those already stated, existed in the case of this colony on account of its position rendering it absolutely necessary that it should always be the last port of arrival and the first of departure, and therefore placed at a greater postal distance from Europe than the sister communities. Coming to the next resolution he thought that the language employed was not too strong when it stated that it was in the highest degree necessary that immediate steps should be taken to prevent the public inconvenience and injury resulting from an interruption of the mail service. Having already established a mail service which, when the terms of the contract were fulfilled, put this colony within two months' communication with Europe, and even when the terms were not absolutely fulfilled gave them the course of post in five months, he thought it was impossible for the colony to go back to any less regular system of postal communication, such as it would obtain if necessitated to resort again to sailing vessels. It certainly seemed to him that it would be altogether impossible for them under any circumstances that might arise to go back. Up to the present time the balance between the relative positions of the two colonies of New South Wales and Victoria was not determined. It was not yet decided which was to take the lead amongst the Australian colonies; and therefore anything this country could do to determine the balance in its favour it undoubtedly was justified—and no time ought to be lost—in doing. It appeared to him, moreover, that in making the trans-Pacific mail route peculiarly their own, they were not acting with any narrow-minded or jealous feeling toward the sister colony of Victoria. It seemed to him, and he thought the House and the country would agree, that a generous rivalry was a right feeling to exist between the two colonies. In this and all other matters they should do the best they could for their own interests; and they would be doing no more than their duty in their attempts to maintain for themselves the leading position amongst the Australian colonies. Then, opening up steam communication between Sydney and Panama would give them, securely and continuously, the valuable trade of New Zealand; for in every sense the colony of New Zealand had always looked towards us with the most friendly feelings. A large part of our trade was derived from New Zealand, and there was a greater degree of commercial friendliness subsisting between that colony and New South Wales than between any other two of the colonies. With New Zealand in the course of time we should no doubt connect ourselves with the innumerable fertile islands of the Pacific, which were destined to yield to the waves of European civilisation ever rolling in upon their shores. The fourth resolution affirmed that there was a reasonable probability of a large volume of voluntary immigration of a desirable character setting in, as one of the consequences of establishing the proposed line of mail steamers. Now some two or three years ago a gentleman named Cameron, an Englishman, settled in the United States, put forth a prospectus for establishing a line of steamers between Panama and Sydney. This gentleman had personal friends in this colony; he was a man of great enterprise and intelligence and of much practical information. In the prospectus put forth by Mr. Cameron at that time he (Mr. Parkes) found this paragraph with respect to the almost incredible amount of traffic existing between California and Panama :—

"California now contains a population estimated at 250,000—suppose it even to be 300,000—and turning to the report of a committee of the stockholders of the Pacific Mail Steamship Company appointed at the annual meeting, May 1855, we find it stated that there are 30,000 to 40,000 people who travel annually to and from California by the two steamship lines from New York, that is to say, at 30,000—the lowest estimate—one-tenth of the whole population, estimating it at 300,000 ; while, adding the passenger traffic from other countries, you may safely estimate the whole at one-seventh to one-eighth of the population."

To show that this traffic has not lessened since 1855, when this statement was made by Mr. Cameron, he would state some additional facts. He found by the latest dates from Panama that on the 30th April two steamers arrived at Aspinwall with 1230 passengers. On the 15th of May the "John L.

Stephens" arrived at San Francisco with 255 cabin passengers and 800 in the second cabin and steerage, in all 1055; in addition to this on the 5th of May, only ten days previous, the "Golden Gate" left San Francisco with 644 passengers. The one steamer, leaving the 5th of May, had 644 passengers; the other, arriving only ten days after, had 1055. These steamers ran twice a month between Panama and San Francisco, and were generally freighted with passengers to the extent he had indicated. There was not alone a sufficient amount of population leaving the Isthmus of Panama to freight these ships, but there was also a monthly line of steamers running between Panama and the various ports of Peru and Chili, also carrying a large number of passengers. Now so far from this incredible and unprecedented traffic across the Isthmus of Panama being likely to subside it was likely to increase. A short time since he had a conversation with a gentleman recently arrived from Europe who had had frequent interviews with the Emperor of the French on commercial matters, and he had learned from Louis Napoleon that at the present time there was building a line of steamers which were intended to run between Havre and Chagres, being one of four lines intended to connect the principal ports of France with other commercial countries. It must be to a large extent an unprofitable undertaking, but it would add to the commerce of France, and it would be carrying out a wise policy for the general welfare of the nation in the estimation of the present ruler of that country. He found also from the latest files from San Francisco, that agents of European merchants were in that State endeavouring to establish lines of steamers between Southampton, Havre, Bremen, and Aspinwall. He would read an extract from the *San Francisco Herald* of the 20th of May as follows :—

"How easy it would be to divert some of the immense tide of immigration which now surges in such mighty waves upon the Atlantic seaboard to these shores. Southampton, Havre, or Bremen, are not much more distant from San Francisco than New York. There is at present a line of steamers from England to Aspinwall, touching at the West Indies, and by that route we occasionally receive the latest news from Europe. The number of immigrants who are annually landed at the Atlantic ports averages, at least, a quarter of a million, and it is but reasonable to calculate that if there were cheap and regular communication between California and Europe, at least twenty or thirty thousand of that vast number would turn their eyes in this direction. Under these circumstances, we learn with great pleasure that it is contemplated by great capitalists in England to establish a line of propellers between the principal European ports (Southampton, Havre, and Bremen) and Aspinwall, and between Panama and San Francisco, and that, in all probability, before very long a steady stream of immigration will set in direct from Europe. Dr. Huddart is the agent of the company in this State. He is an old Californian. He goes to Europe by the steamer of to-day to report, and many months may not elapse before we are in direct and regular communication with the ports above-named. The recent gold discoveries in the British possessions will give an additional impetus to the project, and contribute not a little to its speedy realisation. An annual addition to our population of fifteen or twenty thousand by this new route would do much to promote our prosperity as a State."

They also knew that on the other side of the Isthmus there were even now the greatest opportunities to travel by steamers that were to be found in any part of the world. The celebrated Cunard fleet had its head-quarters at New York. It entered 35 steamers—17 screw and 18 paddle. These steamers ranged from 1000 to 4000 tons burthen. Their aggregate tonnage was 45,198 tons and their aggregate horse-power 12,770. The company had an established name. It had held contracts from the British Government for eighteen years, and he believed that so far from creating the disappointment which this colony had experienced, it had not only performed the services within the terms of the contracts, but had on many occasions reduced the time below that specified. Now that company, if sufficient inducement were offered, could take up this line at once, and in the hands of such a company they would beyond all chances of failure have the service carried out. The facts he had stated to the House, he thought, would show that there was an amount of population constantly passing over the Isthmus of Panama which was almost incredible, and which was of a kind not to be found in any other part of the world; that in no other quarter was there the same number of persons from the great commercial countries of the world constantly arriving and departing in search of some new project or enterprise for advancing their personal fortunes. He contended that if they had a line of steamers between Sydney and Panama, they would be certain of attracting a large portion of the population arriving at the Isthmus with the intention of going to San Francisco. When they found an easy means of transit to Australia they would come to these shores. Seeing the vast extent of traffic from Panama to San Francisco this country might expect in a few years, not perhaps 2000 a month, but at least one-fourth of that number. If steamers ran from Panama to this colony, instead of bringing thirty or forty persons—the most they would bring from India—they would bring four or five hundred every month, and these persons of a most serviceable class; in all probability they would generally be men of intelligence, men of energy, men of enterprise, men of considerable capital, men who would introduce with them all the improvements of civilisation, and conduce in various ways to develope the natural resources of this country, and so increase its industrial avocations and material prosperity. The fifth and last resolution affirmed, "That in coming to a right determination on this subject, the question of cost is not the first for consideration, but that the efficiency of the service to be performed should be secured beyond probability of failure, and that especial regard should be had to those social and commercial consequences which would tend most to the progress and prosperity of the colony of New South Wales." He thought that if it were granted that it was desirable to open up this means of communication no argument was required to show the necessity and wisdom of opening it up well and efficiently. He had endeavoured to show that in all probability the colony would gain incalculable benefits if this means of communication were opened up; that by no other means could they gain anything like a corresponding amount of benefit. It would increase the intercourse with New Zealand. It would tend to increase their intercourse with the islands in the Pacific—with which they must ultimately have large and valuable commercial intercourse as those islands became settled by a European population. He affirmed that it was to the interest of this country to get such a means of communication established at the earliest possible moment; and if it were to the interest of the country to do this, the necessary cost was not the first thing they should regard so long as there was no waste. Being determined by this means to maintain the colony in a leading position, they should secure this end without a niggardly regard to price so long as they secured efficiency in the performance of the contract, without which it would be comparatively useless. For his own part he thought that if this could not be obtained at less cost, it would be wise for the House to vote half a million of money to have this communication established without the possibility of interruption. He believed, so far as the subsidy was concerned, it would be wise to give whatever sum was necessary to have this communication in their own hands; and, depending—as they might reasonably do—on receiving a contribution from New Zealand, and perhaps something from the southern colonies, it would not be a very costly undertaking for the Government of this country. But he felt persuaded that the cost would be as nothing compared with the benefits to be derived, not only from the improved means of postal communication and the additions to our population, but from the new spirit which it would be the active cause of infusing into the commercial enterprise and social life of the colony. They had here a country richer than any other of the colonies, notwithstanding the rapid strides which Victoria had made in colonising enterprise. The natural resources of New South Wales were inexhaustible: its varieties of soil—its marvellous wealth of minerals—its many other advantages—made it second to none. And this highway across the Pacific seemed pointed out as by the hand of Providence to connect them with other countries— other countries, too, where the grand experiment of founding new empires, with a common origin and a common destiny, was going on. Those lands must be the teachers of this, for in no other part of the world were English liberty and English commerce transplanted to work out their ends on a new soil. Under these circumstances he felt that by affirming these resolutions they should affirm principles justifying the Government in taking immediate steps to supply the advantages of regular communication between Panama and this colony. He felt he had to apologise to the House for the time he had occupied, and also for the inefficient manner in which he had dealt with the matter. He felt that an apology was due to the House for his want of ability, more on this than on any other occasion, because he considered that this question was one of greater importance than any submitted for consideration during the session. They might pass their electoral bills, they might extend the franchise to the inhabitants of hovels, or give a vote to all over twenty-one years of age; they might provide for open or secret voting; they might take what course they chose in reforming their political institutions, but all this alone would be inoperative in securing the lasting prosperity of the colony. They required to people the colony with persons of the most enterprising and reputable character—a race of men sprung from the same stock as that from which they themselves were sprung. By making a highway through America to Europe, thus connecting themselves with the peoples of the only other countries where free institutions were successfully planted, and where manufactures and commerce, learning and science, had taken root and advanced together, would their efforts be best directed to the establishment of their own freedom and prosperity. It was the grand result which Australian statesmen should aim at. The resolutions were intended to give authority to the Government to take prompt and vigorous measures in opening this great work. He asked the House to say that it ought to be carried out to the advantage of the country without reference to the men who might hold office, and he felt that if any Government did not effect this consummation it would of itself be a sufficient ground for displacing them, because the service contemplated by these resolutions would be of greater advantage to the colony than anything else they could achieve. It would give the colony its proper position by bringing to its shores a large population of the very best class, infusing a more active spirit into its commerce, developing more rapidly its resources, raising its reputation to a higher level, and gaining for it the first position in this part of the world. In this spirit he regarded the resolutions, and in this spirit he moved them.

DEFENCE OF THE COLONIES.

SPEECH

Delivered in the Legislative Assembly, December 20th 1859, on moving the following resolutions:—

"That this House, having had under its consideration the subject of the defence of the colony, resolves as follows :—

" 1. That having regard to the present complications of foreign Governments, and the hold which the great maritime powers have in the seas of this hemisphere, it is impolitic and unsafe to neglect the means of preparation at our command for protecting the colony in the event of its being attacked by an enemy.

" 2. That the maintenance of regular troops in the colony for its protection is unwise in policy, and cannot be effective without becoming an excessive burden on the public revenue.

" 3. That the true principle of military defence, and the only course which would ensure effective resistance in extreme circumstances, is to habituate the subjects of the Queen in this colony to the use of arms, and to foster among all classes a loyal and patriotic spirit of reliance on their own valour and military organisation.

" 4. That any opinion herein expressed is not intended to apply to the protection afforded by Her Majesty's ships of war in the Australian waters.

" 5. That the foregoing resolutions be conveyed in an address to the Governor-General, with a request that His Excellency will be pleased to bring them under the consideration of the Executive Council, and also to transmit a copy of the same to Her Majesty's Principal Secretary of State for the Colonies."

MR. PARKES : It was scarcely possible to attach too much importance to the necessary provision for protecting their national honour as a British community. Nor was he amongst those who thought that the time of hostility and warfare amongst the nations of the civilised world had passed away. Looking to the advance of arms in Europe, and to the unscrupulous character of particular Governments, they might be fully prepared to anticipate any aggression that was practicable from those powers ; since the only considerations about such an aggression would be the probability of its success, and whether success would contribute to the end those powers had in view. That this danger—the danger of a rupture between the parent land and some one or more of the great powers of Europe—was admitted by persons most competent to form an opinion on the subject he should be prepared to show. But the most satisfactory way of proving this would be for him to lay before the House the opinions of men entitled by their experience and standing in the political world to be accepted as authorities. He should not attempt to detain the House with any discussion to prove the value of these authorities, but should confine himself to quoting from the speeches made in the House of Lords by Lords Lyndhurst and Ellenborough. The powers from which danger was to be apprehended were France, in the event of a rupture with England, and Russia in connexion with China, although that was a more remote contingency in point of time; but the danger of a rupture with France was imminent, and the relations between the two countries were uncertain from one day to another—whilst from intelligence received mail after mail it seemed to be an almost universal opinion that war was imminent. He would now read a few short extracts from the very remarkable speeches delivered in the House of Lords on the occasion alluded to. He need only premise that Lord Lyndhurst occupied a peculiar position amongst the statesmen of Great Britain. His great age, his splendid abilities, the distinction he had won in the highest offices of State, and his personal authority as a public man, together with the truly British spirit that always animated his conduct—these special features of his life placed him in the position of a national watchman, giving a tone and feeling to the national mind and the national heart. In his speech of the 5th July Lord Lyndhurst drew a vivid and powerful picture of the mother country, in regard to her capabilities of coping with the power of France in the event of a rupture. He said :—

"Last year we were in this position : France exceeded us in line-of-battle ships in a small proportion, but she exceeded us in an enormous proportion in steam frigates. At present we surpass her in line-of-battle ships considerably, but we are still greatly inferior in those important vessels, steam frigates. We shall, in the spring of next year, surpass her still more in line-of-battle ships, but we shall still be inferior to her in steam frigates. This is a point for the consideration of your lordships and the consideration of the country."

He then spoke of the comparative naval training that was undergone in France and in England, and said:—

"The French for several years have had a system of training of a most perfect kind—training in the conduct of a vessel, and training not only in the conduct of the vessel, but in gunnery. The moment a French ship is afloat that moment they have trained men ready to go on board the vessel. I am sorry to say, from all I hear, and all I observe, we have not such a system as that to which I have referred—a system of the utmost importance, but which in this country, hitherto, has been almost entirely neglected."

There were other passages showing the uncertainty of victory in the event of a rupture and the danger that must in any case attend such a rupture. After having urged the Lords to sanction the motion for putting the country in a more efficient state of defence, Lord Lyndhurst said:—

"But I may be asked, 'Why do you think such measures requisite? Are we not in alliance with France? Are we not on terms of friendship with Russia? What other power can molest us?' To these questions, my lords, my answer shall be a short and a simple one. I will not consent to live in dependence on the friendship or the forbearance of any country. I rely solely on my own vigour—my own exertion—and my own intelligence. Does any noble lord in this House dissent from the principle which I have laid down? I rejoice, my lords, to find that such is not the case. But while this is a matter for congratulation, I regret to be obliged to say that we do not stand well upon the continent of Europe. I do not think late events have improved our position in that respect. But I go further, my lords, and express my belief, as the result of my own careful observation, that if any plausible ground of difference should arise between this country and France, and that difference should lead to hostilities, the declaration of war with England on the part of the Government of that country would be hailed with the utmost enthusiasm, not only by the army of France, but by the great mass of the French people. If I am asked, 'Will you not rely upon the assurances and the courtesy of the Emperor Napoleon?' I reply that I have a great respect for that high person, and that I will not enter into any explanation on this subject, but will leave every noble lord to draw his own conclusions, and to form his own opinions. This, however, I will say, and I can say it without impropriety. If I am asked whether I cannot place reliance on the Emperor Napoleon, I reply, with confidence, that I cannot place reliance on him because he is in a situation in which he cannot place reliance on himself. He is in a situation in which he must be governed by circumstances, and I will not consent that the safety of this country should depend on such contingencies."

He thought it was Lord Cowley who stated it as the result of his observation as a resident in France that there was not a widowed mother in the country who would not give her last son for a war against England. That was the state of feeling in France according to the authority he had mentioned, and higher authority could not be found throughout the length and breadth of English society. In another portion of the debate to which he had alluded, and in which some of the first men in England took part, Lord Ellenborough used these remarkable words, referring to Lord Lyndhurst who had opened the discussion :—

"My noble and learned friend has put an end to that fatal course of self-deception in which this country has for so many years been indulging. He has distinctly placed before the House and the public the pictures of what we were and what we are—of what we are under circumstances the most perilous which have occurred the last half-century."

In a later part of his speech Lord Ellenborough continued :—

"We hear the war declared to be for the purpose of changing the existing distribution of power in Europe, which has lasted untouched from the treaty of Vienna to the present time. We see it conducted by such an extraordinary force as naturally to produce alarm in the mind of anyone in this country. France in this war appears almost as a new power in Europe. If it be true, and I accept the declaration of the Emperor that he made no preparations, it is on that account I entertain the greatest alarm. If, without any previous preparation, the Emperor of France can in six or eight weeks place 200,000 men, perfectly equipped for military operations, in the centre of northern Italy—if he can send 80,000 men by sea, most rapidly, with most perfect arrangements, with all that is required of munitions of war and provisions carefully packed, as if there had been forethought, and as if intended for transmission by sea—if in addition to that, in a small space of time, he can place from 30,000 to 40,000 men in a powerful fleet in the Adriatic, and there effect a descent and a rehearsal of the invasion of this country—when I see these things done, when I see the diminished force of this country, as detailed by my noble and learned friend, in comparison with the force of France, I do feel apprehensive, and I do feel that it is the bounden duty of Government and of Parliament to place this country in a state of unattackable security."

He thought that these extracts, embodying as they did the opinions of the highest authorities in the mother country, were sufficient to show that we ought not to lull ourselves into a sense of fancied security. Now he maintained, and he appealed to the common sense of every hon. member who listened to him, that the colony at the present time was in a perfectly defenceless state. We hear that after expending enormous sums for the construction of batteries,* they were of scarcely any use unless much greater expense was gone to in providing men to man them—that they

---

* The expenditure incurred under the administration of Sir William Denison in constructing Fort Denison and other batteries.

Defence of the Colonies.   101

were not alone of no use but in the event of an attack they would be worse than useless—they might be turned against us by an invading force. From what we knew was going on in Europe we were aware that an attacking force could be landed here by two or three transport vessels containing four or five thousand men. He believed that France at the present time was constructing, if she had not completed, several steam transport vessels capable of carrying about 3500 men each. Of course he would be met with the assertion of the unlikelihood of such vessels coming to these seas. But in the event of a rupture in Europe he apprehended that one of the first movements would be a well-organised attack on the Australian colonies. And he also apprehended that in carrying out such a well-organised attack by such a power as France—which, as Lord Lyndhurst said, had appeared in this age as a new power in Europe with an enormous increase in all the preparations for war—it would not be inferior vessels that would be sent to these waters, but that even if the vessels he had referred to were not sent, those sent would be of very great power, capacity, and speed; so that in all probability two vessels would land on our shores, without warning or note of preparation of any kind, a force of from three to four thousand well-disciplined men. Let them look at the situation of the colony. We had at the present time an artillery corps containing a trifle above a hundred men, who were supplemented by the infantry at the barracks, making the number altogether about 583 men. Now he could not believe that in any attack that might be made upon the colony, this force would be of much avail to the community. He had every confidence that these men before an army of soldiers sixfold their number, or perhaps a greater proportion, would do their duty; but he thought they would lead a very forlorn hope, and the result would be their own destruction without any protection to the country. The cost of these men, comparatively speaking, was enormous; the sum placed on the estimates for the payment of the 583 men was no less than £16,308, and we were paying only the artillery in full, giving an allowance to the infantry in barracks. So that for this distant colony the cost of a very small and inefficient force was £16,308. It struck him very forcibly that a long residence in a colony was not the best possible mode of discipline for regular troops, and he should scarcely be inclined to expect the same amount of efficiency in troops lying idle in the colony for a number of years as in those under a more regular employment, and who had more frequent opportunities of going into active service. But be that as it might, these regular troops were not formed of a different class, of a different nation, of a different birth, of a different material from the common population of the colony. They were recruited—as all persons acquainted with recruiting operations in England would know—chiefly in the English towns; and there was nothing in the circumstances, or condition, or character of the men who formed the standing army of England that could place them in a better position for effective service than any body of our fellow-colonists who might be enrolled and disciplined in the same manner here upon an altogether different principle. If this system continued we must have a sufficient number of these troops in the colony for the effective resistance of such a force as would be sure to be collected for an organised attack on the part of any of the great maritime powers; and thus, by incurring an enormous expenditure, unnecessarily burden the resources of the colony. There was no argument that he could discover why an Imperial force should be more effective for the purposes of defence than a force composed of residents in the colony. That we ought to raise such a force he did not think required any argument. Even the advocates of the Peace Society in England deemed that England ought to be placed in a state of effective preparation against attempted invasion. Both Mr. Bright and Mr. Cobden had within the last few months expressed their opinion that the country ought to be placed in an effective state of defence; and this being admitted so generally, argument was not required to show its necessity here. The question he wished to raise was, whether it was advisable to create a force of our own by enrolling the inhabitants of the colony, or to depend upon the armed forces that were eating out our vitals without contributing to our industrial powers or being of sufficient strength for our defence. It might be thought that the mother country would contribute to the maintenance of the necessary troops for our defence, but he was disposed to doubt that altogether. The tendency of feeling in the mother country, and especially in the Imperial Parliament, would not lead any one to expect that England would consent to incur any great expense for the defence of the colonies. Moreover,

Defence of the Colonies. 103

the Imperial Government had directly intimated on more than one occasion that the colonies must provide for their own defence. In a despatch from the Secretary of State for the Colonies under the late Government, which he believed had not yet reached His Excellency the Governor, this was alluded to. And in a despatch from Sir Bulwer Lytton addressed to the Governor of Antigua only last year the subject was more definitely treated, and the feeling of the British Government was expressed in a very marked manner, to the effect that the colonies must rely for their general defence upon their own resources. It appeared to him, then, that if we were disposed to rest upon the protection to be afforded by the Imperial troops we should rest upon no certainty. They might and most likely would in time of war be withdrawn from us for more urgent purposes; and not to raise the necessary means of defending ourselves would be in reality to leave ourselves at the mercy of any attacking power in a war between the leading countries of the world at the present time. There was the more reason why we should take this course, in consequence of the intimate knowledge France and America had of our shores and the neighbouring islands, every available inch of ground being known to them as well as to ourselves; and in many respects he was inclined to think they had a much more correct knowledge. Then, France had a port of refuge within a very few days' sail of our own harbour—a port of refuge which he was given to understand was so well protected by forts that it would be almost impossible to follow vessels into the harbour of New Caledonia. What were the military forces of France at New Caledonia he was not in a position to say, nor was it of much consequence; for with the great facility that country possessed for removing military forces we could not be certain from one week or day to another what power might not be at her command in these seas. We know that no power in the world has greater means than France has of providing the necessary forces for a successful attack upon the Australian colonies; nor was any other power so well protected in the Australian seas, as she always had the convenience for a hostile force in a port as contiguous to our shores as an enemy could wish it to be. With regard to the affirmation in the resolutions, "that the maintenance of regular troops in the colony for its protection is unwise in policy, and cannot be effective without becoming an excessive burden on the public revenue"

—that was apparent from the knowledge we had of the expense as shown by the estimates for the military, taken into consideration with the numbers required. It was estimated by the Governor that the annual expense of a battalion of 658 men with officers would be, in round numbers, £40,000. This expense His Excellency calculated would be reduced by the proportion to be contributed by the Imperial Government, leaving the colony to pay £24,000. But we could not depend upon any portion of this expense being sustained by the Imperial Government; for the whole tendency of English feeling was to throw the work of defence upon the colonies themselves. But even this land force could not be effective for the purpose of successful defence against invasion. He would here remark that Colonel Percival had, at His Excellency's request, prepared a very interesting paper on our means of defence; that officer was of opinion that if the colony were attacked, it would be after the manner he (Mr. Parkes) had endeavoured to describe, by a force of some thousands; and he was also of opinion, confirmed by other military authorities, that there would be a combined attack by sea and land. In our harbour and along our coast infantry would be landed so that we should be attacked in front and rear simultaneously. He saw also that Colonel Percival, to a great extent, raised precisely the same question as was raised by these resolutions. He would read a few short extracts from Colonel Percival's paper : —

"The manner in which the Governor proposes that this force should be constituted, in as far as the regular troops and police are concerned, I also fully concur in; but as I consider that this force is calculated at the lowest number that it would be prudent to attempt the defence, I cannot concur in the expediency of introducing volunteers into the calculation.

"Taking, therefore, for granted that the regular force of the garrison will be provided, as recommended by the Governor, and that the police are also made available for duty, there would still be 220 men required."

Again he says—

"The militia is a truly constitutional force, and although in times of peace the expense may be felt to be burdensome, yet as it engenders that spirit by which alone the efforts of a free people can be directed to the defence of their country and institutions, its true value must be at once perceived, especially when war threatens."

In another part Colonel Percival says—

"I will now refer to the possibility of a combined attack by land and sea. This, I consider, not only possible, but in the event of this port being attacked, I am of opinion that this would be the mode adopted by the enemy."

Defence of the Colonies. 105

Therefore so far as they could reconcile the opinions of these military authorities, a force of 2000 men is necessary for the effective defence of the country. There was one other observation made by Colonel Percival which he should quote:—

" The effect, therefore, of an organisation to the extent named, would be to deter any enemy attacking this place without an organised force of at least double the number, and thereby diminishing the probability of an attack at all."

One great advantage of their placing themselves in a state of defence was that to the extent this was done they decreased the probability of being attacked at all. Now if any question was raised as an objection to his resolutions, that the regular troops would be a more effective protection, he would be disposed to appeal to the teachings of all history to the contrary. In their own country, in particular, they had found that the militia and the volunteers had been the mainstay of the country in times of war, and they had in reality supplied a force on which the country fell back with reliance. It was found in one important battle—the battle of Talavera—where a great number of the forces were drafted from the English militia, that they had the advantage over the military. They knew that the revolutionary regiments under General Washington, although newly enrolled, imperfectly clothed, imperfectly fed, displayed superior valour to, and fought successfully in every collision with, the more fully organised enemy with whom they had to cope. Why was this? It was not because they were a revolutionary body, but because they were identified with the country for which they were fighting; and this would be the case with us as with them, because in defending our homes we should be identified with precisely the same principle—the principle that links us to the country, and places before us everything that is dear to us in civilised society. The American war would afford us an example in almost every step we took; and in saying this he was only uttering the sentiments of an English statesman. Mr. Gladstone, some years ago, in alluding to the establishment of a Constitution in these colonies, said there was no other part of the world where we could better seek instruction than the United States of America. In the nature of things there was no other country with analogous circumstances and with kindred feelings; and as the progress of America afforded them lessons in nearly all the events of the peaceful history of the colony, so it afforded them a lesson to depend on themselves for their military defence. The troops of Washington were in some cases reduced to such a state of distress that they were utterly destitute of food, almost uncovered, without ammunition, without shoes, and in the midst of all the severity of a deep winter—at times they could be traced by the blood on the snow, flowing from their feet. Yet these troops never exhibited insubordination, and were as effective as any troops in the history of the world. To quote the words of Webster, the troops of Washington were destitute of everything in the world except their sacred cause and martial demeanour. If men were engaged in a cause which carried their hearts with it, they would be good soldiers; and it was impossible to suppose that a military force locally raised would not be just as effective in defending the country against an enemy as any number of Imperial troops. Within the metropolitan districts there must be 20,000 men capable of bearing arms. He could see no reason, therefore, why they might not have a militia force of 10,000 men at least. The enrolment of these men would do good to society, and would infuse a truer public feeling among all classes, because it would cultivate a juster appreciation of all the institutions of the country and a stronger attachment to the soil. It would make every man proud of the country where his home was fixed; he would have a new interest in his home by becoming a defender of the country in which he was living. The present standing army of the United States was not more than 10,317 men. It consisted, he believed, at the present time of two regiments of dragoons, 1300 men; mounted riflemen, 800 men; four regiments of artillery, 2808 men; eight regiments of infantry, 4464 men; ordnance department, 585 men; engineers, 143; general staff, medical department, and pay department, 217 men; altogether, 10,317 men. The standing army of the United States—the greatest commercial country next to England in the world—consisted then of 10,317 men; but the militia force of the United States consisted of 2,704,454 men, so that the country, with its inexpensive standing army, had a militia force that could be called out at all points and at an hour's notice overwhelming in number compared with any regular army in the old countries of Europe. It would be interesting to see the proportion of the militia force to the population raised in the several States. In 1850 in Maine the militia force was 44,665, and the population was about half a million. New Hampshire

Defence of the Colonies. 107

militia, 29,639, and population just about the same as this colony; Massachusetts militia, 95,893, and population a little below a million. In Rhode Island the militia was 15,786, and population 147,544. In Connecticut the militia was 58,220, and population 370,791—very little over the population of New South Wales. In the State of New York the militia force was 165,544, and population a little over three millions; and so on in proportion throughout all the States of America, making altogether a collective force of over two millions. In 1857—seven years later—the militia force had risen to nearly three millions. Now this proportion of the militia force of the country has been steadily maintained with regard to the population from the foundation of the Union. He found that twenty-five years ago when the population was only 13,820,000, the militia amounted to 1,300,000. In Canada a similar principle obtained. The estimated expenditure for the maintenance of the militia in Canada in 1856 was £36,107 14s. 11d. He had not the number of militia before him, but the estimated expenditure would show it must have been very considerable. As he thought it was a very great matter how a force of this kind was composed, or rather of what particular character it was constituted, he would read how the State Militia was distributed. He found in Connecticut there were 53,241 infantry, 692 cavalry, 2583 artillery, 1704 riflemen, making a total of 58,220. It would be seen the great majority consisted of infantry. So in Maryland the force consisted of 46,866, of whom 41,952 were infantry, 2094 cavalry, 1640 artillery, and 678 riflemen, showing that the United States Government were sensible of the use of the bayonet. It appeared to him that any force raised in this colony, to be effective, must consist mainly of infantry corps. He maintained that for them to depend for protection upon the Imperial Government was in itself contrary to the constitutional liberties of England. As they all knew in the Bill of Rights, under which their present liberties were founded, it was strictly stipulated that no standing army should be maintained without the consent of Parliament. This was violated by maintaining troops here, because the Legislature could have but little power over the troops of the Imperial Government. Although the principle in the Bill of Rights had not been literally carried out, it had been acted upon to this extent, that Parliament would only vote the supplies for the army from year to year; and it was only by holding this power that troops could not be maintained without the sanction of Parliament. Here we had no such power. He held it would be unwise and inexpedient—denationalising the country, stripping it of its highest attributes, emasculating it of the British spirit which was its safety—if they depended upon the troops of the Imperial Government. The right course to take was to depend upon themselves; it would tend to the advancement of society, creating a healthy feeling through all classes, and they alone could defend themselves in case of an attack either by France or America. He observed that the hon. member for Newcastle (Mr. Hodgson) had placed upon the paper an amendment he intended to move upon the resolutions. He would state at once he should divide the House against that amendment. He had always been under the impression that the hon. member belonged to one of the gallant professions, but he supposed he was mistaken in that belief, because he did not think it was the characteristic of British soldiers or sailors to parade their loyalty. He did not think it was the weakness of those gentlemen to suppose the loyalty of the English people was ever at fault, or had been put to the question. Their loyalty had always consisted in defending their country and Queen when called upon, but not in parading their sentiments before the world. He would say there was no occasion for such an expression of loyalty; it would be most gratuitous, and would lay the House open to the suspicion that after all it was not so very loyal. There was nothing in the proceedings of this House or the colony that should induce anyone to question its loyalty to the mother country, or to lead any observer to suppose that they were not a part and parcel of the British people. In submitting these resolutions he wished to raise the question whether they were to go on trusting to a handful of English troops which in time of danger or invasion would be of little use; or whether they were to follow the example of the American colonies and Canada, and the example set them by the mother country in times of great danger, and depend upon their own arms. Whether the House agreed with him or not, it could not at all events take exception to his bringing the question of the defences before the country. A matter of such consequence might have been better brought forward by some member more acquainted with the subject; but if that was not done who was to blame? It was open to any member to introduce the question, but

Defence of the Colonies.

as it was left for some time after the House met he took it up, and whilst he laid claim to no privileges beyond other members he was not disposed to throw off the obligations that rested upon him as upon other members. That it was not introduced until he took it up was sufficient reason for his taking up the question. He therefore should expect and had the fullest confidence that the House would address themselves to the subject he had brought under its notice calmly and dispassionately, fully alive to the dangers of the present moment and actuated by no feelings but those of true patriotism, and with no other object but to preserve the honour and security of the country.

[A lengthy debate ensued upon the motion made. The Colonial Secretary moved an amendment on the second resolution in the following words :—" That the maintenance of regular troops in the colony ought to be supplemented by the formation of a national militia, composed of citizens of the country." This amendment was carried by 39 to 11 votes, and the resolutions as so amended were then adopted by 42 to 8 votes.]

SUBSTANCE OF SPEECH
In reply on the debate which arose on the foregoing resolutions.

MR. PARKES in reply said: He would first notice the singularly cool spirit in which the Premier had addressed himself to this question, considering it as something inferior in importance and urgency to other motions on the business-paper. If the premisses upon which the motion rested were admitted, and they were not denied, how in the name of common sense any member, especially a Minister of the Crown, could consider them inopportune he was at a loss to conceive. Was the motion on the paper which affected the honourable gentleman's own position more urgent than this? Surely he would not say it was. What did he mean by saying the motion was not one of urgency, when it was acknowledged in all parts of the mother country that events were now taking place of the most momentous character, and that must be momentous here so long as this colony remained a portion of the British Empire. If the crisis were urgent in London so it was in Sydney, and ought to be viewed in as anxious a spirit by our Ministers as by the statesmen of England ; and so it would be if they were statesmen instead of merely gentlemen holding the offices of Government. He would now reply to an observation which fell from the honourable and reverend gentleman (Dr. Lang.) He argued that it was a species of cowardice and disloyalty to call upon the Imperial forces to defend us in time of war, and that it would savour of a want of true loyalty. He then went on to say he had no faith in our ability to defend ourselves, and he drew the extraordinary conclusion that if we were separated from England we should be perfectly safe. Surely he had read the fable of the wolf and the lamb, and must know that between different states as between man and man, if one desired to pick a quarrel with the other, a sufficient cause of quarrel would soon be found. If we were worth plundering there would be found governments and states not sufficiently scrupulous to abstain from plundering us. They might have their city desolated contrary to the wishes of those powers that held the forces at command, through a mere caprice of an officer or in violation of an expressed command. This might be done and had been done in hundreds of cases. Their only safety was in being prepared to fight and to defend themselves with their own right arms. Why, while hon. members talked of this motion being a waste of time they were in this position—with 500 armed men they had batteries which the highest military authorities told us might be taken possession of by an enemy. We were not safe from one day to another, but an armed power might be landed on our shores, our property taken, and our homes laid at the mercy of our invaders. Surely this was no exaggerated picture. Experience told them that the great powers, however advanced in civilisation, were not the less unscrupulous ; there was as much barbarity amongst them as in former times although glossed over by higher civilisation. Then the hon. member (Mr. Campbell) had told us that we would be apprised of preparations for war by the electric telegraph. He must have great faith in our enemies to believe that they would spare the electric telegraph. It appeared to him that this question ought to be taken up seriously—if the Government had not taken it up he was not to blame for that. He appealed to the House to adopt the resolutions, which did not assert that they were to dispense with the military force in the colony all at once, but simply asserted that it would be unwise to maintain regular troops for our defence, and that as soon as we were able to defend ourselves they ought to be withdrawn. They would never make the effort necessary to their defence unless they were driven to the necessity of making it. One hon. member had dared to say the people of this colony would as soon fight under the American as the English flag. He disbelieved it; and the sentiment uttered by the hon. member had not even the credit of the courage of rebellion. He could understand him if the hon. member himself was prepared to take up arms against the Government under which he lived, but he could not understand such sentiments as an idle utterance. He disbelieved that any such feeling pervaded any class in this country. The language of Wordsworth applied to us—

> "The land we from our fathers had in trust;
> And to our children will transmit, or die:
> This is our maxim, this our piety;
> And God and Nature say that it is just.
> That which we would perform in arms—we must!
> We read the dictate in the infant's eye;
> In the wife's smile, and in the placid sky;
> And at our feet, amid the silent dust
> Of them that were before us."

STATE OF POLITICS IN 1860.

SPEECH

Delivered at a Public Meeting of the Electors of East Sydney, November 1860.

[A MEETING of electors of East Sydney, convened by the friends of Mr. Parkes, was held on the evening of Monday, November 29th, 1860, in the Temperance Hall, Pitt-street, which was crowded to excess. On the platform were the Mayor of Sydney, Mr. Windeyer, Mr. Harbottle, and a number of gentlemen who had 'been in the habit of supporting Mr. Parkes. Mr. W. Henty, the Colonial Secretary of Tasmania, was also an auditor. Mr. Parkes was enthusiastically cheered on entering the hall; and a large number of persons were unable to obtain admittance. On the motion of Mr. Mountcastle, the Mayor took the chair. The Chairman read the advertisement calling the meeting, and introduced Mr. Parkes.]

Mr. PARKES said he should perhaps be believed by most persons when he assured them that it would be in vain for him to attempt to find words to convey to them his gratitude for the cordial reception he had met with that evening. There were many circumstances connected with his public life and with his personal history which rendered this reception peculiarly gratifying to him. Before he proceeded to what was his proper business as a candidate for their suffrages, perhaps he might for a few minutes be permitted to explain the exact position in which he stood before them. About eighteen months ago they returned him at a general election as one of their representatives. In the course of events a dissolution took place. That dissolution took place after a peculiarly laborious and harassing session, and he at once confessed that he then felt too much weariness and too strong a desire for repose to think much about his re-election. At the beginning of last week he was waited upon by a deputation from a meeting held in this city to know if he would consent again to become a candidate. He stated to the deputation that, looking upon a dissolution of

Parliament in this constitutional light, that it was a declaration that the members had lost the confidence of their constituents, and no longer represented those opinions which it was supposed they represented at the time of their election; looking upon a dissolution as referring them back for the expression of the opinion of the electors, as to whether they had performed their duty faithfully or not, he should have considered it his duty to offer his services again to the electors of East Sydney, without reference to any other consideration whatsoever. He regarded the case as one in which men who had any public reputation at stake could not feel at liberty to shrink from the responsibility before the country which they had incurred. Therefore he told the deputation that, whether they had moved or not, he should have placed himself in a position for the electors to pronounce their verdict upon his conduct. He at once consented, with an expression of gratitude for the trouble the deputation had taken, again to become a candidate. Since then he knew nothing whatever of what had taken place, except what he had learned from the newspapers. No member of the committee sitting in Sydney, acting for him, had ever written to him on the business of the election. His only channel of information in reference to the steps which had been taken on his behalf had been the public press. This was his first personal association with the election, beyond the assent he gave to the deputation. Perhaps they would indulge him a little further in the preliminary remarks he wished to make, while very briefly he retraced his political connexion with this city. He was by far the oldest representative of Sydney now in the colony. More than seven years ago he was elected in opposition to a very upright and worthy gentleman by a majority of two to one. He was again elected after the establishment of responsible Government, being only eighteen votes from the head of the poll. He was for a third time elected in the early part of last year. He was now therefore asking them, if they had confidence in him, and if they thought there were no four of the other gentlemen tendering their services to them fitter for the trust than he, to elect him for the fourth time. During this long period—a long period of political history in the colonies—he had been very intimately mixed up with all that concerned the city, and he thought he might almost say with most questions of importance that concerned the country. It had been said—he had noticed—at some meetings which had been held,

I

that he had been very regular in his attendance in Parliament, and he had heard it hinted that this might be attributed to some peculiar reason. But if they were to take the trouble of searching the records of the former Legislatures, they would learn that his attendance did not begin with last session. From the first day that he took his seat in the Legislature he felt that it was his bounden duty to be present on all important occasions, and to absent himself on no occasion unless for reasons which admitted of no denial. The legislative records for the last seven years would show that his name appeared in nearly every division list from first to last. He did not believe that throughout the many hundreds of divisions which had taken place during those seven years his name would be found absent from twenty. He therefore might very well refer the electors of Sydney for an exposition of his views—for an explanation of his principles—to the votes he had unflinchingly recorded in the Legislature of the country. It was from a feeling of this kind, and from a sense he had always entertained and cherished that a public distinction was no distinction at all unless it was won boldly and independently, that he determined on this occasion not to go beating about the constituency of East Sydney for support. His public conduct was before the citizens of Sydney and before the country. He had scarcely any opinion to modify—scarcely any vote recorded that he would wish to change, and he appealed to the parliamentary history for an answer to all inquiries as to his fitness to represent the city. But while taking that ground—though it was high ground, he believed it was equally honourable to them as to himself—he considered it to be the duty of every man seeking the suffrages of his fellow-citizens to come before them face to face—to allow them every opportunity of questioning him as to any of his public acts —to let them hear fully what he had to say for himself, and to put him through whatever test or trial their ingenuity or patience might invent. It was to afford them this full opportunity, and in discharge of what he conceived to be a duty that belonged to his position as a candidate, that he presented himself before them that night. He might refer specially to some of his own acts in the Legislature of the country if time permitted. He had been in every session what was known in parliamentary circles as a pretty regular committeeman. He had been chairman of some seven or eight committees during different sessions, and if he only enumerated the designations of some of those committees they would serve to show the direction which his labours—whatever they were worth—had taken in the Legislature. One committee was to consider the propriety of establishing a nautical school in the country, with the view of collecting the numerous class of friendless boys cast upon this large city, and of converting them into what the country will stand much in need of in future years—a colonial marine. Another committee was to consider—(he was speaking of some years ago)—the capabilities of this country for agriculture. That was appointed, at a time when it was influentially promulgated that New South Wales was only fit for pastoral pursuits, to endeavour to collect information counteracting that impression. And at this stage he might perhaps be permitted to say that one of the most valuable witnesses examined before that committee was the present Secretary for Lands, Mr. John Robertson. Another of the committees was to inquire into the subject of the adulteration of food—a subject which, as many of them would be aware, had attracted great attention and most deservedly so in the mother-country. Another committee was to consider the subject of the introduction of the electric telegraph, and it was upon his report that the first electric telegraph in the colony was established. Another of the committees, in the late session, was appointed to inquire into the social condition of the working-classes. He had just enumerated the heads of the various inquiries to show the direction his labours had taken in committee business. He might go further, but time would not permit. He now came to what was peculiarly part of his business there, to give some account (and that would necessarily be hasty and imperfect) of his stewardship in the last Parliament. He was elected in June last year. Parliament met at the end of August. The first motion that he submitted to the Legislature was for the repeal of the duties on tea and sugar. Many of them would recollect that this was in accordance with views which he expressed during his election. His motion was carried, and thereupon the Government of the day took it into their heads to be embarrassed; there was not the slightest necessity for their being embarrassed, but they thought it a good opportunity to get into a state of political embarrassment, and after declaring that if he (Mr. Parkes) had only waited a few days longer they themselves should have done the very thing he did—they resigned, because he had strengthened their hands by a parliamentary vote to do it. They had gone on for eighteen months, and yet the Government that had been in power pretty well from that time to this had not done much towards repealing those duties up to the present time. The next vote of importance was given against the Government Education Bill, the second reading of which was negatived by a majority of something like fifty-seven to eight. There again the Government determined to be embarrassed, and they resigned. On the first occasion the Government of the day, as many would recollect, resigned, but owing to circumstances which time would not permit him to explain now, even so far as his knowledge extended, they were recalled to power; on the second occasion there were men found sufficiently desperate to take office and to prevent their recall. Then they had what would be known to all as the Forster Ministry, and he should take the liberty of briefly entering into one or two explanations with regard to the formation of that Ministry, because in consequence of the course he thought it his duty to take towards that remarkable political combination he had been much misrepresented. He did not mean that he had been extensively misrepresented, but that statements had been made very much opposed to the real state of the facts. For instance, it was promulgated that he opposed that Ministry through wounded vanity because he was not consulted in its formation. He had never chosen to explain or to refute that charge, or even to speak of it in public at all until the present moment, but the fact was that Mr. Forster met him in the street in the course of the formation of his Ministry and told him that he was then seeking him to explain to him what he had done, and to ask his advice. He (Mr. Parkes) had heard the rumour—for rumour, as they were well aware, is very prevalent on occasions of such a kind—of what Mr. Forster had done, and he put a question to him with the view of eliciting whether such was the case. Mr. Forster then repeated to him the names of the gentlemen he thought of inviting to join him in the Government of the country—names which rumour had previously assigned to him. He instantly and without a moment's deliberation said to Mr. Forster—"The course you have taken, and the names you have selected to form your Government, so entirely surprise me that I must decline offering you any advice on the subject." He thought it but justice to himself to explain thus much, but perhaps he should not have deemed it necessary if it were not for going on to state why he felt no friendly disposition towards the Government from the first. He had always considered it a principle in constitutional government—wanting which constitutional government would be in danger of running into one of the worst forms of mis-government—that men who had won the public confidence fairly—by ability, fidelity to principle, and by valuable services—should be called upon to govern the State. And without wishing to say a word in disparagement of the gentlemen whom Mr. Forster chose to invite to form his Ministry, he could not detect in them or in their lives one single qualification such as he had always been led to suppose are the qualifications which entitle men to be called upon to take part in parliamentary government. He could not understand how any gentleman, whatever might be the amount of his intelligence—however high might be his character—who had never taken any active part in public affairs—who had come out of a mercantile counting-house a day or two before and had been nominated to a branch of the Legislature generally unpopular—he could not understand how any gentleman so circumstanced could be suddenly elevated to one of the most responsible offices in the country. He therefore disapproved altogether of the manner in which that Government was formed, as ignoring what he maintained lies at the very root of parliamentary government—that the country should be governed by men who have fairly won the confidence of their fellow-citizens. Having, as he said before, been unable to approve of this Government from the first, he determined to meet it on neutral ground. He determined that if the Government after it was formed showed an aptitude for public business—if its members showed that they were masters of the situation which he conceived they had usurped—if they produced sound measures and carried them out with an intimate knowledge of the Parliament with which they had to deal—then he would allow himself to be won to their support. He would allow himself to be won by the merits of their measures. He met them therefore with no very friendly feeling, but with no unfriendly feeling; with a desire, however, to watch them closely: to criticise their conduct, it is true, but to find out what was good in them and to support it. But he would appeal to any man—he cared not whether he agreed with him or not—who had made it his business to watch the proceedings of the Legislative Assembly, whether that Government did not prove itself so utterly impracticable—whatever might have been their good intentions or their intelligence—as to make it apparent to common sense that they could not possibly carry on the business of the country. One thing that a Minister under responsible government ought to know above all things they did not appear to know at all—namely, the character and genius of the Assembly by whose permission they held office. They were constantly thrusting themselves into hot water when there was no necessity for it. They were constantly damping the support of their friends and bringing upon themselves the ridicule of their opponents. It was solely on account of the utter impracticability of that Government, not from any distrust of their honesty of purpose, that he gave his vote at last to displace them from office. The Bill upon which the Forster Ministry was driven from power was one to Reconstruct the Legislative Council. It was in character somewhat like the present Land Bill, containing a considerable amount of good and a considerable amount of mischief. It was indeed a very impracticable measure—crude, unstatesmanlike, and destitute of one important principle without which no second House he firmly believed could be constructed—the principle of indissolubility in connexion with rotatory election. Altogether the measure would have been quite unworkable unless amended in committee. He saw then—as he had seen for twelve months before—the urgent necessity of reforming the Legislative Council so plainly, that he was a long time before he could determine to vote against that measure; and if it had not been for the impracticable character of the Government, added to the crude and unworkable character of the measure itself, he should have voted for the second reading, in order if possible to have made it in committee such a measure as might have averted a calamity that was now inevitable. But he reasoned thus: that it would be impossible, in the existing state of things, for this abortive measure ever to be moulded into a better shape—that if we went on with it time would be lost, and we should be brought to the period when it would be impossible to work out this reform at all. A consideration of this kind, he confessed,

State of Politics in 1860.

largely influenced him in the vote he gave on the occasion. During that Administration he (Mr. Parkes) introduced and carried by a large majority a series of resolutions affirming the principle that this country must protect itself from foreign enemies by its own inherent strength. He viewed that question, after much consideration, in this light—that if we were ever invaded, we should be invaded by so formidable a force that no number of the regular troops which we could afford to keep would be sufficient to stand against the invaders. But the county of Cumberland would supply us with 10,000 men within easy distance of Sydney who were capable of bearing arms. Half this number properly disciplined to the use of arms would be able to repel any foe likely to attack us from without. He also held this as a general principle—that the inhabitants of all free countries —so long as nations settle their disputes by appealing to the sword—should be trained to the use of arms. We wanted no incipient standing army amongst us : but by our young men learning the use of arms, learning to depend upon their own bravery for the defence of their friends and relatives, their homes and altars, a prouder spirit would be fostered in the community and we should stand a chance of attaining a much higher elevation as a nation. Those resolutions were carried by a majority of something like three to one a very considerable time ago, but up to the present time no steps had been taken by the Government to carry them out; the only movement had been made by members of the general community in forming volunteer corps. But the encouragement given to the formation of those companies, he very much regretted to say, had not been so cordial in all respects as he thought it ought to have been. After the resignation of Mr. Forster there was much shuffling of the cards before another Government was formed, but at length Mr. Robertson took upon himself to form the Government we now had presiding over the destinies of the country. The session was continued avowedly on the principle that nothing should be done except the passing of the Estimates, with the view of having an early second session to pass a Land Bill and provide for the expenditure of 1861. The session was nevertheless continued for several months, but the Government consistently adhered to their first announcement that they would introduce no important measure, in order that they might bring the business to a close as soon as they could, so that the second session might be commenced as early as possible afterwards. The session went on for altogether a period of ten months, and Parliament was prorogued on the 4th of July. He amongst others, and he more especially, had lost no opportunity to warn the Government throughout the session then closed, and in the course of previous sessions, of the necessity for legislation to reform the constitution of the Legislative Council. In some words that he had found it necessary to address to the House before the last prorogation he had pointed out the necessity for as short a recess as possible, merely as a matter of form, so that the Government might at once and without delay take up this question of reforming the Council. But notwithstanding that this protracted session terminated only in July, the Government unwisely allowed a recess of eighty-one days to take place. They allowed this although they had the question of reform of the Council staring them in the face, and had had it staring them in the face for the last seven years, for the Constitution Act, be it remembered, was passed in 1853. They had the fact before them, then, that in the early part of May next the Council must be nominated for life if not reformed before that time, and no earthly power could prevent it. Yet notwithstanding this the Government inflicted a recess of three months on the country. The late Assembly was called together for its second session on the 25th September. After all this unnecessary delay the Government met the Parliament and the country with a Land Bill that had been delayed from day to day, from month to month, and from year to year, ever since the establishment of Responsible Government. They met Parliament with this Bill on their hands—with a Council Reform Bill on their hands which it was almost impossible to pass in time—and with the Estimates to be carried through Parliament. He could not believe that any body of men, forced to the grave consideration of this question as Ministers from their position must necessarily have been, could seriously expect to pass their Legislative Council Bill at this late season; and he would tell the meeting why. The Constitution Act under which we lived provided in its 1st, 2nd, and 3rd sections that the Parliament of the country should consist of two Houses—the one, the Assembly, being elective; the other, the Council, being nominated for five years. Of course it followed from this that no legislative business could be transacted without

State of Politics in 1860.

these two Houses being in existence, because without the two there could be no Parliament at all. Thus if the Legislative Council ceased to exist the functions of the Parliament would be gone. Under the Constitution Act it was provided that these nominations for five years should take effect from the day on which the first nominations to the Council should be made; consequently on that day five years the whole Legislative Council fell asunder by effluxion of time. But it was further to be taken into account that the 36th section of the Constitution Act provides that any Bill for altering the constitution of the Council should be sent to England for her Majesty's assent, and that a copy of such Bill should be laid upon the table of both Houses of the Imperial Parliament for thirty days before the Queen could be asked to give her assent to it. Therefore it was almost out of the range of possibility, after the commencement of the session just terminated, for the Government to have given effect to any reform of the Council, even though the Bill had been passed with the greatest rapidity, since they could not have sent it home for the Royal assent, allowed it to lie thirty days on the table of the Imperial Parliament, and have received it back by the 3rd of May next. Thus it had been from the first certain that we were to be afflicted with these nominations for life. The Constitution Act was framed by Mr. Wentworth, and he by introducing the unpopular provision of nomination into the Bill had, notwithstanding his great talents and his many past services to the country, incurred almost universal condemnation. Mr. Wentworth however argued the matter thus:—" I believe in this nominative principle. You say it will not answer. Well, to satisfy you I will insert a provision that it shall only last for five years. You will then have tested it, and if you do not like it you will have the opportunity of changing it. But if you do not avail yourselves of the time thus given you to change it you will have the second nominations made for life." That was Mr. Wentworth's argument, and it must be acknowledged that there was reason in it; and he would fearlessly say that since the Constitution Act had been in force, though we had had liberal Ministries in power all the time, no worthy attempt had been made to alter the constitution of the Upper House, nor had any Bill been introduced to effect this object whose statesmanlike character would justify the belief of any reasonable man that the Ministry which introduced it had thought at all seriously upon the subject. These were facts that formed part of the country's history. They were facts which could not be obliterated from that history, and by this "inexorable logic of facts" let the blame rest on the head upon which it ought to fall. He spoke in strong terms on this subject, for he felt strongly upon it. He looked on it as an impending calamity, and as he had taken a most active part in opposing this provision seven years ago and had done all he could to urge on legislation upon this subject, he naturally felt bitter disappointment at the result. It was quite certain that blame must rest somewhere. Any one of common sense who would look at the facts could trace it to the right quarter. This continued neglect with its fatal result was treason against the liberties of the country. It was treason against the liberties of this country far greater than that for which Ministers of State in earlier times had been impeached and had lost their heads. However, to pursue the thread of his observations on the business of the late session, amongst other motions for which he was largely answerable was one for connecting this country with America and Europe by means of steam communication across the Pacific. He believed that in this he had acted in unison with the feelings of the most intelligent members of the community. At all events he had been backed up by an influential petition which bore upwards of a thousand signatures, amongst which were those of most of the leading firms of the city. Nor was this a new subject with him, for years ago he had maintained that to give New South Wales her proper place in the Australian system steps ought to be taken—whatever might be the amount of trouble or the cost in money—to make her known amongst the great nations of the world; that she ought not to submit to being the last port of communication with the great seats of civilisation in the other hemisphere. And whilst he could see no large benefit accruing to the colony from the expensive system of steam communication by way of India—for New South Wales had no sympathies in common with the nations of Asia and very little commerce with Continental India—no benefit in fact beyond the mere advantages of a postal service, he thought he could see, on the other hand, very great advantages to be attained by bringing New South Wales into closer communication with that great nation of Anglo-Saxon

State of Politics in 1860.

origin and of British blood—the United States of America. Nature had pointed out to them a way across the Pacific by which they might connect themselves with the United States in their intercouse with the mother country; and such connection he believed would be fruitful of advantages incalculably valuable to them as a growing people. He had supported these views whenever occasion presented itself, and in the late Assembly he succeeded in carrying a resolution embodying the views he had now expressed. At the commencement of the second session he determined to take this course on account of the necessity for legislation on the land question, and of the near approach of that fatal day on which these nominations to the Council must be made for life. He occupied as little as possible of the time of the House, though there were many subjects which he desired to take up simply because he considered them of very great importance and because he saw no one else attempting to deal with them. But he had restrained himself in order that no obstruction might be thrown in the way of the Government, and he would appeal to those around who had noticed the proceedings of Parliament whether during the last session he had not been less active than formerly. The Land Bill was then introduced, and he believed the gentleman who was understood to be the author of that Bill was sincerely anxious to make provision for the settlement of the people upon the public lands of the colony. He said thus much because, as he should have to speak of the Bill in a manner that might imply that he entertained a hostile feeling to Mr. Robertson, he wished the meeting to understand that he had no feeling of such a kind; but when men became public men and undertook the responsibilities of governing a State they must not expect to be spared from mere considerations of private friendship. They had to be dealt with as steam-engines that are set up for the accomplishment of a given work; and we had to look to their effectiveness, unrestrained by considerations of personal feeling. He would say, then, that he believed that Mr. Robertson had been for years anxious to effect the ends his Bill was supposed to provide for. Instead of occupying the time of the House by the expression of his own opinions on the Land Bill, he determined to watch its progress in committee, to support those provisions which he honestly approved, and to use his utmost endeavours to amend it in those parts where he thought he saw ground for improvement. He steadily pursued this course, and although he spoke on the second reading he did not occupy more than fifteen minutes of time. When he saw the pastoral tenants of the Crown who had seats in the House opposing the Bill he thought at first that it must be a sham fight got up for a diversion; for the measure, taken in connexion with the Occupation Bill, appeared to him to be so entirely favourable to their interests that he could not believe in the earnestness of their opposition. But when he saw Mr. Rotton commencing at the 6th clause with his amendments for the purpose of shutting out the people from the unsettled districts, and that he was followed up by an insidious but determined effort from another member to alter the 13th clause so as to obliterate the most popular feature of the Bill, he was forced to the conclusion that the object of these gentlemen in assenting to the second reading was to alter it to their own liking in committee so as to convert it into a complete squatting measure. Mr. Robertson's Land Bill did not touch the existing pastoral leases in any respect; and those who told them that the effect of the Bill would be to let loose upon the runs of the squatters a horde of persons with ugly names who would despoil all pastoral property, were in reality simply deceiving them. The leases of the squatters would be left intact; every lease and every promise of lease would be faithfully maintained. In no way could the selector invade land under lease so long as that lease continued in force. Thus every condition was kept with the squatter that he could justly claim, and it was not a very unreasonable thing to expect that, whilst the wild grass was given on the easiest terms to any person who might choose to invest his capital in the rearing of stock, the rest of the people should be allowed to select homesteads, especially when the object was to turn the land to better account than could possibly be done by pastoral occupation. He had supported free selection before survey, not because the Ministry had told him to do so, nor yet because he thought it would please his constituency, but because he thought it would be the means of removing many families from a state of helpless dependence—from stifling hovels engendering disease and premature death to spots where their children might grow up in robust health and might become useful citizens, whilst the land itself would be made more productive by their labour for the general purposes of society. And he would say that free selection after survey would amount to no selection at all. Who was it that it was wished to place on the land by this principle of free selection? Not the man of capital. Not the man with his few hundred pounds; but the man whose capital was his own strong arm and his own stout heart. It was the man who would carry little with him, in founding his home in the wilderness, beyond the strength of his own indomitable energies and his powers of endurance—whose capital was in his thews and sinews; the man who nevertheless had strongly rooted and glowing within his bosom, and rising above all other feelings—to use the language of the poet—

The pride to rear an independent shed,
And give the lips we love unborrowed bread.

But this class of persons who would be most anxious to avail themselves of the right would be those whose vocations had been out in the wilderness, and who consequently would know where to find land that would be useful to them. And if such a man as he had attempted to describe were willing to stake his all, the very hazard of his life, on such a venture—for be it remembered that to the selector it must be success or ruin—if he were willing to stake the welfare of his family, the investment of his capital, which was his labour—by what authority were they to stand in his way and arrest his progress by artificial obstacles? It was in the very fact that he ventured his all—knowing that the result must be success or absolute ruin to him—that they had the best guarantee they could have that he would select well. He could not believe that a staff of ill-paid surveyors, who had to struggle with their Government pay to make provision for their families, would ever be able to find land suitable for the agricultural operations of the selector as well as the man himself would be able to find it. And after all, as had been repeatedly stated, this free selection was only what the squatters themselves had been enjoying for years past. Where would have been the great and important fabric of pastoral industry if the squatters had had to wait for a staff of surveyors to point out their runs to them before they occupied them? It would never have existed. It was because their own enterprise had been allowed full play and they had been encouraged to push forward and discover for themselves the localities that were best suited to them, that they had become the wealthy and powerful class they now were, and that the squatting interest had grown to its present magnitude. And in the same way if it were wanted to settle a race of intelligent, enterprising, self-reliant freeholders over the face of the country, they must be allowed to go and select the spots which they conceived would be the best suited to their purpose. But was it not humiliating to think that the argument against this right of the industrious population should be based on the assumption of the vice and iniquity of human nature? It had been stated that free selection would let loose a herd of cattle-stealers upon the squatting runs. Now he had heard others say—intelligent men who had, what he had not, extensive experience in the ways and practices of the interior—he had heard it said by people of this class that the greatest cattle-stealers in the country were the large cattle-holders themselves. He did not say this, he only repeated what others said; and perhaps he might be permitted to add that he did not believe it. But they said that if the poor man stole a cow it was seen immediately in his four or five; but if the big fellow stole one it was hard to be found amongst his four or five thousand. There was some show of reason in this; and at any rate he thought he was justified in the retort upon those who without any reason at all made such wholesale charges against the industrious classes of the colony. This principle of free selection was defeated, Mr. Hay having moved and carried an amendment to insert the words "after survey as hereinafter provided," thereby destroying the principle. During the progress of the Bill he had told the House that he regarded this feature of it as of so much importance, that if the Ministry consented to its obliteration he should withdraw his support from the measure. He was therefore very glad when he found the Ministry taking the stand they did, and declaring they would not after this alteration go on with the Bill; and possibly he had been one of the first to make a suggestion to the Ministry that the best course for them to take would be to dissolve the House. The amendment to this clause was carried on Friday night, and early on the Saturday morning he conveyed to Mr. Robertson his opinion that the best course would be to dissolve. However, the Government took time for consideration, and on the following Wednesday they came down to the House and stated that they had tendered their advice to the Governor-General that the Assembly should be dissolved, with an opinion that the Estimates for 1861 should be first obtained, and that His Excellency had concurred in this advice.

State of Politics in 1860.

They then announced their intention not to go on with any other business, but simply to get the supplies necessary to enable them to appeal to the constituencies. The Opposition had openly stated that they would not allow the Government to take this course—that the Land Bill was before the House, and that if the Ministry chose to drop it, the Opposition would take it up and "make it a perfect measure." In this way a fortnight was lost in a course of proceeding which he would be quite unable to describe to them, as it was impossible at times to say who were the Government and who the Opposition. At last the Opposition took the very ill-judged step of moving a vote of want of confidence. Now had he been an enemy of the Ministry, this would have been the very last thing he would have recommended or would have thought of doing; for the Government were then tottering, and if left to themselves in another week would have fallen to pieces. Well, when that vote came under consideration, he tried to elicit from the Government whether they intended to put an end to the disgraceful state of things which had arisen—a state of things calculated seriously to endanger the safe and efficient working of our institutions, and which would supply most mischievous precedents for the action of Governments in future, if it were tolerated. He considered it of vital importance that they should preserve those political landmarks which had been left for their guidance by the great statesmen of the mother country, and he considered the state of things to which he referred was destroying all the rules and forms of Parliamentary Government and bringing contempt upon their political institutions. He tried to ascertain what course the Government were prepared to take—whether they intended to dissolve or whether they intended to resign. And what answer did he obtain? The hon. the Secretary for Public Works replied in the language used by Mr. Pitt, the Tory Minister of George III. He received the answer that Mr. Pitt gave to Mr. Fox, who was regarded as the champion of freedom in the mother country; such was the model chosen for the answer with which he was honoured by a member of this democratic Administration. Up to the moment of receiving that answer he did not believe there was one member in the House who knew which way he intended to vote; but he immediately turned to his honourable friend, Mr. Windeyer, and informed him that he should vote for the motion. And he would tell them why he did so. He believed, though the members of the Opposition did not, that the Ministry had the power to dissolve. He knew too that his vote would have the effect of settling the matter one way or the other—that they must either dissolve or relinquish their places. He knew there was a handful of persons eagerly watching for any vote of his on which they might fasten their misrepresentations, but he never yet was deterred from giving a vote by any fear of the consequences. He knew well the heart of the city and of the country, and he had no apprehension that a false construction would be put upon his vote, though he happened to be the only member on what was termed the Liberal side who voted for that motion of censure. There were several other votes given by him in the late session to which he would like to refer. He had voted to exclude the Chinese, although his vote was given on this and the former occasion when the subject was introduced for reasons very dissimilar from those advanced by other gentlemen who opposed this species of immigration. The general outcry against these people was that they were a poor miserable race of beings. Now he thought this was a mistake altogether. He regarded them as a sober, educated, cunning, strong, ambitious, and calculating race. And seeing that they came from a country situate only a few weeks' sail from our shores; that their country is estimated to contain a population of 300,000,000 or 400,000,000 souls, while the total British population of the whole of these colonies did not exceed 1,000,000; he confessed he entertained serious apprehensions—Quixotic as it might appear to some persons—that, if not prevented, they might come here in numbers sufficiently formidable to swamp us as an Anglo-Saxon community. He regarded the influx of these people—all of one sex and in such large numbers, moving amongst us in a dark mist, speaking a language we did not understand, holding a faith we could not comprehend, with characters formed under laws and institutions alien from ours, and all bound together by a secret means of intercourse—not as a subject for jocularity or idle disparagement, but as a matter of the gravest moment and demanding the most serious attention. These were his reasons, as far as he could briefly state them, for wishing to exclude the Chinese altogether. He had wasted a deal of time—so it was said—by undertaking a railway inquiry, of which no doubt they had heard. As this had been referred to frequently in terms of censure in the House he desired now to refer briefly to it. The Legislature they were aware had voted upwards of £800,000 for the purpose of extending the three main lines of railway to the distance of about an hour's drive into the interior. This money was being expended in a manner calculated to awaken anxiety as to the trustworthy character of the works in course of construction. The contractor (who represented one of the largest and most influential firms in the world) and the railway officers were at loggerheads; serious allegations of professional neglect and incompetency were openly made and widely credited. The complaining contractor applied to him to bring his grievances before Parliament; and after hearing his complaints he told this gentleman that his best course under the circumstances would be to come to the bar of the Assembly and make his own statement. It was then seen, however, that this privilege could not be given to the one side and refused to the other; and the investigation was necessarily lengthened out beyond the limits at first intended. But he felt satisfied that no impartial person who read the evidence would consider that the inquiry had been a waste of time. Up to the present moment the railways had not progressed at the rate expected by the public; and as this £800,000 had been borrowed, the colony was at the loss of the interest accruing through the delay in their completion. And what was of greater consequence than the loss of interest, the facilities for traffic so much required and to secure which this heavy debt had been incurred were indefinitely delayed. Looking to all the facts he thought it would be admitted that the inquiry was a very proper one. But he was now about to leave the past and to speak of the future. He was a candidate for their suffrages. He did not think in making this announcement that he could be accused of thrusting himself on the electors, or of presumptuously standing in the way of better men. As a citizen of the country he deemed it so essential for the public welfare that they should preserve the character of their institutions, that if he saw in the field four men of superior stamp in mind and education he should at once consider it his duty to give way. But in the present state of things he did not think it would be contended that there was anything in the character of the gentlemen offering themselves as candidates before which he ought

K

to bow his head and retire. Though he had three times been honoured with their confidence, he might say he had never personally solicited a vote. He would not do so now. In taking this course he was bearing the very highest testimony in his power to their intelligence and independence. It was said that they were now living in the time of party Government; but he thought it would puzzle a philospher to show the lines of demarcation separating one party from another. For example, he often found himself voting on questions with the Government of the day which many of their regular supporters opposed, notwithstanding that those questions involved the most vital principles of the Government policy. Nevertheless he admitted we lived in a time when men sought to attach themselves to parties. But he would at once tell them he did not stand before them as a Ministerial adherent. He stood before them as an advocate of those principles on the strength of which the present Government obtained power; and if he went into the House as their representative he should keep a strict and rigid watch over the proceedings of the Government for the preservation and vindication of those principles. He should give his ready and willing support to such of their measures as were calculated to advance the principles with which he believed were identified the true interests of the country. But he would not blink the matter; he should never connive at any abuse or outrage his conscience for the purpose of keeping a particular set of men in power. He considered the first qualification to be looked for in a representative was inflexible independence; and he thought he might say, without being accused of immodesty, that he had had sufficient experience of public life and had succeeded in winning for himself a sufficient hold upon public confidence to be very slow in finding a leader amongst the public men of the present hour. He had already explained his views on the popular part of Mr. Robertson's Land Bill. There were, however, some portions of that measure of which he did not approve. He was not friendly to the residence condition nor the principle of deferred payments, and if he saw any way of getting rid of these objectionable features he should use his endeavours to have them done away with. As far as he had been able to arrive at a decision on what was certainly a matter of detail as compared with the principle of unfettered selection, he should be disposed to give

State of Politics in 1860.

to the agricultural freeholder the fee-simple without any further payment beyond the first deposit of 25 per cent. He could not see why they should sell to the pastoral occupant at five shillings, and at the same time insist upon £1 an acre from those who were to make the soil in the highest degree productive. The one was going to produce a surface of bloom by instilling into every spadeful of earth a portion of his own sweat; the other meant simply to consume the natural grasses. He should be desirous therefore of facilitating as much as possible the acquirement of freehold possession in the case of the *bonâ fide* agriculturist. The Bill made provision for the sale by auction of pastoral lands at an upset price of five shillings per acre; if they had reached that clause in committee he should have voted against it, since he could not see what advantage was to follow from allowing the pastoral tenants to assume the position of territorial families, as they would doubtless do under such a provision. In the settlement of the Land question they had to consider not only the welfare of all classes of the present day but the interests of their posterity; and looking to the future he could not see his way clear to consent to reducing the price of pastoral land to five shillings an acre. He adverted to these matters now with the view of showing the course which he intended to take when the Land Bill was again introduced. He would now pass to other questions, for there were several great questions which he implored them not to overlook. There was the reconstruction of the Upper House—would any one say now how this was to be effected? There were the means of communication with the interior to be provided for; and there was the question of education, without which they would never be able to secure the settlement of a happy, thrifty, and industrious population on the lands of the colony. They must not thrust the people back into a state of semi-barbarism; education must go on contemporaneously with the occupation of the country. These were subjects which he would not be disposed to let the Government neglect. The arming of the people for their own defence was another matter which he thought the Government should not be allowed to sleep over. A general reform in the management and discipline of our prisons was also a subject which pressed for immediate attention. These were all matters respecting which a candidate seeking their suffrages should be called on fully to explain his views. He now came to a question in which they had a special interest—he meant the endowment of the city. He had always discountenanced the false policy of sectional interests in the Legislature. Though in the electoral system members were chosen by particular districts, the plan was adopted to secure in the general representation the various interests of the country. The members of a legislative body were not on that account to study unduly the local interests of their immediate constituents; they were elected to perform far higher functions —to consider and adjust questions relating to all classes of the community, without reference to geographical boundaries or social conditions or any distinctions whatever. In his own case, though . sitting for Sydney, he had always considered it his duty to study the interests of the remotest district in the colony equally with the claims of the metropolis. His votes would show that he had uniformly acted in accordance with the view he now expressed. It was as a representative, not as a member for Sydney in particular, that he took up the question of the city endowment because he believed it rested upon just grounds. The complaints frequently made that the country districts unduly suffered by reason of the large expenditure voted for the city were in many instances inconsiderately and loosely put forth, and were destitute of any reasonable foundation. Country members, who were loud in these complaints, appeared to forget that there were many institutions (the Government Establishments, the Courts of Justice, the Military Barracks, and the Fortifications, for example), which were necessarily established in the city, because it was the metropolis of the country and the sea-gate through which its commerce flowed and re-flowed, and through which the assailants of its honour and security would strike if a time of danger from without should ever come. They were established not for the special advantage of the inhabitants of Sydney, but for the protection and good government of the country generally. There was a connexion of mutual dependence between the metropolis and the country which neither should violate nor attempt to ignore. On this broad ground the claims of Sydney on this question of endowment were just. The city had grown up, as they were well aware, without any regular system of management— without plan or specific provision for its growth. Its first elective municipal body fell into disrepute and was abolished; and the Legislature of the day, in which the citizens had scarcely any voice, substituted for it an irresponsible Government Commission. The city had been plunged into a debt of upwards of £400,000 by that Commission, and the money had been improvidently if not wastefully expended; the citizens themselves having had no voice at all in the matter. They were taxed almost to the last point of endurance, and yet the city was unable to bear up against this gigantic burden. In this state of affairs the Municipal Council had prepared a Bill for their relief, which they had done him the honour to place in his hands. This measure, if passed, would give the Council power to tax unimproved lands within the municipality, and also to rate Government buildings and properties that were at present exempt from taxation. It would endow the city with certain public lands now lying in an unproductive state within its boundaries, and it would empower the Council to redeem the land at the head of Darling Harbour, so as to increase the conveniences of trade as well as the civic revenues. He was not disposed to throw the burden of this debt on the country at large, but believing as he did that the city would be willing to bear it he should be quite ready to increase its means of meeting it. For these reasons he cordially supported the Bill and should use his best exertions to have it carried into law. If they were not already fatigued, there were one or two topics of a general nature on which he wished to say a few words. They had heard much of late of the decline of their political institutions and of the degeneracy of public life. They were continually reminded in mournful words of the high character of their first Legislative Council—" there were giants in those days." But let them look into this matter and compare notes in a spirit of impartiality. He thought a comparison might be instituted between the first Council and even the late Assembly by no means to the disadvantage of the latter. He admitted at once that there was no man in the Assembly just dissolved who was endowed like Mr. Wentworth with that subtle and wonderful order of ability which is comprehended in the word genius—no man who possessed the classical attainments and dazzling talents of Mr. Lowe; but he maintained that there was in the late House a far larger amount of debating power and constructive legislative ability than could be claimed for the early Legislature in which those eminent men sat. If they carried out their comparison to inferiorities, he had no hesitation in saying that the first Legislature was equal in illiterate, stupid, incapable members with the last. And if they looked in upon their social state did they find the signs of the "downward tendency of democracy," of which they heard such doleful warnings? He had lived in the colony twenty years—in the days which he supposed were, by comparison, aristocratic days. But in those days you could not see a sign of cultivation or taste in the homes of the working classes. Now, travel in what direction you might you saw among the poorer classes little plots of cultivation, evidences of household cleanliness and comfort, flowers about their homes, indicating a love for the pure and beautiful. It was obvious that the growth of democracy had done this for the great body of the people—it had increased their self-respect; it had quickened their domestic affections; it had softened them in feeling and elevated them in sentiment. Then they were told of the disastrous consequences in America—how democratic principles had resulted in the exclusion of superior education and intellect from the Government of the nation. Why, that young republic possessed a line of illustrious statesmen not surpassed by any nation of ancient or modern times. Beginning with the incorruptible Washington, she had John Adams, Jefferson, Hamilton; and coming down to our own times, Calhoun, Webster, Clay, and Everett. Nor was the social condition produced by American democracy a theme for lamentation. De Tocqueville the philosophical observer did not tell us that; Mr. William Chambers of Edinburgh, who visited the United States a few years ago, did not tell us that. Mr. Chambers, speaking of the new city of Cincinnati, described the condition of its mechanics and artizans as very much superior in character and physical well-being to the same class of his own countrymen. It might be in America, as it was elsewhere, that intellectual men who devoted their highest powers to science or literature did not find their way into the Legislature or the offices of Government. In England the men of highest literary fame, the most distinguished men of science and the most accomplished scholars, seldom obtained seats in the House of Commons; but successful prize-fighters and retired shop-keepers—men who began the world in rags and in the lowest depths of obscurity—had found their way into that august assembly. The English Parliament was not filled with University men; but its members for the most part were men who possessed an aptitude for public business and the practical sagacity which could successfully deal with the realities of the state of things in which they lived. This country was unalterably a democracy. All that could be said would not do away with the fact. Its opponents might for a time succeed in throwing odium upon it, and might cause it to work ineffectually for good for a while, but they would never succeed in substituting for it their own counterfeit principles of government. He did not wish to speak otherwise than respectfully of those who differed from him on this subject. He believed they were mistaken in their views, and the sooner they came to understand their true position the better it would be for themselves and the country. It would be the fault of these gentlemen alone if education and property were lost to the councils of the country. There need be no fear of such a result if they would accept the institutions of the country as they existed, and co-operate in good faith in working out those institutions for the welfare and advancement of the people. Instead of hopelessly whining over what was inexorably fixed as their destiny, let them awaken to a healthier sense of duty, and use their utmost exertions to elevate our institutions and improve the condition of the people by a sound and diffusive system of education, and by fostering amongst us correct principles of political honour. He was drawing to a conclusion. If they elected him as their representative, he should esteem the position one of the highest they could bestow. There was no office of greater distinction in this country than that of a representative of· the people ; and most of all was it a great distinction to represent the eastern division of the metropolis. That electorate contained their seats of government, their seats of justice, their seats of learning, and their seats of commerce. Their professional classes for the most part resided within its boundaries. It was a constituency remarkable for the large number of its electors who were individually influential by their talents, education, and social standing. But there was to him a still more gratifying feature in the character of the electorate—its clusters of happy little freehold homes—homes won by the honest industry of its mechanics and labourers. To represent such a constituency was indeed an honour. He sought no higher distinction. To represent them in the Parliament of the country—to represent faithfully their varied interests—so as to be able to come back and be rewarded by the voice of their approval, was the highest possible honour to which any man could aspire.

[A resolution in favour of Mr. Parkes was carried unanimously.]

THE PRICE OF LAND.

SUBSTANCE OF SPEECHES

Delivered in the Legislative Assembly when the House was in Committee on the Crown Lands Alienation Bill of 1861.

[THE 17th clause of the Bill as originally framed, providing for "deferred payments" of the balance of the conditional purchase-money, was under consideration March 6th, and was met by several amendments. Mr. Parkes moved that on satisfactory evidence being received by the Government that the conditions of residence and improvement had been complied with by the free selector, a grant of the fee-simple of the land should be made to him without any payment other than the original deposit of five shillings.]

Mr. PARKES said: He denied the sound policy of a free trade in the public lands of the colony. He drew a wide distinction between the nature of those lands and the nature of personal property. The Legislature in dealing with the virgin lands of the colony was bound to consider what would be the effect upon society in all time to come of the mode in which those lands were now alienated. No doubt land ought to be open for disposal to all who desired to purchase, but its disposal did not stand on the same footing as other property created by human labour and skill. The amendment he now submitted would give the free selector who should effect the required improvements the land in fee-simple without any further payment than the first five shillings deposit. No stinted liberality ought to characterise the manner in which they approached the question of the alienation of the public lands to that class of colonists who by their industry and discernment would make them most productive for the whole. When they were satisfied that there was a *bonâ-fide* purpose to improve and cultivate, all further payment should be remitted. It was doubted by many hon. members whether payment would be made if the system of deferred payments were adopted—(Mr. ROBERTSON: Not by me)—at all events there was provision made for such payments

The Price of Land.

standing over for an indefinite period. He contended that no persons ought ever to be placed in individual and direct subordination to the State—in a relation different from that occupied by other classes. Under all the circumstances the justice of the case recommended the adoption of a wise liberality in dealing with this part of the subject.

[The amendment was opposed by the Government. Mr. Robertson declared that if "the purchase-money for land should be under £1 per acre, the land would not be worth anything at all." Mr. Arnold argued that the "deferred payments" would "enable the State to raise by a sound system of loans the money they required for their public works."]

Mr. PARKES said: The Committee would not have failed to notice how the Government had changed their ground in reference to this Bill. Hitherto the principle was not to derive revenue from the sale of the lands, but the greater though more remote advantage of settling the people on the soil. Now, however, the Government based their arguments on the money value of the land. The Committee must decide whether they were going to lend themselves to create an interminable class of Crown debtors in the country—upon whose indebtedness loans were to be contracted: for the Government contemplated paying for their railways out of the proceeds of those debts which were to remain for ever! (Mr. ARNOLD: At the option of the debtor.) The way to obtain railways was not by the miserably inadequate revenue to be derived from the land itself, but by increasing the population, and by the consequent natural increase of the revenue from the legitimate extension of taxation over as wide a surface as possible. Then it had been said that an upset price of 5s. would be unjust to those who had purchased at a higher price; but he maintained that if the 20th clause were carried, and if there were only one case where land was purchased at the upset price, the objection would be just as powerful. The course pursued by the framer of the Bill could only be defended on the ground that these sales to free selectors were special and for special objects. Notwithstanding what had been said by the hon. Secretary for Public Works (Mr. Arnold), he should think that a free selector would not fail to appreciate the difference between the semi-serf condition which it was proposed to create for him and the possession of the fee-simple of his land. Under the conditions proposed, would the persons who free-selected land know whether they were living under the blessings of the hon. gentleman's government or under the Czar of Russia, when they had to go year after year with their 9d. per acre to some Government official, while they called land their own which was in fact not their own? The advantage to be gained by the State from insisting upon this money balance from the free selectors would be trifling and embarrassing, and the provision would take away to a great extent the sweetness of possession, which it should be one of the objects of their legislation to encourage the free selector to desire.

[Mr. Parkes' amendment was lost on division by 39 to 11. On the following day, the 7th, Mr. Robertson moved the 20th clause, as follows:—

"20. Crown lands intended to be sold without conditions for residence and improvement shall be put up for public auction in lots not exceeding three hundred and twenty acres each, at such places and times as the Minister shall direct, to be notified by advertisement in the *Gazette*. And the upset price per acre shall not be lower than—for town lands £8, suburban lands £2, good lands having frontage £1, inferior and back land 5s. Provided that the upset prices may be respectively fixed at any higher amounts."

A long debate ensued, in the course of which Mr. Parkes opposed the reduction of the price of "back lands" to 5s. for the reasons stated in his speech. The words "inferior and back lands five shillings" were omitted on division by 38 to 18, Mr. Robertson voting for the amendment.]

MR. PARKES said : He should give his vote in the same manner as the hon. member who had just sat down, and he felt somewhat at ease to learn from that hon. gentleman (Capt. Moriarty) that he was at liberty to express his opinion in reference to this matter ! It relieved him from a good deal of embarrassment, coming as it did from so authoritative a quarter. He should give his vote so as to continue the upset price—if they were to continue to sell lands by auction—at £1. This might appear inconsistent with the course he took last night, when he moved an amendment to remit the balance of 15s. for land taken up under free selection, but on that occasion he acted on the special grounds that those who free-selected land would enter upon it under conditions enforcing them to its improvement. But here it was proposed to pass a provision which would open the door to mere trade in land —a thing entirely different from possession on condition of cultivation and improvement. It seemed to him that the class of persons they should encourage above all others by their legislation was the small cultivators of the soil—the men who

The Price of Land. 139

by their industry would turn the land to the best possible account. If, however, they were to reduce the price in alienating the land to 5s. they would open the door to great abuse. The only argument in support of such reduction was that some of the land was not worth 5s. But that argument might lead to the adoption of an upset price of one penny, because he believed that there was land in this country not worth having at a gift on terms of compulsory occupation. Five shillings per acre would not reach the real minimum; it would only be an arbitrary price. What they had to fear under this provision was that some of the richest and most valuable tracts of land would be alienated as inferior land. The condition of this country was likely to facilitate such abuse. We had here a number of old and wealthy families with numerous connexions— numbering in some instances as many as one hundred persons. In addition to these we had another class—the pastoral tenants— who by reason of their pursuits had also a practical acquaintance with the country. So that, although we were a small community, we had among us a comparatively large number of wealthy people who had the colony, as it were, at their fingers' ends. And this clause, just as though it had been framed on purpose, would suit the purposes of those speculative persons. They would not desire to purchase land in large blocks. Hon. members had been told over and over again that the good land of the colony lay in patches, and the provisons of this Bill would enable persons to pick up all the choicest spots from one end of the country to the other. He would tell the Committee how the law had operated with an upset price of £1. A gentleman holding a subordinate public office but whose business required him to travel over the county of Cumberland—although his salary was small—had in a few years amassed a small fortune in this way. He made himself acquainted with the land wherever he went in the county, and whenever he found a small block of rich soil he had it put up to auction, and generally got it knocked down to him at £1 per acre. That gentleman had pointed out to him one block situated in North Harbour which he (the speculator) had purchased in this way, and which he described as covered with a splendid ironbark forest. If under the present system these things could be done in the County of Cumberland, surely they could be done in the remote interior of the country. He believed that this provision of the Bill, if carried, would not have the effect of alienating from the Crown land which was not worth more than 5s., but it would be operative in alienating land in the highest degree valuable, but the valuable qualities of which would be known only to a few persons at the time of sale. It seemed to him very inconsistent to take such a course as that, when they had extracted the 20s. per acre from the *bond fide* cultivators. Surely, in alienating the public land for the good of all, they ought to consider the use to which it was to be applied. They were not to obstruct the operations of the capitalist in any way, but at the same time it was no part of their duty to smooth the way for his making a large fortune out of the public lands. And then with regard to the argument which had been used respecting the attraction of population by lowering the price of land. Good agricultural lands could be bought in Canada at the present time at 2s. per acre. He knew a person who had purchased 240 acres of rich land in Canada for £24. While we kept up the price of agricultural land to 20s., how could we compete with the state of things in Canada? There were strong reasons, however, why they should not reduce the price as proposed by this clause. We had the means of attracting population already. It was not merely by the price of land that people were attracted to new countries. We had one of the finest climates in the world. We had the greatest variety of mineral riches of any country in the world—to say nothing of our magnificent goldfields. And he believed that by having some agency at the great seats of population in Europe to make known the advantages of this country as a field for the emigrating portions of the European populations—to make known also the provisions of this land bill, and the facilities—even encumbered as they were by deferred payments—for settling on small farms, that we should stand as good a chance as any country in the world of attracting population. But if we proceeded on the principle of outbidding a country which, within ten days' sail of England, could offer fertile land at 2s. per acre, we should fail. Upon a careful consideration of this matter he thought it would be better as the question now stood to maintain the upset price of land by auction at 20s.

NEW SOUTH WALES AS A FIELD FOR EMIGRATION.

[A PUBLIC meeting was held in the Town Hall, Derby, on Monday evening, October 7th, 1861, for the purpose of hearing an address from Mr. Henry Parkes on the claims of the colony of New South Wales as a field for British emigration. There was a large attendance, the hall being well filled. The chair was occupied by W. T. Cox, Esq., High Sheriff, who on introducing Mr. Parkes assured the meeting that that gentleman appeared before them duly accredited by the Colonial Government. He hoped and was sure he would receive an impartial hearing.]

SUBSTANCE OF AN ADDRESS
Delivered at Derby in 1861.

MR. PARKES said: The heading of the notice by which the meeting had been called it must be owned was an attractive one—" Freehold homes in a gold country ;" but it might very properly be taken as the text for his comments that evening. He was there to tell them of 200,000,000 acres of land fresh from the hand of the Creator waiting to be distributed among His creatures, and hundreds of miles of that land richly impregnated with gold. It was no mere catch-phrase he had used, but the words correctly described his subject. It would be best however to begin with the beginning, and to tell them why he was there at all. He came from a place that lay as it were in the dim distance of the habitable globe, and was known by the confused general name of Australia. The colony of New South Wales was the first settled portion of Australia, and was founded seventy-three years ago ; within that period—a single life-time—every appliance of civilisation had there taken root and grown up. There were now five other Australian colonies besides New South Wales, and he would name them in the order in which they had come into existence. There was Tasmania, which was a separate island, divided from the mainland by the well-known Bass's Strait, and of which Hobarton was the capital. There was Western Australia or the Swan River settlement, on the west coast of the island-continent. There were South Australia, of which Adelaide was the capital; Victoria, of which Melbourne was the capital; and the newly-created colony of Queensland, of which Brisbane was the capital. It would be necessary to bear these facts in mind clearly to understand his subject. All these colonies were distinctly separate; they had separate legislatures and separate forms of government, and had full power to legislate on all matters exclusively affecting themselves without reference to England and without reference to one another. Well, among the colonies—he believed among all of them—an impression prevailed that they were very imperfectly known in the mother country. This was not without foundation, for works of authority described them very erroneously, and English statesmen had made blunders in speaking of them which were singularly absurd. Even the poet Campbell, in some lines descriptive of New South Wales, says,

> What spacious cities with their spires shall gleam
> Where now the panther laps a lonely stream!

Why, there was not a panther nor a wild beast of any kind except opossums and kangaroos in the country. With the desire of making their colony better known the legislature of New South Wales in May last passed a resolution—which was subsequently embodied in an Act of the local Parliament—authorising the appointment of two commissioners to visit England for a limited time to diffuse information concerning the country and its capabilities derived from the Government returns. He held one of these appointments, and it was in such capacity that he appeared before them that evening. Let them recollect that he represented New South Wales, and had nothing to do with any other colony. He certainly was not there to say a single word in disparagement of the others, but simply to speak the truth of his own adopted country. Ten years ago Victoria was created a separate colony out of the southern territory of New South Wales, and last year the extreme portion of their northern territory was cut off and converted into the colony of Queensland. Still they possessed 207,000,000 acres of land which with its

N. S. Wales as a Field for Emigration. 143

varieties of soil and climate was capable of growing wheat, Indian corn, sorghum, millet, turnips, mangold-wurzel, barley, oats, peas, beans, and most of the vegetable growths of Europe, with the tobacco plant, the cotton plant, and the sugar-cane. The orange and the grape flourished with them as in their native clime; nothing could excel their lusciousness and beauty. Many of their vineyards were ten, sixteen, and twenty acres in extent, and in 1859 they had a total of 1100 acres under the cultivation of the vine, yielding 96,000 gallons of wine and 1300 gallons of brandy, besides upwards of 500 tons of grapes for table use. He had himself known the proprietor of a single orange grove to sell his year's crop hanging on the trees without risk or trouble for £2000. But they had abundance of other fruits; the lemon, fig, guava, loquat, banana, peach, apricot and nectarine, as well as the apple and pear and most of the fruits grown in England. The bowels of the earth were teeming with minerals. Within seventy miles of Sydney an iron mine had been discovered of great extent, from which fine steel had been manufactured and worked up into knives, razors and similar articles of excellent quality. They had several workable copper mines which were already in the hands of organised companies, and silver, tin, platina and other metals had been discovered. Their gold-fields had a world-wide celebrity. It was in New South Wales that the first discovery of gold was made. They had at present fifteen established gold-fields the aggregate yield from which in 1858 amounted to the value of nearly £1,000,000 sterling. In New South Wales the gold-digging population was generally speaking of a very settled and orderly character. There had been some disturbances lately arising from the feeling of aversion entertained by the European diggers towards the Chinese; but with that exception the goldfields were well-ordered and peaceable. Indeed good order and respect for the law prevailed throughout the colony as much as they did in England, and the attendance at places of religious worship and all Christian observances was quite as general. In their colony too they had some social advantages which the younger colonies did not and could not in the nature of things possess. They had many old settled homesteads, the heads of which were possessors of large property and had reared families of sons and daughters with all the attachments and home associations that sprung from being natives of the soil, and in many cases with a fair amount of education. This gave them a kind of social maturity—a likeness to England herself —which could not be found in a colony just settled, where all were strangers to each other and all were smarting under the bitter recollection of the severance of early ties. These sons and daughters of the soil in New South Wales were, as a whole, an active and intelligent race—handsome, spirited, fond of out-of-door enjoyments, proud of their country and alive to the higher demands of humanity. Returning to their goldfields, they had at Sydney in connexion with their gold-producing interest a branch of the Royal Mint, and at this Mint in 1858 they coined 1,101,500 sovereigns and 483,000 half-sovereigns, and melted 14,927 ounces of gold into bars and ingots. New South Wales also possessed extensive coal-beds, which could not be worked out for ages to come. They exported coal to the other colonies and to China and India. In 1859 they raised a total of 308,213 tons of coal. Their chief export however was, as many there would doubtless be aware, fine wool for the Yorkshire manufacturers. The unsettled lands of the colony were occupied by a class of gentlemen called "squatters." Many of these gentlemen held from the Government at a mere nominal rent a quarter of a million of acres—and in some cases much more—over which they depastured immense herds of cattle and almost countless flocks of sheep. In 1859 the colony exported 17,000,000 lbs. of fine wool besides large quantities of tallow and fat stock. Their possessions in live stock were almost fabulous. The population of the colony was only 350,553 souls, and this handful of people held in 1860 no less than 214,684 horses, 2,190,976 head of horned cattle, and 5,162,671 sheep. They would expect to hear that beef was cheaper there than in Derby; no fear of people being starved in a country where to every head of the population, man, woman, or child, there were six head of horned cattle and fifteen sheep. They would not be surprised to hear that the commerce of a country so rich in its natural resources was very considerable. He was only saying what any well-informed commercial man would confirm when he told them that the Australian colonies were, in proportion to their population, the best customers England had. In 1859 New South Wales imported goods from England and other countries of the declared value of £6,772,049, or to the amount of £19 7s. per head of her population. Her

N. S. Wales as a Field for Emigration. 145

Her exports of raw produce for the same year amounted to £5,800,926, or £16 11s. 6d. per head; but it must be recollected that the real value of her produce ought to be estimated in the market of consumption, not at the port of shipment. Their merchants, many of them, were engaged in very extensive transactions and were men of large fortunes. In the city of Sydney they had retail establishments in as imposing edifices and with displays of as much splendour as any similar establishments could boast in England. They had their Chamber of Commerce in a magnificent building, and they had eight banks, each carrying on its business in a palace. They were the builders of their own ships to a great extent, many of the vessels engaged in the intercolonial trade—schooners and brigs of large burden—being built of the hard timber of the Australian forest. Their manufactures were of course in their infancy, but he believed New South Wales was destined to become a great manufacturing country. She had in rich abundance nearly all the minerals, and her soil could produce nearly all the vegetable growths that were required in the chief manufactures of the civilised world; and he believed the time would come when she would pour out from her looms and engines all the various fabrics of mechanical skill to supply the wants of the new populations that would yet swarm over the Indian Archipelago and the countless isles of the Pacific. But already they had some manufactures; they worked up their own wool into fine tweed, which was worn by many gentlemen of fortune in the colony. They made their own soap and candles, their own leather, and their own cabinet-ware. They had some extensive iron foundries and occasionally they built their own steam engines. Such, then, were some of the facts of the case to show what kind of a place was this New South Wales of 1861, which in 1788 was founded by a few outcasts on the edge of a wild forest, up till that time only trodden by the wild blacks. They would now see at Sydney Cove a great city of 95,000 inhabitants, with all the conveniences and elegancies of English civilisation, surrounded by its suburban palaces, and with a breadth of cultivated country studded with rural homes stretching far inland; and beyond this a vast territory that wanted only the labour of man to make it fruitful, where twice the population of the United Kingdom might find room. Nor had the people of New South

L

Wales amidst their natural wealth neglected the means of education. They had spent more than £100,000 on the building of a University which was presided over by professors who ranked as first-class scholars. They were erecting colleges affiliated to this University, and they had in Sydney a public Grammar School largely endowed by Government. Besides these establishments, by which a high-class education could be given to their aspiring youth, they had numerous good private schools. Then there were two classes of schools to supply the means of primary instruction which were mainly supported by government; of one class connected with different religious denominations they had 217 schools; of the other class, founded on Lord Stanley's Irish national system, they had 125 schools, in which a purely secular education was imparted. With private establishments there were altogether in the colony 739 schools, and the Sunday-schools, which had spread to the number of 313, mustered 16,590 scholars. He had told them that New South Wales was under a separate form of government. It had a Parliament consisting of two Houses—the Lower House, or Legislative Assembly, being elected by manhood suffrage and the ballot. This House stood in the same position as the House of Commons and had similar power over the public purse. The Executive consisted of members of Parliament who could command a parliamentary majority. They took office and were displaced from office by the will of the Legislative Assembly, in the same manner as Ministers were raised to power or removed from power in England. And though a good deal of party feeling and squabbling, as it was called, had sprung up under this system, as might have been expected, it had upon the whole worked successfully. The people at large had more power under it and particular classes had much less; and of course those particular classes said it was a bad thing. It was a bad thing for them no doubt; but the colony had progressed under it, and there were more comfortable homes and a more independent feeling among the people. Some bad men were returned at the elections, but if good men presented themselves who had manifested a common feeling with the people they were almost certain to be chosen in preference. He now came to the land policy of the Government. The present Ministry had Bills in their hands for regulating the sale and occupation of the public lands, and on the main principles of these Bills they had dissolved

Parliament, and taken the sense of the country. The constituencies in almost all cases had returned members to support those Bills, and he believed they would become law during the present year. These Bills provided that, except within certain limitations, any person wanting agricultural land might go anywhere over that immense territory of 200,000,000 acres and select what in his judgment was the very best piece and most suitable in situation and other respects for his wants at 20s. per acre, 5s. to be paid down and 15s. at the end of three years, no interest being charged. He could not select less than 40 or more than 320 acres, and he must occupy it within one month and must cultivate a portion of it. He could not select within a certain distance of the towns, as the towns of course must have room to grow, and he could not select on lands which had been leased by the Crown in certain cases during the currency of those leases. With these exceptions he was left free to take his pick of the land; it was his own fault if he did not pick wisely. There were other provisions, some of which were important, such as granting the right of commonage to the selector over the unsold Crown lands adjacent to his little freehold; but he had explained the great leading principle of the scheme. The avowed policy of the Government was to distribute as widely as possible the cultivable lands into the hands of freehold cultivators; in other words, to create in the country a freehold peasantry. The provisions limiting the quantity and compelling residence were to prevent the rich lands being monopolised at this fixed price by large capitalists. He was not there to take any extraordinary pains to persuade them to emigrate. People in Old England seemed very little alive to what was going on in Australia. The grandest work that man could be engaged in was being done there. While in the great English towns they were busily employed in manufacturing ribbons, calicoes and woollens, fire-arms, musical instruments, and edge tools, those far-off little communities on the bosom of the Pacific were building up new nations, which a few generations hence would take a leading part in the affairs of the world. He thought it was a proud thing to have a share in this work of founding nations in a land so blest as the one he had imperfectly described. Perhaps others thought differently. If they were satisfied with the old beaten paths and the keen competition for life that hedged them in on every side in England, let them stop in the good old country,

which few loved better than he did ; but if they aspired to work
out for themselves and their children a happier destiny—where the
race of fortune and distinction was fair and equal to all—let them
come and take their fair share in the hard but well-rewarded work
that was waiting to be done by enterprising and industrious men
in New South Wales.

SUBSTANCE OF AN ADDRESS

Delivered in the Town Hall, Birmingham, October 22nd, 1861.

MR. PARKES said : In the first place he would explain why he
appeared in the town of Birmingham a second time, a reason that
had been partially explained by his Worship the Mayor. After
his arrival in England he held his first meeting in that town, and
since then he and his colleague in London had received such a
large number of applications from the inhabitants of Birmingham
and the neighbourhood asking for further information that it
appeared to him that the best course he could take would be to
appear again before a public meeting of the inhabitants of the
borough. He should try to repeat himself as little as possible,
but it was absolutely necessary that he should briefly recapitulate
a few of the leading facts he had before stated with respect to the
colony. Facts could not very well be altered for the purpose of
affording variety. The colony of New South Wales was the first
English settlement in point of time in Australia, and was one of
six separate colonies, each under a separate Government. It was
on the eastern side of the great island continent, and had a coast
line stretching over 10 degrees of latitude, from Point Danger in
latitude 28° to Cape Howe in latitude 38°. It ran back from the
Pacific Ocean 500 miles into the interior and had an area of
country as large as Great Britain and France. The population of
this vast country was only 350,500, or very little larger than that
of the town of Birmingham, and these inhabitants possessed the
true Anglo-Saxon spirit to surmount difficulties and extend their
race, and of course there was plenty of work for them to do in
subduing those almost boundless wilds of Nature. The soil of
New South Wales was in many parts rich and fruitful and
it embraced many varieties, while the climate was generally

N. S. Wales as a Field for Emigration. 149

genial and healthful, though different as a matter of course in different districts. In the neighbourhood of Sydney, for instance, gooseberries and currants would not grow, while they would grow very well fifty miles off in the south-western interior. The city of Sydney, which was the capital of the colony, was situated a little north of the 34th parallel of latitude, and to the north of Sydney there were no fewer than nine rivers, all pretty well known and all with more or less of agricultural settlement along their banks. There were the Hawkesbury, the Hunter, the Manning, the Hastings, the Macleay, the Bellenger, the Clarence, the Richmond, and the Tweed; and it was a popular mistake to suppose that these rivers were not valuable waters, though it must be admitted that they were insignificant—as indeed their English rivers also were—if compared with those of America. The Clarence was half-a-mile wide, and was navigable for sea-going steamers nearly fifty miles, while the Richmond was navigable for a still greater distance. Steamers traded regularly between the port of Sydney and the rising towns on the Hunter, the Manning, and the Clarence, and the settlements on the other rivers were connected with the seat of Government by sailing vessels regularly engaged in the trade. On the more northerly of these rivers, through four degrees of latitude at least, the soil and climate were beyond all dispute admirably adapted for the growth of cotton, which had been grown as far south as the Manning in latitude 32°, in sufficient quantities to establish the fact. The tobacco plant also flourished in those parts of the colony, and the sugar cane and nearly all tropical products might be successfully raised. The estimated area of land under cotton cultivation in the Southern States of America was not equal to the extent of soil capable of producing cotton of as fine staple in New South Wales. Nearly all the grain products of Northern Europe might be raised from other parts of the soil. In the South-Western interior there were large tracts of country as suitable for agriculture and as capable of production if properly cultivated as any in the world. Then on the Southern coast Illawarra and the Twofold Bay district had an Australian celebrity for the rich and productive character of their soil. He would read from the returns of the Registrar-General the principal items of the agricultural produce of New South Wales in 1859, which would be sufficient, if they recollected the fewness of the inhabitants, to justify the description he had given of the country. In 1859 the colony produced 1,605,353 bushels of wheat, 1,602,630 bushels of maize or Indian corn, 64,411 bushels of barley, 90,213 bushels of oats, 3641 bushels of rye, 1862 bushels of millet, 20,537 tons of potatoes, 3194 cwt. of tobacco leaf, 16,298 cwts. of sorghum and imphee, 60,873 tons of hay of different kinds, and 490 tons of grapes. Wheat grew as fine in grain in Australia as in England, though not in such heavy crops; labour was scarce and land was abundant, and the consequence was that the method of farming hitherto had been slovenly, but there was every reason to believe that as years rolled on and improved means of cultivation were introduced, the soil would be made as productive as the old cultivated lands of Europe. The cultivation of the sorghum and imphee which, as the meeting would be aware, were the sugar canes of China and Africa had only lately been introduced, and they were grown chiefly as green food for cattle. Then look at their grapes. If 350,553 persons possessed as one season's growth 490 tons of grapes—that alone was not a bad substitute for gooseberries and currants. But their fruits in richness and variety surpassed England altogether. Apples and pears grew in the colony as fine in size and flavour as in England. A gentleman from Yorkshire who was a fellow-passenger with him returning from Australia four months ago was bringing home some Australian pears to exhibit at a horticultural show, he believed at Selby, and six of them which he weighed on the passage were a stone weight. In addition to these and other English fruits they had the orange, lemon, guava, fig, banana, pomegranate, loquat, apricot, peach, nectarine, and every variety of the melon; and they had other fruits in great abundance. Ripe peaches were often sold for 1d. and 2d. a dozen, and in 1859 they had 1100 acres of grapes. Let them keep in view that this extensive country, thus bountifully blest by Providence and capable of producing all that was required for the sustenance of man, was inhabited by only 350,553 souls—men, women, and children. Sink below the surface of the soil and mineral treasure was to be found in all directions. Everybody knew that New South Wales was a gold-producing colony, and it was a fact that solid lumps of gold over a hundred ounces in weight were dug out of the soil by miners who had not a shilling at the time of the golden accident. He did not want to entice men to New South Wales with any hope that they would gain these golden prizes on the gold-field, where all was a lottery and the chances were a thousand to one against them; and he was not over-anxious that people should go to the gold-diggings at all. It was at best an unsettled and a precarious life, where roving habits were acquired which unfitted men for the more regular pursuits of society. But the fact was as he had stated it. Besides their gold, they possessed iron, copper, tin, lead, platina, and inexhaustible beds of fine coal. The Registrar-General gave among the articles of export £178 for horse-hair and £45 for rags; it were worth while to dwell for a moment on these two little items: they contained much meaning. It would be recollected that the colony contained 214,684 horses and yet they had only £178 for horse-hair; and of course the colonists threw away their clothes more prodigally than people in England, yet they had only £45 for rags. The fact was that these things, with many others that in England were collected into the channels of commerce, were allowed to waste in the colony; there was a large field there for the students of the "philosophy of small things." There were rag-merchants in England but not in New South Wales, though he supposed by this item that some enterprising Londoner—a native of Field Lane, perhaps—was turning his attention to this source of profit. He would now tell them what kind of people were not likely to succeed in New South Wales, and what kind of people were sure to be successful. It was of very little use for the idle, the drunken, or the self-sufficient and conceited to go out there. The one class would find the common lot of the idle and drunken even at the Antipodes, and the other class would simply get laughed at and their company be avoided. There were men everywhere who shirked the hard and unpleasant duties of life; when the work they had to do was found to pinch, they set about devising some other means of doing it. Now those ingenious people had better stay in England, where there was a larger field than in the colonies for the employment of their inventive faculties. There was another description of persons who were often sent out to the colonies by their friends—the inert in character and unfortunate in judgment, who had scarcely the spirit to do anything and always made mistakes in doing the little they attempted. He would say to the friends of these people that in sending them out to the colonies, they were doing little less than slowly murdering them. If such unfortunates missed all their opportunities at home where they had the counsel and assistance of their friends, how were they to manage in a strange country where they would be friendless? It was these classes principally which supplied the complaining sufferers that hung about the great colonial cities, and such persons there always were, always complaining and always in necessitous circumstances. The persons who would succeed in New South Wales were plain, plodding, hard-working men of sober character and careful habits, who had sufficient common sense to see their own opportunities and sufficient moderation to wait patiently for the fruits of their own industry. Men who were afraid of hard work or of a few privations ought not to go out to a new country. The other night he was asked in a neighbouring town whether the mosquitoes were not very troublesome at Sydney; and at another place he was asked whether the heat and the sand were not very distressing. Now he would say at once that New South Wales did not want her population recruited from men who were afraid of mosquitoes or overwhelmed by a gust of sand. There were mosquitoes at Sydney; and he would tell the ladies who had done him the honour of coming to that meeting that, if they went to Sydney, however pretty they might be on landing, their faces would present all the appearance of a smart attack of measles before they had been there four and twenty hours; and all through the love of these mosquitoes. But this effect—very calamitous no doubt while it lasted—did not continue long, and the poor little mosquitoes really were not worth talking about. Then in Sydney there were occasionally strong winds from the south which carried with them clouds of sand, but these disagreeable winds were unfrequent and of short duration. There were many things in an Australian life not over-pleasant, especially to those who were fond of pleasure and amusement. If you lived in the bush you could not go to the theatre or a concert every night, that was certain. There were theatres and concerts in Sydney. He was sorry to say they had too faithfully copied all the varieties of English city-life. But he was not very anxious for persons to go out to swell the population of Sydney; what they wanted was industrious striving families to settle upon the land to become freehold cultivators. To a man of this class the road was clear and open, and he cared not what the man's previous occupation had been—whether he had been a tinker or a

N. S. Wales as a Field for Emigration. 153

tailor—if he was prepared for hard work and willing to learn, with common sense enough to see what was for his own advantage and patience enough to wait for the natural operation of time and circumstances, he was sure of success. He would not allure any such man with the prospect of finding lumps of gold at the diggings or of making a fortune in a few years by trade; but he would promise to any such man that in New South Wales he would be able by his own exertions to obtain a secure home for himself and his family, supplied with all the substantial comforts of life, unclouded by the fear that it might fail him in the future, and without having to thank other men for their assistance in obtaining it. There was a field in New South Wales for the man without money who was anxious to convert his labour into money, and there was a field for the man who possessed money who was anxious to turn it into more; but in either case nothing could be done without the home-spun qualities of industry, sobriety, and perseverance. Since 1855 there had existed in New South Wales a Parliamentary Government, as in England, to which had been handed over the entire management of the affairs of the colony with the right of disposing of the public lands and the control of the colonial revenues. If any person seriously thinking of emigration thought fit to see him personally, he would, so far as he was able, afford any information that might be required. If people liked to stay in England all he had to say was God bless them in the dear old country. He was as much an Englishman as any man present. The people in Australia were as thoroughly English as the people of the mother-country; they had forfeited nothing by going to a distance of 14,000 miles. Shakspeare and Milton belonged as much to them as to the people of England; they possessed by right of inheritance an equal share in the grand traditions, the old military renown, the splendour of scientific discovery, and the wealth of literature, which had made England the great civilising power of the world.

LECTURE

Delivered before the Working Men's College, Great Ormond-street, London, May 17, 1862.*

MR. PARKES said: It is not perhaps unfitting to take the eldest of the Australian colonies to illustrate the history of the English people in that part of the world. If any *one* were selected for such purpose it would surely be the one where English colonisation first took root, where the colonising spirit had to struggle with difficulties unknown to the offspring colonies, all of which have at least enjoyed one incalculable advantage not among the early experiences of the parent—the advantage of an English neighbourhood. There are moreover some peculiarities in intercolonial relationship up to the present time which would seem to point out New South Wales as the representative colony in any general discourse on Australian progress. For many years her capital was the *entrepôt* for Australian commerce ; even now she is the principal market of supply for some articles of the first necessity, including animal food and coal. She alone possesses the royal power of coining money, and the gold coin generally current in the other colonies is issued from the Sydney Mint.† It was in New South Wales that representative institutions were first transplanted to Australia, and in matters of Government she exercised an early paternal influence, which in some measure shaped the political course of the younger communities. In no other Australian colony have the associations of home so widely diffused the charm of their existence. There we have men and women grown grey through the happy toils of a well-spent life, whose steps have never wandered beyond their own sunny shores, who have never seen other skies or constellations than those which brightly opened upon their childhood and still beam above their honoured age. The social

---

*The following was the list of lectures for the season :—The Meaning and Use of the Word "Civilisation," by the Principal (Rev. F. D. Maurice, M.A.); The Mexican War, by J. M. Ludlow, Esq.; Life and Character of Sir John Falstaff, Knight, by William Malleson, Esq.; The Gold Coast and the Future of the Negroes, by Thomas Hughes, Esq.; A Greek Play, by J. W. Hales, Esq.—or Robert of Brunne, an Early English Life (1303), by F. J. Furnivall, Esq., M.A.; The Poet Wordsworth, by J. R. Seeley, Esq., M.A.; Thomas Carlyle, writer of books, by Vernon Lushington, Esq., B.C.L.; New South Wales, by H. Parkes, Esq., Government Commissioner from the Colony.

† A mint has since been established in Melbourne.

N. S. Wales as a Field for Emigration. 155

amenities that flow from family life are naturally most genuine and matured in the oldest colony. It is therefore not unfortunate for me that my personal experience coincides with these circumstances of Australian life, in pointing out New South Wales as the colony to be kept in view in what we have to say about Australia this evening.

The different terms of designation which geographers have employed sufficiently show their perplexity in correctly describing Australia. We find it variously set down as an island, a continent, a continental island, and an island-continent. Without attempting to trace the discovery of this new southern world, we may admit that the English who are fast peopling it were not the first discoverers. The great land itself lies between lat. 10° 39' and 39° 11' south, and long. 113° 5' and 153° 16' east; and it is from east to west about 2400 miles long, and from north to south 1800 or 1900 miles broad. It has at least 8000 miles of coast, and is computed to contain an area of 3,000,000 square miles.

It was upon the eastern coast of this immense island that the first English settlement was formed in January 1788. After the disruption of the North-American colonies the Imperial Government considered it necessary to find some other outlet for the convicted criminals of England; and in consequence a fleet of eleven transport vessels was fitted out in 1787 under Captain Phillip, who was ordered to sail for Botany Bay, on the coast of New Holland, and there form a new penal settlement, of which he was commissioned as first governor. The great navigator Cook had come to an anchor in Botany Bay, which received its name for a reason more poetical than is generally supposed. Sir Joseph Banks, who accompanied Cook as botanist, so named the place in consequence of the variety of new flowers which he discovered in its primeval forests. Captain Phillip was directed to sail for Botany Bay for the very simple reason that it was the only place of anchorage on the coast of New Holland then known to the authorities. It is not generally known in Europe that no settlement was ever formed on the shores of this bay. Captain Phillip, without landing his people, came to the conclusion that it must ever remain an insecure harbour, while its shores presented no very eligible site for a settlement. After some delay an inlet of the sea was discovered a few miles further north, which is now admitted to be one of the finest harbours in the world; and on the shores of the splendid harbour of Port Jackson the exiles were landed, and a few tents and rude huts occupied a gap in the wild woods where the populous city of Sydney at present stands. The convict colony of New South Wales thus founded seventy-four years ago was the only occupant of this vast unexplored world until the year 1803, when a second convict colony was established under the name of Van Diemen's Land. We cannot stop to notice the chequered history and slow progress of these communities while they remained the receptacles of British criminals, though it will be necessary to revert to the matter for a moment to show how faint are the traces now left of the origin of Anglo-Australia, so rapidly growing up to the dimensions and attitude of empire. The third Australian colony was founded on the western coast in the year 1829, under the name of the Swan River Settlement, or Western Australia. Five to seven years later the colony of South Australia was established, making a fourth separate community. The fifth in point of time, the great colony of Victoria, dates its separate existence from the year 1850, up to which time it formed a part of New South Wales. In the latter part of 1859 the northern extremity of New South Wales was cut off and proclaimed a separate colony under the name of Queensland, forming the sixth and last of the Australian group.

From the repeated severances of territory which the parent colony has undergone, an idea of confined existence might possibly be entertained. But "life has ample room" still within the boundaries of New South Wales. The colony as now constituted contains an area of 300,000 square miles, or upwards of 207,000,000 acres—more than five times as large as England and Wales. I for one believe that it is far better for the parent colony that those distant regions, at one time included within her territorial limits, should be politically separated and erected into independent colonies, and that the springs of prosperity for all will gain in vigour and elasticity by the separation. The interests of the separate communities will naturally act and re-act on each other to the general advancement, increasing the established channels and creating new outlets for trade and intercourse, and at the same time best developing the natural resources and distinctive advantages of each for the good of all.

Having glanced at the far-off group of political independencies which are revelling in freedom under the British flag in the southern hemisphere, and where the Anglo-Saxon spirit lives as sound and healthful and is as gloriously battling for moral empire as within the British Isles, we will confine ourselves for the rest of the evening to a view of Australian progress, sketched from life in the parent colony, the Mother of the Australias, as she may be fitly named.

New South Wales has a coast-line extending from Point Danger on the north in lat. 28°, to Cape Howe on the south in lat. 38°; and as the colony runs back to points 500 and 600 miles from the sea, it contains many varieties of soil and climate. Though it is more than five times as large as England and Wales it is occupied by a people much weaker in numbers than the population of Glasgow or Manchester. I apply the term "weak" to this handful of colonists in contrast to the vastness of the field before them, where in every direction nature is asking for human strength to render her riches available for mankind. If we go back forty years we find that in 1822 the population of New South Wales was 30,756; that was in fact the total population then in Australia; for at that time there was no other settlement on the mainland. Now the united population of Australia may be set down at 1,250,000.* The present population of New South Wales is 350,553. The principal staple production of New South Wales for years past has been fine wool. In 1822 the number of sheep in New South Wales, which means in fact the number then in Australia, was 138,575. Now the number of sheep in the four colonies of New South Wales, South Australia, Victoria, and Queensland—leaving Tasmania (as Van Diemen's Land is now called) and Western Australia out of the account—is 18,187,451. The number of sheep at present owned by New South Wales is 6,119,163, being 325,036 more than is possessed by any other colony. In 1822 the number of vessels which arrived in New South Wales, which means the number of arrivals during that year in Australia, was 71, giving an aggregate of 22,924 tons. In 1860 the number that arrived in New South Wales alone, to say nothing of the other colonies, was 1424, giving the aggregate of 427,835 tons. The same surprising results would be shown by comparisons drawn from the same period in other main elements of material progress. But comparisons compassing a wide space of time in Australia

---

* The total population of the Australian colonies and New Zealand at the present time (1875) is estimated at not less than 2,250,000.

give an average of progress which, owing to the slow and impeded course of colonisation in the days of convictism, affords no true indication of the rapid strides made during the last few years. Let us therefore take the intervening five years which lead from the cessation of transportation in 1849 to the introduction of Responsible Government at the close of 1855, and then the succeeding five years, during which the colonies may be said to have been struggling with the novel task—so difficult on account of its novelty—of governing themselves.

I shall commence with the returns for 1851 to avoid the confusion that would surround the use of the figures for 1850, in which year the statistical returns were largely affected by the separation of Victoria. In 1851 the population of New South Wales was 197,168, the land under cultivation was 153,117 acres, the number of horses in the colony was 116,397, the number of horned cattle 1,375,257, the number of sheep 7,396,895, the number of vessels inwards 553, the number of vessels outwards 503, the amount of imports was £1,563,931, the amount of exports £1,796,912, the revenue was £486,698, the expenditure £444,108. In the same year the number of schools in the colony was 423, and the number of convictions in the Supreme and Circuit Courts and in the Courts of Quarter Sessions was 574. In 1856 the population had increased to 286,873, the land under cultivation to 186,033 acres, the horses to 168,929, the horned cattle to 2,023,418, the sheep to 7,736,323, the vessels inwards to 1143, the vessels outwards to 1219, the imports to £5,460,971, the exports to £3,430,880, the revenue to £1,986,553, the expenditure to £1,835,134, while the schools had increased to 565—showing an addition of 142—and the convictions in the criminal courts had been reduced to 461—showing a decrease of 113. In 1860 the population was computed at 348,546—more than double what it was in 1844, notwithstanding that Victoria had set up on her own account with her 70,000 inhabitants in the interval. In the same year the land under cultivation was 260,798 acres, the horses were 251,497, the horned cattle 2,408,586, the sheep 6,119,163, the vessels inwards 1424, the vessels outwards 1438, the imports amounted to £7,519,285, the exports to £5,072,020, the revenue was £1,880,508, and the expenditure £2,047,955. The schools had increased to 798, while criminal convictions had been still further reduced to 405. Let us pause here to see more clearly

N. S. Wales as a Field for Emigration. 159

some of the results exhibited by these figures. New South Wales was a convict colony up to 1849, a period of 61 years; though it is proper to state that the prison stream had flowed into it in diminished volume during the last 6 or 7 years of that time. In 1851, the second year after its emancipation, the land which had been brought under cultivation in 63 years was 153,117 acres. In 1860, the eleventh year after its emancipation, the land under cultivation was 260,798 acres, showing in the 9 years an additional acreage more than equal to two-thirds of all that had been done in the first 63 years. In 1851 the schools were 423, in 1860 the number was 798—an increase in 9 years of nearly 90 per cent. on the result of 63 years, to say nothing of the improved character of the schools. In 1851 the number of criminal convictions was 574, with a population of 197,168; in 1860 they were reduced to 405, with a population of 348,546. If it were my purpose to show the impolicy of planting colonies as places of penal servitude, at least so far as the progress and welfare of the colonies are concerned, perhaps these expressive figures would go far towards carrying conviction on that point to impartial minds. Happily in our case that is not called for, as the colony of which we are speaking is fairly started on the broad road of freedom, and may rank itself with the most favoured in the measure of self-government it enjoys. These figures however will serve to show how rapidly the convict taint is disappearing before the enlightened activity of a free British population. The actual number of Imperial prisoners now in New South Wales is very small; in 1860 it had dwindled down to 186. It would be difficult indeed for the most fastidious of social critics to discover in the face of things in the colony at the present time any visible traces of its penal origin, or any marked features distinguishing its cities and towns from the cities and towns of England, except it be that they generally are cleaner and look much happier.

It has been already stated that the territory of New South Wales comprises 207,000,000 acres. Of this vast area of land, in 1860, 7,170,690 acres had become private property by grant and purchase, 49,068,941 acres were held under lease chiefly for pastoral purposes, 1,808,640 acres had been reserved for public purposes, and 148,951,729 acres were lying unoccupied. Some of the pastoral "runs" in the interior comprise 250,000 to 500,000 acres; and the quantity of cattle and sheep chiefly possessed by these Australian squatters, as already stated, would give an average of more than 7 head of horned cattle, and more than 17 sheep for every man, every woman, and every child in the colony. In 1860 the principal items of pastoral produce exported were 12,809,362 lbs. of wool, amounting to £1,123,699 in value; 13,647 cwts. of tallow, amounting to £28,794 in value; and green hides to the amount of £68,576. It will be seen from the figures already used that the number of sheep in the colony had declined in 1860 to 6,119,163 from 7,736,323 in 1856; but it must be recollected that the new colony of Queensland—eminently a pastoral country—had just been partitioned off from New South Wales with a number of sheep estimated at 3,000,000. It may be fairly admitted, however, that circumstances, not the least of which is the healthy growth of other interests, render "squatting" or sheep-farming on a large scale in New South Wales less progressive than other departments of productive industry. The mere "squatter" naturally prefers a country where the inconveniences of civilisation are farthest removed from him, and for this reason many "run-finders" among the class have latterly migrated to the vast unexplored regions in the north. Still, the capitalist who prefers this kind of colonial investment, and who can content himself with less than extravagant returns, may find a wide and profitable field in New South Wales. The land under cultivation in 1860 yielded 1,581,597 bushels of wheat, 1,484,467 bushels of Indian corn, 39,801 bushels of barley, 98,814 bushels of oats, 28,127 tons of potatoes, 9704 cwts. of tobacco, 50,927 tons of hay, 99,791 gallons of wine, besides other produce. The grapes raised for table use amounted to 366 tons, and other green fruit, including oranges, lemons, figs, bananas, guavas, loquats, nectarines, apricots, peaches, plums, pears, and apples, must have reached a total value of over £100,000. The value of the fruit—chiefly oranges—exported was £61,466. It may be confidently expected that every kind of cultivation will extend with comparative rapidity under the new Land Acts which came into operation on the 1st of January this year. These Acts enable the agricultural settler to select for himself a farm of not less than 40 nor more than 320 acres, at a fixed price of 20s. per acre, giving him three years' credit without interest for 75 per cent. of the purchase-money. Recent advices from the colony report that within two months

N. S. Wales as a Field for Emigration. 161

conditional purchases had been made by 1222 persons not previously freeholders—the area selected being 104,405 acres, and the portion of the purchase-money paid up £26,275, while 219 purchases had been effected by small freeholders, adjoining their freeholds; so that the total number of conditional purchasers had been 1441, the area selected 117,949 acres, and the deposit paid £30,033.

The first discoveries of Australian gold were made in New South Wales, and the gold produce has of late years largely increased; but the colony contains also rich mines of coal, copper, and iron, and recently an extensive silver-mine has been opened. In 1860 the colony raised from its mines 356,572 ozs. of gold, valued at £1,359,823; and 369,827 tons of coal, valued at £228,187, besides a small quantity of copper ore.

The value of the gold raised during last year was nearly £2,000,000, and so far as this year had advanced, at the date of the latest intelligence, the yield was still largely increasing. This will be seen by comparing the results for the first two months of the last three years. For January and February, 1860, the escorts delivered at the Sydney Mint 40,354 ozs.; for the corresponding period of 1861 the delivery was 54,109 ozs.; for the corresponding period of 1862 it amounted to 82,424 ozs.—more than doubling the yield of 1860. It is worthy of note that while this remarkable increase is shown in New South Wales, the yield in the other gold-producing colonies of Australia is sensibly declining. A few months ago a new gold-field in the Lachlan district was discovered, which there is reason to believe will prove of wonderful extent and richness. At our latest dates the gold found there had reached an amount actually beyond the power of the escort to bring it to Sydney. A telegram received by the Government in March states "that 17,000 ozs. had been placed in the hands of the commissioners to be sent to Sydney by escort; that upwards of 5000 ozs. had been lodged with or purchased by the banks, and that about 8000 ozs. additional was known to be still in the possession of the diggers, who were waiting an opportunity of sending it down." The silver mine already alluded to has been discovered on the southern coast, about 200 miles from Sydney, and the assays that have been made give a yield of 40 to 100 ozs. of pure silver to the ton of ore. The copper mines opened in New South Wales are eight in number, and the latest advices show great activity in setting up machinery and preparing to work these mines. Copper ore is certain to form an important item in the exports of the present year.

Some of the minor productions of New South Wales may be pointed out as showing the various channels into which colonising enterprise is directing itself. Colonial manufactures are of course in their infancy; but we have among other establishments of this kind 10 breweries, 62 tanneries, 8 tobacco manufactories, 8 cloth factories, 15 foundries, and 34 soap and candle manufactories. In the year 1860 we manufactured among other things 118,500 yards of tweed, 57,080 cwts. of soap, 35,485 cwts. of candles, 1695 cwts. of tobacco, 113,600 cwts. of refined sugar, besides 17 sea-going vessels of different sizes, and 1,573,500 sovereigns and 156,000 half-sovereigns—the coinage of the Mint. In the same year we exported articles of colonial growth or manufacture of the following estimated values:—Beer, £5314; butter and cheese, £33,527; carriages, £1681; carts and waggons, £5744; eggs, £5324; fish, £7212; Indian corn, £92,450; leather, £11,866; machinery, £8393; timber, £27,210. These are only a few of the minor exports, and are quoted simply to show the more infant forms of productive industry. It may be further added that in 1860 there were in the colony 193 mills for grinding corn (of which 134 were worked by steam power), 230 reaping and threshing machines, 41 saw-mills, and in connexion with the port of Sydney, two patent slips, two dry docks, and a fleet of 51 steam-vessels.

Sydney, the capital of New South Wales, is a city containing with its suburbs 93,000 inhabitants. It may be said to occupy several rocky ridges of land radiating from its southern limits to the waters of Port Jackson, the waves of this noble bay beating into its bosom up a succession of beautiful deep coves. No finer site for a great city could be imagined. Many of the streets are well formed, and the houses of business are of considerable architectural pretensions, and are as well stocked with merchandise as similar establishments in England. The city, being the seat of Government, contains all the public buildings of a national character, and among its other edifices may be enumerated two cathedrals, upwards of twenty churches and chapels, the University, the Exchange, and eight handsome banking-houses. The suburbs of Sydney present on all sides delightful pictures for the admirers of Nature in her different forms of beauty. There is an almost

N. S. Wales as a Field for Emigration. 163

endless variety of sea and shore; and the romantic inequality of the neighbouring country has been taken advantage of in many instances, with the eye of the artist, for the erection of rural villas, and in some cases quite lordly palaces, which greatly heighten the landscape under a blue and cloudless sky. Many persons will be surprised to be told that some of the proprietors of these suburban palaces are gentlemen in receipt of incomes varying from £20,000 to £40,000 a year, and that some of them are "sons of the soil," who have never been out of the colony.

The principal country towns are Parramatta, Bathurst, Goulburn, Maitland, Newcastle, Grafton, Armidale, and Albury, the populations of which range from 3000 to 8000; but there are many other townships. In 1860 there were in the colony 287 post-offices, and the mail routes added together gave a distance of 1,461,518 miles. The statistics of the Post-office for that year afford some proof of the growth of intelligence; the number of letters conveyed was 4,230,761, the number of newspapers 3,668,783, the number of book and other packets 83,736. In illustration of the intercourse between the colony and the mother country, it may be stated that the mail steamer which arrived at Sydney in March last carried to the colony 21,014 letters, 26,452 newspapers, and 271 packages of new books and printed papers. In Sydney there are two large daily newspapers, and nearly every country town has its local journal. In 1860 the scholars attending the 798 schools were 34,767, and there were in the colony 329 Sunday-schools, with 21,104 children attending them. The University of Sydney, which occupies a noble Gothic building that London would not be ashamed to possess among her public edifices, includes Professorships in Classics, in Mathematics, and in Physics, and Readerships in Jurisprudence and in -Modern Languages. Its constitution is purely secular, and so catholic in principle that, while it is open alike to students of all creeds, the son of the shoemaker has as easy admission as the son of the millionaire. The Colonial Government has founded this great institution, as I hope it will be admitted, in a spirit of wise forecast, and with a patriotic munificence, to afford the means to superior native talent of fitting itself to serve the country in the different provinces of knowledge and of public life. If such an institution should appear to some above the wants of the colony, I would ask them to reflect upon the value of a single mind richly gifted—such as rises upon the world as the luminous accident of a hundred years—if fully armed for the "battle of life," in a country which has everything of good and renown to achieve.

In the early years of New South Wales the forms of Government were of an arbitrary character. The Governor for the time being was a little despot; men were tried for their lives by benches of military officers. Trial by jury was at length introduced, and a local Legislature was established, which however was at first composed of gentlemen appointed by the Crown, and presided over with closed doors by the Governor himself. The representative principle was not introduced till the year 1843, when the colony was 55 years old. The Legislature then created still retained a large infusion of the nominee element, and it possessed very few of the substantive powers of legislation. It had no voice in the disposal of the public lands; no effective control over the public revenues; no check whatever on the public service. The representative part of it was mainly based upon an electoral household qualification of £20, and a freehold qualification for members of £100 a year. This form of Legislature continued with some modifications till the close of the year 1855, when new constitutions of a very comprehensive and liberal character were conferred upon all the Australian colonies. Kept in leading-strings until then, with even their Custom-house officers appointed by the Imperial Government, they were suddenly raised to a state of the fullest freedom with constitutional power to fill every office from the Chief Justice downwards; to raise and appropriate the public revenues and to dispose of every acre of the public domain. It would not be a matter of surprise to thoughtful men if these complete powers of self-government were used with some abuse and some folly by a people into whose hands they came so suddenly, and who had been so little trained for their wise exercise. But it would be an easy task to show conclusively if time permitted that Parliamentary Government in Australia instead of proving a failure, as English libellers have asserted, has been a remarkable success. It has done one thing however in which may be found the secret of much of the abuse indulged in by returned colonists; it has removed from active public life many of the persons who formerly enjoyed the "loaves and fishes" of Government and Government patronage, not by the confidence of the people, but by a petty kind of Court favouritism

N. S. Wales as a Field for Emigration. 165

and by their official connexions. It is natural perhaps that these persons should complain, but in their morbid descriptions of the political condition of the colonies they should at least adhere to the facts.

The present Parliament of New South Wales consists of two Houses—a Council appointed by the Crown and an Assembly elected by the People. In the constitution of the Lower House there is no qualification for members, the elective franchise is extended to all permanent residents and all persons holding a "miner's right" on the gold-fields, and the votes at elections are given by ballot. This House claims the exclusive exercise of the money power, and four out of the five Cabinet Ministers sit here at the present time. It is desirable to distinguish between the residential suffrage existing in New South Wales and "universal suffrage;" for the simple qualification of residence, while it admits all who can entertain any serious desire to be upon the electoral roll, effectually excludes persons of no settled abode or occupation. In 1860 the number of registered electors was only 77,945, while the adult males could not be fewer than 130,000.

It must be admitted that men of questionable fitness have been elected to the Legislative Assembly, but it is also a fact that some of the best-qualified men in the entire colony are members of that body. But notoriously unfit men were returned to the early colonial Legislatures; and are no unfit men returned to the House of Commons? Then with respect to the Ministers who enjoy the confidence of this Legislature, the present Prime Minister is one of the oldest Australian representatives, having been returned to the first elective Council in 1843; he is admitted on all hands to have been one of the most useful public servants, and is undoubtedly the most experienced administrator in the colony. In social standing Mr. Cowper is the son of an archdeacon of the Church of England who laboured through a long life universally respected. I may disapprove, as I certainly do disapprove, of much in Mr. Cowper's political life, but surely the circumstances I have stated should point him out as one of the men entitled to aspire to Ministerial office. If not to men like him, where should we look for our Ministers? It is a stereotyped phrase with English newspaper writers, who write without knowing the facts, that every mail brings a Ministerial crisis in Australia. Why, Mr. Cowper has been Colonial-Secretary, with the exception of a short interval of some four months, ever since 1857. Your Palmerstons and Derbys don't last longer than that. Many persons indeed think he has been too long in office.

We do not pretend to say that blunders have not been committed in the management of our affairs, or that faults of a more serious nature may not be singled out. Other considerations as well as fitness for the office may have weighed with Ministers in making appointments to the public service. Unsound principles may have received an insincere support because their advocacy insured a passing popularity. But still we ask, do these things not occur among your old and highly-disciplined politicians in England? and why do you not pluck the motes from your own eyes? And we answer your affected satires by telling you, in a tone of reproach which we think can be better justified, that we have no bribery and intimidation at our elections, such as your parliamentary committees—to the shame of the nation—have disclosed. But parliamentary Government in Australia has not been an inoperative, unproductive thing. We appeal to the British people, and ask to be judged by what *we have done*. Not by the words of the *Times* newspaper, but by the acts of our own Parliament. Since the introduction of Responsible Government we have established District Courts throughout the colony, enabling suitors to obtain justice without being ruined by long and costly journeys to Sydney; we have brought into existence no fewer than twenty municipal bodies for managing the local affairs of the principal towns; we have greatly multiplied the means of public education; we have improved the management of the gold-fields and rendered them much more productive; and we have opened the public lands on an easy and equitable plan for the settlement of industrious families. One consequence, which cannot be easily summed up in definite terms, is the wide diffusion of feelings of contentment and attachment to the country, and the growing up of a robust spirit of independence. More men look abroad with the consciousness in their looks that they have a rooted interest in the land; more poor women plant flowers at their doors and decorate their rooms with pleasant pictures; there are more neatly-clothed and happy-looking children. Surely these are results to test the value of a political system. Surely these are goodly fruits to spring from our governing ourselves.

We have been charged with disloyalty. We answer, when did

any great event stir the heart of the fatherland and we not give brilliant proof of our consanguinity and our loyalty? The Australian Governments have been charged with repudiation. We say, simply, the charge is false. No public man amongst us has ever breathed a thought that could be tortured to mean repudiation of our public engagements. On all occasions the public faith has been scrupulously kept, even in cases where it is popularly believed that corrupt bargains were made by leading men of the former *régime* who are now among the loudest traducers of the colony. Every true Australian is too confident in the glorious destiny of his country to wantonly sully her early fame by a public act inconsistent with public honour. A few generations more and that destiny will place the Australias amongst the foremost of free and prosperous Christian states.

FRIENDLESS CHILDREN.

SPEECH

Delivered at the Annual Meeting of the Sussex-street Ragged-schools held in the Hall of the School of Arts, Sydney, July 1st, 1863.

MR. PARKES said : I have been requested to move a resolution which I am sure will be adopted by you with your perfect concurrence and your unqualified sympathy. It is my privilege to ask you to acknowledge in a special manner the services of those ladies and gentlemen who visit and teach in these ragged-schools, and who by various means contribute to their success. In this city, so admirably adorned by wealth and surrounded by such multiplied forms of beauty, there is nothing richer or more beautiful to an enlightened mind than the unostentatious care and teaching bestowed by these ladies and gentlemen on the forlorn and forsaken children of our streets. Thanks, I say, thanks from warm and grateful hearts to these good teachers. And it reflects honour on our city that among her sons and daughters living in affluence and ease there are not wanting those who quietly come forward to undertake this task, and in circumstances which would be irksome and repellant to their minds if it were not for the practical philanthropy by which they are sustained. I would venture to say to them, that though they may pursue their work apart from the bustle and parade of this world; though by it they may acquire no fleeting reputation among their fellow-creatures—still their labours are not unnoted and cannot be obscured ; still they are building up for themselves the best and only satisfying reward of human action—the consciousness on leaving the world that they have striven to improve it. These ragged-schools—those 230 little children—what a history is there ! Closed and sealed at present, and only to be unfolded by the rolling course of years. Imagination alone can help us now in estimating the manifold results that will be borne forward on those 230 streams of life. How largely will those 230 children influence society ? Who dares to look upon them with a feeling of indifference or pass them by with an idle scorn? Why, those little helpless creatures who now excite no higher feeling than pity, will one day step forth into the world to stir the strongest passions of our kind—it may be to leave a visible mark for good or evil on their generation and time. The report of the Sussex-street school quotes the words of Mr. Kingsley, that "The most precious thing in the world is a human being." And is not this the sum of all experience and all knowledge? What larger golden truth relating to the affairs of this life can we learn? What thing can we find of purer interest? What is there in the dainty outlines of the loveliest poodle that ever was nursed in lady's lap to compare with the mantling cheek and soul-speaking eye even of a scantily-clothed and neglected child? What is there in the glory of the rose or the sweetness of the lily to compare with the heart-fragrance which is stored up in one of those little ones? Nay, more; who shall say, while contemplating some goodly work of human intellect, that the undeveloped capacity does not exist in some child before him which shall expand and strengthen till it confers a yet greater service on mankind? Let us then take care of these precious things, remembering always that those we rescue with the left hand not only lessen the sum of vagrancy and vice, but they are passed on to society by the right hand to lighten its burdens, to increase its powers of industry, and to defend its interests. Practically considered—in a business sense of what is practical—it is indeed surprising how largely the ragged-school teaching is calculated to benefit society. Few persons perhaps have estimated the amount of mischief which a few criminal children may cause to the State. By a return furnished to a committee of the House of Lords I find that 530 children under 16 years of age were committed for trial at the Middlesex Sessions during one year. The total value of the property stolen by these 530 children was only £158 7s. 9d. But what was the cost of their punishment? The cost of prosecuting them was £445 17s.; the cost of their maintenance in gaol after conviction was £964 12s. 2d.—making £1410 9s. 2d. Thirty-six of their number were transported, and the estimated cost of transporting and maintaining these was £3952—making a total of £5362 9s. 2d. But who can calculate the cost of those 500 children to society? This £5000 was only the beginning. How much better to teach the child than to punish the hardened youth; how much cheaper to provide schools than to build gaols;

how much more creditable to us as a community to have a long roll of schoolmasters than a longer list of gaolers and turnkeys. I hope and believe we have no criminal classes here such as exist in the old cities of Europe. Our little vagrants for the most part are the children of parents who have fallen in their own lives through being removed from the restraints of family and friends, and exposed to ruin and temptation—rather than the children of parents who were themselves born to an inheritance of homelessness and crime. If this be so, the more encouraging is the work of rescue; and not less imperative is the necessity of staying that course of degradation which will otherwise settle down into the permanence of a criminal class. If my voice could be heard beyond this meeting, I would appeal to those gentlemen throughout the colony who are at the head of large establishments. These ragged-schools are deserving of their attention, and may I be permitted to say? ought to command their aid. They might do much for the children, for themselves, and for the colony, by opening avenues of useful employment to the inmates of these schools when they arrive at years fitting them for service. A few months ago I passed a short time as the guest of an English nobleman, who was something more than a peer of the realm—one of the finest Englishmen I ever had the happiness to meet. This nobleman, who was a model farmer, had on his estate a private Reformatory of the simplest but the most beneficial character. He takes poor boys at an early age, provides them with a home under sound domestic discipline, has them taught practical farming, while he gives them the means of a good primary education. The result is that there is quite a competition among the farmers in that part of England for the boys reared on the estate. Why should not gentlemen in Australia imitate that excellent example, and relieve the ragged-schools by drafting off the older boys to a still healthier atmosphere, while the girls might be absorbed by a similar principle into domestic service? A hundred young men and women thus added to our real colonisers would be a saving of more than £1000 in our immigration grants, to say nothing further of the other and higher benefits to society at large. It is impossible to over-estimate the value of these efforts of unpretending philanthropy. Let us all help to the extent of our opportunities and our means. In few things— perhaps in nothing—can we be of more use to our country.

THE FIRST YEARS OF RESPONSIBLE GOVERNMENT.

[IN the early part of 1864, after his return from England, Mr. Parkes was invited by a numerously signed requisition to become a candidate for the representation of Braidwood, and although he declined and refused to give his sanction to any of the proceedings that followed, he was placed in nomination. An avowed candidate was in the field who prosecuted an active canvass on the spot, and this gentleman was successful by a majority of twelve votes. After the election Mr. Parkes was invited to a public dinner. He arrived at Braidwood late on Wednesday the 30th of March; and though the night was dark and rainy a number of gentlemen met him several miles on the road and accompanied him into town, where a crowd of about 200 persons assembled in front of the Doncaster hotel received him with three hearty cheers. The public dinner to which he was invited took place on the following evening, and the large room of the Doncaster was completely filled, not fewer than 200 gentlemen sitting down to the good things provided. The chair was occupied by James Rodd, Esq. After the usual loyal toasts, the chairman proposed " The Guest of the Evening and the True Principles of Parliamentary Government," which was received with much enthusiasm.]

SPEECH

Delivered at a public dinner given by the people of Braidwood, 31st March, 1864.

MR. PARKES said: He felt it difficult to find language to express his grateful sense of the reception he had received at Braidwood. He felt that he stood before them that evening under circumstances of a gratifying character, which very seldom occurred in the lives of public men. Either in the colonies or in the mother country it was not often that men engaged in political life received a compliment—he might say an ovation—in its nature and its significance like that with which they had honoured him. It was no uncommon thing for members of Parliament to be fêted by those whom they immediately represented, or by masses of men interested in some cause with which they were specially identified. It was no uncommon thing for Ministers of State in the zenith of their power and popularity to be banqueted in a national spirit by a grateful people. But it was a rare occurrence, and one that carried with it the most gratifying reward that a public man could receive for years of labour and sacrifice, to be drawn back as it were after he had retired from public view—not by those with whom he had been intimately connected, not by those to whom he had been personally known, but by a remote part of the community, all strangers to him, who have brought to bear on his character and conduct something of that scrutiny which is exercised in its complete justice by posterity alone—to be drawn back, and publicly honoured for services rendered years ago, which perhaps his opponents were beginning to hope were forgotten. He felt that in their generous reception of him that night he received no mere empty compliment, but a publicly avowed recognition of efforts he had made and of weary days and nights he had consumed to benefit the country. His labours might not always have been well directed—his best efforts might have been crowned with unequal measures of success. Indeed he was free to confess that his past public life, in his maturer judgment to-day, had not been without mistakes—perhaps serious mistakes.

> Vain was the man, and false as vain,
> Who said, were he ordained to run
> His long career of life again,
> He would do all that he had done.

He acknowledged that if he had his lost opportunities before him again he would try to use them in some instances more wisely. But still he believed the good people of Braidwood recognised, in their warm and generous welcome, the purity that he hoped had regulated his political life and the usefulness that as a general result had attended it. They did this in a way so spontaneous and unsought that instead of invoking jealousy it ought to be an encouraging assurance to others engaged in the toils and anxieties of political warfare, that public gratitude was not a mere figment of the imagination but a living principle of English society; which like all good seed repays the sower according to the amount of faithful labour he bestows upon the planting. A public dinner was a thoroughly English mode of testifying respect for a public man; and he for one did not wish to see this hearty custom

First Years of Responsible Government. 173

effeminated into a custom of pic-nics. These gatherings had their uses, and in English history they had been often made instrumental in giving new direction or new impulses to the public mind, and in accelerating important events. He did not for a moment believe that the gentlemen who had originated the present dinner had no object to promote by what they had done—no end which their meeting here to-night might tend to accomplish. In the first place, he understood this demonstration, in reference to himself, as telling him plainly that in the opinion of a large portion of the people of Braidwood it was his duty to do something more than he had lately been doing ; that in some way or other he ought to be more actively participant in the progress of the country. In the second place he understood it as meaning plainly enough that they were not quite satisfied with the state of political affairs at the present time ; that they wanted in some way or other—as Englishmen always wanted when politically dissatisfied—to find voice for their opinions and sentiments ; and that among other things they wanted to hear what he had to say. Well, he had to say that the men of Braidwood were noble fellows, and that the women could have nothing better said of them than that they were worthy of the men. But there were other things to be said. In some sense this was a trying and dispiriting time, but it was a period in our political history full of interest and instruction, and leading, although unperceived by the noisy actors of the day, to important changes in our condition. They might rest assured that political life with us was in a state of silent but rapid transition, and that before a very long time should elapse things lately done with complacency would be undone with general approval ; and names now conspicuous would be lost sight of, perhaps for ever. He did not however think it was a time to despair of the working of liberal institutions, or to doubt the ultimate triumph of liberal principles. But it was a time for men to pause and review the past ; to ask themselves as honest citizens whether all had been done for the best ; whether no pernicious extravagances had been committed ; whether no false standards had been set up. It was a time for men to inquire into the fitness of things, and to be satisfied that their strength, as a community endowed with all the immunities of freedom, was being wisely applied. He wished to speak to them as electors, and through them—if any words of his might reach so far—to the constituencies that lay beyond them. He was not there in a contested election; happily he had no foe real or imaginary to battle with him—no political party to attack. But as one who had laboured hard to extend their political liberties, and who was largely responsible for the present state of the electoral law of the country, he hoped he should be heard with indulgence, not only by those present but by others elsewhere to whom his voice might not reach. If the present Legislature were to be accepted without question as the natural fruit of the existing Electoral Act, he feared their reforms must be pronounced a failure, for a more mischievous and dangerous body than the Assembly as it now existed could scarcely be imagined in a free country—mischievous and dangerous alike from its inexperience, its self-conceit, and its utter want of self-respect and just sense of its duties and responsibilities. He knew it was the fashion to attribute this to the Electoral Act. He did not believe it. He would not say that the electoral law was perfect, or that it did not contain serious political errors. But he was satisfied that the admitted failure of the present Assembly was of itself no proof of the failure of the Constitution under which it existed, but was attributable to a variety of causes, some of them lying remote and not likely to be investigated or noticed by the mass of the community. The chief of these causes he thought rested with a class of gentlemen who were loudest in their condemnation of the existing state of things, inasmuch as instead of remaining at their posts and patriotically fighting out the "battle of the Constitution," which was inevitable on the introduction of responsible Government, they spiritlessly abandoned the contest when the first storm of popular displeasure rose against them. If they, like true English gentlemen, had kept their ground and fought on bravely through the struggle for power, the mere conflict of disciplined minds and the opposing of one set of principles to another would have preserved a higher standard of public life, and would have effectually repressed that low order of time-serving and shameless insensibility to the public interest which were the most conspicuous characteristics of the present Assembly. True, they might have been defeated in the House and on the hustings, but the defeat of to-day would have been followed by the triumph of to-morrow, and many men who were now encumbering seats in Parliament would never have found their way to a place for which they were so utterly unfitted. Another fruitful

First Years of Responsible Government. 175

cause of our present confusion was to be found in the conduct of the men who obtained possession of the high offices of Government by giving undue prominence to mere creatures of the hour, for the unworthy purpose of having their assistance as mere political creatures. These short-sighted Ministers were now justly punished by seeing their tools transfer themselves body and soul to the "new men," apparently without feeling a touch of shame in openly avowing that the only condition of their subserviency was the possession of power by their masters. Another cause was the very censurable apathy of many intelligent men in not recording their votes at the elections, and the profligacy of others who under any system of suffrage would be electors and possess influence, in jockeying the elections to serve temporary and selfish objects. And one cause of this unhappy state of things, interwoven with and influencing all other causes, was the immense patronage which had sprung up of late years, and which under any electoral system would have been sufficient to corrupt both Parliament and people. It was a most dangerous thing for any Government, whatever might be its theoretic form, to possess the amount of patronage enjoyed by the Government of this colony, and the large increase of this patronage consequent upon our coming into our political inheritance of self-government had never been sufficiently considered. Its baneful effects followed quickly upon our learning the art of governing ourselves, and had undoubtedly done much towards vitiating the current of political life amongst us. Before we joined in blaming our institutions for the excess of freedom they guaranteed to the people, we ought to reflect a little and think what would have been the excesses of the old order of Government if our rulers then had possessed the gigantic patronage of the present day. Or let us try to imagine what a Government with the same powers of patronage, the same powers of propitiating, intimidating, and silencing, would be likely to do if they had to deal with a close Legislature based on a narrow property suffrage. Did any sane man believe that a happier state of things would be the result? How were we then to remedy the evil? The remedy was in the people's own hands. Let men of property and intelligence mix with the people and take a steady and consistent interest in their affairs, and on all occasions afford them the teaching of example in the single-minded performance of public duty. Let the electors as a body learn to value the political trust confided to their keeping and to treat with a just contempt all who would wheedle them out of their rights for sinister ends. Let the men who fill the high offices of State enforce a higher standard of political conduct; and instead of tampering with members of Parliament and packing the Assembly with mere tools, let them boldly seek support by the soundness of their measures and the purity of their administration. The real power of remedying the evil was in the hands of the electors. A weak and mischievous Assembly might be brought into existence, but it could only live its little day. Ministries might rise and fall, but the electors remained the real masters of the political situation. It might sound strangely as coming from him, but he did not fear being suspected of subserviency to any particular class in advising them to be cautious in trusting their liberty to men newly sprung from amongst themselves, or to men who evinced too great an eagerness to secure their votes; but rather on all occasions let them select as their representative the true English gentleman if they could find him—the man who by education and association was alive to his own honour, and who valued his name and personal independence above the favour of any Government. In England there were gentlemen who held their simple names too high to be ennobled by the Sovereign. If they could obtain the services of a man of this stamp, cast in the mould of the immortal Hampden, their interests would be safest in his keeping. But they must be careful not to mistake the parvenu for the gentleman—they must have the real pearl and not the counterfeit. He had seen the results of the mistakes made by the constituencies in electing new and inexperienced men on the mere strength of their loud professions. These men were thus thrust into situations of importance for the first time in their lives; and when they got to Sydney they were pounced upon by Ministers and political manipulators, and in their ignorance and self-conceit they mistook the attentions that were only designed to wheedle them out of their votes for a kind of homage to their genius. Too often these loud talkers about the rights of the people, who had been too readily trusted by the electors, became the veriest of time-servers and sneaks. Instead of talking about narrowing down the liberties of the country it would be wiser to educate the people up to the proper exercise of their rights. In America there was a great law-book, *The Commentaries on the Constitution*, by Mr. Justice Story, an abridgment of which was used as a text-book in the public schools in order to instruct the rising generation in the duties of citizenship. Why should not we have a political text-book in our schools to teach our boys to understand the duties and to value the rights of a free subject? Let us extend our system of common schools, and make the range of instruction more comprehensive and useful. In connexion with the education of the people, he could not but express his strong regret at a recent Act of the Legislature which, without adding materially to the public revenue, must tend to impair the usefulness and limit the circulation of the public press. Even admitting that there was room for improvement in the character of colonial newspapers, still the newspaper was a powerful instrumentality in keeping up our civilisation in a country where the population was so scattered and the means of communication so difficult, and where the circumstances of daily life tended so much to rudeness and semi-barbarism. The newspaper was our great political educator, and political education was the one thing absolutely necessary to the successful working of our institutions. Let us for a moment try to imagine the moral eclipse that would suddenly darken this country if the two Sydney daily newspapers were stopped. Would life in the interior be tolerable under such a condition? If there were no means of knowing whether the Governor was dead or alive; whether the courts of law were sitting or not; whether the markets were failing or were well supplied; whether the Legislature was passing wise laws, or the members were locked up in the watchhouse. Why, life in the interior would be so irksome in such a state of things that half the inhabitants would leave it. And by imagining this extreme case they might see what, in a less degree, would be the consequence of this recent Act of an Assembly that was clinging to a feeble existence under a sentence of popular condemnation. If the consequence of this measure was to withdraw the light of the press only from a single family it would be a calamity, and one which it may be the duty of the Legislature especially to remedy, seeing that it was the duty of the Legislature to extend popular education. When lately in England he had paid some attention to the condition and character of the provincial press of the mother country, and he had no hesitation in saying that the colonial press need not fear a comparison with it. The Newspaper Postage Act would never have been passed if the Legislature had understood the true interest of the country. The constituencies must prepare for the general election, which could not be delayed beyond another year. The greatest and most interesting of colonial questions—the administration of the public lands—was not yet settled. Much had yet to be done to perfect the means of easy and secure settlement on the public lands, and to provide for the improvement of the interior of the country. And then the question of taxation was waiting for examination and readjustment, and a fiscal policy for the country had to be established. He had long held the view that the land revenue ought not to be applied to current expenditure, but ought to be set apart for the permanent improvement of the interior. It was not enough to settle men and women on the waste lands, but every means ought to be adopted to keep up their civilisation and to promote a healthy development of society. In settling the principles of taxation, while they provided liberally for the current expenses of government, they ought to take especial care that the expenditure was not in excess of their real wants, and that the public burdens were imposed equally upon the people and in no way tended to cripple the industry or impede the progress of the country. And let them not commit the mistake of fettering their external commerce. No man could be more anxious than he was for the introduction of new employments, for the implanting of new manufactures amongst them, for the opening of new avenues of industry in the country. The human organisation was so various, the capacity for usefulness was so different in different individuals that, as generation after generation arose, if their intellectual and physical strength were forced into only one or two broad channels of employment, the future nation must become degenerate. One boy had a turn for mechanical invention, another for commercial enterprise, a third had a love for agricultural life, a fourth for the study of law or the investigations of science, a fifth had a genius for the higher arts ; and unless they found means of affording congenial employment to all, their noblest resources as a civilised community must be in a large measure wasted. But anxious as they all ought to feel for improvement in this respect, they must not seek to bring it about by endangering their commercial freedom. Rather than resort to any unhealthy prohibitory or protective policy, let them adopt some judicious system of bounties for the encouragement of their infant industries until those industries could take root and exist on their own support. They were aware that he had lately had something to do with immigration. They had been told something about that on a recent occasion in his absence, and now he was here perhaps they would allow him to say something for himself. He did not know whether anyone there was opposed to immigration, but he believed a greater mistake could not be committed by the working classes than to suppose that the introduction of new population within just limits could be injurious to them. It was ridiculous to say that this colony, with a territory five times as large as England and Wales, was in a natural state with a handful of inhabitants fewer in numbers than the population of Manchester. The sooner the country was adequately peopled by industrious men and virtuous women the sooner would it arrive at a state of social happiness—the sooner would the enjoyments and the refinements of civilised society be within the reach of all. He for one however did not approve of the spasmodic importation of large numbers for the mere purpose of supplying the "labour market" as it was called, and thought that much temporary mischief arose from the system—or rather want of system—which was allowed to operate in our immigration of past years. If we could originate a system of voluntary or self-supporting immigration, it certainly would be the most beneficial in all respects for the colony. This was the object of the mission entrusted to Mr. Dalley and himself two years ago. It was an unreasonable thing to expect much from their efforts in the short time that was allowed to them. He was convinced that this mission had not been altogether unsuccessful; but whatever success might attend it, the results could never be traced by the public. Persons coming here in consequence of the efforts made by himself and Mr. Dalley would not arrive in immigrant ships or be announced in the *Government Gazette*. They would naturally arrive in small numbers and mix unobserved in the general mass of society; and many persons had undoubtedly so arrived. He noticed that a ship now in harbour, one of the line of the London firm with whom he and Mr. Dalley made arrangements for the conveyance of steerage passengers to Sydney, had brought to the colony twenty-five steerage passengers, and several persons with whom he communicated in England had called upon him since his return to the colony. He firmly believed that it would be greatly for the benefit of the colony to maintain a permanent agent in England to diffuse correct information respecting the colony, and to promote the emigration of those persons who had the means of defraying the cost of their own passages—a class of emigrants who would bring more or less of capital with their labour, and which consisted mostly of men of enterprising spirit and provident habits. He again thanked them for the great honour he had received at their hands. He was not there with any view to future events—he had no political object before him. Possibly he might never again occupy a seat in Parliament, and he had lived long enough and had been sufficiently cooled by experience not to be particularly anxious for that honour. But he hoped he might yet be of some use to the country, and they might be assured that their generous recognition of his past services would stimulate him to stronger exertions whenever opportunities presented themselves. He hoped this meeting would induce them all to act more steadily and consistently in the performance of their duties as citizens and in promoting the freedom and prosperity of the country.

PUBLIC AFFAIRS IN 1865.

SPEECH

Delivered to a meeting of the electors of Kiama held at Shell Harbour, August 10th 1865.

MR. PARKES said : He did not appear there so much to give "an account of his stewardship" as it was termed, as to explain his views on those political questions which were likely to come under the consideration of Parliament at the present time. Of what had been done in the session lately closed and the part he had taken in the proceedings, the public press had made them already acquainted, and it certainly was not within his present intention to take any trouble to place his conduct in a more favourable light than that in which the means of knowledge generally accessible to the public might place it. He had opinions of his own and he generally acted upon them without much regard to consequences, and he believed his constituents would not consider it an honour to be represented by any man who did not value his own political independence. He should make but slight reference therefore to his votes in the recent session. He had recorded his vote on nearly every question of importance that came before the House, and he was quite willing to leave those votes to speak for themselves. He did not expect that his conduct would meet with the unqualified approval of all who supported him, nor yet that the opinions of his warmest friends would accord with his on all occasions. The principal measures of the late session were the Felons Apprehension Act, the Stamp Act, and the Acts for imposing new Customs duties. He was ready to confess that he regarded the first of these measures with a very unsettled state of mind, and he could not envy those gentlemen who professed to deal with the matter without doubt or hesitation. What they called vigorous treatment, he took the liberty of calling recklessness. He was sufficiently imbued with the traditions of the past to make him fearful of touching any of the guarantees of personal liberty established by the common law and the jurisprudence of England. And the novel character of this measure—its fierce spirit and desolating provisions—awakened in his mind many reflections at war with his strong desire to support the Bill. It never entered into his imagination that such a measure would be considered on party grounds. On the contrary, he thought that if there ever was an occasion when it would be open to members of a deliberative body to act on their convictions as they might be modified by fuller consideration or larger information on the subject, such a measure as the one proposed afforded that occasion. He voted for the second reading of this Bill from an unwillingness to throw obstacles in the way of a Government charged with the responsibility of suppressing the monstrous evil of bushranging. After a careful examination of the arguments adduced against it and a reconsideration of the whole subject, he felt constrained to vote against the third reading, however much his course might subject him to attack, from a conviction that we were not justified in violating principles of high moment for the sake of an object that could not with any certainty be accomplished by the terrible provisions of that Bill. He maintained that the result had fully justified the doubts entertained by himself and others. There was no proof that this sanguinary Act had done anything whatsoever in the suppression of bushranging. Ben Hall and Gilbert were both shot in pursuance of the ordinary operations of the police laws before either of them had been outlawed under this Act, and Dunn was still at large, and of course harboured notwithstanding the frightfully penal clauses against harbourers. No doubt, thoughtless people would say that bushranging had been put down by this measure, but the facts when examined spoke for themselves; and if they were to admit the statement as true it would prove too much,—that the Government had asked to be armed with this extraordinary and un-English measure to enable them to get rid of two men. He next came to the Stamp Act, of which perhaps they had heard. It had been told everywhere and therefore the people of this district must be aware of the circumstance that the Government were next door to a dead-lock for want of money. When the Treasurer came down with his budget he was in a plight very much resembling that of a schoolboy who has got into a predicament where he is forced to disclose something very bad of himself. As the words came out of his lips the tears were all but coming down from his eyes, and he told the House with fear and trembling that he did not know what to do for money. There were many others in the same bad way it was to be feared. Well, as the Government must have more revenue, he voted for the plan they proposed for raising it by a system of stamp duties. It was right that the electors should know that in these money-measures the Assembly must either accept or reject the proposals of the Crown. Members could not substitute financial notions of their own for those of the Minister, and thus when the Minister told them that the public credit was at stake in their measures a great responsibility was cast on the Legislature. He did not much approve of this system of stamp duties. He feared it would be found very vexatious in its working and he expressed himself to that effect at the time, but he voted for the Bill from the case of necessity put forth in its support and he was there to take his full share of responsibility in assenting to it. There were some considerations too which induced him to assent to the Stamp Act on its merits. The public burdens hitherto had fallen very unequally on the different classes of society. The possessor of large properties and the man who only possessed a tobacco-pipe and pannikin paid the same rate of taxes, which was not just; and these stamp duties, objectionable as they were in many respects, would certainly fall principally on the classes identified with property. Still, upon mature consideration of the subject, he thought a system of stamp taxes was not suited to the circumstances of a new country, and the sooner a better system was substituted for it the better for all. But something else came after the Stamp Act. That wonderful financier, Mr. Smart, had a wonderful way of doing business. One morning when he thought the session was drawing to a close, he read in the newspapers that Mr. Smart was about to come down again upon us with a second budget. Two budgets in three months was enough to frighten us from our propriety. And sure enough Mr. Smart came down with two new Bills for imposing more burdens. He again pulled a long face and said he thought he had enough, but he found he had not. The first dip into the people's pockets was unsatisfactory, and he must dip again. We then had the famous Package Bill, which in its first inception imposed an equal duty on all packages of goods coming into the country, whether a case of gooseberries or onions from Tasmania, or a case of gold watches or silks from England or France. But the greengrocers rose up as one man, and the fruiterers moved in deputation upon the Treasury. It was represented that the gooseberries coming in one day would spoil before the Customs could be moved to permit their landing on the second, and the great gooseberry interest was too much for the Minister. The Government could not stand up against a cargo of rotten fruit and vegetables, and so gooseberries and other articles of colonial produce were exempted from the operation of the Bill. But the Package Act as it now stood levied the same amount of duty on a parcel worth ten shillings as it did on a parcel worth £500. Then there was another Bill for increasing the duty on all articles then dutiable. He had from first to last opposed both these Bills. He based his opposition on the ground that this bit-by-bit plan of submitting the financial measures of a Government was foreign to the parliamentary practice of England, and ought not to be tolerated. But if this objection had not existed he should have opposed these measures on their merits, as about the rudest and clumsiest ever devised by any Government. He should now with their permission say a few words on the present state of things, and the public questions presenting themselves for consideration in the future. The present condition of the colony demanded an earnest and honest investigation of the causes of the prevailing depression. And this was clearly the duty of the politician. Men who undertook the responsibility of interfering with the public interests beyond the province of the ordinary duties of the citizen were clearly bound to free themselves as much as possible from prejudice, to close their eyes to consequences affecting their own individual interest, and to endeavour to bring whatever ability they possessed to bear faithfully on all questions which they had power to influence. But at a season of popular discontent like the present, when it was felt on all hands that the affairs of the State were seriously disordered and the forces which were available for giving us strength as a community were in a large measure misused or lost, it specially behoved public men to do their utmost in justice to themselves and to the public to discover why we are passing through this period of unnatural adversity, and then endeavour to supply the natural remedies. How was it that 400,000 people of British origin, in free possession of a territory capable of sustaining a population of 40,000,000, and in a land abundantly blessed with all the natural elements of wealth, were nevertheless in a condition of commercial stagnation and suffering, in some respects positively worse than that superinduced by the accumulated mismanagement and improvidence of ages in older countries? This could not be the normal state of things. The colony had suffered heavily of late years from the visitations of Providence; but neither failing crops nor floods nor droughts were sufficient to account for the long-prevailing depression that spared no branch of industry and seemed to afflict the most valuable classes with the greatest severity. In this working-day world of ours the most valuable thing—and viewed in its true light the most honourable thing—was human labour; and in a new country this precious attribute of man which dimly reflected Divinity itself in its creative power, ought to find endless employment. One could not travel through any district of this colony without seeing a thousand things which required to be improved by human labour. No man possessed houses or land which would not be rendered more valuable if more labour were expended upon them. No man occupied any position which subjected the forces of nature in any degree to his control who would not be able to improve that position if he had more labour to assist him in his operations. And yet the fact could not be explained away that in this rich and extensive country, occupied by a handful of population, and where of all precious things labour was the most precious, and of all the things wanted labour was most wanted, there were men willing and able to work who had great difficulty in finding employment. This was one of the strange and startling facts of the present time. Could it be that there were too many industrious men in the country—that we had too much of what we most wanted? No man not very ignorant nor absolutely insane would say that such was the cause. The cause was to be found in the defective nature of our industrial machinery and our economical agencies. In every occupation of life our energies were impelled by a too speculative spirit, and the idea of permanency had not sufficient hold of the mind. Our aims were too extravagant and our efforts in consequence were to a great extent spasmodic and self-exhaustive. A colonising population had a natural tendency to waste its strength in this direction, constantly striving to grasp too much and constantly missing the true end of all exertion—that secure possession of a sufficiency of earth's blessings which, tempered by repose and enjoyment, constitutes happiness. Everywhere we might see objects commemorative of this waste of life; houses built in inaccesssible situations, works begun to remain unfinished, traces of enterprises that started to life on the wildest calculations and failed. These ideas of extravagance and this misdirection of energy infected the Government as well as the people, and the consequence was that in proportion to these fruitless efforts the productive power of the community was lost. If we could not find employment for all our able-bodied men at the present time, it was that we had not properly employed them in times past. Human labour rightly directed would multiply the demands for its continued exercise. But the Government was not free from blame in our misfortune. An enormous public debt had been created, the interest of which was draining the life-blood away from us, and the money thus raised had in too many instances been lavishly and wastefully expended. Scores of examples might be given where this had undeniably been done. At the present time they were pulling down the building used as the General Post Office in Sydney. Only a few years ago a large sum was expended in the erection of an ornamental front to that building, and not more than three or four years ago a new Telegraph Office was built adjoining to it, with a great deal of ornamentation in front. All of this was sold the other day for a mere song—less than the price of the stones. Surely the Government might have looked ahead three or four years and saved the country some of this expenditure. This was only one instance out of a hundred. He would take another of quite a different kind, and one close to their own doors; he meant the harbour works at Kiama. He believed a very large sum of money had been thrown away upon those works, and that the works when completed would not be of so much value to the place as a far less costly work might be, while the less costly work would have been completed long ago and the inhabitants now enjoying the benefit of it. The evil did not stop with the wasteful outlay of public money. All the labour which had been thus wastefully consumed if it had been directed to productive pursuits would have added to the riches of the country instead of making it poorer. In like manner every policeman and every Government clerk taken into the public service beyond what was clearly necessary was not only a wasteful drain on the revenue, but an abstraction of so much muscle and sinew from our producing power. The business of men in a colony was to colonise. The sudden acquisition of political power in this country had produced one enormous mischief—it had deadened our love of hard work. In other words it had done something to weaken the spirit of self-dependence among the people, and there were now too many eyes in all ranks of life turned in the direction of the public service. It was said by English economists that the army and navy were kept up to a war-footing for the purpose of finding employment for the younger branches of the governing families. In these Australian colonies there was already too much reason to fear that the Government departments would be unduly extended for the purpose of finding employment for the friends of members of Parliament and leading politicians. We were in great danger of being too much governed. The male adults of our population could not be more than one-third, and 130,000 or 140,000 men could not endure many thousands of rulers. Somebody must do the work necessary to keep us together as a community, for we should not keep together long if we were all Ministers of State, police magistrates, clerks and policemen. Those classes who went on doing the work would act wisely by seeing that there were not too many set over them to keep order whilst they did it. He had admitted that there was a want of employment partially felt at the present time, and yet he contended that we wanted nothing so much as an increase of population. The general force of circumstances in a young country always tended to precipitate population on the capital. Dislike of the rough solitude of the interior, not less than love of the bustle and popular excitement of city life, helped to crowd the city, and the chances were more frequent than in old countries for persons of limited means to gratify their desire of gain by embarking in branches of business which only flourished in thick populations. The goldfields in our case had aggravated these tendencies, and nothing but a steady stream of new population would rectify the social derangements that now existed, to say nothing of that sustained growth of people which was necessary for the progressive development of our resources and our gradual elevation into a nation. Immigration was the life-blood of a young country. But this immigration, if promoted at the public expense, ought to be placed under conditions consistent with the welfare of the immigrants themselves as well as with the interest of those already settled in the country, and ought to be regulated with sufficient wisdom and foresight not to cause "gluts in the market," if he might employ such words on such a subject. And something more than this was wanted. The greatest care possible should be taken to see that the immigrants were of a class likely to succeed in colonial life. The present system so far as it went secured in some measure the first of these conditions, but it certainly gave no guarantee that the immigrants would be the kind of persons best suited to the work of colonisation. Now if they turned their eyes to other British colonies, they would see that matters were managed better than with us. In Canada for example some 20,000 immigrants were received in 1863. Of these between 7000 and 8000 were male adults; and this number of men are thus classified in the public returns :—2198 farmers, 3147 labourers, 2098 mechanics, 10 professional men, 28 domestic servants, and 203 clerks and traders. These figures gave us the thews and sinews of a colonial population. The nationality of these 20,000 new comers was stated to be as follows :—4830 English, 5508 Irish, 3949 Scotch, 3047 Germans, and 2085 natives of other countries. So far as we could form an opinion from a statistical view of the question this was a healthy stream of immigrants, in which the principal colonising nations of the old world were fairly represented, and of which the great producing ranks of society constituted nearly the whole. He was in favour of an entire revision of our system which should embrace the selection by our own agents of such persons from the agricultural class and the useful trades of the three kingdoms as could find a portion of their passage-money. He entertained no doubt whatever that a sufficient number of the very pick of the United Kingdom might be found to absorb our immigration grants, and men who by supplementing those grants from their own resources would make the money go much further. And who could doubt but that if we had a steady influx of population of this character the beneficial effect would soon be felt in the increase of the producing classes of the country and the general progress of settlement? At present we had too large a proportion of the population cooped up in Sydney and the other large towns, trying to live by any means rather than productive employment. Who could doubt that if the large tracts of fertile land on the Murray which would be open to free selection in January next were all taken up by new comers, the colony in all the elements of material prosperity would be vastly benefited by this increase of its population ? This brought him to the land question. The pastoral tenants of the Crown were striving hard to obtain a firmer hold of the public lands. They were now powerful in the Legislature, they were powerful by the advocacy of one portion of the press, and they were powerful by the support of the banks and the other great monetary institutions of the country. No doubt they would fight a desperate battle, for the prize to be contended for was magnificent in its magnitude. He denied entertaining the slightest enmity towards this great interest, and he had many personal friends among the squatters; but he had no hesitation in saying that they occupied a position so peculiar, in which the interests of individuals were so obviously opposed to the interests of the public at large, that they required to be watched with the utmost jealousy and vigilance. When their claims were again put forth, as no doubt they would be, he for one should keep his eyes on the other interests of the colony which had few advocates, as he knew the squatters would be sufficiently cared for by the powerful support which they were able to command. What we had to do in their case was not to grant them more protection, but to guard the general community against their attempts at infringement. He was prepared to support in their integrity the Land Acts framed by Mr. Robertson, and passed into law under the auspices of that Minister—at least for a period sufficient to give the system they embraced a fair and intelligent trial. He did not look upon the Acts as perfect pieces of legislation, and very possibly a system might yet be introduced which would tend to promote the settlement of the country more satisfactorily and rapidly, which ought to be the great end of all legislation on the land question; and he was inclined to think a measure of the character of the Homestead Act of the United States would be a great improvement. But the Land Acts of Mr. Robertson were in force, and the system had already produced the most hopeful results. He fully shared in the public gratitude that was felt towards that Minister for the beneficial policy he had introduced, and if any attempt were made in the ensuing session to interfere with that policy he should be found its consistent supporter. He felt that he was addressing men who took a higher view of the duties and responsibilities of a member of Parliament than to regard him as a mere delegate to attend to their local wants. Though he was returned to Parliament by the district of Kiama, he had to assist in passing laws for the whole people of New South Wales, equally for the residents at Wagga Wagga and in the city of Sydney as for his own electoral district, and he could not consent to be sent into Parliament on any condition subversive of this national character of the trust reposed in him. He knew that the intelligent men of this district understood and appreciated this as well as he did himself. If his conduct in this capacity, independently pursued according to his own judgment, and by an honest use of what little knowledge and ability he possessed, was acceptable to them, and secured to him the continuance of their confidence, he should esteem it a great honour, and should endeavour to show his sense of it by a faithful discharge of his public duties. The post of a representative could not be held with honour on any lower conditions.

THE WORKING OF FREE INSTITUTIONS.

SPEECH
Delivered at a public dinner given by the electors of Kiama,
August 15th 1865.

Mr. PARKES said : He could not profess inability to find words to convey to them his sense of the warm and generous manner in which they had drunk his health, because the simplest words would be the best to express his feelings on such an occasion. He knew this gathering represented the district. He saw many gentlemen around him who from their character and intelligence enjoyed largely the respect of their neighbours, and who at considerable inconvenience to themselves had come many miles to be there that evening, and he felt very sensibly the high compliment paid him in making his visit to the district the occasion of this representative gathering. But he was not vain enough to assume that any personal consequence attached to himself in this movement in this quiet community. He believed the independent men of this happy and prosperous district had made his visit the occasion for celebrating in this true British fashion their adherence to the progress of liberal principles. That was a phrase often on the lips of public speakers, and it was used so vaguely that it often meant almost anything and sometimes nothing at all. But a great master had lately taken upon himself to define what was understood by " liberal principles." Some three months ago Mr. Gladstone had defined liberal principles to mean " the principle of trust in the people, only relieved by prudence," and the opposite to it as " mistrust in the people, only relieved by fear." He accepted this definition, and he asked their attention for a few minutes to a brief review of the last nine years to see what the success of liberal principles had done for this colony. It had multiplied the fields of industry, it had spread intelligence, it had increased the comforts of the homes of the people, and in every condition of life it had largely added to the conveniences and the elevating influences of society. What man was there amongst them who thoroughly knew the state of things under the old system of Government, when we possessed none of the parliamentary privileges of freemen, who would not admit that the country had been greatly benefited in all that related to our social condition by the introduction of Responsible Government? But let them examine the Statute-book of the colony and see what the actual legislation had been since they had enjoyed the privileges of governing themselves. They had planted municipal institutions among the people, securely rooted and with prosperous growth. The powers of local management thus extended among the people had been zealously and beneficially exercised, and while innumerable public improvements had been carried out successfully, the available talent of the different districts had been trained and accustomed to the duties of self-government. They had passed Acts for opening the public lands, and promoting the settlement of an agricultural population in their vast interior, and let any unbiassed mind institute a comparison between the results of their present land policy and the state of things which previously existed, and it would be seen at once how great an improvement had taken place, and how hopeful were our prospects for the future. We had effected a great change in the electoral law of the country, conferring the right of the suffrage on all men of whatever condition of life who were settled amongst us. Many other measures wisely conceived, and sound and liberal in their scope and tendency, had been passed by the legislature. And let it be admitted for the sake of argument that we had been too precipitate in some of these Acts, and had gone too far in our liberal tendencies. Could it be reasonably expected that we should commit no blunders in the great task of governing ourselves, to which we were so suddenly called, and for which in a great measure we were so unprepared? Was it reasonable to expect us to do better than the great people in the old country? Coming into possession of our political birthright so suddenly, after so long a period of disfranchisement, with all the powers of Government conferred upon us as it were in a day, and with our new Legislature necessarily composed of men for the most part little accustomed to employ their minds on questions of Government and subjects of State policy, it was a matter of surprise that we had committed so few blunders, had manifested so much wisdom, and had so clearly comprehended the course of public duty. But how stood the case in comparison with the political state of things in the mother country? Our elections were free from the disorders and riots, and untainted by the bribery and intimidation, which unfortunately still disgrace Parliamentary elections in England, and when the fastidious political moralists of the House of Commons—Mr. Lowe and his sympathisers—pointed with affected scorn at us, they should recollect the flimsy glass-houses in which they live themselves. From what he had said on other occasions during his visit to Kiama they would not understand him to approve of all that had been done in working out the free institutions. On the contrary, he freely granted that, in his judgment, many mistakes had been committed, much had been done which might have been more wisely left undone, and much public mischief had arisen as a consequence; but he maintained that the general result was a great success such as ought to make them prize the blessings of the political liberty they enjoyed, and that ought to invigorate their efforts to improve their institutions and consolidate them on a sound liberal basis, as the best means of ensuring the happiness and prosperity of their country. People of a British origin, in whatever clime they live, must be free to be prosperous. If in the course he had taken during the last few years his humble efforts had contributed to the great end he had feebly sketched as the one to which the exertions of all ought to be directed, he should be amply rewarded by being permitted to hope that year by year they would make a nearer and still nearer approach to the great end of enlightened government—human happiness. As their representative in Parliament he should endeavour, by bringing what little knowledge he possessed to bear on the public business, by exercising his judgment with independence, and by acting fearlessly in the course he believed he ought to take—he should steadily endeavour to advance the cause of true liberalism in this country, not being ashamed to retrace his steps when he found himself in error nor afraid to meet popular displeasure when he believed himself to be right. He had great faith in the judgment of the popular mind as ultimately pronounced, but he was fully alive to the broad fact that popular opinion often erred and often committed acts of temporary injustice. Edmund Burke was rejected by the people; Lord Macaulay was rejected by the people; and, still later, Richard Cobden was rejected by the people whom he had served so well. But in all such cases the people, when they came to understand the error they had committed, were eager to make a generous atonement. Lord Macaulay was carried back to Parliament by the repentant electors of Edinburgh with a unanimous triumph; and Mr. Cobden, who had availed himself of his release from the labours of public life to recruit his health in a foreign country, returned to find, as he planted his foot on his native soil, that he was again a member of Parliament and a Cabinet Minister. But in one respect affecting men engaged in political life, popular opinion was an inexorable taskmaster—it was never satisfied with the past. Men engaged in literature might safely rest on their reputation if they succeeded in producing one great book, and happy it would be for the fame of most authors if they were so content to rest. In like manner the successful soldier might rest on his laurels, if good fortune favoured his rest, and still enjoy an undiminished fame. So also might the competitors in the other great walks of intellectual activity. But year after year the public demanded from the prominent politician renewed pledges for their continued confidence, and if as time wore away and his strength became impaired he relaxed in his exertions, they only remembered his former services to point the sharpness of their rebuke of his present inactivity. For the active politician to stop in his career was to commit political suicide. He was fully sensible of the hard conditions of the life he had entered upon as their representative, and he did not shrink from the consequences. It might be that he should consider it his duty to take a public course which would subject him to their disapproval; but should the time unfortunately arrive when he might lose their political support, he hoped the independence of his conduct would still entitle him to their respect. He desired above all things that in matters of this kind they should all exercise their own independent judgment on his conduct. He should never shrink from any public scrutiny; all he asked was that he might be treated justly, and that a fair interpretation might be put upon his public acts. One word on the state of things in which he should be soon called upon to take an active part. They would recollect that when they did him the honour of first electing him last year, the Government was in the hands of gentlemen* who were now safely removed from power. He had contributed his efforts to remove those gentlemen from the seats of government. Their Administration was now a thing of the past and might be referred to somewhat in the light of history, and certainly he had no wish to speak harshly of any of those gentlemen. He was ready to admit that in his judgment their intentions were in the main honest, but from first to last in their Administration they displayed an utter inability to comprehend the conditions of power—a lamentable want of a true understanding of the interests of the country and the character and genius of the people. This was the only title of men to govern a free country, and this thorough understanding of the nation was the secret of the eminent success of Lord Palmerston. Well, another Government† had been formed under circumstances favourable to the construction of a vigorous Administration. But was the country satisfied—ought it to be satisfied with what had been done? He believed the present holders of office, when Parliament reassembled, would have to take a course very different from the course pursued hitherto, and would have to produce measures very different from their measures of last session, to prove to the satisfaction of the Legislative Assembly and the country their capacity to deal with the difficulties of the time. He should be prepared, however, to give a fair support to the present Administration, hoping that their conduct of affairs would justify the continuance of his support, and he acknowledged that he should not hesitate to strain a little rather than risk the possible chance of a return to office of such statesmen as Mr Geoffrey Eager. So far as he was concerned, he desired no higher position than being the freely chosen representative of one of the happiest and most intelligent constituencies in the colony. He felt no small degree of satisfaction in the circumstances giving a distinctive character to this representation. The two gentlemen now near him, who formerly represented Kiama, were both men of such personal qualities as made it an honour to be their successor. Their excellent friend in the chair (Mr. John Marks) had brought the weight of a very high character and no mean ability to bear on the business of legislation, and Mr. Gray was the son of one of their oldest and most respected residents, had grown up amongst them in their esteem and confidence, and was unquest-

---

* The first Martin Administration.
† The Ministry formed by Mr. Cowper in January, 1865.

ionably a gentleman of ability. He was afraid there were constituencies which from caprice or some other cause had elected members whom it would be no very attractive distinction to succeed. He was proud of his constituents, and he hoped he should be able to pursue a course which would make them not ashamed of the association of his name as their member. He hoped he should be privileged to contribute in some limited degree to a course of political life in the country which would preserve the purity and increase the stability of their institutions, promote the cause of popular instruction and intelligence, and tend to the permanent prosperity of all classes and their gradual elevation into a great and happy nation.

AD VALOREM DUTIES.

SUBSTANCE OF SPEECH

Delivered in the Legislative Assembly, December 20th, 1865, on the motion submitted by Mr. Cowper to impose a duty of 5 per cent. *ad valorem* on imports.

MR. PARKES said that when the hon. Chief Secretary submitted his resolution, amidst the rather noisy cheers of the House, he thought the hon. gentleman must have felt rather uncomfortable. At all events there were heard most distinctly amidst those loud cheers two separate sets of voices. There were the cheers of self-gratulation and rather pardonable exultation on the Opposition side of the House, amongst the late Ministry and their friends, who had succeeded in imposing their protectionist views on this Free-trade Government; and there were the insolent cheers of an unintelligent triumph on the other side—the triumph of the successful double-dealing and manœuvre of their slippery chief. But this kind of thing was only a thing of the hour, and there would come a sober time of reckoning even if they were successful to-night. If he could have been induced by any considerations, in view of something less desirable that might be substituted, to have given his vote for doubling the tea and sugar duties, he certainly should have been prepared to have voted for doubling those duties rather than for the proposition that had been made to-night. But he certainly could never have been induced to do that, because it did not follow that if this thing was intolerable we should accept something that was scarcely less tolerable. He did not wish to misstate the arguments that had been urged either for or against the proposition; he did not wish to mislead the sense of the committee. He was fully aware that the arguments, whatever they might be worth, against the proposition submitted by Mr. Samuel, the hon. member for Wellington, were based upon what were conceived to be an inequality in the incidence of taxation. But quite a different class of arguments rose up against such a proposition as this. Here we have a proposition for increasing the burdens of the country in a manner that, even if it should be successful in raising the trifling sum estimated, would carry with it derangement and injury to the infant commerce of the country in all its branches. Any interference with that very tender and important branch of the public interest—the intercolonial commerce—was to be deprecated in the strongest possible terms. And all this was to be done for the purpose of raising £130,000 ! Because, after listening with the greatest attention to the hon. member for West Sydney (Mr. Joseph), he was much more inclined to take that hon. gentleman's estimate of the probable revenue from these new duties than that of the Collector of Customs. Large deductions would have to be made for the free list, and for the large amount of goods trans-shipped to other parts of Australia ; and there would also be large deductions by reason of the system that now obtained of overvaluing the imports, which of course would prevail no longer. He would call attention to the remarkable speech by which this proposition was submitted. A great deal was said to us about schemes of retrenchment, but these schemes were indicated in such dim phraseology, and were propounded in such a hypothetical way, that scarcely any hon. member could expect to see them carried out. Then there was something said about an income tax. But how was it that there was no promise of bringing in such a tax? All that was said was that it might be desirable to see whether the House would consider the propriety of giving their support to an income tax. But there was no mistake whatever as to what the hon. gentleman said about the *ad valorem* duties. They were submitted all ready to be crammed down the throats of the people because it was known that on the Opposition side of the House there were certain gentlemen who could not do other than vote for these duties. Did any hon. member believe for a moment that, if these *ad valorem* duties were passed, there would be any great pains taken to make reductions in the public service, or that any serious attempt would be made to introduce an income tax? But we were asked to swallow this nauseous dose of *ad valorem* duties, surrounded as it was by a coating of promises of the most vague and dim character. Were the committee prepared to accept these *ad valorem* duties ? Let it never be forgotten that the whole of the members who sat on the Government side of the House who

Ad Valorem Duties. 199

had seats in the late Parliament opposed the very same proposition as this when brought forward by the Martin Ministry. Let it never be forgotten that the Free-trade Association movement was based upon direct opposition to this kind of taxation; and were the hon. members who were returned under the auspices of that Association prepared to support the Government in this proposal, after having opposed their predecessors when proposing precisely the same policy? If they would really do that, then farewell to all consistency in public life in this country. Would either of the hon. members (Mr. Caldwell or Mr. Neale) have been returned for East Sydney if they had avowed to their constituents their intention to vote for a 5 per cent. *ad valorem* duty? He was perfectly satisfied that neither of those gentlemen would have been elected upon that avowal. This scheme was brought down by a Government that only twelve days ago introduced a scheme of a precisely opposite character. Surely the hon. member for Wellington did not continue to hold office as Colonial Treasurer until his successor was appointed. He felt certain that the hon. gentleman would never have thought of submitting such a scheme as this. Was it right that he should sanction such downright political profligacy as there was in the bare proposal of this scheme? What could be more profligate than to go before a constituency professing one set of principles, and within twelve-months after—without publishing any recantation—to support a measure based on diametrically opposite principles? Could the credit of the country be sustained by such legislation as this? Confidence in the affairs of the country would be restored when the affairs of the country were managed by men who recognised political principles. He was at a loss to know how gentlemen engaged in commerce could support this scheme. He had been accused of having expressed views in favour of Protection, and he would take this opportunity of making some remarks upon that accusation. Whatever his views were six years ago, as expressed in bringing up the report of the committee of inquiry respecting the condition of the working classes, and whatever interpretation had been put upon those views, he still entertained them. He maintained that if there was any new product or manufacture by the pursuits in connexion with which a large number of persons would find employment and the colony be largely benefited, the fostering of that product for a time would be perfectly justifiable. These *ad valorem* duties would not confer any benefit of that kind, but they would be a source of great annoyance and loss to those who had embarked their capital in commercial pursuits. Why should these gentlemen have every £10 worth of their property subjected to the interference of perhaps some drunken Custom-house officer? The duties would not do any permanent or appreciable good whatever. Our intercolonial commerce was one of the most valuable things we had, and this would be seriously damaged by the imposition of the proposed duties, for it would be impossible to obtain drawbacks on many articles. By far the greater portion of this trade was made up of broken packages. With the existing competition a large amount of trade was carried on at a profit of not more than 5 per cent., and under these proposed duties the importer would have to sink an amount of duty equal to the profits on his trade. The result therefore would be that the trade of this infant city would be destroyed. He maintained that to raise revenue in this way would be madness. The statesmen of England, before introducing any new measures of taxation, first considered what effect they would have upon the commerce and prosperity of the country. It was not simply how they could raise revenue that they considered. They knew that even if they raised millions of money but inflicted an irremediable injury on the country, no amount of money would compensate for the wrong. But here all at once this monstrous measure was brought forward, and all considerations of the trade and prosperity of the country were forgotten. He could not believe that there was any necessity for this scheme. We should not rise in the estimation of the people of the mother country by these wild schemes. After seeing what the House did last week, and what it would probably do to-night, they would say that we were a Chamber of madmen. He voted against the former propositions for reasons amply sufficient to his mind, and he should vote against this also, but from entirely different reasons, which yet to him were amply sufficient. He understood that at the meeting of the private friends of the Premier some promise was given or implied that along with the *ad valorem* duties there would be a proposition for imposing direct taxation. He was also told that it was understood that a small percentage of duty would be proposed. But these were only specious delusions. Feeling so strongly opposed as he did to the scheme, he could not move an

Ad Valorem Duties.

amendment with a view to any modification; and he should not feel it his duty to raise his voice again if a majority of the committee thought it their duty to agree to this scheme. He protested against the proposed duties as unsound in themselves, and on the ground that they were not justified by the necessities of the time, but were calculated to inflict a greater injury on the country than any revenue derived from them could possibly counterbalance.

THE BORDER DISTRICTS.

[MR. PARKES, then Colonial Secretary, being at the town of Yass, received an invitation to visit Albury, which after some hesitation was accepted. A deputation consisting of the Mayor and one of the resident magistrates met Mr. Parkes with a carriage and pair at Wagga Wagga, and drove him from that town, a distance of ninety miles, to Albury. At Eight Mile Creek he was met by an escort of the townspeople, consisting of ten carriages and about twenty horsemen, and conducted into Albury, then across the Murray into the colony of Victoria, and back to the Exchange Hotel. At three o'clock there was a general meeting of the inhabitants at the Court House, when addresses of welcome were presented to Mr. Parkes from the Municipal Council, from the inhabitants of the district, and from the German vine-growers. The banks and places of business were closed on the day of Mr. Parkes' arrival, and in the evening he was entertained at a public dinner. The following was his reply to the first address.]

SPEECH

Delivered in reply to an address of welcome from the Municipal Council of Albury, May 15th, 1866.

Mr. PARKES replied as follows:—Mr. Mayor, members of the Municipal Council, and gentlemen. If I should fail to find language sufficiently adequate to express my sense of the very warm reception you have accorded me, you must attribute it in part to my little expectation of such a demonstration. I can only return my kindest acknowledgments, and assure you I duly appreciate the kind and generous feelings which dictated this reception. On receiving this address from the municipal body whom you have chosen to represent your interests, it will be most convenient for me to reply at length on the several topics introduced, instead of replying in detail to each of the other addresses which I understand are to be presented. The same questions are touched upon in the address from the people of Albury; but I am quite sure the citizens at large will take it in good part if I

The Border Districts.

reply to their municipal representatives. The great grievance brought under my notice as a member of the Government—and I admit it is a grievance—is the imposition of Customs duties on colonial produce crossing the frontier. I call it a grievance, because it certainly appears to me to be a result in the enforcement of the law which is vexatious and oppressive. This is the only grievance touched upon in the address which assumes a constitutional character, and I think the people of Albury have fair ground to stand upon in requesting its redress. You have settled here, you have bought land, you have established households, you have converted the wilderness into a garden, you have raised produce by your honest industry, and that produce has found a market in a neighbouring colony—a much larger market it appears than exists on this side of the boundary. It is impossible to trace out the causes which operated to bring about this result of which you complain; but it is sufficient for me and for the Government to know that you have found a market in a colony subject to another Government, which Government imposes a duty of 3s. per gallon on the main produce of your district. I can easily see how destructive this must be to your interests, and I repeat that the existence of such a state of things is a great constitutional grievance. But I wish to call your attention to the fact that this grievance does not arise from any new action of our Government—that it is not a special grievance arbitrarily imposed upon your district in particular. Certain Customs duties were established in each colony, chiefly with a view to obtaining revenue from the commerce of the seas. Probably not a thought of the effect of these duties upon land boundaries was entertained when the tariffs were under discussion. But when these duties came into force they were in time found to operate in unforeseen quarters in a way that was not anticipated. One duty cannot be levied in Melbourne and another in Belvoir, and the question arises, in what way can the remedy be applied? The Constitution Act, which gives us the right of dealing with our lands and revenues, imposes the obligation that we shall not do anything at variance with the legislation of the parent country, which, as you are aware, prohibits differential duties. Therefore no power exists to relieve you by a lighter and exceptional duty, but the Constitution Act in no way prevents us from entering into an arrangement with

Victoria to allow colonial produce to pass the border free of duty. As a colonist I say we should at once enter into such an arrangement, and as a Minister of the Crown I will use whatever abilities I possess to represent this matter fully and fairly, both at Melbourne and to my colleagues and to the Legislature. As regards the Circuit Court, I am inclined to think the Supreme Court should be carried to every important district. This sentiment I did not come here to express. I expressed it years ago in a very different place. I was not favourable to establishing the District Courts, because I could not see how there can be two qualities—a first quality and a second quality—of justice. I was inclined to think, and think still, that the wiser course would be to carry the superior Court to every district in the colony. No pains and no cost should be spared by any Government to secure the completest administration of justice, and to obtain the services of the ablest men for the judicial bench. I will not say I will go back to Sydney and immediately take steps to procure the opening of a Circuit Court in your district; but I say your claim is a fair one, and if you persist in it I have no doubt it will be recognised. As regards an amended Municipalities Act, I may say it is the intention of the Government to introduce a Bill for the better government of municipalities. This will be not a mere amending Bill, but a comprehensive measure of reform.

[Some other matters of merely local interest mentioned in the address were referred to, and Mr. Parkes then proceeded.]

I have gone through the list of your grievances, and am glad to find them so shadowy. There is only the one grand grievance, the taxes on your produce. In coming to this district, although it had attracted my attention for years, I was most agreeably surprised. Had I not seen it I should never have known what a glorious land you possess. Perhaps I may be pardoned if I say that years ago, as a public journalist and as a Member of Parliament, I strongly supported your interests by advocating the formation of a main trunk railway to the Border. At all stages of that question I have never been silent, and I have always urged that it was a grand mistake to undertake three lines simultaneously. Seeing that only 130,000 or 140,000 souls contribute to the progress of the colony as producers, it appears enormously burdensome to undertake three railways at once. It always appeared to me best to concentrate all our energies on one main line. But if I had known what a beautiful district extends between Gundagai and Albury, so eminently designed to sustain the industries of a thriving population, I should have redoubled my efforts. Ever since I have taken an interest in questions affecting the public, I have realised the possibility that my influence might be felt in localities distant from where I exercised it; and I have therefore kept myself perfectly untrammeled by local predilections. I have been bound by the limits of no district; I have known no sectionalism. I have felt that a community cannot be too united, while its industries and its productions cannot be too varied or even too contrary in many respects. Thus your vinegrowers are more favourably situated by having extensive mineral and pastoral country in their vicinity than they would be if the whole country was capable of producing only the same thing. But our resources are so varied and so extensive that we could almost exist without communication with the rest of the world. We are so capable of producing corn in one place, wine in another, the raw materials for clothing in another, minerals for the metal manufactures in another, that we have a much greater chance of growing into a happy, prosperous, and great people than if the country was exclusively mineral, exclusively pastoral, or exclusively agricultural. At Sydney we have one of the finest harbours in the known world, and when I look at the natural wealth of the interior, when I see the fat of the land, I cannot but admit that the sterile tract of country around Sydney seems designed especially to point out that the produce must come down from the interior to employ the shipping in that magnificent harbour. Sydney is all the better for having this fine back country so productive of wealth ; and the back country is all the better for having a rendezvous for commerce like Sydney. I am happy to find you apparently so prosperous. If I understand you rightly, you favour the view of still belonging to the old colony, and I am glad of it. But I say you must be justly dealt with. You are entitled to have at least the amount of your land revenue spent upon your roads and other improvements. For years past I have been opposed to spending a single shilling of land revenue for any other purpose. We are unworthy of the great country from which we are sprung if we cannot support the civil government of the country by taxing ourselves. The land is the inheritance not only of the present people, but of future generations; and it is our duty to see that this inheritance is handed down unimpaired and not unnecessarily encumbered. This can only be done by laying out the produce of our land sales in improving the country. I think an outlying district like this is not only entitled to a fair share of the revenue, but something more. We should do all in our power to make the inhabitants of such districts feel that they are not separated in their affections from the Government. Gentlemen, again I thank you for your cordial welcome. I shall not fail to represent to my colleagues what I have seen and heard, and I shall do so in the common interests of the whole country. The Government has no object in view superior to doing what is beneficial for the colony at large. For my part, I should not value office if I could not do something to raise my own reputation and character. I always regard official position as a prominence which exposes a person to the public gaze, and unless such person possess a fair share of ability and that public confidence which integrity only inspires he must fail, and the prominence to which he has attained will only expose more glaringly his want of capacity. I would not hold office a single day unless I felt I was capable of doing something for the good of the country—unless I had resolved to know no friend, no district, no sect, in carrying out my public duties.

SUBSTANCE OF SPEECH

Delivered at a public dinner given by the inhabitants of Albury, May 15th, 1866.

MR. PARKES said: It is the characteristic of the Anglo-Saxon race to propagate the principles of freedom and progress wherever their steps are planted. The great people of which we form part had been designated by an eminent man, "the English-speaking nation," as that people is now rooted in every quarter of the globe, carrying its institutions and its language to the uttermost ends of the earth. One of the institutions of this nation, and he believed a good one, was to be found in its public dinners. This was a peculiar but a great institution, which often

The Border Duties.

produced results of the most beneficial character. It might be that the banquet that evening would serve as a link to attach and draw closer the older parts of the colony to the newer and more distant. He ventured to express a hope that the trouble they had taken and the pains they had gone to in procuring his attendance would not be altogether fruitless. On one matter, he might state that a week before he left Sydney he had a conversation with the head of the Government, Mr. Martin (not knowing at that time he himself was likely to visit Albury), on the subject of the apparent greatest cause of their complaints—the Border Customs. His colleague and learned friend then expressed his earnest desire to have this important question satisfactorily settled, and on his return to Sydney he trusted that he would be able to do something to help in that direction. He saw that they stood on the borders of a country, young comparatively, but destined to be great hereafter: they looked across a narrow stream to a younger country, destined also to become great, and they naturally felt annoyance and discontent that they could not convey their produce across that narrow stream to the nearest market. The people here had already designated their town the Border City, and it was scarcely possible to estimate its future importance. It was quite possible that it might become the seat of a Federal Government, and might acquire a lasting eminence in Australian history. When they looked around and saw the elements of happiness and greatness they possessed, they might well be pardoned for entertaining bright anticipations of the future. He had been delighted with his journey to Albury. They had supplied him with a comfortable carriage, good horses, very fair horsemanship, agreeable companions, and he hoped the journey would not only be one of pleasure but of instruction. He had often wished to come so far to make himself acquainted with the capabilities of the district and the characteristics of its inhabitants; and he might say, now that he had met them, that he had never seen a fairer country or a finer people. With regard to what they required of Government, he feared he could not promise everything. That Government was always the best which interfered least with the interests of the several classes of the population, and that session of Parliament was in the main the best which passed the fewest laws, if those laws were only good ones. A Government in a young country should interfere as little as possible with the operations of industry, and avoid all action savouring of a paternal and patronising Government; the very perfection of free and good government consisted in letting people alone to do the best within the reach of their own capabilities for themselves. They had an example of a paternal Government in Russia, but that was not what was wanted here. No doubt the Government of a colony like this had a highly-responsible task to perform in the alienation of the lands. They had cast upon them a duty in this respect very different from that of the Government in the mother country. There the alienation of the land had taken place centuries ago, and he believed it was a fact that in the island home of which they loved to speak with so much delight the soil was in the hands of half a million of persons, leaving twenty-six and a half millions without an inch of land to call their own. Here the duty—and it was a solemn duty—of alienating the lands required greater capacity for legislation than was often demanded in the affairs of older countries. Everything came from the land; it was the great element of existence, and the task of alienating the virgin soil of a young country was one of the highest that could be conceived. So far, under Responsible Government, they had no cause to be ashamed of their advance; upon the whole the colony had become a better, a happier, and a more cultivated community. But still there was a great deal to be done, and, unless the constituencies did their duty in sending proper representatives to Parliament, they could not expect good government. They should set a high value on the rights of citizenship, and return only honest and independent representatives, otherwise government would cease to be pure, sound, and vigorous. He should return to Sydney with a lasting recollection of the district and its resources. If he should ever be permitted to visit them again, he fully anticipated he should be surprised by still greater manifestations of progress and by a fuller development of the great advantages with which Providence had so abundantly blessed them.

VISIT TO MUDGEE.

[IN May 1866 Mr. Parkes received an invitation to visit the district of Mudgee, but his engagements did not permit him to make the journey until the beginning of July. On his arrival he was enthusiastically received. He was entertained on the 3rd at a public dinner by the principal residents of the district, and on the following evening at a second public dinner by the working classes. The following is the substance of speeches he delivered at these entertainments.]

SUBSTANCE OF SPEECH

Delivered at a public dinner given by the magistrates and other residents of Mudgee, July 3rd 1866.

MR. PARKES said : I have read somewhere or other, though I don't know where, of a blooming young maiden who had a bashful deaf and dumb lover. A number of her associates who had more experience than she, took her to task and asked her how she could think of tolerating his addresses. She tried to write the alphabet on the carpet with her toe, and at length simpered out, " Joseph cannot express himself, but I am sure his intentions are good." I must say that the position I hold this evening is very similar to that of the deaf and dumb lover. I cannot express my deep sense of the honour done me this evening by an assemblage where the wealth and intelligence of the district are so worthily represented. But if I cannot express myself, my " intentions are good." And when I take into consideration that these cordial greetings have not come alone from one section, but from the bulk of the population, I think I may without exaggeration term my visit a public triumph. I am not vain enough to assign this cordial welcome to personal merit. I am not vain enough to attribute it to any particular merit of the Administration to which I have the honour to belong ; but I do attribute it to a cordial feeling of love for established authority and the organisation of

Responsible Government as the embodiment of the will and power of British people. I accept it as such, and I believe that the present Government will to the best of its judgment and understanding advance the general interests of the country; that it will do all that lies in its power to educate the rising generation, and to encourage the settlement of the country with an industrious and virtuous population. In coming into this fine district I can hardly believe that there is any desire on your part that I should visit your district merely to learn what are your particular local wants, but rather that its capabilities and resources should be thoroughly understood. You desire that your riches should be known in other parts of the country, and by the Government of the whole. I came here under the firm conviction that it is the duty of rulers of such a country as this to try to understand its various wants and capabilities. I did not come with the idea of gratifying local advancement at the expense of the whole, but to understand this one district as part of a whole country that I am called upon to assist in governing. Though my visit is short, I hope it will prove to be not wholly without instruction, and that I shall go away with a more practical knowledge of the country, and able to contribute more effectively and justly to the relief of general wants. In the several districts of the colony the people should learn to co-operate with each other; each class should discriminatingly appreciate the importance of every other class, each interest the importance of every other interest. It is only by the union and harmony of industrial efforts that a nation can hope to be sound-hearted and prosperous. Be the day sooner or later, this colony will yet be a distinctive nation. We have to-night drunk the health of Her Majesty. No man in the colony has a stronger feeling of loyalty than I have, and to none will I yield in my admiration of the illustrious qualities of our Queen; but as surely as the sun will rise to-morrow so sure am I that ere long this colony will be a free and independent nation. This is as clearly foreseen by British statesmen as any other of the great political developments during the last fifty years were foreseen; and when the event shall have become a matter of history, it will be found that it is as much to the interest of England as to the interest of the colonies themselves. But why do I foreshadow this event while the population of the colony is not more than that of Manchester or Glasgow? I refer to it because it should impress

Visit to Mudgee.

upon all those who have social and political influence the duty of laying sure and deep the foundations of the future nation. It devolves on all ministers to keep in view this great eventuality, as in this regard their duties are not less lofty than those of English statesmen; for, although the interests in the mother country may be greater and more varied, still the path is more broadly defined. We in a comparatively infant country have to mark out our own pathway and to set up our own landmarks. Therefore, although it may appear presumptuous, I would exhort all, in whatever capacity, to do their utmost to bring together the elements of a robust and independent national character. Do it by finding out the best industrial appliances to develop our natural sources of wealth. Contribute to education by all possible means, and use every possible influence to give the best direction to human energy. Let all do something towards forming a state worthy of the mother country. Much has been said in disparagement of our institutions. But it is in the nature of things for individuals to underrate the advantages they see under their own eyes. There has been much captious criticism respecting the management of our affairs. Now, could we only turn up the records of the English Revolution, we should find that the very same terms of abuse had been applied to the actors in that great drama of history. Turn to the life of Washington, and we should find that the patriot and statesman whom the universal voice of posterity has assigned a place among the highest was during his lifetime assailed by every species of calumny. I will venture to say that more improvement has been spread through the country and has permeated through all ranks of society since the inauguration of Responsible Government than there did during the whole period previous to its existence. I have now been long enough in the country to speak definitely on this point. I was here when the first representative form of Legislature was established in 1843, and I have watched its course attentively since, and the advances of the last ten years in moral and social improvement supply an ample vindication of the wisdom of free institutions. I shall leave the district of Mudgee fully impressed with its importance. You know you have a land flowing with milk and honey, and you are proud of it. I think you are all the better for knowing this, and being determined to assert its importance. But my advice to you is to endeavour to do what you want for yourselves. I find that my friend Mr. Dalley, whose silvery laugh is easily detected, is inclined to put a different construction upon my words to what I mean. I say, do what you want for yourselves, and by this I mean, if you see anything you are entitled to, do not sleep over your claims and rights. Agitate! agitate! Impress on the minds of the Government the justice of these claims, and do not rest until you get it recognised. If you sleep, you will never gain your object. It has been said by the wise man of old, "Put not your trust in Princes;" and I say, "Put not your trust in Ministers." If you have a good cause, never rest till you succeed. If you have a grievance, insist upon its. redress. That is an Englishman's advice, and I give it to Englishmen. I thank you for your kindness, and in return I wish you prosperity. If you only understand aright the interests of the country, you will find that there is no richer land under the sun. Regard it as your motherland, and cherish it with the affection of brothers. Do this, and you will eventually make it the pride and admiration of the civilised world.

SUBSTANCE OF SPEECH

Delivered at a public dinner given by the Working Classes of Mudgee, August 4th, 1866.

MR. PARKES said: I can assure you I hardly know what to say, or how to acknowledge the proud distinction you have conferred on me on this my first visit to your town and district. I believe I am right in regarding this entertainment as emanating from the great body of the people. I notice that in the public announcement it is called the Working Men's Demonstration. If, therefore, I address myself to that class, it must not be supposed that I have any intention of slighting any other. I consider it a special honour to-night, to be entertained in this sumptuous manner by the class who support themselves by their daily labour. I am willing to attribute it to anything but my own personal merit. Still there is something in this entertainment of a peculiar character. Yesterday I was entertained by the leading members of your community, and I take this as a mark of extraordinary distinction that it is made an object of emulation on the part of two sections of the community as to which shall honour me most. I am sure I only interpret your feelings when I say it does not arise out of any feeling of antagonism—that there is no class-conflict in this rivalry of welcome. I have already said in a public gathering in your town, and I say it again, that I fully appreciate the value of the labouring classes in every English community. I hold nothing more sacred or honourable than the labour of an honest man. I hold that there is a divinity in hard work. Just in proportion to a man's capacity for work does he possess the control of the destinies of the world. A man who can rise two or three hours before his fellows every morning will ascend above the level of his fellows in the social scale. The most illustrious of our fellow-countrymen, the statesmen who by the magnitude of their performances and the profundity of their wisdom made themselves not only objects of admiration but authorities for all time, have on all occasions frankly and eloquently acknowledged the value of the working-class as the foundation of all other classes. It has only been shallow minds, unable to comprehend the great producing power of society, that have undervalued it. How could it be otherwise? Without that class which Sir Robert Peel said was "the foundation of every other class," neither the privileges of property nor the elegancies of culture could exist. The working-classes of England may justly boast that the most illustrious characters among poets, statesmen, and the conquerors of the material elements of the world, have sprang from them. A few generations ago a new world was opened in America on British principles. It was founded on the peaceful principles of industry and commerce. Yet when a terrible time of war came it was found able to sustain one of the most gigantic struggles ever known. One of the wisest men among the founders of that great republic was a journeyman printer—Benjamin Franklin. Again one of those conquerors of space, who have made known to us rich divisions of the globe which were unknown to our forefathers, went forth to discover new lands, and among others he discovered that on which we now stand. He was the son of a farm labourer—the illustrious James Cook. In our own day, we have had a new era in the facilities of locomotion; wings have been given to civilised communities by railway communication. This revolution has brought about mighty changes in all the relations of society; and who was the pioneer of all this but a poor labouring man?—George Stephenson. Without instancing other cases, have we not all seen in the labouring-class their admirable thrift and common sense; the timely intercession and delicate help of those who are continually assisting each other? Look at the Lancashire co-operative scheme, brought to its present state of perfection entirely by the wisdom and foresight of working men. In Rochdale there is now established an almost princely establishment, a benefit to four-fifths of the whole population, and managed entirely by bands of artisans —managed, I say, with judgment, integrity, and ability not exceeded by any other class. No one need be ashamed of being a working-man. It is the non-working man that needs to be ashamed. If there is an unworthy object in the world it is the non-working man—the man who rises late and consumes the day heedlessly and unprofitably to himself, and who lays his head on his pillow at night without the reflection of having performed a single generous act or done one useful thing to lull him to sleep. I am one of those who think that hard work is necessary to give happiness. Some may inherit great wealth, but they cannot be truly happy without hard work. Those who have enjoyed the advantages of wealth have at varous times been the hardest workers. Perhaps it is a condition of property and honour that a man should work, for if we find a man of property habitually idle, or a man in a place of distinction giving way to self-indulgence, the chances are that he will pass away like the grass of the fields. It is only by using opportunities that we can hope to be happy ourselves, or confer happiness upon others. I hope that my visit to this district will not be without some beneficial effect. It is not for me to say too much, or make promises that I may not be able to fulfil; I can simply say that if it should be in my power to serve your interests without sacrificing those of the country, I will to my utmost do so. I have noticed several things during my tour through the district, and you will pardon me for referring to one of them. I cannot understand why the houses of the poor men should have so few comforts about them. I should like to see more attention paid to the small comforts of daily life. I should like to see the cottages surrounded by small flower-gardens; to see trees planted and more attention paid to those little natural elegancies which have so great an effect in bringing out the finer feelings. You live in a rich and fertile district;

Visit to Mudgee.

there is none richer under the sun. You have a fruitful soil and a healthy climate. Your condition of life is as free as possible. Why, then, not endeavour to be as comfortable as possible? One great defect of Australian habits is overlooking the common advantages of daily life, without which it is but barren and to a great extent miserable. Men only look to sleeping and feeding. Life loses a great portion of its elevating influence unless the gifts of Nature are cherished and enjoyed for the sake of beauty alone. I have often thought it a great mistake to neglect small industries. It is not quite wise to simply depend on growing wheat or potatoes and the produce of a cow or a pig or two. A number of other things might be introduced by which a man would make himself more comfortable and respected. Instead of the unsightly bark huts with little about them but broken bottles or old tin cans, we might see pretty cottages from one end of the country to the other; and would not such a picture have a more elevating and refining influence upon our children? Better for them and better for the parents! Depend upon it that we are laying the foundations of a nation, and whether it is to be one of first or inferior rank rests with ourselves. We can't escape our destiny. We are the forerunners of generations that shall be reckoned by millions of dwellers in this splendid territory, and we need to look well to our efforts and their contributive influence in the formation of our national character. Remember that you are all answerable for good or bad government. Every man possesses the franchise, and if Government is not what it ought to be the fault lies with yourselves. You are the fountain-head of power. No Government or Parliament which does not represent you could exist if you rightly understood your own power. There is no hope for a country except by an incorruptible exercise of the franchise. We may have an incompetent Administration or a corrupt Parliament, but if the constituencies were only pure they could not last for a single day. If a country is corrupt in the exercise of the franchise it is impossible to foretell the evil that may overtake it. The present Administration is composed of men who are mostly well known, and who for one reason or other have, I believe, enlisted the public confidence on their side. I think I may say they have no desire for power unless by its exercise they can be of advantage to you and the country. For myself I can say that, whether I am a member of a Government, or simply a member of Parliament, or a private citizen, I will ever labour so far as I can to promote the education of the country and its settlement with happy homes. I know of no higher duty before us than to devise some better means of education. Situated as we are, with a widely scattered population, it is incumbent on us to devise some measure for the extension of the means of education to every corner of the land. If parents are not alive to their own responsibility and will allow their children to grow up without any education, we cannot be surprised if the fire in their young blood finds a vent, or if, removed from the better influences of society, they turn out offenders against law and swell the roll of bushrangers. To prevent crime we must enlighten the people. Better have schoolmasters than gaolers; better schools than gaols. The honours and distinctions of this country are open to all, and no man, however humble his lot, may not hope for his son to attain the highest position. There are no obstacles in the way of advancement; therefore hold fast by your institutions and transmit them to your children as their proudest inheritance. I have seen your district and enjoyed your hospitality, and I can only say that I shall ever remember the cordial reception I have received, and will do my best as far as I can to serve you.

PUBLIC EDUCATION IN 1866.

SPEECH

Delivered in the Legislative Assembly on moving the second reading of the Public Schools Bill, September 12th, 1866.

ON the Order of the Day being read by the Clerk,

Mr. PARKES rose and said: Mr. Speaker, I beg to move that the Public Schools Bill be now read a second time. The subject to which I desire to invite the attention of the House is, as I think it will be admitted on all hands, one of surpassing importance. My best apology for undertaking to deal with it is that it is no act of individual presumption on my part, but a duty that devolves upon the office I hold. In addressing myself to the question, I am sincerely anxious to temper my own opinions with the results of experience, and to meet the opinions of others with consideration and respect. I am sensible of the many difficulties that surround the question—that must surround it at all times—and in view of those difficulties, the actual state of the country, the necessities of the rising generation, and the duty incumbent upon the Government to do something for the purpose of extending the means of instruction to those who now do not possess them, I have undertaken this duty. I am equally sensible that I shall not be enabled to deal with it in a manner that will be satisfactory to myself or the public unless I am supported by the attention of honourable members. The attention which might not be due to myself is due to the subject under notice; and I trust I shall receive the indulgence of honourable members, though I may be compelled to detain them at greater length than is my custom. I think it will be advisable, before going to the immediate subject with which we have to deal, to glance at the progress of education during the last half-century in other parts of the world. Up to the beginning of the present century education—what is known by the term "Popular Education"—had scarcely taken root in the civilised world. In our own country, as we are all well aware, the most barbarous laws existed. Men and women were tried for their lives, and condemned to the forfeiture of their lives, for what are now considered almost trivial offences; men were hanged for stealing a sheep, and young girls were hanged for stealing a few yards of calico from a shopkeeper's counter. Yet, contemporaneous with these savage laws, statesmen held the opinion that it was dangerous to instruct the people of the country. That opinion prevailed in the mother country until a comparatively recent period; and even now I believe men in positions of authority are still of opinion, though they do not often express it, that it is dangerous to diffuse education too widely among the people. If it be really a duty to educate the whole people of a state, I think it must follow that that duty devolves upon the Government of the state. There are, I am aware, men of very considerable influence in the present day who, though strong and zealous advocates of education, yet maintain that the Government ought not to interfere in the work, which should be left exclusively to individual exertion. Now, unless it be admitted that it is the duty of the Government to undertake this work of education, I feel that I shall have a very poor cause to bring before the House; and I prefer stating the argument in support of the Government undertaking what is called popular education, or in other words the education of the whole people, upon some higher authority than my own. I shall therefore trouble the House with the argument advanced by a man whose name is an authority in all departments of knowledge, and especially a weighty authority on this question of education. I will read what Lord Macaulay urges to prove that it is the duty of Government to educate the people. The short passage I am about to quote contains the gist of his argument in support of the view that this duty devolves upon the Government. Speaking in support of resolutions submitted to the House of Commons, he says:—

"This, then, is my argument. It is the duty of Government to protect our persons and property from danger. The gross ignorance of the common people is a principal cause of danger to our persons and property. Therefore it is the duty of the Government to take care that the common people shall not be grossly ignorant. And what is the alternative? It is universally allowed that, by some means, Government must protect our persons and property. If you take away education, what means do you leave? You leave means such as only necessity can justify—means which inflict a fearful amount of pain, not only on the guilty but on the innocent who are connected with the guilty. You leave guns and bayonets, stocks and whipping-posts, treadmills, solitary cells, penal colonies, gibbets. See then how the case stands. Here is an end which, as we all agree, Governments are bound to attain. There are only two ways of attaining it. One of those ways is by making men better, and wiser, and happier; the other way is by making them infamous and miserable. Can it be doubted which we ought to prefer? Is it not strange, is it not almost incredible, that pious and benevolent men should gravely propound the doctrine that the magistrate is bound to punish, and at the same time bound not to teach? To me it seems quite clear that whoever has a right to hang has a right to educate. Can we think without shame and remorse that more than half of those wretches who have been tied up at Newgate in our time might have been living happily—that more than half of those who are now in our gaols might have been enjoying liberty and using that liberty well—that such a hell on earth as Norfolk Island need never have existed—if we had expended in training honest men but a small part of what we have expended in hunting and torturing rogues. I say, therefore, that the education of the people is not only a means, but the best means of attaining that which all allow to be a chief end of Government; and if this be so, it passes my faculties to understand how any man can gravely contend that Government has nothing to do with the education of the people."

It seems to me that the argument thus briefly stated by this celebrated man is conclusive that it is the right and the duty of the Government to take in hand the education of the people. I have just said that popular education belongs to the present century. It is a reflection upon our great country that this cause first took root and first spread its luminous power in other countries of Europe—for instance, in Prussia, Holland, and in the northern nations of Norway and Denmark. In the last-named state, of which so little is known, it took root and diffused its influence among the people at a much earlier date than in our own country, and it has effected its work much more completely there than in Great Britain up to the present day. In Denmark it may be said that the whole of the children of the country are instructed. As far back as 1817, the population being then 2,000,000, the pupils were 278,500 against some 300,000 children at that age when children ordinarily go to school. So far back as this, the proportion of uneducated children of the age at which they usually go to school was exceedingly small. In Holland, as we all know, one of the most complete systems, probably the most complete system of popular education in the world, came into existence at the beginning of this century, and has been making steady progress up to the present day, till it has, as it were, embraced the whole population. The state of education in that country affords so much instruction to us, that I beg to be permitted for a short time to bring it under the special notice of honourable members. The largest portion of the population of Holland are Calvinists, the next largest Catholics, and the next Lutherans; but throughout this century the children of all these churches in Holland have been educated in the same schools. So far back as the great education law of 1806, it was laid down that all disputable points of doctrine should be avoided in education, and that law and the famous education law adopted by Prussia in 1819 have been spoken of by a distinguished French philosopher as the noblest monuments of public education ever raised in the world. Education there has been going on with almost uninterrupted harmony among the different religious sects, and indeed, instead of differences widening any breach between these religious sects, a law was passed about three years ago amending the education statute of 1806, so as to render the whole of the education of Holland, both primary and secondary, of a purely secular character. In 1806 the Government of the Netherlands issued an address to the heads of the various religious bodies inviting them to come forward and take upon themselves the duty of imparting religious instruction to the children in the schools, and stating in plain and distinct terms that the Government intended especially to exclude religious education by the teachers. They invited in this express manner the heads of the various denominations to come forward and assist in the education of the children by giving proper religious instruction. This invitation from the Secretary of State, addressed to all the Synods of the Reformed Church and to the prelates of the Roman Catholic Church, runs thus :—

"THE SECRETARY OF STATE FOR THE HOME DEPARTMENT.
" To all Synods of the Reformed Church, both Dutch and Walloon ; Consistories of the Lutheran Church, Remonstrants and Mennonites, and Prelates of the Roman Catholic Church.

" Gentlemen—The great importance which the Government attaches to primary instruction in this Republic cannot have escaped your observation. None of its duties are held by it in higher estimation. May the improved establishments for education yield, under the divine blessing, the fruits which they seem to promise ! They will arrest the progress of immorality in our native land, and the pure principles of Christian and social virtues will by their means be implanted and nurtured in the hearts of future generations. It cannot be doubted that such at least is the most ardent wish of Government, and its chief aim in the improvement of the primary schools. In the decree of the 3rd of April last, concerning primary schools, that intention is made manifest by the clearest evidence. The school is not viewed as a means of conveying useful knowledge only, but is established as a powerful auxiliary in the improvement of morals.

" Upon the same principle, the Government expects that you will give your support and assistance to these educational establishments, and invites you by the present communication to employ your powerful influence for that end.

"There is one especial part of the education of the young in which the Government claims your co-operation, namely, their instruction in the doctrines of the different communions.

" You must be well aware that throughout the whole extent of our country there has hitherto hardly existed a single school in which the master has given a properly regulated religious education. Religious instruction in the schools has gone no farther than to impress upon the memory of the children and make them repeat the questions and answers in some catechism. There was, however, no ground to expect more from the master, for several reasons. Although the Government indulges the hope that the newly established schools will lead to the salutary result, that a regularly organised system of instruction in the Christian religion, in so far as concerns the historical parts, and Christian morals, will be gradually introduced ; but in the present state of things it does not consider itself entitled to impose an obligation upon the masters to teach the doctrines of particular sects.

" If Government has thought it necessary on that account to separate instruction in particular doctrines entirely from ordinary teaching in the school, it does not attach less importance to the duty of providing that the children shall not be deprived of that instruction ; and therefore, having full confidence in your good dispositions to promote these salutary ends and the welfare of the young, Government has considered that it could adopt no measure more effective than to address the different ecclesiastical bodies in this Republic, and to invite you, as I now do by this letter, to take upon yourselves the whole religious instruction of the young, either by properly arranged lessons in the catechism, or by any other means. I shall be glad to learn what measures you may adopt—whether they are to be new, or the revival of former methods.

" As you will doubtless consider it important to communicate the contents of this letter to the different ministers of the congregations within your several jurisdictions, I request you to inform me what number of copies you wish to have for that purpose ; and I conclude with commending you to the protection of the Most High.

" (Signed) " HEND. VAN STRALEN."

Now the whole of the heads of the different religious denominations of Holland replied to this address of the Government by undertaking the duty. I will quote one of these replies ; that from the head of the Roman Catholic Church is in these terms :—

"Sir—In reply to your communication of the 30th May last, which I had the honour to receive on the 10th instant, I have the honour to state, that as good schools cannot but produce the most desirable results in preparing the young for the exercise not only of social but of religious virtues, there cannot be a doubt that all the ministers of the different religious communions in general, and those of the Roman Catholic persuasion in particular, will attach the highest interest to the measures which have been or may hereafter be taken by the Government for that object, and that they will consider it a matter of duty to co-operate on their part, as far as it is possible for them to do so.

"I request that you will supply me with sixty copies of your letter, that I may distribute them among the clergy of the church to which I belong.

"The Roman Catholic clergy will most willingly undertake to instruct the children in the doctrines of their religion, and will teach them the catechism in the churches on such days and at such hours as shall be considered best suited to the circumstances of their respective parishes; and I shall communicate on the subject with the priests who are under my jurisdiction. I embrace the present opportunity to take the liberty of calling the attention of your Excellency to a circumstance deserving of notice.

"Sunday is the only day, especially in rural districts, on which religious instruction can be regularly given to the children of labourers and artisans; but an abuse which becomes more and more prevalent throws a great obstacle in the way of the efforts of the clergy—working on the Lord's Day becoming more and more general among all classes of the people. Artisans of all descriptions frequently work in public on Sundays, and if notice be taken of it they excuse themselves by saying that a refusal on their part would be followed by a loss of employment; others follow the example, and thus a large number of children are cut off from religious instruction.

Now as in all Christian communities Sunday is consecrated to religious instruction and religious duties, and most assuredly the clergy have ample need of that day to teach the young, and especially the lower orders of the people, it is to be wished that Government should adopt some effective measures to facilitate the duties of the clergy in this matter, and to eradicate the evil I have just pointed out.

"I pray you, Sir, if possible, to bring the subject under the paternal eye of the Government, in order that it may be attended to.

"I have, &c.,

"J. VAN ENGELEN, Chief Priest."

"Mannsen, 13th June, 1806.

This occurred in the year 1806, and from that time to the present, this system of education, so happily established in Holland, has gone on progressing from year to year, until it has overcome all sectarian impediments, and embraced the whole of the rising generation. I have before me a work by an eminent man in the mother-country, published only a few months ago, which gives some account of the present state of education in Holland, and I will read a short extract from this book to confirm the statements I have just made. It will be known to honourable members that the state of education in Holland is perhaps better understood by the English people than that of any other Continental nation. At different times men of intellect and character have visited that country to investigate the state of education there, and their valuable reports have explained it with lucidity and truthfulness to every part of the world. The great naturalist Cuvier was one of these, the great philosopher Victor Cousin was another; the popular English writer William Chambers visited Holland for the same purpose some years ago, and later still that eminent scholar Mr. Matthew Arnold was despatched by the Committee of the Privy Council to ascertain the facts under the stamp of authority. The opinions of these men are widely known, and they place the education of that country beyond all misconception or doubt, and with great fulness and clearness before the world. The Home Secretary of State in 1857 stated the principles of education as carried on in Holland in these words:—" 1. Culture of the social and Christian virtues; 2. No dogmatic teaching given by masters; 3. It respected all beliefs, and inculcated a spirit of tolerance and charity." Now what I have said of the state of education in Holland so far, applies in a special manner to primary education, to elementary instruction. The secondary schools and the universities were reported by the distinguished men whose names I have mentioned as not in so satisfactory a state. But in 1863 a law was passed so amending the great law of 1806 as to apply the same principles to the secondary schools, and at the present time the whole of the education of that nation is secularised and entirely freed from sectarian incumbrance. I hold in my hand a book by Mr. Grant Duff on Continental politics, published in the beginning of the present year. This book explains in a few words the nature, character, and condition of these secondary schools of Holland; and as the character of most of these schools as they are here classified is new to the Australian public, and as they seem at the same time to offer excellent models for our imitation, I desire to read Mr. Grant Duff's description of them. There are four classes of these secondary schools :—

"The first, a school with a two years' course for those who were to live by some handicraft, trade, or by agriculture, taking up their education at the point where the primary school stops.

"The second, a school for boys who desire a good, but not a learned education. In this class are two divisions :—
"A. The school with a three years' course
"B. The school with a five years' course."

Thus we see how this graduated system of secondary schools is carried out so as to fit every man for his calling, and to enable him to apply his faculties in the best manner in performing the special duties of his daily life. The writer proceeds :—

"The third, or Polytechnic school, which is intended for those who mean to devote themselves to the higher walks of manufactures—engineering, architecture, and the like. The fourth, or Agricultural school, intended for those who desire a thorough knowledge of that science, which since the decline of Dutch commerce in the last century has made immense progress in Holland, and is—now that Dutch commerce is reviving under the happy influence of free-trade—advancing alongside of it to new victories in the wide heaths which occupy so much of the soil of the Netherlands, and contrast so painfully with the riches of those districts of the country with which travellers are most familiar. All these various schools are strictly superintended by the Government, and—enthusiastically supported by an intelligent people—are working admirably. We need hardly add that the whole system found bitter opponents in the same section which is opposed to religious and to political progress; nor need we mention that no attempt is made to discourage private efforts for the establishment of other secondary schools on other principles. As a matter of fact, many such exist, though few of them we believe have much merit. It is only just to say that the staunchest and most celebrated Conservatives in the Netherlands speak, as we know from personal experience, with good-natured pity of the antique and barbarous system which still disgraces our most famous schools."

The system of education in Prussia is very similar to the system in Holland; but on the whole I believe it has not been so successful. But in Prussia a few years ago, when the population stood at 14,000,000, there were 22,910 schools and 27,575 teachers, which gave one teacher to 78 scholars. One very important point for us to decide in this discussion is the number of children who may be safely entrusted to the teaching of one man. In the kingdom of Prussia, with its 14,000,000 of persons and 22,910 schools, the average was 78 children to every teacher. There were at this time children from five to fifteen years of age—that is, of the school age—2,830,328, and of these 2,830,328 children there were 2,289,727 receiving instruction, leaving only 540,601 who were not attending school. At the present time—according to this book on the state of the Continent—there are in the Prussian army, of the power and prowess of which we have lately had signal examples, only four recruits in every thousand men who cannot read, write, and cipher. In the great empire of France education is very much behindhand. It is, I fear, even worse upon the whole than it is in our own country, although the French have made prodigious efforts of late years in the cause of popular education. The same principles of education as are in operation in Holland and Prussia have been introduced into France, and it is hoped that in a few years they will produce results highly gratifying to every enlightened mind. A few years ago there were 2,654,492 children attending school in France, and there were at the same time 4,800,000, or nearly double that number, who were receiving no education at all. I now come to the mother country, where the progress of education has not been such as ought to give us any strong feeling of satisfaction. I consider that the Privy Council system—which I take leave to say is no system at all—has proved to a great extent a notable failure. I think I shall be able to show that it was only devised by the eminent statesmen who brought it into existence as a make-shift, with the hope that in the course of time something like a general system would be brought forward and receive the sanction of Parliament; and that the Privy Council scheme itself was never intended to be anything more than a machinery for dispensing the Parliamentary grants devoted to education. Small grants were given by the Imperial Parliament for the purposes of education so far back as 1833, but they were so small as to appear insignificant even beside the grants of money devoted to the same purposes by the Parliament of this country. These grants were handed over by the Treasury to the school societies of the time and expended without any effective supervision, without any real discretion in the manner of their disbursement, and it was the dissatisfaction arising from the improvident and uncontrolled expenditure of these insufficient grants of money that induced Lord John Russell and Lord Lansdowne to originate the mode of disposing of the money by the Committee of the Privy Council. The first grant I think was moved by Lord Althorp in 1833, when £20,000 was voted for England and £10,000 for Scotland. When it is borne in mind that this Legislature voted the magnificent sum of £80,000 for public education this year, the early English grants appear insignificant—I might almost say paltry—taken in connexion with the educational necessities of the United

Kingdom. These grants, as I have just stated, were very improvidently and unsatisfactorily expended. There was no proper authority to expend them; there was no proper supervision exercised over the expenditure, and the dissatisfaction felt by the Government of the day led to the institution of the Committee of the Privy Council on Education. At the time the first of these votes was passed by the House of Commons, the population of England amounted to 14,314,102. There were in the country children from three to fifteen years of age numbering 4,294,230, but the children then receiving instruction in England did not amount to more than 1,276,947, leaving 3,017,283 between the ages of three and fifteen without instruction of any kind. The Committee of the Privy Council on Education began with a comparatively small grant of money, but this went on increasing in magnitude till in the year 1849, ten years afterwards, it reached £75,000, and it has since risen to the sum of £840,000. Since the revised code was introduced in 1861 the vote has been sensibly though not to any very great extent decreased. That scheme was never intended to supply the place of a general system of education, as was amply proved in the evidence given by Earl Russell and other eminent men—who have been occupied with the business of the Committee of the Privy Council ever since it was instituted—before a Committee of the House of Commons last year. Earl Russell supposed that after no long period from 1839 some general system of education would be submitted to Parliament, but the same kind of difficulties which surround this question here have surrounded it in England, and those difficulties proceed in the main from the various Christian Churches. The reason that no general plan of popular education has been assented to by the Imperial Parliament, such as would reach the whole of the children of the country, is that the various churches can never be prevailed upon to give their united assent to any honest comprehensive system. That this expenditure of money—for I refuse to call it a system of education—this irregular expenditure of the Parliamentary grants under the supervision of the Committee of the Privy Council on Education—has not answered the purposes which a general system of education should answer, may be seen from one fact alone: last year there were in England 11,000 parishes—after the expenditure of the Parliamentary grants had been going on from the year 1839 under the super-

Public Education in 1866. 227

vision of the Committee of the Council on Education—there were 11,000 parishes, with 4,000,000 of population, who had not derived one farthing's benefit from these grants. Now, I think there could be no more striking evidence that England is still utterly destitute of any system of public instruction for the people worthy of the name. She is utterly destitute of any system at all, and this device of the institution of the Committee of the Privy Council to expend the education grants—though it has been instrumental in improving the quality of education, insuring more vigorous inspection, providing a better class of teachers, and extending the advantages of education to a much larger number of children—has yet lamentably failed in meeting the wants of the rising generation of the mother country. Earl Russell, in his evidence before the Committee of the House of Commons, clearly shows that when he devised and assented to the formation of the Committee of the Privy Council he only looked upon it as provisional. Mr. Lingen, the secretary of the Committee of the Privy Council—whose name is, perhaps, better known than any other connected with education under the action of the Privy Council—shows in his evidence that he considers the scheme only provisional. Earl Russell says repeatedly, in his answers to various members of the Committee, that he always looked forward to the undertaking of some large general system, and that sooner or later this large general system must come into play before the wants of the rising population of the mother country can be provided for. If I did not fear trespassing on the time of the House, I should like to read some of the evidence given before this Committee. Earl Russell is asked by the chairman, Sir John Pakington—

"Were those large proportions foreseen by your Lordship at the time as likely to be administered under the system which you then created for the existing state of affairs?"

Lord Russell replied—

"I cannot say that they were; but the question arose after a time whether or not it was desirable to go on with the system as then established, or to attempt, by bringing a Bill into Parliament, to apply a more general system over the country. It was then on consideration thought impossible to carry a Bill for a more general system, and that it was better to go on with the existing system. Sir James Kay Shuttleworth, I remember, thought that the expenditure under the present system might be carried on to three millions or three millions and a-half of money, and that in that way the education of the whole country might be provided for; but that was not the view, I think, of those who founded the Committee of Council."

When asked whether he would recommend the appointment of a Minister of Education, he thus expresses his dissatisfaction with the existing system :—

Q. "May the Committee understand that your Lordship is not of opinion that the establishment of a sole Minister of Public Instruction would be an improvement upon the present system of administration?"

A. "I think that so long as the present system continues it would not be an improvement. If you were to make a change, I think you should begin with establishing a new system by Act of Parliament. And when you have done that, you might find that a Minister for the sole purpose of education was desirable, and almost necessary."

This answer clearly shows that Earl Russell, who had more to do than any other living statesman with the formation of the Committee of the Privy Council, always contemplated that this arrangement should be provisional only, and that some general system should be organised afterwards. Again :—

Q. "When you speak of a change of system by Act of Parliament, may I ask what kind of change of system you are contemplating?"

A. "The sort of change of system that I was contemplating is this : At present you give aid to those who are willing to help themselves ; that is to say, to those who are willing to subscribe, and to the parents who are willing to pay for their children's schooling. The State comes in and says, 'we will help you with another portion of your expenditure ;' but supposing that the persons that are to found the school do not care about the subject of education, and that the parents do not care about their children being educated, they have nothing at all. That is the cause of there being such a vast number of parishes as I see are mentioned in the report as not having any efficient schools. If you alter that system, you must not be content with subscriptions from persons who are willing to aid education ; but you must certainly have a rate ; you could not have a rate imposed generally upon the country without satisfying those who are to pay the rate and the minds of the people in general, and the House of Commons, that it was fair to all the religious bodies in the country ; otherwise you would have, as I have heard it remarked with regard to the question of a rate, the disturbance which there has been about church rates. These are very great difficulties which would have to be got over. I do not know that they will be got over in my time ; but if they ever should be got over, then I say that a Minister of Education would be desirable."

Q. "May I ask why you think a Minister of Education would be more desirable in the event of a rating system being adopted, than it is now, to attend to all the complicated questions which under the existing system come before that department?"

A. "I think in the first place that education, as extended to the whole country and to nearly every parish in the country, would be far more important; and in such a condition of things Parliament would look for the responsibility of a single Minister."

Q. "Then your Lordship admits that the responsibility would be greater in the case of a single Minister than it is under the present divided system of the department?"

A. "I think it would be so."

Mr. Lingen, the Secretary to the Committee of Council, states his opinion thus :—

Q. "Would you concur in the opinion that it is impossible for the advocates of general education to rest content until some system reaches the whole of the country?"

A. "I should have, I think, to answer that question rather at length if I stated what are my views on the subject. It has always seemed to me that the present system was adopted on the theory that the main part of the education in this country would continue to be voluntarily maintained, and almost in despair of arriving at any national and complete system. I have always understood the idea of its framers to have been that it was possible to improve a certain part of the education which was voluntarily maintained, and so to create throughout the country a standard of education, and promote a desire for education, the means being a very direct and a very minute action on part of the Government. The system seems to me to be essentially a provisional system, and good from that point of view; but its continuance must depend very much upon the state of public opinion. I never expect to see it become a complete and national system without (to say the least) great modification."

While some of the Continental nations have made such rapid and commendable progress in popular education, those offshoots of the mother-country across the Atlantic, the United States, have also done a noble work in this cause. Without troubling the House with more than a mere glance at the state of education in America, I will briefly describe the condition of seven of those States, taken almost at random. Some few years ago in Connecticut there were 1656 public schools, with 1787 teachers and 71,269 pupils. The population at the time amounted to 370,792, and the persons who could not read or write were only 4739, or $1\frac{1}{4}$ per cent. of the whole population. In Kentucky there were 2234 schools, 2306 teachers, 71,429 pupils; the population was 982,405, of which 210,981 were slaves; the number of persons who could not read and write was 66,689, or only $6\frac{3}{4}$ per cent. of the population, notwithstanding this vast number of slaves. In the state of Maine the number of schools was 4042, the number of teachers 5540, the number of pupils 192,815; the population was 583,169, and the number of persons who could neither read nor write was only 6147, or 1 per cent. of the whole population. In Massachusetts the number of public schools was 3679, the number of teachers 4443, the number of pupils 176,475, the population 994,514, and the number of persons who could not read or write 27,539, or barely 3 per cent. of the population. In New York the number of schools was 11,580, the number of teachers 13,965, the number of pupils 676,221, the population 3,097,394, and the number of persons who could neither read nor write was 91,293, or 3 per cent. of the population. In Virginia the number of schools was 2930, of teachers 2997, of pupils 67,353 ; the population was 1,421,661, of whom 472,528 were slaves, and the number of persons who could neither read nor write was 77,005, or 5½ per cent. of the whole population. In Rhode Island the number of schools was 416, of teachers 518, and of pupils 23,130 ; the population was 147,545, and the number of persons who could neither read nor write was 3340, or 2¼ per cent of the population. There are some peculiar features in connexion with the public schools of the United States; for instance, in many States large grants of public lands are made for educational purposes. In Missouri in 1855 the grants of land were 1,199,139 acres for common schools, and 23,040 acres for a university. In Mississippi 837,584 acres of land were granted for common schools, and 23,040 acres for a university. In Boston there is a School Board consisting of 74 members—the mayor, president of common council, and 6 persons elected from each ward, 2 members being elected each year and retaining office for 3 years. There is a Superintendent of Schools, who receives a salary of 2500 dollars, and who has constantly to give his assistance to the School Board. In 1855 the number of children between the ages of five and fifteen in Boston was 29,092, and the number of pupils 25,500, a comparatively small number of those who were of school age not receiving instruction. I have gone over this ground because I think it must be of advantage to us to see what has been done in this cause in other parts of the world, and to compare our efforts with those that have been made by others, especially in countries that are kindred to our own. Passing from the United States to Canada, we find magnificent provision made for the education of the people. In 1855 the public schools in Lower Canada were divided into three classes—the superior, the secondary, and the primary; the superior embracing universities and special schools ; the secondary consisting of colleges, academies, and convents for girls ; and the primary consisting of model schools and elementary schools. There were of the superior class 12 schools, with 54 teachers and 331 pupils; in the secondary class there were 140 schools, with 767 teachers and 20,245 pupils; and of the primary class there were 2736 schools, with 2850 teachers and 112,193 pupils. Then there were in Upper Canada 3325 common schools, with 222,864 pupils, supported at an expense of £224,818, and 65 grammar schools, with 3726 pupils, the expense of which amounted to £13,535. There was one normal school, with 124 pupils, the expense of which was £5576. Besides this there were in Upper Canada at this time 179 municipal libraries, with 116,762 volumes of books in them, costing £13,870. The total cost of education in Upper Canada in the year 1855 was £288,998. The proportion of scholars to children of school age in the United States and Canada was—in Upper Canada, 76 per cent.; in Lower Canada, 43 per cent.; in the United States, 66 per cent.; and in the State of Maine, which was the most highly-educated State of the whole, 93 per cent. Having thus cursorily glanced at the state of education in other parts of the world, I will only delay honourable members for a moment longer by enumerating the ratio of education in some of the leading countries of the world. I have a table showing the proportion of scholars in the elementary schools to the whole population of the respective countries :—Switzerland, 1 in 5; Prussia, 1 in 6; Norway, 1 in 7; Denmark, 1 in 7; Austria, 1 in 10; Belgium, 1 in 11; France, 1 in 17; Roman States, 1 in 50; Portugal, 1 in 88; Russia, 1 in 367; United States, 1 in 5; England, 1 in 11; Scotland, 1 in 10; Ireland, 1 in 18. Now, I think, if honourable members have done me the favour of endeavouring to follow me through these dry figures, they must see that in many parts of the world education has made more rapid progress than in our own country. Notwithstanding the great things which Englishmen have done, notwithstanding the glory which surrounds the English name, notwithstanding that the British nation has undoubtedly been the pioneer of liberty in all parts of the world, still for some reason or reasons which I do not pretend fully to explain we have not been foremost in this great work of educating the people. We have seen that Prussia, Holland, and the United States are before us, and if we were to judge by the munificence of the grants in New South Wales in this respect our colony would appear to be in advance of the mother-country; and I think that on the whole this infant community may be said to have addressed itself in a larger spirit to this work than the parent-land has done. I wish now, without detaining the House further, to speak of our own colony. I find that in 1829, when the population of New South Wales stood at 41,450, there were 54 schools in the colony, with 2003 pupils, and the percentage of scholars to the population was about 4¾ per cent. Ten years later, in 1839, when the population stood at 114,386, there were 166 schools, with 6790 scholars, giving about 6 per cent. of scholars to the whole population. Ten years later still, in 1849, when the population had risen to 246,299, there were 558 schools, with 25,682 scholars, giving 10 per cent. to the population. Ten years later, in 1859, when the population stood at 336,572, there were 739 schools, with 32,840 scholars, giving 9¾ per cent. In 1864, when the population had risen to 392,589, there were 1022 schools, with 48,427 scholars, giving about 12 per cent. of scholars to the population. In this country the public provision for education was very limited until of late years. In 1846 Mr. Robert Lowe, who was then a member of our Legislature, and who has since distinguished himself as one of the ablest advocates of popular education in England, moved the first resolution in favour of establishing education in this country on what was known as Lord Stanley's National system, and in the following year the old Legislative Council voted £2000 for establishing what is now the Board of National Education in this colony. The Board consisted of the late Mr. W. S. Macleay, Mr. Plunket, and Dr. Nicholson. In the same year I think the Denominational School Board was organised by the Governor for the time being. The two Boards have gone on progressing and receiving increased grants of public money until last year, when the National Board had 386 schools open with 18,126 pupils, and the Denominational Board 445, with 23,746 pupils. Last year there were new schools opened by the National Board to the extent of 44, and only four schools were closed by that Board during the year. The pupils attending the denominational schools were 23,746 against 22,297 attending schools in the previous year. If we group together all our means of education partly supported from the public revenue, we find the total cost for last year was £134,858 5s. 1d. I mean the total amount as supplemented from private sources. This was expended in the following manner:—Orphan schools, £7500 5s. 4d.; Destitute Children's Asylum, £6413 8s. 7d.; denominational schools, £53,580 4s. 10d.; national schools, £49,927 18s. 1d.; University, £11,226 13s. 9d.; St. Paul's College, £810; St. John's College, £500; and the Sydney Grammar School, £4899 14s. 6d. It may be as well that I should state to honourable members the particulars in the cases of the University, St. Paul's College, St. John's College, and the Sydney Grammar School. I find that in the case of the University the amount raised by contributions, fees, and from other private sources was £6226 13s. 9d., in addition to the public grant of £5000, making £11,226 13s. 9d.; and the number of scholars was 43. St. Paul's College received from the Government £650, and from private sources £160, making £810, and the number of scholars was 8; St. John's College received £500 from the Government, and nothing from private sources, and the number of scholars was 10. The Sydney Grammar School received from the public revenue £1500, and from private sources £3399 14s. 6d., making a total of £4899 14s. 6d., and the number of scholars was 141. I have in my hand a decennial return of the number of schools and scholars down to the close of last year, and I find that within ten years we have nearly doubled the number of children attending schools in this country. That certainly is a gratifying result. It shows a rate of progress in the cause of education amongst us which will bear favourable comparison with the state of things in other parts of the world. The number of schools in this country last year was 1069, and the number of children attending those schools was 53,453. Besides this number of day schools we had 35,556 children attending Sunday-schools. It is very satisfactory to learn that within seven years the number of children attending the Sunday-schools of the country has more than doubled. In the year 1859 the Sunday-scholars numbered only 16,590; at the close of last year the number had risen to 35,566. The private schools in the country last year numbered 443, with 10,331 pupils. The latest estimate of the state of education as applied to the number of children in the colony I will now place before honourable members. The children under fourteen years of age in the country at the latest date to which our statistics come was 150,845. I invite the special attention of honourable members to these facts. Of this number there were attending school 53,452, leaving the enormous number of 97,393 with no education whatever. This return comes down to the close of last year. Making allowance for the increase of population to the time I am speaking, it is very probable that in this colony at present there are 100,000 children under fourteen years of age destitute of all instruction whatsoever !* I think then that I have made out a case for interference. If we are here with a population little over 400,000, and if one-quarter of the whole are children in a state of educational destitution, with no provision at all for their instruction, I think it will be admitted that I have unanswerably made out a case for interference. I think the argument of Lord Macaulay shows conclusively that it will not do to leave this matter to parental care, to private charity, to the wise efforts of benevolent and enlightened individuals; but that it is the duty of the Government, on the clearest grounds of statesmanship and political economy, to make every effort possible to reach a larger number of these destitute and neglected children. The obligation rests upon this Assembly to endeavour to arrive at that result apart from all other considerations. The importance of educating these children and rescuing them from possible ruin rises immeasurably above all subordinate objects. No higher duty can engage the ability of Parliament than supplying these 100,000 unhappy children with the means of instruction. That the necessity has been widely felt for a long period is well known to every honourable member who hears me. For a number of years effort after effort has been made by succeeding Governments to deal with this question. So far back as the year 1859 the honourable member for East Sydney (Mr. Cowper) brought in a Bill, which I understood at the time was intended to introduce something like the machinery of the Committee of the Privy Council; but that system it was found impossible to introduce into this country. The Bill was defeated. In the same year another Bill was framed by the honourable member for the Hastings (Mr. Forster) to deal with this question. In 1862 Mr. Cowper again introduced a Bill into the Assembly to deal with the subject. The Bill provided that a Board of Education should be called into existence, to consist of eleven persons; and I think from a hasty glance over the measure that this was its most remarkable feature.

---

*This estimate included infants not yet arrived but every year arriving at school age.

Public Education in 1866. 235

In the same year the Government of Victoria dealt with this matter. Though they took from us our national system and denominational system, they found, as we have found, that the two systems together were at the same time expensive and ineffectual. They abolished the two Boards and constituted one system of schools under the name of common schools. In 1863 Mr. Cowper again introduced a Bill, which any one acquainted with the Common Schools Act of the sister colony will see at a glance was mainly founded on the law of Victoria. In the same year the honourable member for the Hastings (Mr. Forster) again prepared a Bill, which however I believe was never introduced. A Bill was also brought in by another honourable member (Mr. Sadleir), the fate of which I am not acquainted with. It will be seen therefore that there have been six or seven Bills framed for the purpose of dealing with this question. No other evidence is necessary to show that it is one which Parliament has for a long time considered it ought to deal with. The mere fact that scarcely a year has been allowed to pass without an attempt to grapple with the subject shows as completely as it could be shown that dissatisfaction exists and is deeply felt, and that there is a widespread desire to substitute for the two existing systems one system which will be more beneficial to the public. As I understand the opinions of honourable members and the public, the disadvantages of the present systems may be summarised thus :—(1) That education thus carried on is unnecessarily expensive ; (2) that it is, consequent on the very character of the systems, of an inferior quality ; (3) that the present method is calculated to engender jealousies and uncharitable feelings among the different sections of society ; and (4) that our present education is in an alarming degree limited in its supply. I think I can show to the conviction of every honourable member who will attend to me that our schools are unnecessarily expensive to a degree that ought not to be permitted to continue. I have a return here of a large number of the schools scattered over the colony, both national and denominational. This return has been prepared at great trouble and I believe it is in every case perfectly accurate. It supplies information which cannot be obtained from any public source, and perhaps on that account alone honourable members will give me their attention. I find by this return that in a district close to the city of Sydney, within an hour's walk, there are three schools supported at the public expense which contain only an aggregate of 91 children; in another district, about thirty miles from Sydney, I find three schools supported by the public money, with separate teachers and machinery, and the number of scholars in the three schools is only 73. Passing to another district, I find two schools supported at the public expense, with separate appliances and separate teachers, the two schools together containing 51 children. Passing on again to a populous town within two hours' journey of Sydney I find three schools supported at the public expense, where the children number in all only 130. I find in another district two schools supported at the public expense where the scholars number 61. In another district I find two schools with 82 children; in another two schools with 71 children. In another district I find three schools, side by side as it were, supported at the public expense, with separate school arrangements and separate teachers, which only muster amongst the three 79 children. In another district (an old township with a thriving population) there are three schools supported at the public expense which contain only 61 children. In another district (an old settled town) there are two schools which muster only 45 children between them. In another district, in a town, there are side by side two schools, and the two contain between them only 85 children. In another town there are two schools side by side which only contain 60 children. In another town two schools side by side contain only 67 children. In another town (and a large one for our country towns) there are two schools side by side, and they only contain 61 children. In another district there are two schools close together which only contain 94 children. In another district, little more than an hour's journey from Sydney, there are three schools supported at the public expense, with separate teachers, which contain amongst the three only 101 children. In a thriving town, which can well afford to educate all its own children, there are three schools supported at the public expense, and containing between the three only 99 children. In another town there are two schools side by side supported by the public money, which only contain between them 58 children. In another town there are two schools which only contain 61 pupils; and in another there are two schools close together which only contain between them 48. In another town —a town of great prosperity among the young rising towns—

there are two schools side by side that contain only 81 children. In another town there are two schools with only 85 pupils; in another there are two schools which together contain but 59 children; in another town there are two schools which contain only 71 children; in another town there are two schools with only 94 scholars; in another there are two schools with only 54 children; and in another there are two schools which between them contain only 43 scholars. I have only given a few of the instances contained in this return, but these are quite sufficient to show the extravagant manner in which the education grants so munificently voted by this House have been dispensed. I must state that the return extends only to a portion of the schools, and the reason it does not extend to all is simply the want of time in its preparation. As far as it extends, it shows that the saving which might be effected in each case if these schools were consolidated, so as to have only one teacher to a sufficient number of pupils, would amount to over £7000. The only way in which the difficulty is to be got over is by establishing schools under some condition that shall leave one school to do the work of education in a district that can only supply a sufficient number of children for one school, without this unnatural competition. If the Government is to undertake the great duty and responsibility of educating the children of the country, they must do it in a manner that shall be effectual and just to the taxpayers of the country—in a manner that shall be effectual both in teaching as many children as possible and in providing a quality of education as high as it can possibly be raised, and at the same time by economising the funds so as not to expend a single shilling more than is necessary in the work. It must be positively sinful to expend a single shilling unnecessarily upon educating 50,000 children so long as 100,000 children are destitute of education. It must be wrong to administer the Parliamentary grants in a way that shall in any respect impair the quality of education; and it must be wrong to administer them in a way that shall in any degree limit and impede the progress of education. Now the causes that lead to the existence of these small and inefficient schools (for it must be borne in mind as a rule that every small school must be inefficient) will suggest themselves to the minds of all honourable members. The main cause of the multiplicity of small inefficient schools is the unseemly contention amongst those members of society who ought above all others to lend their efforts to promote harmony and goodwill amongst the people, I mean the clergy of the various churches. In this colony, as well as in the mother country, they are the most inveterate as they are the most powerful enemies that popular education has to fear. What is the spirit calling into existence these small and inefficient schools, which are swallowing up the beneficent education revenues of the country? Why, nothing but the petty desire of every parish clergyman to have a school of his own. If in a locality where there is only a sufficient number of children to form one good school the clergy would exercise that Christian charity which they ought to be the first to inculcate, and consent to the children being educated side by side, extravagance would be avoided, and the means of education would be extended to a number of other children who, whilst ministers of religion are cavilling over a division of the spoils, are left destitute of all instruction, and often sink into the worst courses of evil as a consequence. With regard to some of the victims of capital punishment within the last few years, it cannot for a moment be doubted by anyone who knows the country that if education had been extended to those unfortunate young men they might have been still alive, and, as Lord Macaulay says, enjoying liberty and using that liberty well. We know that some of those young natives, led step by step in crime till they forfeited their lives on the gallows, never had the slightest chance of instruction; that there was no helping hand extended to them to point out the way in which they should go. Should the disposition be still indulged to seek local and sectarian advantages by the establishment of two or three schools where one is sufficient, our funds will still be wasted and the cause of education will still be sacrificed. I do not believe that the parents in this country have any serious objection to sending their children to good schools, though those schools may not be of a denominationl character. I do not believe these sectarian objections arise in the minds of the fathers and mothers of the country, and I have a return in my hand which will conclusively prove that I am right in this belief. I have had prepared a return showing the percentage of the denominations of the country to the entire population, and another return showing the percentage of children belonging to those various denominations attending particular schools. I find that the percentage of the Church of England is 45, that of the Roman Catholics 28, that of the Presbyterians a little over 9, that of the Wesleyans a little over 6, and that of all other denominations a little over 9 ; and I find, looking to the national schools of the country—and I refer to them now because they most closely resemble the schools which I think ought to be established all over the country—that parents of all denominations do not object to send their children to these schools. I venture to assert that there is hardly a parent in the country, belonging to whatever church he may, who if left to himself objects to send his child to these schools. Who then is it that objects ? Who are they that interfere with the control of the parent, and tear the child away from the education which the parent would be glad to give ? The children on the rolls of the national schools of the country four years ago represented the denominational elements in the whole population in the following manner :—There was a little more than 41 per cent. of children of the Church of England ; a little more than 20 per cent. Roman Catholics ; 15¼ per cent. Presbyterians ; a little more than 15 per cent. Wesleyans ; and a little more than 17 per cent. of the children of other denominations. That was in 1862. In 1865 there was 41 per cent. of the Church of England, 21 per cent. Roman Catholics (showing an increase in the number of Roman Catholic children who attended these schools), 15 per cent. Presbyterians, and 14 per cent. Wesleyans (showing a decrease of children of this denomination). If we come to particular instances, the percentage will be more striking as showing the willingness on the part of parents of all denominations to send their children where they can receive the best education. I dare say some honourable members will hardly credit it when I tell them that in one part of the colony the percentage of children of the Roman Catholic Church attending the national schools is larger than that of any other denomination. In one of the country towns there is 60 per cent. of the children of the Roman Catholic Church attending the national school. In another town in the interior there is 49 per cent., or nearly one-half Roman Catholic children attending a national school ; and in another town in the southern district, of considerable importance, the number of children of the Roman Catholic Church attending the national school is 86 per cent.

Mr. DIGNAM : Perhaps they are all Catholics there.

Mr. PARKES : Then why do they not go to a Roman Catholic

denominational school? This supplies a conclusive argument in support of my statement that if parents were left uninfluenced to send their children where they could receive the best education, they would not hesitate to send them to that school, without reference to their associations with the children of other denominations. I must decline to name publicly any of the particular localities to which I have alluded, and I will tell you why. I did state publicly only a few weeks ago one or two instances in which Roman Catholic children were attending national schools, and immediately afterwards the parents were compelled to withdraw their children, and only last week a large number of children were forcibly taken from one of these schools, not by the parents, but by a power which I think ought not to be allowed to interfere. I now come to the Bill before the House. I must be permitted to say that in the preparation of this Bill no member of the Government has sought to carry out his individual opinions or any pet theory; but the purpose of the Government has been, looking fairly at the complications of the question, recognising the interests of the great denominations of the country, and consulting even the prejudices of the people, to meet the difficulty in the most practical manner they could devise. I hope the House will still favour me with that attention which I confess it has through a somewhat wearisome time given me beyond my expectation, while I go through the Bill and state the objects and intentions with which it has been framed. The first clause provides for the formation of a Council of Education, of which the Colonial Secretary for the time being is to be *ex-officio* President.* The simple idea in this provision is to have a Minister of Education. It has been felt that this education grant is now of such magnitude, that the interests connected with it are of such vital consequence to the present generation and to posterity, that it should no longer be administered without some person being made directly responsible to Parliament. The idea is to ensure this responsibility without creating a new Ministerial office. If this Bill should become law, the Colonial Secretary will be known in this House as the Minister of Education, or as President of the Council of Education, and in that capacity he will be responsible to Parliament for the

---

*This provision was carried in the Assembly, but it was struck out in the Council and power given to the Council of Education to appoint their own President.

administration of the grant. That is exclusively the intention of this provision. I pass on to clause 5, which provides for the appointment of the council. Whilst it appeared to the Government that no better authority of appointment could be devised than that of the Governor with the advice of the Executive Council, it was felt that it would be better to appoint members of this important body for a fixed term. At present the members of the two Boards are appointed for an indefinite period, and if not removed by the same authority as that by which they are appointed they remain members for life. It was thought that it would be an improvement on this mode to appoint members for a limited term, and the term was fixed at four years. It was then thought that it would still be an improvement upon this arrangement to have the members retire by rotation, so that whilst the members periodically retired the body itself might be perpetually in existence. It was considered also that a great convenience might arise from this mode of appointment. It is not beyond a probable case that, though all the members of the Council might be men of standing, of good education, and in every way desirable persons, yet there might appear some person of such high ability and such great devotion to the cause of education that his superior qualifications would justify his appointment in place of a retiring member. Of course no Government would attempt the invidious and offensive course of removing a member for the mere purpose of appointing another, however superior that other might be; but if members retire from their seats by the operation of time it will neither be invidious, offensive, nor inconvenient to appoint any such person as I have supposed may arise amongst us in place of some one retiring. This might be done in such a case without calling for severe criticism, and the Council might thus be invigorated by the infusion of the highest talent and fitness that could be found in the country; so that by this system of rotatory retirement and appointment for a fixed term great advantages might arise, and no serious disadvantage could possibly be feared, because, unless in such a case as I have supposed, the members retiring would as a matter of course be re-appointed. Then it is provided that no two of the five members of the Council of Education shall be of one and the same religious persuasion.* I believe this is in the Common Schools

---

* This provision was given up in deference to the sense of the Assembly.

Act of Victoria, and I think it was a provision in the Bill introduced by Mr. Cowper; and the object, I presume, is that no undue denominational element should operate in the Council, such as might withdraw from it public confidence. Of course, if this provision be carried and it becomes part of the Bill, the Church of England, the Roman Catholic Church, the Presbyterian and the Wesleyan will be represented, and there will be some gentleman selected to represent the Congregational and other religious denominations of the Protestant Church. The 6th clause gives to the Council the necessary powers to appoint and remove teachers and inspectors, to expend the money voted by Parliament, to establish and maintain public schools, to frame rules for their own guidance, to train and examine teachers, to examine scholars, and to provide for the discipline to be enforced, and so on. I have read the petition presented by the honourable member for East Sydney (Mr. Hart) and signed by a number of the Roman Catholic clergy; but this petition—I don't know whether we are to understand the petitioners as representing the church— would render it utterly impossible to carry out any scheme of public education. The petitioners say plainly that the denominational system of education is the only system under which what they call their freedom can be enjoyed. It would be absolutely impossible to carry out in our limited community, with our limited revenue, and with the vast number of children that we have to educate, any denominational system of education. These petitioners, for example, want to have a denominational training-school for the education of teachers, but in order to place all on equal terms it would be necessary to have eight or ten such schools, for I imagine that the Catholic clergymen would not arrogate to themselves the right of training teachers for the Protestant denominations. They take up this position, that we must have ten training-schools instead of one. It would therefore be impossible to carry out the views expressed in the petition. Then these petitioners, and those who act with them, claim the appointment of the teachers. Now I should like to know how any Parliament, chosen as this Parliament is, entrusted with plenary powers in disposing of the revenue of the country, could vote away the public money for education while the teachers were appointed by the various religious denominations? Practically, in the denominational schools that will be aided under this Bill the clergy will have considerable influence in the appointment of the teachers, because, as a matter of course, if they recommend to the Council persons suitable for teachers the Council will, on being satisfied of their competence, appoint them. The 7th clause gives the Council of Education power to frame regulations, but these regulations are not to have the force of law until they have been before Parliament a whole month, during which time Parliament can exercise a direct power of disallowance. I now come to the soul of the measure, if it has a soul, in the 8th and 9th clauses. The 8th clause provides that a "public school may be established in any locality where, after due inquiry, the Council of Education shall be satisfied that there are at least forty children who will regularly attend such school on its establishment." Now by referring to the other clauses of the Bill it will be seen that this public school is to be one in which secular education is to be carried out during four hours every day; but provision is made that clergymen, or other religious teachers, may attend and instruct the children of any particular denomination in their own religious doctrines. If the clergymen of this country could rise to the height of their duty, as they did in Holland, they would see that the best system of religious instruction could be combined with the most effective system of secular education that the country can supply. But if they must claim the sole control, while in fact they leave religious instruction to be carelessly imparted by the schoolmaster, they will simply exhibit themselves as stumbling-blocks in the way of education, as they have been times out of number before. It must be apparent to the common sense of every honourable member who hears me, and of every member of society out of doors, that the only way in which we can provide education in small thinly-peopled districts is by refusing our sanction to more than one school. The consequence would be, if we allowed more than one school in such district, that the money voted by Parliament, no matter how large the grants, would be wholly insufficient to provide schools for the colony. If the clergy were bent upon carrying out the true principles of Christianity, if a high sense of Christian duty guided them in their daily life, they would find sufficient time to attend the schools, and to instruct the children in the faith of their forefathers. But with a view of meeting the denominations as far as possible, the next clause provides that they may have a denominational school wherever they can find children to support it, in addition to the number of children fixed for the public school. When they can find forty* children to form a school they may have a teacher of their own persuasion, and they may then remain themselves in the school and teach religion from morning to evening; the only thing that the Government insists upon being that the standard of secular instruction shall be as high as in the other schools—that it shall be sound and efficient. The 9th clause provides that "it shall be lawful for the Council of Education in any locality where a public school may be established which has in attendance thereat not less than eighty† children to certify as a denominational school any school situated not more than five miles from such public school, on such Council being satisfied after due inquiry that there are at least forty children in regular attendance at such school." I have shown that in Prussia and in some other of the large states of Europe, the average number of children allotted to a teacher is 70 in one case and 78 in another; and so, in order to prevent the unnatural competition that has been consuming our education revenues, it is provided that a second school shall not be established until the first has reached a scale of numbers equal to the attendance of pupils in the great countries of the Old World. What could be more reasonable? When the school to which all can have free and equal admission is filled up, if forty children belonging to one denomination can be found in excess of the eighty in the first school, the clergy can claim another school for them; and this school will be to all intents and purposes a denominational school, the only conditions insisted upon by the Government being that the same course of secular instruction shall be taught, and that it shall be under the same regulations and inspection. But even the regulations will be modified to suit its denominational character. The 10th clause provides for the appointment of teachers of the same religious persuasion as that of the denominational schools in which they will be employed to teach. I am told that some denominations, if they have a good teacher of another denomination, do not care to part with him; so that this clause is so framed as to be put in force upon application from the persons interested. The 11th clause provides that in all certified denomi-

---
* The number was reduced to *thirty.*
† The number in this case was reduced to *seventy.*

national schools the religious instruction shall be left entirely under the control of the heads of the denomination to which any such school may belong. The 12th clause is, as far as I am aware, new in Australian legislation. It provides that—" In districts where, from the scattered state of the population or other causes, it is not practicable to establish a public school, the Council of Education may appoint itinerant teachers under such regulations as may be framed by them for that purpose." I am told that in several districts in this colony this system of ambulatory teaching is carried on to a considerable extent, and that its advantages are felt to be considerable. In Norway, which is one of those northern nations that have paid great attention to education, the population is thinly scattered over wide mountainous districts, and the bulk of the children are instructed by itinerant teachers. This system, therefore, is not new. In 1833 the population of Norway was 1,000,000 and it had only 183 fixed schools, the pupils numbering 13,693; but there were 1610 schools carried on by itinerant teachers, and the children connected with them numbered 132,632. This is an illustration of the successful working of the system of ambulatory schools in thinly-populated districts, and will at once set aside all objections to it. Looking at the state of our country, and the similarity of many parts to the physical characteristics of Norway, I think we may be able to reach some of the children in this way that could not be reached in any other way. It will be far better to afford them this imperfect means of instruction than to leave them to grow up totally uninstructed. I anticipate, therefore, that not a single vote will be recorded against this provision. The next clause—the 13th—provides that—"The Council of Education shall establish a training-school for the education of teachers, both male and female, and shall prescribe the course of studies and the examinations in such school; and the teachers so educated shall be classified according to their attainments and skill in teaching, and shall receive certificates of efficiency which shall entitle them to corresponding grades in the schools service." I desire particularly to call attention to the words " skill in teaching." Mere accomplishments, or aptitude in special branches of learning, will not be sufficient; but these teachers, in addition to proficiency in general knowledge, must establish their " skill in teaching " before they can obtain their certificates of efficiency. It has been well said by Earl Russell, that if we want good schools we must have good teachers, and there is no possible way of raising up a body of efficient teachers except by some such institution as this. The 14th clause is one upon which I am aware there is much difference of opinion, and gentlemen entitled to the highest consideration, who agree with other parts of this Bill, object to this clause. I am fully aware that much can be said against it, but I also feel that much can be said for it. The clause is as follows :—" The salaries of teachers in all cases shall be fixed and not supplemented by fees, shall be regulated by the number of pupils, and shall be increased by every addition of ten to the average attendance over a period of three months." * Well now, it is objected to this clause—first, that the arrangement of supplementing the salary by fees gives the teacher at once an interest in promoting the progress of the school. It is said he would never take the same amount of trouble to collect fees if his own interest in them were removed, and the amount received for education from this source would consequently fall off. It is thought, moreover, that there would be some risk in remote districts of the fees being misappropriated. The Government in considering this provision were desirous of raising as much as it was in their power to raise the social status of the teacher. They think that his office is a high and noble office, and that the person to whom you entrust the education of your child should cultivate in himself as nice a sense of personal honour as possible. They think he cannot stand in the independent position which he ought to occupy, and must resort to conduct inconsistent with a fine sense of honour, if he is paid by fees. It is known to be a fact that if, as is always the case, the parents of one portion of the children pay regularly, and the parents of the other portion pay irregularly, the teacher will insensibly, and perhaps not unnaturally, take care of those children whose parents pay regularly, and regard with disfavour those children whose parents do not pay regularly ; and thus two classes will rise up in the school, against which mischievous contingency you can make no provision. It is thought, then, that by giving him a fixed salary you relieve him from this invidious position. You above all things protect the unoffending children from any neglectful treatment which might arise from the conduct of their parents, and ensure their being received

---

* This clause was struck out in the Legislative Council, and a new clause authorising the collection of the fees by the teacher substituted for it.

on grounds of equality. Then we say that if we make the increase of his salary dependent on the increase of his school, we supply that stimulus which he has now in connexion with his fees. It is said that if you release the teacher from the obligation of collecting these fees they will fall off, and thus the State would be a loser. It is very probable the fees may fall off, but if we secure to the teacher a better position—if we protect the children from any unfair treatment arising from the manner in which the parents pay or do not pay—we say that the amount of good that we obtain will be altogether beyond any falling-off in consequence of this arrangement. These are the main views which actuated the Government in the preparation of this clause; and, after having listened to the objections consistently and forcibly urged against it, we still think that our views are sound. The next clause simply provides for a scale of fees to be paid by children. Clause 16 provides that notwithstanding any regulations that may be made for collecting school fees, any children whose parents neglect to pay the fees shall be received and educated. It has been and will probably be again alleged that these clauses are inconsistent, inasmuch as they provide for the payment of fees, and at the same time, as it is alleged, supply a loophole for evading payment. The question again arises, what are the objects of Parliament in making this provision for public education? Is it to compel the parents to pay school fees, or is it to save the children and to make them useful members of society? If the primary object which rises above all others is to educate the children, then I say that the non-payment of fees, in exceptional cases, ought not to be considered for a moment against the attainment of that object. Because a drunken father or an ignorant mother neglects to pay the fees which he or she has engaged to pay, are their children to be deprived of education and turned adrift? It is said that all parents will refuse or neglect to pay the fees; but I say that honourable members who take this ground of objection know nothing whatever of the character of the British people. There is among the great masses of our countrymen and countrywomen in the lower walks of life as fine a sense of honour, as true an appreciation of their obligations, as great a desire to occupy a position of respect and influence, as exists amongst any other class of society; and I say that nine-tenths to British fathers and British mothers who have once engaged to pay these school-fees will no more think of classing themselves with drunkards and worthless persons for the mere purpose of evading payment than they would of forfeiting their right hands. Amongst the respectable portion of the working-classes and the tradesmen of this country no person—or not one in a hundred— will attempt to shirk the payment of these fees simply because this provision is made for children who have disreputable parents. To escape the payment of these fees they would have to class themselves with these worthless persons. They think as much of their position, of their character, of their honour, as the nobles in the old world or the richest and most influential persons in this. I feel therefore that these objections are perfectly groundless, and that it will be found that the persons who engage to pay these school-fees will pay them just as regularly as they would if this provision did not exist. We provide education for a class of children who require it most, because if any child requires the intercession of the State, if any child has a claim upon its bounty, it is the poor child whose parents neglect to provide for him and refuse to pay the ordinary school-fees. We thus provide in the only manner in which it is possible for these children who, if you deny them this, will have no other means of education. To refuse this, you simply refuse to educate the children who are placed in the most necessitous circumstances. You educate those whose parents are anxious to take care of their precious intellect and develop it, but you refuse to educate those children whose natural guardians desert them and leave them to the fate of ignorance. I feel that the operation of this provision will be beneficial, and that it will be followed by none of those inconvenient consequences to which some honourable members seem to fear that it will lead. Clause 17 provides that four hours in each day—two in the forenoon and two in the afternoon—shall be set apart for secular education in public schools. It goes on to provide that one hour shall be set apart when the clergyman or other religious teacher of any denomination may visit the school and instruct the children belonging to his religious communion in the faith in which it is desired that they should be trained. But there is a proviso to the effect that if the clergymen do not avail themselves of this hour, the precious time shall not be lost, but shall then be devoted to the ordinary instruction of the school. The 18th clause enacts that no applicant shall be refused admission into any public school on account of the religious persuasion of such applicant or of either of his parents. I imagine that no one will object to that. The 19th clause gives power to the Council of Education to dispense with the attendance at the training-school and with all examination, in the case of national and denominational school teachers now appointed, where it may be expedient to retain these teachers in the school service; so that unless their removal is rendered necessary on the ground of inefficiency they will be retained, and will not necessarily be subjected to the inconvenience of passing the examinations. The next clause provides for the creation in any district where Public Schools shall be established of a Public School Board. There is a departure from the existing plan in the creation of this Board. At present the local patrons are appointed on the recommendation of the community where the schools are established. This Bill provides that they shall be appointed by the Governor with the advice of the Executive Council, on the nomination of the Council of Education. It is intended practically that the persons whose names may be submitted by the community where the school is established shall be appointed, on the Council of Education being satisfied that they are proper persons. It was thought that the appointment by the Executive Council would give as it were something more of standing and authority to the persons nominated than attaches to the present mode of appointment. This was the only reason for the departure from the present practice. I am aware that many excellent persons are in favour of these local boards being elected, but I am not sure that any process of popular election would be so safe as the plan proposed. The next clause empowers the Council to erect public buildings on sites vested in it for public school purposes. The next clause after that provides that in the establishment of new schools or in the certifying of denominational schools the intention of the Council shall be published four consecutive times in the *Gazette*, the object being to afford the public time to remonstrate or to offer any objection to the action proposed to be taken. I have now got to clause 23, which gives power to the Council of Education to sell property and reinvest the proceeds for the purposes of public schools. The next clause simply provides for the due preparation of annual reports. Clause 25 provides in a more liberal spirit than any other Bill of the kind that the whole of the schools now existing shall be taken over and allowed twelve months to conform to the provisions of the Act. In Victoria only six months were allowed, and the schools there had to conform to more stringent provisions. If by January 1868 the schools do not come up to the moderate minimum of forty pupils they will be dropped. The other two clauses simply fix the time for the commencement of the Act and define the short title. I think that if this Bill has the good fortune to receive the support of the House and to become law, it will do much eventually towards economising the public school expenditure, and ensuring education of a higher quality by reason of raising up, I hope, a class of trained teachers to carry on this education. I have clearly shown that it would extend the advantages of education to a far greater number of the children of this country. I think that its provisions are calculated, beyond the possibility of controversy, to extend the advantages of education to thousands upon thousands of children who at present receive no education at all. I trust that the measure will be considered in the same spirit in which it has been framed—with no desire to carry out any pet theory, with no desire to overlook the predilections of large bodies of the people, but with an anxious and sincere desire to ensure the administration of the Parliamentary grants so as to provide the largest amount of education, and education of the highest quality that we can reach, to the largest number of the children of this country. I now offer my apologies to the House for the imperfect manner in which I have treated this question; and, deeply sensible of the momentous interests involved in its settlement, I submit it for your deliberations, not without serious apprehension of the dangers to which it may be exposed from an advocacy so weak as mine, but with perfect confidence that it will receive justice at your hands. This cause connot suffer from the feebleness of my appeal; the voices of a hundred thousand children appeal to you and implore you not to allow any secondary consideration to impair your generous exercise of power in saving them from neglect and ignorance. By what you do now you may render a service that will be felt hereafter in the aspirations of a hundred thousand human lives—of that unknown multitude arising in our midst who have yet to employ their faculties in moving the machinery of society, and who for good or evil must connect the present with the future. They will come after us, in the field and in the workshop, in the school and in the church, on the judgment-seat and within these walls—a mighty wave of intelligence that must receive its temper from you, but whose force you will not be here to control. I leave with you this question, so pregnant with social consequences, relying on your enlightened patriotism to approach it in a temperate spirit, to consider it dispassionately, and to arrive at a decision upon it which shall inspire the people with renewed confidence in the wisdom and integrity of Parliament.

THE
FEDERAL & SEPARATE INTERESTS OF THE COLONIES.

[ON Saturday March 16th 1867, a number of gentlemen connected with New South Wales entertained the Hon. Henry Parkes, the Colonial Secretary, and the Hon. Joseph Docker, the Postmaster-General of New South Wales, at dinner at Scott's Hotel, Melbourne. After the usual loyal toasts had been proposed, the Chairman proposed the healths of his honourable friends, the Chief Secretary and Postmaster-General of New South Wales. The toast was received with all the honours.]

SPEECH

Delivered at Melbourne, March 16th 1867.

MR. PARKES said: I am sure I express the feelings of my colleague as well as of myself, when I say that we are deeply gratified by the kind and cordial manner in which you have drunk this toast. We were told when we were invited to this entertainment that the gentlemen inviting us were colonists of New South Wales,—gentlemen having a deep interest in the prosperity of that colony. This circumstance invests the present gathering with peculiar interest, because we ought not to forget —and I admit it freely and generously—that we are assembled in the capital of another colony, which is at the same time the greatest city in Australasia. The circumstance that we, the members of the Government of New South Wales—the parent of all the colonies—are met in this room in so cordial a manner by our fellow-colonists, is one that I regard with special interest. In returning thanks for the compliment you have paid us, I set a special value upon this circumstance. Our worthy friend the chairman—and I am sure you must be wise men to place this

Federal & Separate Interests of the Colonies. 253

gentleman in the chair—has told us pretty distinctly the occupation in which you are all engaged. I give our worthy friend the utmost credit for ingenuity and good nature; but if he expects me to make any serious revelations regarding the land policy of the Government, I fear he will be disappointed. If in the exercise of his bounteous good nature he has any design of tying me to a buggy and carrying me on to Fort Bourke, in order that I may acquire a knowledge of Riverine interests, all I can say is, he will not catch me on the other side of the Murray. I appreciate his kindness but would rather be excused from his services. Gentlemen, considering the few opportunities that I have had of understanding the country with which you are more particularly identified, considering that I have no personal interest in common with yours, I think there are few persons who have shown more consideration for the exceptional circumstances of the Border districts, or more sincere anxiety to do all that can be fairly done to place you on a level with the people of the other portions of New South Wales. On the question of the Border duties I have always felt very strongly the impolicy of collecting those duties along the River Murray. Years ago, before they were collected in accordance with law—for nothing could be more irregular than their collection at that time—I felt that if continued for any length of time they would be fraught with such serious evils that it would be better to lose the revenue than risk the danger of their collection. I have always regarded the establishment of inland Customhouses as a positive evil which no circumstances could to any great extent modify or decrease, and I would rather have assented to any imaginable arrangements than see a whole body of customhouse officers stationed along the narrow river dividing the territory of Victoria from New South Wales. We know that the duties entrusted to officers at a remote distance from the central authority are seldom well performed; but however well they may be carried out, they must necessarily and inevitably lead to bickerings, to bad feeling, to much of that kind of evasion of the law which, if it goes on for any length of time, settles down into the inveterate vice of smuggling; and rather than see a numerous class of petty smugglers disseminating the virus of their bad habits and disaffected feeling throughout society along the banks of a river like the Murray, I would submit to almost any conceivable law. This is and always has been and always will be my view of the question. I expressed this view to the colonists on both sides of the Murray when I had the honour of visiting those districts during last year; and I am sure my honourable colleague will say that I did not lose any opportunity of enforcing those views upon the Government on my return to Sydney. With regard to distant portions of these Australian colonies, I am one of those who believe that where self-government can be carried out it is better that it should be carried out. I am a colonist sufficiently old to remember the time when the country which is now the colony of Victoria was part of the colony of New South Wales. I took some interest in public life when the agitation was going on for the separation of this portion of the territory. I was in this city of Melbourne on the very day when the separation from New South Wales was celebrated, and all my sympathies were with my fellow-colonists in this part of the territory. I thought it was only just to them, and must necessarily be beneficial to the whole of the population, that they should be separated from the old colony and erected into a separate community. Later still I was in the Legislature of the colony when the separation of Queensland took place, and if any one chooses to search the records of Parliament he will find that my vote was recorded for motions previously made in favour of the separation of that colony. I believe that persons considerable in numbers, considerable in property, and considerable in their industrial enterprises, who are carrying on the work of colonisation at a remote distance of 600 or 700 miles from the seat of Government, should be allowed as they attain to numerical strength sufficient for the purpose—and if other circumstances conform to such a condition of things—to form a colony of themselves. I have great sympathy for any class of my fellow-colonists who are placed under the disadvantages and difficulties which remoteness from the seat of Government will at all times carry with it. I should not like to be misunderstood or to be supposed, even by implication, to be the advocate for the creation of a new colony to be called Riverina. However earnest some gentlemen may be as Riverine patriots, I am sure they will not be displeased with me for candidly declaring my own sentiments; and I do think that the colony of New South Wales, within the boundaries fixed by the Constitution Act under which we now live, has not yet been proved to be too large. I think, before we split up any portion of this territory, we should try better than we hitherto have done—and this I confess candidly—to govern these outlying districts satisfactorily and beneficially for the whole community. I think the Government in Sydney ought to devote all its energies, without the loss of a single year, to connecting the metropolis of the colony with those districts by railway. I am bound to acknowledge that one of the finest and noblest examples of statesmanship that I know of in the Australian colonies is the conception of the Victorian railway from Melbourne to Echuca, and the vigorous action of the Government in carrying it out to completion. I don't know who were the authors of that scheme, but I think it was sagacious in conception, and that it has been carried out with true patriotism; and I give the colony of Victoria every credit for its far-sightedness in this great work. But I should like to see the Government of New South Wales do something more than copy that example. I should like to see the parent colony putting forth all her spirit of enterprise, and constructing a railway to the Murrumbidgee with even double the energy of her ardent offspring. I should go further even than this. I should be disposed to devote all the revenue derived from those outlying districts in the interior to their improvement. I believe it is a sound principle to dedicate the revenue derived from the public lands of a new country to the improvement of that country, and that the mere expenditure incurred in carrying on the civil government should be met by the ordinary means of taxation. The land once alienated can never be alienated again, and the revenue derived from that source is collected once and for all. I think, therefore, it is a correct principle that the Governments of these new countries should devote the whole of this revenue to making the land more accessible for the purposes of settlement and civilisation. I held this doctrine years ago, and I hold it still. At all times I shall be prepared to support the doctrine with reference to the outlying districts of the country. Our worthy chairman has alluded to the occasion which has brought my honourable colleague and myself to the city of Melbourne; and I am sure you possess that interest which intelligent men must feel in anything which draws the colonies into closer intercourse and into a better understanding. For my own part, I do not hesitate to say that I regard this occasion—though I am in no sense the author of it—as one full of interest, as one from which much may be expected, and from which I believe many good results will undoubtedly flow. For the first time in the history of these Australian colonies they have all assembled, including New Zealand—I may say all of them, because they are all represented, with the exception of Western Australia—with no feeling of emulation less worthy than the desire to have the largest share in effecting a common end to promote their common interests. It appears to me a very important occasion; and from my intercourse with the gentlemen who have been entrusted with this important mission I have formed so good an opinion of their judgment, of their sound understanding, and of their disinterested desire to promote the good of the entire group of colonies, to lose sight of individual interests as far as they can be lost sight of consistently with a proper feeling of patriotism; that, although I am restricted from saying anything about our proceedings, I think I may venture to say that the results will not fail to be satisfactory to the Australian people, and productive of great good to the Australian family. Apart from all personal interest I take in this occasion, I think the time has arrived when these colonies should be united by some federal bond of connexion. I think it must be manifest to all thoughtful men that there are questions projecting themselves upon our attention which cannot be satisfactorily dealt with by any one of the individual Governments. I regard this occasion, therefore, with great interest, because I believe it will inevitably lead to a more permanent federal understanding. I do not mean to say that when you leave this room to-night you will see a new constellation of six stars in the heavens; I do not startle your imagination by asking you to look for the footprints of six giants in the morning dew, when the night rolls away; but this I feel certain of, that the mother-country will regard this congress of the colonies just in the same light as a father and mother may view the conduct of their children, when they first observe those children beginning to look out for homes and connexions for themselves. I am quite sure that the report of this meeting in your city of Melbourne, little as it may be thought of here, will make a profound impression upon the minds of thoughtful statesmen in England. They will see that, for the first time, these offshoots of empire in the Southern hemisphere can unite, and that in their union they are backed by nearly two millions of souls. They will see in them in reality an infant empire, and a power which they will feel must be treated with respect, and

Federal & Separate Interests of the Colonies. 257

whose claims must receive a steady and respectful attention. Gentlemen, I have again to thank you for the compliment you have paid us by inviting us to this entertainment; and I can assure you that, if it shall ever lie in my power to serve the district with which you are connected, it will afford me a real happiness to do so. It may be, if we can only obtain a distinct promise that we are not to be carried to Fort Bourke, that we shall venture to cross the Murray on leaving this city; and if we do we shall employ the occasion to make ourselves better acquainted with those important portions of our great colony. Gentlemen, I freely admit the great advantages which belong to this colony of Victoria. I give credit to its people and Government for their enterprise and for the vigour displayed in the management of their affairs; I admit in the fullest degree its ample resources. But unless I am prepared wilfully to shut my eyes, I cannot conceal from myself that we possess a colony much vaster in territory, with much more varied gifts of nature—a colony rich in coal, rich in iron, rich in gold, with pastoral lands unequalled under the sun, and with wide regions fit for nearly every kind of production. With such vast variety and richness of resources, if we don't march ahead of all the other colonies it will be our own blame. We have on our north the young colony of Queensland, which is making vigorous steps onwards, and any man with common sagacity may see that the more rapidly that colony advances the more will it give us a central position in the Australian group. With our splendid harbour, our beautifully situated city, our vast territory, all our varied and inexhaustible natural wealth, if we don't convert our colony into a great and prosperous nation, it will be a miracle of error for which we shall have to answer as for a gigantic sin. I believe in the greatness of New South Wales, and I hope there can be no disrespect, after what I have stated, in expressing the opinion that she will eventually be the leading colony of Australia. I don't think that it is possible to be otherwise. If I were asked to account for the superior progress made hitherto by our younger sister, I should account for it simply on the ground that Victoria has a new population, all whose energies are awakened and directed to a precipitate progress; while the elder colony, having a much larger range of family life and having more stable interests, has been more conservative in all its instincts, and more disposed to question every new idea and every new project. But the time

s

will come when by the very force of enlightenment a new order of things will arise, and the energies of our population will be directed to a wise development of those resources that must yet give us a splendid position in the family of the Australian colonies.

DEFENCE OF THE MARTIN GOVERNMENT.

[THE Legislative Assembly was kept sitting in Committee of Supply the whole of the night of the 9th January, all business being successfully obstructed by the Opposition. At one time attention was called to the presence of strangers, and the galleries were cleared by order of the Speaker. The proceedings, as continued on the 10th, are thus summarised by the *Sydney Morning Herald* of the following day :—" In the Assembly yesterday morning, after our yesterday's issue had gone to press, the same system of moving alternately motions that the chairman leave the chair, and that he report progress, was continued until about five o'clock, the divisions being frequent, and owing to the constant counting of the House the division bell was kept going almost continuously. Shortly after five o'clock the press were again admitted to the reporters' gallery ; by that time a fresh batch of members had arrived, and the speeches began to assume a more sustained character. Mr. Brown and Mr. Robertson spoke in very strong terms of the conduct of the Government, and were followed by other members of the Opposition. About ten o'clock a.m., Mr. Robertson again rose and expressed a desire that some course of conciliation should be adopted. He proposed that the House should adjourn until three o'clock, and that in the interim four or five members from each side of the House should meet and try if some compromise could not be come to, or some arrangement made to extricate the Parliament from the unfortunate position into which it had been plunged. The Government must do something of this kind, or they must go to the wall ; for as they had to keep twenty members present whilst the Opposition only needed two, they must soon be worn out. He made an attack upon the way in which the Government had acted during the session, charging against them that they were not constitutionally in office, that they had not been able to carry a single measure of importance, and that there had never been a Ministry which had done so little public business." Mr. Parkes rose a little before noon, having been in his place since three o'clock the previous day.]

Speeches.

SPEECH
Delivered in Committee of Supply, January 10th, 1868.

MR. PARKES said : If the speech they had just heard was a specimen of the honourable gentleman's conciliation, he hardly knew what shape his hostility would assume. That gentleman commenced by taking great credit to himself for a desire to arrive at some understanding that might be honourable to all parties and beneficial to the country, and he concluded with the same sentiment. He was ready to believe that these were the honourable gentlemen's real sentiments, but he must think that that gentleman forgot the beginning of his speech before he reached the end of it. The speech just delivered had been of as hostile and reckless a character as any other of those which he was sorry to say the honourable member was accustomed to deliver to the House. He should have to say two or three things before he sat down which would probably lay him open to the charge of glorifying the Government. The Government had been condemned all through the night on this occasion, as on many former ones, by honourable members opposite. Generally it was thought scarcely necessary to reply to those condemnations, but it might be as well at once to see what could be said in defence of the Government. The honourable member (Mr. Robertson) had made his attack on three principal grounds :—That the Government was not constitutionally in office; that the Government had not been able to carry a single measure of importance ; and that at no time did a Government ever exist in this country which had done so little public business. He took exception to all these as misstatements of facts. He said that the Government was constitutionally in office, and that the invaders of the Constitution sat to the left of the chair. The present Government had carried more important measures than any other Government that ever existed in the country. He was one of those who did not estimate the merits of a Government or of a Parliament by the number of Acts they might pass. He was inclined to think that a very large portion of the duty of Parliament is to guard against bad legislation—that a Parliament accomplishes one of its highest purposes and best discharges its trust when it takes care that no positively mischievous statute is placed on the Statute Book. He did not therefore set very great value on the mere quantity of work done, if we were to understand the term in its gross sense. The

Defence of the Martin Government. 261

honourable member particularised some individual acts of the Administration during this session. First, the honourable member spoke of the proposed railway loan as if a proposal to borrow money, submitted to Parliament and withdrawn or modified, were a new thing in this country. Why, the Government that preceded the present did this every session. For the fiftieth time the honourable member made a most unfair and ungenerous attack on the honourable member for Northumberland (Mr. Tighe). What his honourable friend did on a late occasion was a strictly honourable and Parliamentary act; and if there was any attempt at sharp dealing, it was on the part of the honourable gentleman who had just addressed the House. What were the facts with respect to this proposal to borrow three millions? A proposal was submitted which a majority of the House manifested their unwillingness to support, including many honourable members who generally agreed with the policy of the Government. Members who had given the Government a general, a consistent, an almost uniform support, objected to give their sanction to this proposed loan. The honourable member for the Clarence, the leader of the Opposition—then consisting of some twenty members—had tried his hand at defeats of the Government, but most unsuccessfully time after time, being in minorities of thirteen to twenty-five, twenty-one to thirty-one, fifteen to twenty-nine, seven to seventeen, and other similar divisions quite as overwhelming. The honourable member, seeing this favourable opportunity of mustering his band, and availing himself of the strength of the Government supporters, eagerly, impatiently, and almost ravenously snatched at it to get a victory over the Government, which would have been no victory to him after all. As honourable members on this side of the House intended to move an amendment, they were not disposed to be jilted out of their purpose in this way, and to be made use of thus adroitly to swell the honourable member's ranks. Although they condemned this particular proposition of the Government, they said in effect—" We will be no parties to giving a seeming victory to the leader of the Opposition ;" and thus his honourable friend for Northumberland took the step of moving his amendment, and so forestalling the leader of the Opposition, which was strictly in accordance with Parliamentary usage and was beyond doubt a successful movement. There was nothing in the result of that proposition that would in any way justify the Government in resigning. The honourable member then went on to the defeat of the Government on the Land Bill. That was a defeat on which the Government might very properly have resigned, but it was not a defeat such as to necessitate a resignation. The honourable member asked when was such a defeat ever heard of in the House of Commons without being followed by a resignation? Why, every session in the House of Commons. If he had time he could produce a score of instances where Bills of great importance had been introduced, and when it was found that they could not pass, had been withdrawn. Need he go further than the great question of Parliamentary Reform? Did not Lord John Russell introduce a Bill to settle that great question, and when he found that it was impracticable to carry it through the House, withdraw it? And did not Lord Palmerston do the same? These were two instances affecting the greatest of all English questions; and as the larger contained the less, it was not worth while to enumerate the smaller. So long as Government was supported by a majority, it was for Ministers themselves to judge whether a measure was essential to their power of governing. The real complaint against the Government was that it had a majority of the people's representatives. Well, he always thought that Parliamentary government lived by majorities. By what other means was Parliamentary government to be carried on if not by a majority of the men elected to represent the country? According to the honourable gentleman, we had 40 in favour of the Government and 30 against them in a House of 70. He would not dispute the honourable member's estimate, because after giving him all those gentlemen whom he did not know to be in favour of the Government for certain, he might have 30 who would at times be found to vote with him. We were not sure that all those gentlemen would go with the honourable member; we knew that he had never numbered more than one-third of the people's representatives in this House excepting on that one occasion of the defeat of the Land Bill. It might be that the majority did not think that the present Administration was composed of the best men in the land, but it was quite clear that they preferred the present Ministers to the honourable member and his friends; and there seemed to be something not only unwise but unseemly in any honourable member thrusting his services upon an unwilling Parliament. What was the complaint against those

Defence of the Martin Government.

who supported the Government? It was that they attended in their places! For what under heaven were they elected if not to attend there? The heaviest shafts launched against honourable members on this side of the House consisted of upbraidings because they attended in their places; he should have thought in his innocence that this was rather to their credit. Supposing it were true that these honourable gentlemen had been asked to attend, was there anything dishonourable in that? Was not their attendance a proof of their preference for the existing Government? If they had been asked to come, and in obedience to that asking had come, had not the members of the Opposition done the same? Was there a single declared follower of the honourable gentleman opposite absent that day? We knew that every effort had been made to assemble the enemy, and it had been rumoured all over the town that on the first day of meeting they would turn out the Government. Thus the disappointment could be accounted for, and the anger almost amounting to savagery which might be seen in the countenances of some gentlemen opposite. The Opposition thought that as honourable gentlemen who supported the Government had to come hundreds of miles from their homes, and as their friends were nearly all resident in Sydney, the chances were that the supporters of the Government would not be in their places; and the Opposition were therefore impatient to snatch what they had sought for so long in vain—a victory. They had not got that, and he thought it was not likely they would get it just at present. The honourable member (Mr. Robertson) had said certain things time after time and week after week as if he wished his remarks to reach the ears of a certain person. The honourable gentleman had told us that it would be unconstitutional to dissolve Parliament twice for one Minister. He was not going to say whether Parliament was likely to be dissolved or not. But it was strictly in accordance with the duties of a representative of Her Majesty to give a Ministry a dissolution whenever they asked for it, if in his judgment of the relations of parties and the situation of the country such a course appeared to be expedient. It was not that Ministers were to have a dissolution in regular turn; but that the man who had the confidence of his Sovereign and the country should be allowed to appeal to the people against the obstructions of faction. The honourable gentleman (Mr. Robertson) expressed his hope that honourable members on the Government side were really acting from conscientious reasons. What right had the honourable member to doubt that those honourable gentlemen were acting from conscientious reasons? Was it not possible for conscientious men to exist without being in the keeping of the honourable member or his followers? And if they looked to the honourable gentlemen who supported the Government, and the honourable gentlemen who supported the member for the Clarence in the course he was taking, it would be seen that they in all respects as fairly and as largely represented the interests of the country. The honourable member said that the present Government had had the best support any Government ever received. Well, if that was so, might it not be accepted as evidence that the present was the best Government? But he would say that the honourable gentlemen who supported the Government were by their standing, their character, and their services, and in all other respects, as much entitled to be treated with the respect which was due to all members of the House as any equal number of men within its walls. The honourable member for the Clarence had also indulged in some strange vagaries which he could never comprehend about the arrival of the Prince and cocked hats. Mental philosophers told us that the human mind was like a storehouse, it could only contain a certain quantity of things. And if the human mind be stuffed with frivolous things there is no room for sound and wise things. Now, the Ministry had never talked about cocked hats and the visit of the Prince, but the honourable member opposite was for ever talking about them. It was evident therefore that those things were always occupying the honourable member's mind—that he thought a hundred times more about those subjects than any member of the Government did. But he thought that on such an occasion any allusion to the son of our Sovereign ought to have been avoided. The Government had never introduced the subject of the Prince's visit, except so far as it was necessary to indicate their views to Parliament; and he should have thought it quite unnecessary to mix up the Royal visit with the persons who happened for the time to hold office so much to the disappointment of the Opposition. He would proceed to show what the present Government had really done. Whilst he felt bound to advert to what had been done by other Governments, he should take that course very unwillingly, because he had no wish to mention the name of a gentleman who was no

Defence of the Martin Government.

longer a member of that House. When the present Ministry, for the purpose of forming a striking contrast, was compared with its predecessors, one could not avoid alluding to former Administrations. He had just looked back over the Votes and Proceedings to see how far his memory served him as to the course taken by previous Administrations; and he found that Mr. Parker's Administration—the first which existed any length of time—took precisely the same course that his honourable and learned friend at the head of the present Government took upon their first defeat on the second reading of important Bills. He had been under the impression that Mr. Parker's Government sustained its first defeat on the second reading of the Electoral Bill, and that the Government immediately resigned. But he found by reference to the Votes and Proceedings that previous to the consideration of the Electoral Bill of the Parker Ministry, on the 27th August, Mr. Donaldson moved the second reading of an important Bill connected with the public revenue—the Revenue Receipts and Payments Regulation Bill—and was defeated by a majority of 22 to 9; the same day Mr. Donaldson moved the second reading of the Light Navigation and Pilot Board Bill, upon which he was defeated by a majority of 21 to 15, whereupon Mr. Parker moved the adjournment of the House until the next day—precisely the same course as had been adopted by his honourable and learned friend at the head of the present Government. This defeat took place on the 27th August. When Parliament again met on the 2nd September Mr. Parker explained to the House that as he had not failed in carrying on the public business, he had not considered it necessary to resign in consequence of the late defeats. An adverse motion thereupon, moved by Mr. Cowper, was lost. Mr. Parker's Administration was as honourable and correct in its conduct as any of its successors. Well, Mr. Parker proceeded with the business, moving the second reading of his Electoral Bill the same day. The debate on this Bill was adjourned to the 4th, when the Government was again defeated, and resigned.* If the present Government had sustained several defeats on important Bills, they would either have tendered their resignation, or have adopted the other course which would have been open to them. On the resignation of the Parker Ministry in 1857, Mr. Cowper succeeded to

* Mr. Parker, now Sir Henry Watson Parker, accepted office as Premier October 3, 1856, and resigned September 7, 1857.

the Government, but before he had been in office six weeks he was defeated more than a dozen times. On the 16th of December he applied for leave to introduce a Bill to establish a new judgeship at Moreton Bay, and he was defeated on the motion for leave by a majority of 24 to 7. And again on the second reading of his Increased Assessment Bill, an amendment that the Bill be read that day six months was carried by 23 to 21. Mr. Cowper's Administration was completely studded with defeats of such significance. Then he came to the honourable member's Administration, and he would select only one instance of that Administration because it so notably refuted his boastful assertion in charging him with the abandonment of a very slight cause. A late honourable member of the House (Mr. Buchanan) recently introduced a Bill to reduce the Governor's salary, and he as minister had voted against it. The honourable member for the Clarence on that occasion made some observations on his course of conduct, characterising it as an abandonment of principle, and taking the opportunity of boasting of his own consistency, and that he was always in favour of this reduction. Well, he found that when the honourable member was in office a Bill of the same character was introduced by Mr. Forster, and the honourable member then at the head of the Government instead of voting for it moved the previous question, the very thing for which the present Government had been so much complained of, on which motion the honourable member was defeated by 21 to 15, and the bill was read a second time. Then he came to the last long Administration of Mr. Cowper. In the sessions of 1861 and 1862 the Administration of Mr. Cowper was, he found, defeated about thirty times. Among these defeats were the following :—His honourable friend (Mr. Wilson) made a motion to the effect that the appropriation by the Government of the revenue arising from the Church and School lands without the sanction of that House was unconstitutional, and the motion was carried by 22 to 14. He should think that was a serious defeat to the Government. It certainly was a distinct vote of censure. Then he found that the Government was defeated on a motion to adjourn the House. Mr. Augustus Morris took the adjournment of the House out of the hands of the Government, and carried it by a majority of 14 to 12. That was a strong evidence of the weakness of a Ministry. And then this troublesome Bill to reduce the Governor's salary was brought on again

Defence of the Martin Government. 267

by Mr. Hoskins. The Bill had been tried by almost all our financial reformers. We had Mr. Forster bringing in the Bill, which when he developed into a statesman he soon abandoned. During Mr. Cowper's Administration Mr. Hoskins took charge of this pet measure of retrenchment, and the Government divided against it, and were beaten by 34 to 7. Then the Government opposed a grant of money for the Queen's Plate, and were beaten on that. It was not of much consequence, but still the Government had given the whole force of their opposition to it. Then there was the Sales of Liquor Bill; the House was in committee, when the chairman reported progress and asked leave to sit again; an amendment was moved, and the Government was beaten by 21 to 19, so that the Bill was lost by the action of the Opposition. Then they were beaten on the appointment of a committee to inquire into the case of Dr. Beer, whom the Government seemed to think had been rightly convicted. They strenuously opposed the motion, and were beaten by 21 to 18. Then there was the Matrimonial Causes Bill, which was precisely the same measure in character as the Bill introduced since by Mr. Buchanan. It was introduced by Mr. Holroyd, and on the second reading Mr. Cowper, not directly opposing the Bill, made a motion to refer it to a committee. That motion was defeated, in spite of all the influence of the Government, by 25 to 14. Well, here was a Bill to alter the marriage law of the country: if that was not an important measure he should like to know what gentlemen opposite considered important. Then the honourable member for Hastings (Mr. Forster) moved resolutions censuring the Government for the appointments made to the Legislative Council in order to swamp the opposition in that branch of the Legislature, and in three divisions the Government was beaten. A message came down giving reasons for declining to produce the correspondence relating to those appointments as ordered by the House, and the honourable member for the Hastings thereupon moved a series of resolutions censuring the Government for its disobedience to the House. The Government was beaten in three divisions one after another. That was on the 29th October 1861, and would be found in the Votes and Proceedings of that date. Surely that was a serious defeat. Then Mr. Dick introduced his Real Property Bill, which the Government opposed, and was beaten by 22 to 11. Then the honourable member for the Hastings, who was certainly distinguished for his industry, proposed a motion ordering the Government to convene Parliament not later than the first week in May, and upon it the Government was beaten by a majority of 30 to 9. Then the honourable member for Hartley (Mr. Lucas) beat the Government, and he was young in those days. The honourable member from that time to this had had his eye upon the public works. The honourable member would pardon him—he merely meant to say that he always looked after their welfare, always took care to see that they were properly constructed. The honourable member certainly had attended to the public works of the country with great industry and intelligence, it might be with great benefit to the country, or it might be that the benefit was to come. The honourable member moved a resolution that in the opinion of the House tenders should be called for in the colony for all railway plant, rolling stock, and supplies of goods intended for public works. The gentleman who now so ably filled the chair was Secretary for Public Works, and he opposed Mr. Lucas—this perfect baby in politics in those days—with all his eloquence and logic, and yet Mr. Lucas carried his motion against the Government by 17 to 12. He thought he had now given evidence that where the present Government had been beaten once, other Governments had been beaten a dozen times. He thought he had proved that other Governments had staggered under a battery, compared with which anything which the present Government had sustained was trifling. He would now show what the present Government had done; and he ventured to say that they had done more for the benefit of the country than any other Government that had ever held office. No man would deny him the right of stating what he could to the credit of the Government, which had been attacked so often and so recklessly. He should begin with a subject for dealing with which gentlemen opposite should be grateful to the Government. We had dealt with the condition of the lunatics. There were honourable gentlemen opposite who, if they ever thought of their own future welfare, should be grateful for that service. It had been a standing complaint with all observant and thoughtful persons that this unfortunate class of our fellow-colonists had been ill provided for in this country. They were ill provided for still; but he ventured to say that they were much better provided for now than when the present ministry entered upon office; and the

Bill of his honourable and learned friend, which had passed both Houses, would when it received the Royal assent place the treatment of these helpless sufferers in a far better state than it ever was placed in before—in a position much more in accordance with the enlightened views of the present age. The Government had succeeded in dealing with another question that had engaged the attention of the Legislature for some years past—he meant the question of industrial schools. Under the recent Act they had succeeded in establishing two schools, which were now occupied by nearly 100 unfortunate young creatures who were formerly on the way to crime and ruin. Honourable members must not confound these schools with asylums for destitute children and orphanages, These industrial schools would in all probability prevent much crime, and save the country much cost in connexion with police and gaols, by rescuing the children from the brink of destruction when no other arm was stretched out to rescue them. If they not only saved these children, but educated and trained them to habits of industry and usefulness, the work was beyond all praise, and reflected the highest honour on the Parliament that passed the Bill. His honourable friend the Minister for Lands succeeded in carrying an Act for the regulation of the goldfields, which he understood was working satisfactorily and beneficially. They had carried an Act consolidating the laws relating to the Post-office, and they had settled on entirely new principles the vexed question of the Border duties. In the negotiation of that arrangement he thought· his honourable colleagues were entitled to the highest praise. No one could understand the difficulty and danger of that question while it remained unsettled, unless he had seen the state of feeling on the spot. He was sure if the question had been left in the state in which this Government found it, it would have engendered and kept alive the greatest heartburnings and disaffection amongst the Border residents. This Government had also passed an Act for amending and consolidating the law relating to the volunteer force, which he believed had given complete satisfaction to the volunteers, and under which the force was likely to be very largely increased. Then he came to the Public Schools Act. He ventured to say that the results of that measure more than justified the warmest anticipations of its warmest friends. He believed that if it had been a more perfect measure it would have been less successful. In his opinion its success arose from the wise, considerate, and equitable compromise which the Act embodied. That it had been generally, and generously, and thankfully accepted by the people of this country facts alone were sufficient to prove. Within one year the Council of Education under the Public Schools Act had established 100 new schools, and the reports upon which those schools were established showed that some of them had been established in spots 30, 40, 60, and in some cases 70 miles away from any other school. The Council of Education had done all this and had savings to the amount of £12,000 to pay back into the Treasury. Talk of retrenchment—the cutting down of paltry sums from salaries! Was not this a wise and, he might say, statesmanlike mode of economy? They had economised these funds, while at the same time north and south and west they had planted new schools. If he mentioned these facts, and they in any way reflected credit on him and those associated with him in the Government or in the Council of Education, had he not a right to his share of the credit? These were some of their measures of legislation, and he ventured to say that no Government that ever existed in this colony could show a more honourable catalogue of measures passed within the same space of time. He should like to know what the honourable member (Mr. Robertson) could show against this long list of measures to the credit of the Government. He had got his Land Bill; but would his Impounding Bill redound to his credit? Talk of bungling measures! Was there ever a more bungling piece of legislation than the honourable member's Impounding Bill? So much for the legislation of the present Government. What had they done in Administration? When they went into office they found the country in a disturbed state from the prevalence of the crime of bushranging. In one quarter of it, embracing as large a tract of country as all Ireland, people were afraid to travel from one point to another in consequence of armed and murderous bushrangers. The present Government had entirely broken up the gangs, and reduced that district to as perfect a state of security as any other part of the Australian colonies. They had moreover planted schools in districts where no schools previously existed, and the very brothers and sisters of the bushrangers were attending these schools. In Ireland there was a constabulary force of 11,000 men, which nevertheless often failed in preserving the public security, yet this Government with a comparatively small force had put down the

Defence of the Martin Government. 271

disorder and crime that disgraced a district as large as Ireland. Persons might sneer, misrepresent, and calumniate, but they could not diminish the force of facts nor take away from the Government the credit which belonged to its members in the light of those facts. True it was that four unfortunate men lost their lives, and the honourable member for the Hastings had charged him with the murder of these men. He was no more answerable for the death of those men than the Inspector-General was for the murder of constables in the regular force; and if the same men had been members of the regular force and had exerted themselves in the meritorious way they did—though in some instances perhaps indiscreetly—they would have been just as liable to fall victims to the cowardly ruffians who murdered them. He had in his hand a return showing the number of policemen on police duty who were killed and wounded during the Administrations preceding the present and during the present Administration. He found that after bushranging discovered itself in this colony in 1862, there had been nineteen policemen killed under other Administrations, and under the present Administration only five. The unfortunate men who were murdered at Jinden volunteered their services to the Government. For some time the Government declined accepting them, but they pressed their services and eventually their offer was accepted, and they were sent to the disturbed district accredited to the officers in charge of the regular police, and they acted with more vigour and determination than any police in that district had done before they appeared in it. When it was said that if these special constables had not gone the bushrangers would have been captured, the thing was manifestly absurd; because the bushrangers had been committing their depredations for three years and had not been captured. If the Government had succeeded in the suppression of crime, he was quite sure it was a service that would not be overlooked by the constituencies. Then what had been done in the administration of justice? Would the honourable and learned member for East Sydney (Mr. Burdekin) or any other member of his profession express a doubt as to the satisfactory administration of justice by the present Attorney-General? The public generally would acknowledge that the best Minister ever at the head of the administration of justice in this country had been his honourable and learned colleague. If they had suppressed crime under disadvantageous circumstances, and restored the country to security so as to bear favourable comparison with other colonies, and had administered justice to the satisfaction of all classes, what had been done in regard to our public institutions? Our public asylums, he ventured to say, were in a far better condition than when the Government took office. Some had been considerably enlarged and altogether put into an improved state, and all who visited them would admit the amelioration that had been effected in the condition of the inmates. He might take credit for some share in prison reform before he became a Minister, for many improvements in our penal establishments were traceable to an inquiry conducted by himself, and the very regulations he found posted up in them were sent out by him from England. The present Government had greatly improved several of our principal gaols. But, of course, they had not been able to do these things without money. He was hardly able to understand the views of gentlemen who seemed to think all expenditure was wasteful. He had always thought that the public expenditure came under two distinct heads—that required for the machinery of the Civil Government in the payment of salaries, and that which was necessary to carry out public improvements and effect purposes of public good. He had thought that that Government was the most successful, and acted upon soundest principles of economy, which spent the smallest amount in salaries and the largest amount in promoting the public benefit. When they were carrying out these useful objects—establishing reformatory schools, making better provision for the insane, and improving our penal establishments—the necessary outlay was rather a credit than a matter of blame to the Government. His aim had been, and would be, to diminish that part of the expenditure which went as a return for services. He would have efficient servants and pay them well. He did not think it wise economy to pay the public servants at a rate below that at which private servants were paid. The paring down of the salaries of high officers endangered the proper conduct of large establishments, involving momentous interests. He would prefer to employ men of talent and character at fair remuneration, and have the smallest number employed consistent with the amount of work to be done. In previous years people had been employed not because their services were required, but because employment was wanted for them, and in deference to the pressure brought to bear in favour of individuals. He did not think the

Defence of the Martin Government. 273

present Government had done much in that way; he was sure he had not. He had not bestowed any situations on persons in any way connected with himself, or in deference to the pressure of influential people. He had offended friends by taking this course, and he had refused the recommendations of the highest personages in the country when he thought others who had no influence were more fit for situations vacant. If they were to carry out the improvements he had referred to, of course they could not do it without money; but the money was applied to the very purposes for which the revenue was raised, and for purposes which would have the unanimous approbation of intelligent men. What was the character of the measure on which the Government sustained its one defeat? Did any one who heard him, any one not entangled in the web of inveterate hostility which kept the Opposition together, not biased by the influence of those around him, suppose that if the same Bill had been introduced by the honourable member for the Clarence it would not have received the support of nearly all on the other side who opposed it? What was there in it detrimental to the interests of the country? If free selection was good, was it detrimental to the interests of free selectors to remit part of their purchase-money? If 320 acres of land be a good thing to have, could it be said that 640 acres is a bad thing? How could this militate against free selectors? He knew as a fact that this valuable class of our colonists considered it a desirable thing to have the residence condition abolished; and he also knew that supporters of the honourable member for the Clarence had expressed to him their astonishment at his opposition to the measure, and had pronounced it one of the best Bills ever submitted to Parliament. He firmly believed that the Bill had been favourably received by a majority of the country. These were some of the things accomplished which the Government could show, not by a mere parade of words, but by a statement of the facts. What was the situation of the Government in relation to the Opposition in this House? Had they been wise enough to leave the Government to its defeat on the Land Bill, that would have been a defeat which he admitted would have weakened the Government. But the Opposition at once brought forward a vote of want of confidence which at once gave the Government a majority of ten. No doubt we might have resigned when we were beaten on the second reading of the Land Bill;

T

but when we received this vote of confidence immediately afterwards it was impossible to resign, unless we were prepared to abnegate our constitutional functions. To allow ourselves to be dictated to by a minority would have been simply abandoning the constitution of the country. From that time to this we have had majorities, and if the whole Assembly were present we should still have a decisive majority. With this large majority, larger than often carried important measures in the House of Commons, were we to dissolve the House? With this majority, in all respects equal to the Opposition—in birth, in education, in social standing, in property, in intelligence, in everything that gives consideration to a citizen—were we to think of tendering such advice? All the instincts of Englishmen understanding constitutional government were with us; with the gentlemen who opposed us there was nothing but the desperate frenzy of unreasoning faction. There was an evidence of that in the proceedings of last night. In the fifty divisions that had taken place there were three to one in favour of the Ministry, and yet the Opposition consumed the whole night in obstruction. When did the House of Commons disgrace itself in such a way? When had it so far forgotten its high duties, its high character, its high mission as to descend to anything like that? We were asked to give way—and this showed the beggarly character of the Opposition—because, forsooth, they could parcel themselves out in relays, knowing that if the Ministry did not keep a quorum together they could break up the House. They told us that they could weary us out in that discreditable fashion. But the high capacity of Parliament was equal to meet even such an emergency. The minority must submit to the majority. A great deal had been said about going to the country. None of those gentlemen who supported us need fear going before their constituents. The honourable member (Mr. Robertson) had submitted a proposal to the effect that the House should adjourn for a short time, in order to allow some six or seven members from the Ministerial and Opposition ranks to hold a conversation, and to see if they could not arrange some sort of agreement. He had nothing whatever to say to that proposal. The honourable and learned member at the head of the Government was in his place, and he might pronounce his opinion upon such a novel proceeding. But he did not think that the proceedings which he had only faintly characterised, or the support of the gentlemen whose confidence we have the honour to enjoy, would counsel us to become a party to any such arrangement.

THE PUBLIC SCHOOLS ACT

AND THE

FIRST YEARS OF ITS ADMINISTRATION.

[FROM January 1869 until the end of 1870 Mr. Parkes filled the office of President of the Council of Education, and during this period he was frequently invited to take part in laying the foundation-stones and the opening of Public Schools. The following speech is selected from those delivered on such occasions.]

SPEECH

Delivered on the occasion of opening the Public School at Dundas, near Parramatta, 4th September, 1869.

MR. PARKES said : I do not think it an unimportant event, the opening of this schoolhouse, though the ceremony is not attended by any circumstances of great display. We have met in a very quiet neighbourhood—a neighbourhood which is not susceptible of much excitement, happily for the neighbourhood itself—and we have met about a business which calls for no excitement; and I think it ought to be accepted as an evidence of the great interest taken in the work in which we are engaged that so many persons are assembled here to-day under circumstances so quiet and unattractive. We are not doing anything calculated to challenge the admiration of the world, but we are, nevertheless, doing one of the most important things that can at any time be done in a state of civilised society. We are endeavouring to supply the means of sound instruction to those who, in a very few years, are to constitute the strength of the country. We know— all of us by rather bitter experience—that time stays for no one. Those advanced in years present to-day will soon be gone from amongst us; those assembled in the full vigour of health and strength will pass away, and these little ones will become the growing nation that we have been. Though it is a silent work—a work from which no one can derive any great amount of reputation—a work from which no one can derive anything but the consolation of doing a little good—yet it is, nevertheless, a great and holy work to try to educate this rising generation. I think all praise is due to the gentlemen resident in the locality who have gone about the business resolute that it should be done. We may fittingly congratulate them that the school is about to be opened, and we may congratulate the parents that it is to be opened under the auspices of gentlemen who, by the evidence of zeal given, convince us that they will still watch over it.

I am desirous on this occasion to say a few words giving something like a connected review of the course of education since the present law was passed, and giving also, so far as I am able, a faithful exposition of the law itself. I have never, though I have had many opportunities of speaking on occasions of this kind, taken this particular range of my subject; but from various indications of a confused notion abroad as to what the law really is—as to what the public school system of this country really is—this confused opinion being no doubt to a great extent propagated by misrepresentations in some quarters—it seems to me not only quite justifiable, but expedient and very desirable, that some clear and faithful exposition of the present system should go forth to the country at the present time. Now the Public Schools Act, as we all know, became law towards the close of the year 1866. Previous to its enactment two educational Boards existed in the colony, which had existed at that time nearly 20 years. One of those Boards, under the name of the Board of National Education, was incorporated by law, and charged with carrying out a system of public instruction analogous to the national system of Ireland. It may be gratifying to many on this occasion to know that this system arose upon an inquiry into the state of education in this colony, conducted by a gentleman then resident among us, and now one of the most distinguished men in England—I mean Mr. Lowe, the present Chancellor of the Exchequer. This Board of National Education, if I remember rightly, was composed of the late Mr. William Sharpe Macleay, Dr. Nicholson, and Mr. Plunket. These gentlemen, from the liberality of their views and their great acquaintance with the subject of education, were perhaps the most acceptable of any that could have been selected to carry out this important work. The other Board, which went by the name of the Denominational School Board, was not constructed under any Act of the old Legislature, but was simply established by the authority of the Governor and the Executive Council; it was charged mainly with distributing the public grants to the various denominations. Whilst one Board was charged with introducing a system of instruction and carrying it out in all its details, the other was practically the means of distributing the public moneys to the various denominations, leaving the denominations themselves to conduct education pretty much as they thought fit. These were the two Boards of Education in existence up to the end of 1866. Though very much good was done by these two bodies, still a great deal of dissatisfaction existed in the public mind, which became evident at different periods in different ways; so much so that various efforts were made for a number of years to pass legislative measures entirely reconstructing the machinery of education. I do not remember at this moment all, but I think not fewer than four or five Bills were introduced into the Legislative Assembly in order to remedy the defects in the systems of instruction under the two Boards; but each of the measures successively failed to become law. I am not going to say a single word in the form of criticism upon one or other of the organised authorities that formerly existed, or of the education carried out by them. I have just alluded to their existence in order to present to those who hear me at the present moment the leading facts regarding the state of things existing previous to the legislation of 1866.

I find by the reports for 1865 submitted to Parliament by the former Educational Boards (the last year previous to their dissolution) that there were then in existence 268 national schools, and 351 denominational schools—making a total of 619 schools. The national schools contained 18,126 pupils, and the denominational schools 35,396 pupils—making a total of 53,522 pupils. Thus you have the results of former efforts up to the time when the present law came into operation. I find by the report of the Council of Education for last year that this body had under its authority 459 public schools, provisional schools, and half-time schools, and 289 denominational schools—making a total of 748 schools. The number of children attending the public, provisional, and half-time schools was 37,990 ; the number of children attending the denominational schools was 35,980—making the total number of children attending the schools under the Council last year, 73,970 ; and showing an increase of pupils during the years which these figures represent of not less than 20,000. As far as these general figures can show, that is the work which has been done since the year 1865.

It is extremely difficult for me to speak of the present law as I should speak if I had not been so intimately connected with it, because persons not very charitably inclined will attribute any praise of mine to a desire to praise myself in connexion with the measure. But still all fair-minded persons will admit that I have a perfect right, and that it really is my duty, to show what has been the actual working of the Public Schools Act and what are its indisputable features. That measure I think has, beyond contradiction, received the support and approbation of the country. We have the evidence here to-day—and we can go to no part of the colony where we shall not find similar evidence—of its having been accepted by the people of this country simply because all who think on this important subject of instruction believe that it affords the best means for training their children up to become useful and respectable men and women. That is the reason why it meets with approval. But notwithstanding the general approval the measure has received, I am not unaware that it has its enemies. I am not insensible to the fact that persons of fair and benevolent dispositions—persons sincerely bent on doing the best they can for the country, even for the cause of education—believe the measure to be in many respects defective ; and I am inclined to think that nearly all the opposition that proceeds from this better class of people is based upon a misapprehension of what the law really is. And without attempting to distort any fact or to give a high colouring to any fact, I am desirous of showing what actually are its provisions. This cannot be done except with a good deal of tediousness ; and I must beg the forbearance and consideration of my audience while I hastily examine this Act of Parliament.

The Public Schools Act of 1866 is a short measure of 32 clauses. Some of the early clauses—the 2nd, 3rd, and 4th, I think— are devoted entirely to the abolition of the Boards which previously existed. By the 1st and 5th sections of the Act the Council of

Education is appointed. The 6th section is important, as it defines the powers given to this Council. In the first place the Council of Education is entrusted with the expenditure of all sums of money appropriated by Parliament for elementary instruction. Secondly, authority is given to the Council to establish and maintain public schools; the words I use, to "establish and maintain," are the words of the Act. Thirdly, the Council of Education has authority "to grant aid to" certified denominational schools, and here again I give the exact words of the Act; the Council is not authorised by Parliament merely *to establish and maintain* them, but *to grant aid to* them. Fourthly, it has authority to appoint and remove teachers and school inspectors, and it has authority to frame regulations which by the seventh section have the force of law if not disallowed by express resolutions of both Houses of Parliament. Here again I have been particular to give the precise language of the Act. The Parliament has deliberately given to this body the power to frame regulations which if not disapproved, not simply by the vote of the Legislative Assembly, but by express resolutions of both Houses of Parliament—will have the force of law—will be as much law as any part of the statute. The Council has authority given to it under the statute to do all matters necessary to be done in carrying out the provisions of the Act, so that if anything was unintentionally omitted, the Legislature has gone so far as to give to this body the large authority to repair the omission. I think it will be seen therefore that the Legislature intended to give this body the most absolute and independent power to carry out the work of instruction without interference from any quarter whatever; that though responsible to the Executive Government for any dereliction of duty or abuse of power, and responsible to Parliament if Parliament should see that anything in the law requires remedy—responsible in this general sense to the Executive and to Parliament—the Council possesses the power, and was intended to possess the power, to do everything in the most independent way for the promotion of education. But what was the intention of Parliament in giving these large powers to the Council of Education? It is expressly declared that this complete authority was bestowed upon the Council in the first instance to define the course of secular instruction; secondly, to provide for and ensure the training, examination, and classification of teachers; thirdly, to cause a proper examination of the scholars; fourthly, to establish a system of discipline to be enforced and observed—not simply enforced upon others, but to be observed by those who enforce it throughout the public school system. These important powers were given to be exercised independently and without interference of any kind, so long as they are not abused. I shall have to return to this clause—and I have been dwelling for the last few minutes upon the sixth section—in the course of what I have to say, but I now pass on to the leading principles of the Act. The 7th clause provides for the legal validity of any regulations which the Council may have occasion to frame; and section 8, one of the most important clauses of the statute, gives the Council of Education direct power, where that body is satisfied upon inquiry that twenty-five children will be found to attend a school, to establish and maintain a public school. The clause is very short, but it is exceedingly important. There is no authority under the law that can determine where this thing is to be done except the Council of Education. Wherever twenty-five children can be found to attend a public school the Council has power from the Parliament to establish and maintain a public school, having by inquiry first satisfied itself of the facts. Passing on to the 9th section of the Act, which is the one most generally misunderstood, we find that it is there enacted that it shall be lawful for the Council of Education to certify denominational schools under certain conditions. In any locality where a public school may be established with an attendance thereat of not less than seventy children, a certificate may be granted to a denominational school at any place not less than two miles distant and within a distance of five miles. We have thus seen that Parliament in considering this subject empowered the Council, upon its own inquiry, to establish a public school where twenty-five children could be collected to attend it. It has no authority to establish a denominational school at all; but it is enacted that it shall be lawful for the Council to grant a certificate to the denominational school, under the conditions named, which has a regular attendance thereat of not less than thirty children; showing that the Legislature was determined that the public school in the locality should not be interfered with until there were seventy children in attendance—seventy pupils being, as we all know, sufficient to support a teacher in tolerable circumstances of comfort. But even then some one else must establish this denominational school. It must be brought into existence by private effort. If there are any persons belonging to the Church of England, or to the Roman Catholic Church, or to any other denomination, who think so much of the value of religious teaching being combined with secular instruction that they wish it introduced into their school, they must, as evidence of their sincerity, set to work and establish the school themselves; and they must have thirty children in attendance there in addition to the seventy attending the public school before the Council is authorised to grant a certificate. So that there must be at the two schools not less than one hundred children—seventy at one, and thirty at the other. If this new school which it is supposed some religious people are anxious should be established in addition to the public school, is *within two miles* of the public school, there must be no fewer than 120 children attending the two places. The Legislature clearly comprehended that a child within two miles of a public school could easily attend that school, and so while a denominational school within five miles of a public school may be certified when there are only seventy children at the public school and thirty at the denominational school, still if it is within two miles the number is increased by twenty, and there must be at the two schools together 120 children. By the original Bill the number was considerably more—I think 200 children; but in the passage of the measure through committee, this number was reduced by amendments in favour of denominational schools to the number I have indicated—that is 120. This being so, it is beyond all question that the intention of the Legislature was to make the first schools in the colony public schools to be established and maintained by law; and that denominational schools should only come into operation when there was room for them in addition to the public schools; and that then they should in no sense be established by authority, but that aid should be granted to them only after they had been established by zealous persons who might think them desirable. But in this 9th section of the Public Schools Act, which enacts that it is lawful for the Council of Education to grant aid to denominational schools, there is an important provision which I wish to point out to this meeting. It shall be lawful to certify the denominational schools only on one condition which is contained in this proviso— that they shall be subject to the same course of secular instruction, to the same regulations, and to the same inspection as the public

The Public Schools Act, &c. 283

schools; with such modifications—not being inconsistent with the express provisions of the Act—as may be judged to be expedient by the Council of Education. This shows conclusively that in these denominational schools aided by the public money, as well as in the public schools established and maintained by the public money, it was the intention of Parliament that the course of the public instruction should be entirely in the hands of the Council of Education. It shows that the course of secular instruction—teaching the children to read, write, cast accounts, and understand their own language, in all of which there is no religious principle involved—was intended to be alike in both classes of schools and for all children, let their religious faith be what it may.

I now wish to call attention to the particular objects defined by Parliament, to which the Council of Education has to direct its very large powers. 1st. To prescribe the course of secular instruction which, as I have already shown, is alike in both classes of schools. 2nd. To adopt means for the training, examination, and classification of teachers. 3rd. To ensure the due examination of scholars, and to establish sufficient discipline. It is clear enough from a consideration of these definite objects of the public school system, that Parliament was resolved that in future the education of this country, so far as it was assisted by public money, should be efficiently conducted; that it should not be left to chance in any way whatever; that the school-houses should not only be constructed on the best plans to promote the health and comfort of the children, but that the persons, men or women, sent into these schools to instruct the children should be properly instructed themselves. It is as clear as if it had been said in so many words, that the Parliament of the country was determined that there should be no longer any man or woman receiving the money of the State to instruct children without some guarantee that they understood what they were doing, and that they were fully sensible of the responsibilities of the task they had undertaken. It is no part of my purpose, nor would it be consonant with my feelings, to dwell at length on a former state of things, but in order to make myself thoroughly understood it is necessary to advert to a time when teachers in this colony, paid from the public Treasury (which means being paid by your money), were appointed to schools for no other reason than that they were the protégés of ministers of religion, or because they were unable to earn a living in any other walk of life. Numerous cases have come within the knowledge of every person at all conversant with the progress of education here, of men having been appointed to schools, the only motive for whose appointment being a desire to do them a good service. Of course we all like to see people benevolently inclined and anxious to assist their neighbours, but let them assist them at their own expense. Because they wish to benefit some poor dependent who has been unfortunate, that is no reason why their protégé should be appointed to teach our children when he needs the hands and perhaps the cane of the schoolmaster upon himself. Parliament has decided that this shall be so no longer, and the Council of Education has to see that all teachers are properly educated for the business of teaching. The objections to which I have adverted—the objections to incompetent persons being appointed to the office of teacher—do not simply apply to persons of inadequate attainments. Men may be even accomplished scholars and yet utterly unfit to teach little children; they may be highly educated and yet have none of that aptitude, that patient power of control, that peculiar sense of responsibility to parents and to society, which are necessary in the management of children. They may know nothing of the varying forms of development of the human mind, but without some knowledge of the capacity of the mind to receive instruction no man or woman can teach little children. The Council have to teach them the art of teaching, and they are classified, not simply upon their ordinary educational attainments, but upon their skill in teaching. A knowledge of history and science, classical learning, the gift of poetry, the accomplishments of the orator, are useless in the vocation of the teacher unless the teacher himself knows how to teach children. That he is skilled in teaching is one of the conditions upon which the teacher now receives his status in the school service of the country. It is utterly impossible to over-estimate the amount of advantage resulting from this one provision, because, so far as I can understand this question of education, it is an admitted law among educators that there can be no good school anywhere without a good teacher. You may build a nice building in the most salubrious position possible, and provide ample funds for maintaining it, but unless the teacher understands his work you will have no good school; and I am happy to think, from my slight knowledge of the teacher of this school,

The Public Schools Act, &c.

that the parents here are likely to have a good school. I was privileged to distribute the prizes at Pennant Hills last year, and was struck with the excellent condition of the school, the proficiency of the pupils, and the evident desire on the part of Mr. Sharp and Mrs. Sharp to do their duty by their charge. I am happy to think you will have a good school, because the Council has appointed teachers in whom they have great confidence. By the 15th section of the Act it is provided that the Council of Education shall establish a training school or schools for the education of teachers, who shall be classified according to their attainments and skill in teaching : that is part of the statute. Not classified according to their attainments alone, but "according to their skill in teaching;" and these trained teachers shall receive certificates entitling them to corresponding grades in the school service, the course of training being purely secular. Well, the Council has established a training school in Sydney, where this provision of the law has been carried out with great impartiality, and with no inconsiderable amount of success, though not with all the success which the Council could desire. By the 21st section of the Act the Council of Education, notwithstanding the provisions to which I have alluded for the training, examination, and classification of teachers, are empowered to dispense with the examination and attendance at the training school in the case of old teachers under the former systems, where it is considered expedient to do so. It has been already pointed out that national schools and denominational schools existed in the country for nineteen years previous to the passing of the Public Schools Act, and in any case where a teacher entered upon his duty upon the first establishment of those schools and was 30 years old then, he would be fifty years old now, and it would be almost cruel to compel these people—old men, women, perhaps, with grown-up daughters—to attend at the training school. They have reached an age when the mind is frigid, when it is no longer pliable, and capable of being moulded. Under these circumstances, power was given to the Council to dispense with examination and attendance at the training school in any case where it should be considered expedient to continue such persons in charge of schools. This shows the liberality of the Legislature in entrusting so much indefinite power to the body which it was about to call into existence. It shows also the consideration and justice of the Legislature—and perhaps I may be pardoned, as a member of that Legislature, in pointing out any of its good qualities—which I am obliged to admit are not too many; it shows the consideration of the Legislature in not compelling these comparatively aged people to go to the training school when they were not able to go there. There are cases where persons, though not trained in accordance with the modern notions, in accordance with those maxims which as embodying general principles are considered necessary, may nevertheless from aptitude and general disposition and fondness for their calling be pretty good teachers; and in cases where the Council of Education are satisfied of the teachers' efficiency, and where it would be a great hardship to pass under training, the teachers are exempted, in conformity with this provision. But it will be seen, I hope, that this in no way affects the school service to be built up in the colony. All young people must undergo this training; and they can only receive their places in the school service, which entitle them to receive corresponding salaries, by reason of their merit; and thus though we have the power to exempt some of these teachers belonging to past systems, that in no way affects the service of the future. Hereafter the teachers will be a body of men and women trained for the profession of teaching, admitted to the several grades of the service by their merits alone. There will be no royal road to the school service. No man—from the Prime Minister downward—will be able to get a boy or a girl made a teacher unless he or she is qualified for the calling. Perhaps at this stage it is as well for me to say that no member of the Council of Education has ever from first to last attempted to exercise the slightest personal influence whatever in any of these appointments. Appointments are made by such a machinery, based upon the regulations framed, that an unknown boy of the poorest parents in the colony would have just as fair a chance of attaining a position in the service as the son of the Prime Minister of the country. The 23rd section enacts that no money shall be expended by the Council of Education upon any building unless the site of such building be vested in the Council for the promotion of public schools. We have recently heard in the proceedings of public bodies complaints put forth by ministers of religion, that it was very unfair that the denominational school buildings should not receive the same amount of support by the expenditure of public money upon them as public school buildings. Even the persons who put forth these complaints must I think acquit the Council of Education of all unfairness, because the provision of the statute is clear beyond all possible question that the Council has no power whatever to expend a single shilling of the public money upon denominational school buildings. But I think the provision of the Act is in itself essentially just. The public schools of the colony, this house just erected and all other public school-houses throughout the colony, are the property of the State. They are the people's schools, they remain the people's property—that is, accepting the Government as being merely the custodian of the people's property, the people's money, and the people's law. These schools, built chiefly by contributions from the public revenue, remain the property of the State or of the people; while the denominational schools belong to the churches as private property. Why, therefore, should the money contributed by the people of the country be expended upon private property? In expending it upon the public school premises it remains the property of the State, and the justice of the principle is clearly manifest. During the nineteen years that the late Denominational Board existed it must have received little short of £200,000 of the public money. Very large were the proportions of that money expended upon denominational school-houses, and I think some of it was expended on chapels also, which it would not be difficult to prove. All these many thousands of pounds have gone to enrich the denominations, while the money expended upon the national schools remains in the form of public schools, which are still the property of the State. From one end of the colony to the other, from the borders of Queensland and the sea to the borders of Victoria and South Australia, the people have their school-houses, built with their own money, and remaining their own property.

I think I have shown that it was the intention of Parliament that the Council of Education should have independent and absolute authority in the matter of education, subject to the control and correction provided by the Constitution, as all other departments of the Government must be. If the Council should so far forget its duty as to abuse its high powers, it is open to the Executive to remove its members; and I hope the Executive will at all times be alive to the fact that it is its duty to remove the members the moment there is any abuse of the kind. But so long as that body acts within the law and discharges its important functions within the letter of the law, its authority is absolute and independent; and it was intended by the Legislature that it should not be crippled by any interference whatever. It is apparent, I think, so far as I have proceeded, that the class of schools to be promoted under the direct authority of the State were to be public schools. Why? We know well enough that certain persons have charged these schools with being godless schools. We know well enough that certain other persons who have been conspicuous in advocating this system have been aspersed as persons indifferent to religion; but we know also that these are mere devices of the enemy—that when men fail in argument they turn to abuse; when they cannot depend upon simple facts supplied by the course of circumstances, they commence inventing facts for themselves. I do not believe for a moment, nor do others believe, that it was insensibility to the interests of the Christian religion which inspired the Legislative Assembly and the Legislative Council with the firm resolution that the class of schools to receive the direct sanction of the State should be these public schools. If there is one characteristic of a deliberative Legislature more apparent than another it is its ultimate action upon the common sense of the country in which it exists. There may be in the Legislative body men of high imaginative powers; there may be visionaries; there may be transcendental philosophers; there may be very stupid people—and generally the electors manage to collect specimens of each of these classes. However visionary or fantastical some may be; however blind in ignorance others may be; the result of the friction of mind and the pressure of public opinion, and of that continual dread of the adverse vote of a constituency, will grind down their opinions into the groove of common sense; and what they find is the common opinion and feeling of the country that, after much piggish resistance and some curious episodes, they will adopt. The recent determination of the Legislative Assembly to enact that these schools should be the schools of the country—the first to receive support from the public revenue—was because they were seen to be the best, and the most acceptable to the common sense of the country. It is common sense to understand that in a community where there

The Public Schools Act, &c. 289

are only twenty-five or thirty children to be instructed, you may instruct them altogether; but if four or five denominations were determined to have their own schools, with seven, ten, or twelve children in each, it would be perfectly impossible for the State to provide the four or five teachers that would be required to instruct them. It is no question of hostility to any religious sect; but it is a question of common sense. We can have one school where we cannot have two or three. When a community is larger and the children all attend one school, you can have an efficient teacher and can afford to pay him well; and the efficient teacher will only go where he can be well paid. A large school can give a better income to the teacher than a small one; and a person of ability will be attracted to the large school, which his ability will not fail to make still larger. You will not find any person—an artisan or a professional man—who will give his services for a guinea if he can get five guineas. I should like to see if you could tempt a lawyer in that way. It is clear that you will get better teaching where there are one hundred children taught together than you would get out of three or four teachers if the hundred were divided into schools of twenty or thirty children each; so that here again it is a matter of common sense. The circumstances of a young country are particularly powerful in rendering this a matter of obligation upon us. The scattered state of the inhabitants gives us numbers of cases where, if we had not a school to which all the children could go, we should have no school at all. Some applications made to the council are of such a startling character in their surroundings that they often strike me with astonishment. We have had applications for the establishment of schools in places where there were no schools—within how many miles should you suppose? Under the law the distance of the nearest existing school has to be stated in the application, and I remember one case in which the nearest school was said to be seventy miles away. I don't think any mother would care to see her little boy or girl going seventy miles to school. This shows the necessity for economising the public money, and the wisdom of establishing schools which will be open to children of all religious professions and of all grades in society. But it is said that this is a godless system—that it is a system antagonistic to religion. There was one gentleman, a most worthy gentleman, the other day at a Bible meeting, of all places in the world—a place where one would

U

think people should confine their attention to the advocacy of the Bible—who moved an amendment to a resolution to the effect that no more Bibles were required in this country, and the reason he gave was that there were no Bibles in the public schools. That is the most remarkable logic I ever heard of. If this gentleman's assertion were right, the deduction should be that more Bibles are wanted. His deduction however was that no Bibles at all are wanted. I think that all attempts to cast this cruel stigma upon he public schools must be futile in the opinion of any inquiring mind. What are the facts? Under the law of the country it is provided by an express section that one hour every day shall be set apart for the teaching of the Bible, that is if our religion be the teaching of the Bible; and while that is the law—not a matter that rests with the judgment of the teacher or the inspector, or the Council, but part and parcel of the law itself—what becomes of the attempt to cast this cruel and unjust stigma upon the system? Any clergyman can come into this school and collect the children of his denomination and instruct them for a whole hour, every day they are in attendance. But not only so; among the books prescribed as books that may be used in the schools themselves, there are Scripture lesson books containing the cardinal truths of the Christian religion—books which have obtained the sanction of distinguished men, including that wise and venerable prelate, the late Archbishop Whately. And when this is the case, how completely contemptible is it to attempt to attach such a stigma to this class of schools! I had an opportunity of understanding what is really meant by some of these objectors a few evenings ago. I was present at a meeting where a clergymen of the Church of England stated, not in direct terms but, what is worse, by inference, that the public schools were training children without the Bible. I ventured—I thought it my duty not to sit silent and hear such an observation made—to make some such explanation as that which I have just given. This gentleman then asked me whether the Bible was a class-book, and I said " Certainly not ; it would be a most inconsistent thing —in this age so filled with the spirit of liberty—to force the Bible upon persons who do not believe in our version of the Bible." The gentleman replied—" There you go, pandering to the Roman Catholics." It is a new thing for me to be accused of pandering to the Roman Catholics. But I saw what was meant. This gentleman would in his liberality force his Bible down the throats of those who refused to have it. He would force his tenets upon people who objected to his tenets. He would return to the times before the Catholic Emancipation Act. Children of any religious faith, however strong their parents' convictions may be, may without danger attend these public schools. There need be no fear that their faith will be trifled with; there need be no fear that they will have forced upon them anything dangerous to the religious convictions in which parents desire their children to be brought up. I think the duty of giving religious instruction to these children rests with the parents and their clergymen, and that the proper supplement to the public school is the Sunday-school. I think a child is more likely to grow up a devout member of the Church of England or the Church of Rome by learning his religion from his father and mother, and receiving his religious teaching from the authorised religious instructor—the clergyman. The schoolmaster has enough to do in teaching the children to read and write, to understand accounts, to become good citizens, able to perform their duty to society; and so long as he does that in a spirit consistent with the Christian religion he does his duty, and we should never throw upon him the work which properly belongs to the clergyman.

It must be abundantly clear, I think, that the course of instruction sanctioned by the State is to be secular, unsectarian, so that all children can be partakers of it. What right would the State have to direct the religious instruction of children? The Administration of the day is composed of five or six persons, and it would be a difficult matter always to ascertain what the religious opinions of these persons are. What right has it to interfere? But it has a right, and it is its solemn duty, to see that the children of this country are so instructed that they may understand the laws, and be competent to take an intelligent part in the work of civil society. We know that education will not always make good men and women, but how can we expect any man to obey the laws if he have not sufficient knowledge to comprehend what they are? It is the duty of the State therefore to see that children are properly instructed to know their duty in order that they may properly perform it. It is, I think, quite clear that it was the deliberate intention of the Legislature that this secular instruction should be given to children by properly trained teachers. It is clear, I think, by the provisions of the Act I have already specified, that the Legislature intended that both classes of schools should be under periodical inspection—that it was not enough to supply school-houses properly arranged and constructed, to supply teachers properly trained and classified, but that the ability to teach could only be kept up by having persons constantly in watch over these schools. We provide for the regular inspection of the schools, because we all know how prone human nature is to relapse into indolence and neglect. It is no reflection upon the teaching profession to say that, after starting upon his work, the teacher's zeal may give way under the various temptations presented to him. These teachers are surrounded by temptations like other men and women, and may from various causes, from domestic discomfort or family bereavement, or from any one of a hundred other circumstances, relapse into a state of indifference destructive to their schools. The Legislature determined that it was not enough to supply good teachers and good school-houses, but that inspectors must be appointed to see that the teachers do their duty, and that the schools are kept full of life and activity. It is clear, I hope, from what I have already said, that so far as the money of Government is expended, there is to be no distinction between the public schools and the denominational schools— that is, that the same course of instruction must be pursued in both—that both must be subject to like inspection, and that the teachers in both must be properly trained. The Council has had no end of difficulty in carrying out the intentions of the Legislature. Clergymen who formerly appointed teachers think that they ought to do so now, and we have the greatest difficulty in persuading them that the power rests in the Council alone. Not that the Council desires to interfere in any irritating manner with these gentlemen, but because it is its duty to obtain results for the expenditure of the public money. We are continually compelled to write polite letters—and we are a most polite set of men—to tell these clergymen that they have overlooked the authority of appointment. We have received time after time intimations to this effect—that some rev. gentleman has appointed a teacher and that we must confirm the appointment. We have to tell him that there must be some error, that he has no power to make any such appointment; yet still he likes to exercise the patronage to which he has been accustomed. It is fortunate for these schools that he has not the power; fortunate even in his own sense, because if ministers of religion had the power of appointment, I think that the efficiency of the public schools would soon drive their denominational schools out of the field. I think the efficiency of the denominational schools is now being kept up by the power of appointment being in the hands of the Council, which appoints only good and properly qualified teachers. By this means some of them are coming into competition with our public schools, because they have teachers trained in the ordinary way under the Council. But if the denominational schools are preserved to compete with the public schools they will be preserved in spite of their patrons, the clergy, who, if we consulted their opinions and feelings, would appoint such inefficient teachers that they would soon fall behind in the competition between the two classes of schools. But while the Parliament of the country was thus firm, and, as I think, sagacious and far-seeing in establishing a system of public instruction so suited to the circumstances of the country —which I venture to say has been so far eminently successful— and while it was thus firm in its determination that the public money should be spent only in achieving sound results, it was at the same time generous to the denominations of the colony in a remarkable manner. Thus, going back to the 10th section of the Act, we find it provided that only teachers of the same denomination shall be appointed in denominational schools, so that it was careful not to give the Council power to tamper with these schools. Where a certificate is granted to a denominational school, it will be a denominational school to all intents and purposes; and thus the Council has only power to appoint a teacher of the same denomination, unless it should be desired by the church authorities themselves to have a teacher not of the same denomination. It was thought there might be cases where there was little difference between the sects, in which a Church of England school might desire the services of some Wesleyan teacher of ability, or *vice versa*. If any such case occurs the Council is empowered to forego this restriction, and appoint the teacher who may be desired, provided the appointment be sanctioned by the heads of the denomination concerned in the matter. Then it is provided that all religious teaching shall be left entirely to the heads of the denomination concerned, showing that whilst the duty of imparting religious instruction is thrown upon the church itself, the Council of Education cannot interfere so as to be in any way the cause of trouble in matters of religious belief. By the 28th section of the Act, notwithstanding the express provisions of the Act in reference to the future, all denominational schools existing at the time of the passing of the Act were entitled to be certified; all existing on the first of January 1867 could claim to be certified. They did all receive certificates, and the Council was restricted from taking them away until they had been in existence twelve months, notwithstanding that the school fell below thirty children. Many of these schools had not more than one-third of that number—not more than ten children in some instances—whilst in other cases there were only four or five. So generous was Parliament—so careful to do nothing which would prevent one child receiving instruction—that these schools were preserved in existence, and they had twelve months to work up to thirty children. After that period it was necessary by law that they should have thirty children, like the new schools.

These are the main provisions of the Public Schools Act of this country which in any way embody matters of principle. These are the only provisions which in any way provoke strong differences of opinion in the country. Now let us dwell for a moment upon the more striking features of this system of public instruction. In order to show whether or not it is suited to the wants and circumstances of the country, it is necessary to understand what those wants and circumstances are. We are a mixed population, made up of the social elements of the three kingdoms, with a good sprinkling of foreign elements. We have a very large number of persons professing the doctrines of the Church of England; we have considerable sections of society professing other Protestant doctrines; and we have a large portion of the community—one-quarter to one-third—professing the doctrines of the Church of Rome. These various classes do not number more than 450,000 souls. They are scattered over a territory where four or five millions might be settled, and yet they would be in a scattered condition still, the territory is so immense. It is very clear that there must be great difficulties in originating and successfully establishing a system of State-paid instruction in a community so circumstanced, which would not exist at all if the community were of one religious faith. I ask anyone capable of dispassionate inquiry and of forming a dispassionate opinion on a subject of this kind, whether there is anything in the system which I have faithfully laid before the meeting that contains the shadow of a principle of hostility to any religious belief. Where can it be pointed out ? What principle in the Public Schools Act comes in conflict with the religious sentiments of any man ? Its great merit is that it is free from all power of encroachment or irritating interference, free from all coercion, that it leaves a man's faith as a matter between that man and the God he worships. This system of education is entirely devoid of any aggressive spirit, free from all suspicion of hostility to any man's religious opinions. If this be so, I ask would it be possible to supplant the system by any other system combining religious instruction so as to be suitable to all classes of the people ? While the system embraces a plan of public schools all over the colony, it recognises in a generous spirit and with fostering care even the denominational schools in towns and districts where those schools can be useful; it recognises them in a spirit of justice by providing that they shall hereafter be efficient. Thus it makes them stronger for the purpose for which the various religious communities desire them, and at the same time it takes care that the children attending them shall receive justice from the teachers who are paid by the Government of the country. I think that any impartial-minded person who will carefully follow me over the ground I have traversed, and who will consider this question, not as between political parties, but as between the little children growing up to fight the battle of life on the one hand and the Government on the other, will agree with me that the system is better suited than almost any other that could be devised to overcome those difficulties which arise out of the circumstances of the country.

There are other provisions of the Public Schools Act very interesting and important, but they do not contain any serious matter of principle. By the 12th section the Council of Education is empowered to establish itinerant or perambulating schools—a means of instruction hitherto unknown in the Australian colonies. This is sending the schoolmaster to the children, instead of the children coming to the schoolmaster. It was thought there might be cases where several families settled in one place, having ten or twelve children among them of a school age, who were so remote from the means of instruction that they would grow up without any instruction at all. As I have shown, the Council has only power to establish a public school where there are twenty-five children—that being the minimum—and to supply some means of instruction to isolated families the system of itinerant teachers was devised. Under the 12th section of the Act, the teacher may go to one group of children and teach them for three days, and then proceed fifteen or twenty miles to another group and teach them for three days. It was thought it would be better to give them half a week's instruction than none at all. By the 13th section of the Act still further concession is made to the necessitous circumstances of our remote settlers. Power is given to the Council to aid provisional schools wherever there may be collected 14, 16, 18, or 20 children, or any number less than 25, the number required to enable the Council to establish a public school. If in any thinly-peopled locality the persons interested will find a schoolhouse and teacher, the Council has power to aid the teacher, so that the school may be supported until a better can be established. The object of the Legislature in this case is very clear. It is that these irregular schools shall be aided and supported until such time as a public school can be established in the district—thus making the provisional the nucleus of the public school. That is clear beyond controversy from the 8th section of the Act, which expressly enjoins that in all communities where 25 children are to be found a " public school shall be established." These provisional schools are supported only in localities where children are not sufficiently numerous to justify under the law the establishment of a public school. But as our rural communities rapidly increase in most cases, these provisional schools will soon become public schools. In the meantime they afford the means of educating—imperfectly it is true, but still educating—the children who would otherwise have no education whatsoever. By the 14th section the Council has power to authorise the establishment of cheap boarding-schools in remote districts, so that an isolated family on a squatting station for example, living at a distance from others, can send their children to be boarded from week to week. In this country children ride on horseback very early, and a journey of many miles twice a week is not a matter of great inconvenience, and this provision will enable them to attend school from week to week in perfect security and at small expense. The 16th, 17th, and 18th sections of the Act give the Council power to authorise a scale of fees to be charged in the schools; but though it has been thought desirable to supplement the salaries of the teachers by small fees —so small that most parents can afford to pay them—and though a large sum of money is raised from these fees to supplement the grant for public instruction, still provision has been made for children to be educated without cost of any kind in cases where parents do not possess the means of paying the fees. One feature of the system is that no child is turned away from the school from any cause whatever. No child can be turned away on account of his religious faith, or the poverty of his parents; and whether he pays the fees or not, if he presents himself to be educated he must be received. The 19th section provides that one hour a day must be set apart for religious instruction; the 20th, that no child shall be refused admission to the public or the certified denominational school on account of the religion of his parents. The 22nd section provides for the establishment of a school board to watch over the public school as soon as it is opened. It is not intended that these school boards shall interfere with the course of instruction. Their duty is to see that the teacher remains efficient, to see that he conducts himself in a proper manner, to see that the school is kept in a decent and orderly state, and to promote its success and prosperity. The teaching is left to the teacher himself, under the regulations of the Council and the direction of its proper officers; and I think most persons will see that it is desirable that this should be so. By the 24th section provision is made that previous to the establishment of any school it shall be notified in the *Government Gazette ;* and here again is an example of the caution that was exercised by the Legislature. Before this school which we open to-day was established, the Council of Education had to give notice in the *Government Gazette*, and if there had been any valid reason why the school should not be established it could have been stated. By sections 25 and 26 the Council is empowered to buy and sell property, the proceeds of sale in every case to be expended in the same neighbourhood for the purposes of public instruction. What was contemplated was that the Council should have power to dispose of property, where other property could be bought affording greater facilities for carrying out the purposes of the Act. The 27th section provides that the Council shall annually report its proceedings to the Government. The 29th makes provision for granting certificates to existing denominational schools, to which I have already alluded; and the 30th enacts that general religious teaching, as distinguished from dogmatic and polemical theology, shall form part of the course of secular instruction. What is meant by this latter provision is, that books which contain the cardinal truths of Christianity, apart from all doctrinal disputation, may be used in the schools, supposing that the parents do not object. If the parents object they will not be used. A Jewish child, for instance, would not be taught these lessons if his parents intimated that they did not wish it. Such then is the system of education supported by the Government of this country. I have slightly alluded to some of the difficulties which had to be met and overcome by the Council of Education. There are some other difficulties to which for a few moments I would like to draw attention.

The Council of Education has now in its service upwards of one thousand teachers. If we had one thousand persons present here to-day we should see great varieties in the individuals forming so vast a crowd; and it must be manifest to all of you that it is a difficult thing to collect one thousand persons with a natural aptitude to acquire the art of teaching children. We thus have a difficulty in getting persons capable of being made into good teachers. This difficulty is increased by the zeal of excellent and worthy persons wishing to become teachers who have none of the qualifications for the office. It is hard to refuse these persons when they are of good character and anxious for employment; and it can only be ascertained by trial in most cases that they are not fit for the office of teacher. Thus we get a large number of persons into our training school who never should be there—persons who after undergoing the necessary probation turn out, in the opinion of the officers of the Council, as never likely to succeed in the art of teaching. But when candidates leave the training school and become teachers, they continue fallible men and women, sent out into the world under circumstances of trial and temptation, stationed perhaps four hundred miles from Sydney, in localities where they become from their demeanour and attainments comparatively important members of society, where they are sought after by some, and perhaps

The Public Schools Act, &c.   299

regarded with jealousy by others, where they are thrown into the company of strangers and are liable to contract habits which may militate against their usefulness. It is hard to deal with all these difficulties. Therefore it is important that every head of a family should be as considerate as he can of the position and character of the teachers; that they should be treated as persons occupying very responsible posts of duty, and engaged in arduous labours for the public good. Persons of influence among whom they are placed should give them advice if they show any incipient tendency to fall away from their duty, seeing the future welfare and happiness of the children greatly depend upon the rectitude and correct conduct of the teachers in their separate callings. I am happy to be able to believe that, notwithstanding the many difficulties in the way of collecting this large body of persons into the school service, and the difficulties in the way of preserving them as efficient teachers afterwards, the teachers under the Council of Education are entitled on their merits to the respect and confidence of the country. Any one who will peruse the report of the Council, which embodies the reports of the several inspectors on the teachers immediately under their observation, will agree with me that we have a valuable body of teachers working zealously at the present time. We have been fortunate in securing in the higher grades of the school service a number of enlightened and upright men to perform the duties of inspection. And these gentlemen—whose duty it is to travel over the whole of this extensive colony and examine into the condition of the schools, with equal justice to the teachers and the children—these gentlemen on the whole have carried out that duty with an amount of intelligent firmness and a studied absence of all kinds of favouritism which ought to be in the highest degree satisfactory. They have reported upon the state of things they have found in different schools in a faithful and independent manner worthy of all praise. I think the Council has been singularly fortunate in securing the services of such gentlemen to act as inspectors. Another difficulty, which is very natural in the circumstances of remote districts, is that of getting proper persons to form the School Boards. Wherever a public school is established the Council has to select several residents to form a Public School Board, whose duties I have already endeavoured to describe. No one, I am sure, can take the slightest offence when I say it is exceedingly difficult in many localities to get suitable gentlemen to form the Boards. Any one acquainted with the interior of this country must be aware that it is not an easy thing to get three or four persons to understand the work of education, in the light I have endeavoured to place it before you to-day—who will understand the nature of their duties and the means of performing them, who will have the requisite amount of mutual forbearance and of consideration for their work to act together amicably. We find that one person will not work upon the School Board because other persons whom he does not like are upon it. It is difficult to get some men to lay aside their local dislikes even for such an important purpose as this. But on the whole we have been fortunate in obtaining good Boards. Then, again, we have the indifference of parents to contend against. I am sorry to say that some parents are not sufficiently sensible of the importance of education. They will allow the child to stay at home too often because he can be made useful. But however useful a child may be at home, his usefulness is as nothing to the good which results from his regularly attending school. Then we have the difficulty which presents itself in the indifference of communities to the importance of education. I believe your friend, Mr. Miller, has experienced it here. When he put his shoulder to the wheel he found many people who preferred standing with folded arms and seeing how well he did it. Though he had worthy coadjutors, still there were many gentlemen who looked on and allowed the work to be done by himself and his friends. So it is always. The selfish man with property, but without children, says, "Why should I give my money? I have no children to educate." But if he could break that hard crust which shuts him in too much within himself, if he could be sufficiently enlightened, he would see that the education of the children around him would be as much for his benefit as for theirs—that it would make his property safer and more valuable from the fact of its lying in the midst of an educated and well-ordered community. Last of all we have the difficulty of the parson, and that is the greatest, because just in proportion as people are ignorant they are generally influenced by their clergyman. If he goes to an ignorant member of his flock and tells him that he will incur his displeasure by doing a certain thing, the thing is likely to be left undone or done badly.

The Public Schools Act, &c. 301

The sending of a child to school may be done badly as well as less important duties. When the parson sets himself against us we have a formidable enemy. He would not be formidable if we could face him and talk him down; but when he goes behind our backs and persuades parents not to send their children to school he is formidable. And when the clergyman tells the people that if they send their children to a particular school he will deny them the ordinances of religion, it is no wonder that parents quail and promise that they will withdraw their children from the school. For my part, I think that in these days of religious liberty when we and our fellow-subjects stand upon one broad level of religious equality, it is a burning shame for parents not to exercise their own judgment and to send their children where they can be best instructed. But notwithstanding all these difficulties, the public school system has made steady progress. That progress will be best seen in the results—in the multiplication of schools, and in the improved teaching. I have already alluded to the number of schools when the Council of Education was called into existence by law. At the present time, without this school—for the figures were put together before this school came into existence—the Council had 810 schools under its control. During the first two years of its existence, 1867-68, that body established 55 new public schools. Fifty-five new schools like this in places all over the colony. These schools in every instance have been established on the application of the people themselves, and for a time those applications fairly represented all denominations. There was as large a proportion of Roman Catholics as Protestants among the applicants; but when this fact became known the heads of the Roman Catholic Church—I am sure no one will suppose that I am saying anything in a manner hostile to them, because I suppose they are prepared to justify what they do—went to the persons who applied, and told them that they must withdraw their names. An instance occurs to me where a school was applied for in the Western District, and where the requisite amount of local contributions towards the building was subscribed and remitted to the Council of Education for the purpose. Plans were prepared by the Council's architect, and tenders were invited for the erection of the building, when the Roman Catholic bishop went to the parents and told them that they must withdraw their names and get back their money. Of course it was easy to withdraw their names, but it was not so easy to get back their money. The Council had called for tenders for the building, and the money could not be returned. That was one case in which one section of the community has been interfered with in the exercise of their authority as parents, and in contravention of that religious liberty which prevails now, and which is quite as much in favour of Roman Catholics as of other sections of the community. It is a fact that this prelate printed and published a document, a copy of which was sent to me, threatening all parents of his denomination who sent their children to a public school with a denial of the sacraments of his church. As far as I understand the Roman Catholic faith, you may almost as well threaten a person with physical death as threaten him with the withdrawal of the ordinances of his church. You are pushing a man to the brink of a precipice, and I imagine he will do almost anything to propitiate his clergymen who threatens to drive him over. If this enormous power of ecclesiastical punishment is brought to bear upon the public schools, it is a matter of wonder that we have any Roman Catholic children still attending them. But notwithstanding this active hostility of their priesthood, Roman Catholic as well as other parents are so thoroughly alive to the advantage of sound instruction, are so sensible that if they wish their children to emerge from performing the lowest drudgery of civilised society they must be as well instructed as others, that they continue to apply for public schools and to send their children to public schools. I do not hesitate to say here that it is my profound conviction that if the parents of the Roman Catholic Church were left free—if it were not attempted to exercise this terrible tyranny over them—they would as generally avail themselves of the advantages of these schools as any other class in the community.

The Council of Education during 1867 and 1868 established 55 public schools, and aided 103 provisional schools. In addition to this it established 38 half-time schools—that is, 38 of that class of schools where the teacher itinerates and follows the children, and carries the blessings of education home to their doors in cases where they cannot attend school themselves. During that time only one denominational school received a certificate. During the present year, in addition to the schools already enumerated, the Council has established fifteen public schools,

The Public Schools Act, &c. 303

fourteen half-time schools, and aided thirty-two provisional schools; giving a total of 257 new schools opened since the 1st January, 1867. In addition to these we have twenty-five new schools being brought together; the schoolhouses are in course of erection, this being one of them. Notwithstanding the allusions I have made, I am very happy to take this opportunity to bear testimony to the liberality of many clergymen in their support of the public Schools Act. There are clergymen of all the Protestant churches, including considerable numbers of the clergy of the Church of England, who view with interest and rejoicing the progress of the public school system. They see that there is nothing here antagonistic to the Christian religion founded upon the Bible—that there is nothing in the system which is not in the highest degree in harmony with the propagation of the gospel of Christ; and that the proper instrumentality to teach that religion is the Sabbath-school system extended throughout the country.

I think it would be very improper for me on an occasion like the present to suffer myself to diverge into anything like party politics; still a public school system in any country is an essential part of its institutions in the large sense of politics. It is part of the policy of the country. It is part of the intention and action of Government, part of the very life of constituted authority; and just in that sense I wish to say a few words before I conclude. We are on the eve of a general election, and in a country like this, where all power is derived from the people, that is a very important event at any time. But it is an event specially important following three years after the establishment of a new system of public instruction, before all the difficulties surrounding its origination have been surmounted, before the lapse of time has been sufficient to test safely its acceptability to the people and its adaptability to the circumstances of the country, before all classes have allowed themselves calmly to ascertain what the thing really is. Well, there is reason to suppose that this public school system will be a cause of conflict on every hustings in the colony in the course of a few months, probably in the course of a few weeks. All I wish to say is, let the people who believe that the system is good in the main, adapted to the country, and calculated to work good results—all who believe that, say so openly and fearlessly. Let us have no concealment or ambiguity on this question. Let those who are opposed to the system come forward and boldly and manfully state the grounds of their opposition. If this question is to be mixed up in the conflict the result of which will be to constitute a Legislature for the next five years that will have the power of life and death in its hands, let us know what we are about. Above all things be careful to understand every man who asks you for a vote one way or the other. Surely that is fair. Do not let us have to fight men in the dark. Do not let us return men to Parliament who promise to do one thing while they are secretly pledged to do another. This thing is worth battling for in the full sense in which an Englishman understands those terms. It is worth while for a man to spend an hour in the discharge of his duty to the country and the exercise of his privilege as a citizen; it is worth while for every man to exercise the suffrage, and it is worth his while thoroughly to understand those to whom he entrusts the power of making the laws for the next five years. The future of this country will be a great future. No one can doubt that. A few years will bring us into the capacity and all the privileges of national life. Whether these colonies go on for a long period of years linked to England, or whether, with the consent of England herself, they take a fresh start with a willingly-accorded separation, one fact is certain. In another ten years these colonies will have grown into the capacity of a nation. Already they number two millions of souls, and in a few years more they will be as large as the American colonies were at the time of their separation from England. Whatever may be our form of Government, the time will come—I hope to live to see it—when we shall take our place with all the real conditions of freedom, with all the immunities of national life, among the free nations of the globe. Let us by every means in our power take care that the children of the country grow up under such a sound and enlightened system of instruction, that they will consider as the dearest of all possessions the free exercise of their own judgment in the secular affairs of life, and that each man will shrink from being subservient to the will of any other man or of any earthly power.

THE
EVILS OF A WEAK GOVERNMENT.

SPEECH

Delivered in the Legislative Assembly (the adjournment of the House having been moved by another member) on the position of the Cowper-Robertson Ministry, April 27th 1870.

MR. PARKES : The Administration as it was originally formed was now simply represented by the Minister for Works, the Postmaster-General, and the Colonial Treasurer. The changes in its component parts had been so remarkable that no one could tell what would happen to-morrow. Parliament would shortly be prorogued, and in all probability when it was called together again we should have an entirely different Government. He did not think that from that state of things we had a very satisfactory prospect before us. When the Government went into office at the end of October 1868, and met the Parliament, they submitted a programme of some twenty-one measures. The gentleman who was entrusted with the formation of the Administration said he went into office in order to carry out his "sincere and earnest desire to unfetter as much as might be the trade and commerce of the country," and to carry out in every possible manner public retrenchment. And that hon. gentleman at the same time reminded the electors that he was one of the historical characters of the country, who had left a straight line of action behind him—a deep sunk line—and that it was known to every one that it was not likely he would depart from the broad straight line. The other leading member of the Government stated that he went into office to restore the Government to its constitutional conditions and usages, to put an end to sectarian differences, to carry out a number of important reforms, and to deal especially with the finances of the country. Those were the professions which were made eighteen months ago. And now it was said that there had been no time to carry out these things because wicked people in Parlia-

v

ment had so obstructed the Government. He had always thought that the very essence of Responsible Government consisted in having such a command and support in Parliament that successful obstruction would be impossible. No doubt if it were not for the magnificent support from the nation which Mr. Gladstone received he would be obstructed in the House of Commons. But Mr. Gladstone was so supported by a compact and intelligent majority, and by the voice of the nation outside the House of Commons, that he could set obstruction at defiance. But was it true that this Government had been obstructed?

Since the session commenced the whole month of February passed away without the slightest effort being made to do public business. With the exception of four nights in the month of February last the House adjourned before eight o'clock every evening. And yet we were told that the array of measures which had been submitted in order to deceive the country, and to make a pretence of earnestness on the part of the Government to do business—that these measures had now been dropped because the Government had no time to carry them into law. Now he ventured to say that there had been no time since the advent of Responsible Government when the Administration had been treated with so much consideration, and had met with so little obstruction of any kind, as had been the case with the Administration now in office during the present session. The present state of the business paper was an example of that. Yesterday, and again to-day, there was no business on the paper beyond that for the day itself.

Mr. GARRETT: That was on account of the action of the House itself.

Mr. PARKES: That only proved what he asserted, that the House had been so considerate and forbearing that no impediment whatever had been thrown in the way of the Government, not even in the shape of private business, but that they had been left to take precisely their own course. It was a fact that a great many things had gone unchallenged rather than that there should be any show of opposition to the Government. Nevertheless, we were brought to that stage that whole measures, involving important financial questions, had been dropped on the mere plea that there had been no time to invite the attention of Parliament to their consideration.

During the first session no impediment was thrown in the way of the Government getting the Estimates and the Appropriation Act. But having been treated with that consideration and forbearance, the Government remained six months in recess, and did not meet Parliament until the 28th of September, notwithstanding that the Parliament must expire by effluxion of time in the January following. During the six months' recess nothing appeared on record to gain or merit the approbation of the country. When Parliament again met, in the latter part of September, the Government came down again with a great array of Bills. They either thought it was possible or impossible for those Bills to be considered. Therefore they submitted them either in good faith or for the mere purpose of making a show of an intention to carry out useful legislation. After a few weeks a dissolution took place. We then had what was a most unusual occurrence—the gentlemen who had charge of the affairs of the country in nearly every instance refused to face their constituents. It was a most unusual thing for gentlemen holding Ministerial offices—having advised the Crown to dissolve—to shrink from facing their own constituents. The honourable gentleman at the head of the Government (Mr. Robertson), instead of going back to the Clarence, appealed to the electors of West Sydney, and was elected. The honourable the Secretary for Lands (Mr. Forster), instead of going back to the Hastings, appealed to the electors of St. Leonards, and was defeated. In the meantime the friends of that gentleman nominated him for his own constituency, where also he was defeated. The only member of the Government who was returned by the constituents who had previously sent him to Parliament was the honourable the Minister for Works. The electors of the country, so far as he could judge, returned a Legislative Assembly unfavourable to the existing Administration. He admitted that the House had resisted any change. But it by no means followed that the members of the present Assembly were supporters of the Administration. If we judged from what honourable gentlemen were continually stating in the House, what they stated before their constituents, and from the indications of their daily conduct, a large majority were not satisfied with the present management of affairs.

In the beginning of the year or the latter part of last year a remarkable change took place in the Ministry, which it would be rather difficult for any one to properly describe. The Premier retired from the Government, and another gentleman who had no connexion with the formation of the Government stepped into his position. Since the resignation of Mr. Robertson there had been no Premier in the Government of the country, no person answering to the head of the Ministry as known in England. The office of Premier was no doubt unknown to the law of England, but by usage the person selected by the Crown and instructed to form a Government assumed the position of Premier, and was held responsible for the policy of the Government. In our case a change had occurred which would be impossible in England, and which had never occurred in any of the Australian colonies. Then we had the retirement from this Administration of the late Solicitor-General. He was not disposed to speak in harsh terms of Mr. Josephson because that gentleman was now absent. He wished to confine his observations to the political aspect of his act of retirement from the Administration. Mr. Josephson was the law adviser of the Crown, and in addition to this a member of the Executive Council, sworn to give his best advice to the Crown on every subject submitted for consideration. This high Minister of the Crown entered into a negotiation with a permanent and subordinate officer of the Government of which he formed a part, by which he was himself to retire from his high position and to accept the lower position vacated by this officer in the service of the country. That was a remarkable and he thought an unprecedented thing. As soon as the negotiations were completed he resigned the high *status* he held as an Executive Councillor to take this paltry position of District Court Judge. The very theory of responsible government assumed that the persons who aspired to these executive offices were actuated by honourable political ambition, and that they were not taking them for the purpose of enabling themselves to obtain permanent employment or personal benefit. The Minister could not have accepted that subordinate office without the concurrence of the Executive Council, and therefore if he took a low view of his position, the other members of the Executive Council must also have taken a low view of theirs to have concurred in it. This came of forming an Administration, not on the plan of English statesmen, but on the plan of men simply determined to grasp and cling to the advantages of office, no matter on what terms. They had also had another retirement—that was

Evils of a Weak Government. 309

the retirement of a gentleman who probably brought more intellect to the Administration than any other member of it; he meant the honourable member for Queanbeyan (Mr. Forster). That gentleman retired about a fortnight ago, and his letter of resignation was read in the Assembly. Yet honourable members were told to-day that he still performed the duties of Secretary for Lands. This, again, was an unexampled state of things. It could never have occurred in the mother country, and he did not think a similar instance had ever before occurred here. Honourable members might be in danger of confusing the resignation of a Government with the resignation of a single member of the Government. When a whole Ministry tendered their resignations they must necessarily hold office until their successors were appointed; but a single member of the Government retiring occupied an essentially different position. When an individual Minister retires from the Administration, it must be understood to be, as a rule, either because he dissents from the policy or conduct of the Government, or because he has had some personal misunderstanding with the Government, or some individual member of the Government. In any one of those cases he would be no longer in a position where he ought to know what the Government were doing. The moment he sent in his resignation he ought to know no more of what the Cabinet were doing than any person in Parliament who had never been connected with the Government.

Parliament was about to be prorogued, and what was the prospect before honourable members? They had here a string of Bills dangled before the House, some of them of the most important character. There was a Bill to consolidate the Customs laws of the colony. It was introduced last session, and had twice gone through the process of being printed. There was a Bill to amend the Stamp Duties Act, an Audit Bill, a Bill to provide for distillation from colonial produce, and a Bill for the management of the goldfields. All these had been promised from the time of the inauguration of the Government, and they would now have to go over. This Stamp Duties Act Amendment Bill was a very important connecting link in the proclaimed policy of the Government. The policy submitted to Parliament this session might be considered as entirely based on the enactment of this Bill. They were told in the financial statement that the *ad valorem* duties would be given up, that the present duties of 5 per cent. would be reduced to 2½ per cent. from the 1st October next, and that from the 1st January the taxation would cease and determine altogether. They had been told that those duties interfered with the trade of the colony, and were only to continue in force until the Stamp Act Amendment Bill passed into law ; and the Government had given the House to understand at different stages of the session that they would certainly go on with that measure. The Treasurer had distinctly stated that he would go on with it, and in adverting to some observations which had been made he added that unless the House allowed him to manage the financial affairs in his own way he would retire in favour of somebody else. He did not believe honourable members were so simple and guileless as to suppose that the Stamp Bill would have been given up had it been found that there was a possibility of carrying it into law. The Government would have been defeated on the second reading, and consequently the measure had been abandoned.

The Government could not point to a single act which would receive the approbation of the country. Prodigal in their promises they had been more than beggarly in their performances. And what position had the Government taken up with reference to one of the most important questions which had been submitted to the House—that of immigration ? A member of the Government had undertaken the duties of chairman of a select committe to inquire into and report upon the question, and the committee reported that it was desirable to bring in a Bill to promote immigration. In pursuance of that recommendation a Bill was brought in, but not as a Government measure. There were remarkable provisions in the Bill which were likely to give rise to some angry feeling, provisions which were in the highest degree debatable, but the Government would not take the responsibility of the measure upon their shoulders. ·The honourable the Colonial Secretary had endeavoured to dissociate himself as leader of the Government from the position he occupied as chairman of the committee, and to make the Bill a private measure. That measure was of more importance than any other which could possibly be introduced. It dealt with a question that was viewed from entirely different standpoints in New South Wales and in England. Here we were desirous of obtaining the best class of persons we could induce to come out—the sober, industrious, and robust—but in England they were desirous of sending out persons who were of an opposite character. It was child's play to talk of our financial difficulties, or the administration of our land laws, as compared with settling over the face of this country a vigorous, industrious, enterprising population. The public debt was spoken of as having its great security to the public creditor in the lands of the colony; but of what value were these lands if they were not made productive by population? They were of comparatively no value as a security to the public creditor, compared with the assurance that would be given by the expansion of revenue with the growth of a prosperous population. The adjustment of this question so as to promote an inflowing and a steady stream of valuable population, without inconsiderately disturbing the interests of labour, was one of the most difficult tasks for Australian statesmen. This question was now upon the business paper in the shape of a private motion, and it might be said in charge of a member of the Government. With all these facts staring us in the face—this total failure of administrative ability, this entire forfeiture of all public pledges ever given, this entire abandonment of all principles avowed as the leading principles of the Administration—we were about to bring the session to a close. He should like any honourable member to go before his constituents and fairly recount the doings of this Parliament, and see whether they would approve of its conduct. He did not pause for a moment in saying that, so far as his experience went, this was the most useless, barren, ineffective session we had ever had in this country. Without the exposition of one sound principle of Government, without passing one useful measure, without carrying into effect one proposal of economy, without any change excepting changes in Administration, which must be admitted by all candid persons to be changes for the worse, we were about to close this session. He did not think that the Government would be able to justify the course they had taken in any stage of our proceedings. Why were all these measures submitted in January last, if it was known that the session was to be so short that there would not be time for their consideration? We had been told that the session was already protracted to a longer period than was contemplated; but that surely was a strange way of accounting for the introduction of a number of measures which we were now told could not be dealt with even in this longer time. During the month of February the House sat only four nights after eight o'clock, and, with the exception of those four sittings, the whole time consumed in public business did not exceed more than twenty-four hours some minutes. In the face of that fact how could it be said that there had been any worthy effort to carry them into law? The question returned—Why were these measures introduced? Were we to go on with gentlemen occupying the seats of Government who never intended to pass any measure, who had no belief in any measure, but who, because a particular question happened to be debated in public, submitted a measure to satisfy expectations which they cared nothing at all about, and who, if they were likely to be placed in an inconvenient position in consequence, were ready at any moment to abandon the measure they had brought forward? This had been the policy of all the Governments of which the honourable member for West Sydney (Mr. Robertson) had been a member; and any one who would turn to the Votes and Proceedings of the House could satisfy himself of the fact. As some honourable member had moved the adjournment of the House, he almost thought that the best way would be to agree to the motion, and allow the Government an opportunity of considering whether they could not carry out some measure which would have the effect of satisfying, if not the Opposition, at least the just expectations of their own friends. Surely there ought to be some faint hope given to the merchants of Sydney of the abolition of the *ad valorem* duties. Surely those gentlemen who had such a sublime faith in the intentions of the Administration ought to have some better reward than being told to still hope.

In October, 1868, we were told that the leading principle of the Premier was a sincere and earnest desire—a rather curious form of expression that, making a principle a desire—to unfetter trade as much as may be, and to free the commerce of the country. We had been eighteen months trying to unfetter trade, and he should like to know whether there was any prospect of trade being unfettered? A year afterwards we were told, in October last, that the *ad valorem* duties of 5 per cent. would be reduced to $2\frac{1}{2}$ per cent. on the 30th of June next; but there was very little prospect of that now. By the second utterance of the oracle we were told that the reduction was to take effect on the 30th of September next; but there was still very little prospect of that second promise

Evils of a Weak Government.

being carried into effect. He thought that the merchants of Sydney would begin to suspect—what many other persons had long ago suspected—that the revenue was such a convenient thing that the duties would be kept in existence until somebody else would have the disagreeable task of repealing them. The Stamp Act was to supply sufficient revenue to enable this repeal to take place; but that unfortunate measure was found to have conjured up so many opponents that it was also to be cast aside. And would any one believe, after the experience before them of the fate of the Immigration Bill of last session, that it would be revived in the next? The House had a right to complain that the Government of the country session after session submitted a number of measures on important questions of public interest, and invited honourable members to the consideration of those measures, and that after all they should, without any reasonable excuse or explanation, abandon them simply because they thought they would have to encounter opposition which might lead to defeat. If government were to be carried on in that way, a Government might exist and do nothing for twenty years. When the complexion of the Cabinet became a little unpalatable or odious, you had only to arrange for one member to go out and another to come in, and then come down to the House and say—" We want a little time ; it is unreasonable to expect that after these important changes we can do everything." If the honourable member for Newcastle (Mr. Lloyd), for instance, wanted an Immigration Bill, the Minister had only to say to him—" We all agree with you. You shall have an Immigration Bill; only be content to wait a little longer and you shall have all you want." But when the Appropriation Bill was passed all these measures would be dropped. Parliament would go into recess. During the recess another member of the Government would go out and some one else come in. Then they would say it was a new Government, and Parliament must give them time. They could not expect much to be done now that such great changes had taken place ; let there be a short session, and let the Estimates be passed. Another session would come round and a new programme be again submitted. The honourable member for Newcastle would be indulged, and great anxiety would be expressed to carry these measures. But as soon as the Appropriation Bill was again passed, away these measures would go. And so on again and again. Then the

Government would say—"Just think, we have been five years in office, and have not been able to pass measures on account of the obstruction we have met with." A dissolution would be obtained and then there would be another change. All these tactics were well known to the honourable member who had been elected "more times than any other man in the country," who had been "in more Cabinets than any other man," who left a track in the public life of the country, deep, broad, and straight, but which nobody but his friends had yet been able to discover.

This was the style of government upon which they had fallen, and if honourable members chose to submit to it, they would have a Government in office for the next ten years with any number of shiftings to gratify the lovers of change; but he would venture to say that the honourable member for Newcastle would not get his Immigration Bill. As long as there were ten sturdy men from the Emerald Isle to be conciliated, they would not be neglected for the Congregationalism of the honourable member. He would be betrayed like many other innocent young creatures, and would get very little sympathy from his betrayers or from other people. He ventured to assert that no single act of administrative reform would be carried out, simply because the Government had not the requisite power. Men who held office by this kind of tenure would never have the privilege of carrying out any measure for the advancement of the country or of their own honour.

THE PROGRESS OF THE EDUCATION SYSTEM.

PUBLIC SCHOOL BOARDS.

SPEECH

Delivered on the occasion of laying the Foundation-stone of a Public School at Liverpool, June 4th 1871.

MR PARKES said : In our youthful days we had all often heard that " the schoolmaster was abroad." When that great movement for the elevation of men set in fifty years ago in England, the originators of it, in order to give a stimulus to the movement, never tired of telling the nation that the schoolmaster was abroad. He was inclined to think, after listening to the speech of Mr Wearne, that what was wanted in Liverpool was a schoolmaster at home. They wanted something that would infuse a new spirit into the town and district. It seemed a lamentable thing that the fine paper mill close to the town should be closed. There must be something wrong in our industrial system when such was the case. When the community was consuming such large quantities of imported paper, precisely the same kind of article that could be manufactured at that mill, there must be something out of gear or the mill would not be closed. It would only be by knowledge that we should clearly ascertain what it was that was wrong ; and the only way of enabling the public to know how to remedy that which was wrong, in every instance, was to educate the whole mind of the country. The public school system which had been established had for its aim the imparting to the men and women of the future the means of elevating themselves, if they were disposed to do so. He knew as well as anyone that education such as was given by our public school system to children would not be sufficient of itself to make men good, prosperous, or useful. But he knew, on the other hand, that there were a hundred chances to one against the human being left destitute of instruction. Let us give the rising generation the means of serving themselves—the means of turning to advantage every circumstance, which, rightly understood, would be to their advantage—the means of knowing how to benefit others whilst benefiting themselves—the means of guiding themselves in a clear course of duty; and if they did not pursue that course, the fault would be with them and not with society. He really thought that our public school system was equal to that of almost any other country, in being calculated to effect those ends. Allusions had been made to the school system of America; and those of us who had given attention to the subject, knew that America had the distinguished glory of being amongst the foremost nations in imparting sound instruction to the people. What was the consequence? With all their faults—with all the faults inseparable from a new state of society—with all the faults inseparable from a nation that was continually planting new banners on new ground, which had continually to contend with special social circumstances—with all those faults, America had made greater progress in wealth and power, than any other nation of our day—he might say, than any nation known to history. There was another nation equally distinguished for her system of national instruction, he meant Prussia. It was the intelligence much more than the numbers of his soldiers that enabled King William to achieve such victories over France. It was nothing but the instruction which the Prussian soldier received that made him so victorious. He remembered reading an account by an American gentleman who passed through Prussia some years ago, before the late terrible war broke out. This gentleman pointed out then that every common soldier in the Prussian army was equal to a French officer —equal by dint of intelligence, and by bringing a well-informed mind and highly cultivated energies to bear upon every duty he performed. In other countries—our own, he was sorry to say, amongst the rest—the soldier was a mere machine, doing that which he was bidden as though he were an inanimate unintelligent machine; not so with those men who formed the rank and file of the Prussian army. We had seen in the late war the effects of cultivated power in a manner which was perhaps unexampled in the history of warfare. He was inclined to think that the system of public instruction established in this remote colony of New South Wales is equal to either the American or the Prussian system. He felt perfectly satisfied that we were pre-eminently above the other Australian colonies in our system of public education. He had recently had opportunities of observing with his own eyes, and inquiring by the aid of his own faculties into the systems of three of the other Australian colonies. And, without desiring to say one single word in disparagement of those colonies, he felt satisfied that our system of education was superior to them all. Now what was this system of education which had been established in the colony? He would in a very few words point out the leading features of the system of education which we had now established amongst us. He should then desire to point out a few of the good results of the system; and then he would make a few remarks on a matter which he regarded of some importance, and which he had come there to-day more especially to speak upon.

Our system of education had this distinguishing quality: It had no aggressive spirit; it declared war against no one; it interfered with no one's preconceived opinions, nor did it in any way impair or tamper with any man's faith. It had also this other distinguishing quality—that it took the best of all possible securities to see that the children of the country were taught by those who had been taught to teach. It had done away for ever with the possibility of any man with wealth, political or social influence, using that wealth or influence in getting a person appointed as teacher of a public school. No person could by any possibility be appointed as teacher under this system unless he had proved, by going through examinations, that he was capable of teaching. That was a priceless security for the proper teaching of our children. He had said that the system was singularly unaggressive. With what man's conscience was it in conflict? With what man's liberty to deal with his children as he thought proper did it interfere? It opened the door to every child without distinction as to creed, sect, country, or colour. It abolished once and for ever the idea that the public school was a poor man's school or a class school. It had so completely abolished that invidious distinction, that the children of the poorest and the richest men could sit side by side receiving the same amount of instruction and yet feeling each his separate independence. He was aware that there were worthy men in this country who think that the public money ought not to be spent in educating the children of those who could afford to educate them themselves; and he had heard people say that it was not right for a person of property to send his children to a public school. Such an idea struck at the root of the public school system. Instruction was given not alone for the benefit of the children but also for the sake of society hereafter. It sought to secure sound primary instruction to all as the basis of character, and at the same time to familiarise the children with each other, so that whether they were rich or poor they should feel themselves members of the same human family and responsible members of society. One of the great advantages of the system was that the children of all classes could be educated under one roof during the period of childhood; and, if the system was properly carried out, they could not get such good instruction anywhere else. It was not because a person of property would wish to evade the necessary expenses of educating his child that he sent his child to the public school, but because his child, so long as it was receiving elementary instruction, could not get better instruction elsewhere; and because whilst attending a public school the child's mind became infused with a sense of his common citizenship. The provision of the law rendered it impossible to establish any other than one of these public schools in any district in the first instance. Wherever 25 children could be found to regularly attend the school the Council of Education was authorised to establish a public school. That school could not be interfered with—no other school could come into unhealthy competition with it by the aid of public money until it had 70 children. Because it was assumed that a teacher could well control 70 children—or rather that less than 70 children would not be sufficient to provide the necessary salary which a man of ability could always command. The unhealthy competition which formerly existed through two or three small schools—presided over by inefficient teachers who could get nothing better to do—being established in the same place was thus prevented. But the system also provided for aid being extended to denominational schools under certain circumstances.

[Mr. Parkes referred to the provisions of the Act relating to denominational schools, and he also explained the careful training which persons had to receive before becoming teachers of public schools, and entered briefly into an exposition of the Act similar to that contained in the speech at Dundas. He then proceeded:—]

Progress of the Education System. 319

Last year there were 359 public schools—an increase in three years of 71 schools, which were scattered all over the country. Just imagine what an instrumentality for good those 71 schools would prove—schools that were thoroughly organised, with trained teachers and local boards to watch over their management and keep them in a state of discipline. The establishment of those 71 additional schools alone was a prodigious work, a work which promised for this country the most gratifying results. At the end of last year there were 164 provisional schools, showing an increase in three years of 133. During the same period the half-time schools increased from 6 to 82. Thus in places where education was most wanted, where men were the furthest removed from the influence of civilisation, where they seldom came in contact with agencies that led to good, where they were left without any of those restraints felt in more settled society, 71 of these half-time schools had been planted. Whilst all that work had been going on the denominational schools had decreased from 317 to 241. That decrease had not been brought about by any adverse action on the part of the Council of Education; but it had been brought about by natural causes. Parents knew their children got on best in the public schools; many of the most intelligent of the clergymen began to see that the public schools were the best schools, and they were willing to have their denominational schools converted into public schools, in order that the instruction given to the children might be more efficient, and that the children might grow up better men and women to form the society of the future. At the end of last year there were 846 schools under the Council of Education, an increase of more than 200 in three years. He thought therefore that the assemblage he was then addressing might congratulate themselves and congratulate the Parliament of the country upon the enactment of the wise and beneficent law that had produced such results.

He now came to the more unpleasant part of what he had to say. It was the more unpleasant because he had to refer to a gentleman whose character he held in profound respect, and whom he regarded with feelings little short of personal affection, and who within the past few days had left the colony. He alluded to Professor Smith. No one could more warmly admire the character of that gentleman, no one could place a higher estimate upon his services to the cause of public instruction, than he did. He esteemed his services so highly that he did not believe his place could be supplied by any other man in the country in this work of education. He had had the privilege of watching his painstaking and anxious labours in that cause for so long a period that if it were possible for him to give his hearers a just idea of those labours they would concur with him in thinking that it was impossible to set too high an estimate upon the good that that gentleman had done. He need only say that it was some seventeen years since Professor Smith became a member of the Board of National Education; and as a member of the Board he laboured assiduously, and at great personal sacrifice, in promoting the cause of education. Having said thus much he was bound to take exception to an opinion which Professor Smith expressed in a public address about a month or six weeks ago, and which he (Mr. Parkes) thought was calculated to lead to great mischief. One provision of the Public Schools Act was to establish, by the authority of the Executive Government, a Public School Board in connexion with every public school, to watch over its interests. That Board was not supposed to interfere with the routine of intruction. Indeed, if any member of the Board was to so far forget himself as to interfere with the properly trained and duly appointed teacher, he would do what was foreign to his duty and quite contrary to the regulations. The Board had to watch over the school, and see that the teacher regularly peformed his work, that the school was properly regulated and ventilated, and kept in a state of cleanliness; but it had not in any way to interfere with the course of instruction carried on by the teacher under the regulations. Professor Smith expressed an opinion that it would be a very proper thing to appoint clergymen to these School Boards. He admitted at once that, in many instances, clergymen were the most suitable for any work of an educatory character. They were educated men, and were more or less trained to the work of educating. But he objected altogether to this opinion of Professor Smith's, and he thought he could show that meeting that if such an opinion were to be carried into practice it would lead to the most mischievous results. The public school system of this colony is non-sectarian. No clergyman ought to be placed in the position of calling the school his, or to have other clergymen calling it theirs. And he appealed to the everyday experience and common sense of those who listened to him to say

Progress of the Education System. 321

whether if there be two or three persons of comparatively uninfluential position and an influential clergyman of the district appointed, the school would not be regarded as belonging to that clergyman by the people who know his influence and power. It would be impossible to dissociate a clergyman's influence from the authority of the school. And when you told a child that it was a non-sectarian school, he would ask at once how came it that the clergyman was a member of the School Board? The utmost mischief would result from the appointment of clergymen to these boards. The moment you appoint a Church of England clergyman you must appoint a Roman Catholic priest, and you must also appoint a Wesleyan minister, and clergymen of other sects. You would then have none but clergymen on the Board, and thus the principle of non-sectarianism upon which the system rests would be virtually destroyed. And if clergymen were to be appointed members of the School Boards, why should they not be appointed members of the Council of Education? What was the difference in principle? He would like to know how we should carry out this unaggressive system of education if we had clergymen upon the Council. It was not that we undervalued the attainments of clergymen, but because we saw that it was utterly impracticable, that we took our stand against clergymen being appointed members of the School Boards. When we reflected that the School Board had really nothing to do with the system of instruction beyond seeing that it was kept efficient, that the teacher did not relapse into bad behaviour, or that the building did not fall into decay, was it likely that clergymen would wish to be on the Board merely to attend to such matters? The clergyman would want to interfere, and tell the teacher what he thought was right, and what he thought he ought to do. That was what the law said the clergyman should not do. Therefore he thought that, coming from so high a source, the opinion uttered by Professor Smith was calculated to do very much mischief; and he was desirous of embracing the first opportunity to express his dissent from that opinion. He believed the opinion was altogether opposed to the principles and spirit of the Public Schools Act.

He understood that this school, the foundation-stone of which had just been so well laid, would accommodate about 120 children. He must say that he felt some pain that it would not accommodate more. It seemed to him that as there were 90 children already on the roll the new building ought to have provided for a much larger number; and he trusted, at all events, that the plan of the building was such that it could be easily enlarged on some future and not very distant occasion. He could suppose that with an efficient teacher it would soon be found that the school was overcrowded. That seemed to him a matter of regret in a town of such importance as Liverpool ought to be. He had now said what he had chiefly come there to say. He had glanced at the origin, growth, and results of the system of education we had amongst us. He could scarcely express an opinion respecting a system with which he had been so closely identified without laying himself open to a charge of being unduly in favour of it. But, so far as he could examine himself, he did not think he should be insensible to its defects, or to anything superior that could be put in its place. At the same time he felt it his duty to caution the people of this country against too hastily meddling with the system. The system had hitherto worked admirably well, and had produced most gratifying results. It had multiplied schools in the manner he had already shown. It had created an army of trained teachers now 1100 strong. The Council of Education had 1100 men and women trained to the business of teaching children. The largeness of such a blessing as that could not be over-estimated; and it must produce most blessed results in the future generation. It had done all this, and the system that had done so much was worth holding fast. It was worth holding fast when persons of a theoretical turn of mind and wedded to one idea talked of altering it. It was worth holding fast against persons who, however benevolent in feeling, looked at the affairs of the world from a narrow point of view. It was worth holding fast against all changes.

The time might come when it would be necessary to enlarge the system so that it might embrace a higher province of instruction for the more gifted of our children, so that it should embrace, perhaps, a larger number of subjects for instruction. But he did not think that time had come yet. And it was one of the greatest consolations to him to see that the Parliament of this country, whilst it was giving public money to this good work, was at the same time firm and resolute in protecting the system and keeping it in existence. He thought he was at liberty to say that about three months ago he received a letter from a Cabinet Minister of

Progress of the Education System. 323

England, the Minister who carried through the House of Commons the present Education Act, Mr. Forster, the vice-president of the Committee of the Privy Council on Education. Mr. Forster sent him a copy of the Act, and in a letter which accompanied it he said:—" I only hope I shall have the same good fortune with the measure I have succeeded in conducting through the House of Commons that you had with the Public Schools Act which you succeeded in passing when Colonial Secretary of New South Wales." He thought he was justified in stating the opinion of that eminent statesman, because it reflected great credit upon this country that England looked to us for an example of this high import. Any interest which he might have in the matter was very small compared to the interest which we all must feel in knowing that our education policy was not unheeded by statesmen in legislating on the same question for the people of England.

THE COMBINATION

BETWEEN

SIR JAMES MARTIN AND MR. ROBERTSON.

THE POLICY AND MEASURES OF THE MINISTRY.

[IN December 1870 Mr. Cowper and his colleagues (one of whom was Mr. Robertson) resigned office on failing to obtain support in the Legislative Assembly. The Governor (Lord Belmore) sent for Sir James Martin, and entrusted to his hands the formation of a new Government. After his defeat in the Assembly, Mr. Cowper appointed himself to the office of Agent-General in London, and in the course of a few days it was announced that Sir James Martin had formed an Administration, in which Mr. Robertson held the office of Colonial Secretary. This sudden and unexpected combination created the greatest political scandal in the history of New South Wales, the effects of which are still visible in the state of parties. In the beginning of 1872 Sir James Martin, having sustained defeat in the Assembly on the question of collecting the Border Customs duties, obtained from Lord Belmore a dissolution, which resulted in an overwhelming majority opposed to the Government. The following speech was delivered during the election for East Sydney, where Sir James Martin and one of his colleagues—Mr. John Bowie Wilson—were candidates, and where both Ministers lost their seats :—]

SPEECH

Delivered at a meeting of the electors of East Sydney, February 10th 1872.

Mr. PARKES said : I have come here to-night to support Mr. Alderman Macintosh as a candidate for East Sydney. I do not desire to be understood as pleading my own cause in coming to this meeting ; but as a citizen I come, by my presence and by any influence I may possess, to support the claim of this gentleman.

Alderman Macintosh has told you that if he were to be defeated it would be no disgrace to him, but rather a disgrace to those who brought him forward. I dissent from that altogether. There is no disgrace attaching to defeat. What we have to do in any great national struggle is to select the right side, to do our best to win; and, whether we succeed or not, if we have performed our duty there can be no disgrace. I am not in favour of men who, before engaging in any cause, take particular pains to be certain of success. It is a much more wholesome thing when they take pains to be right; and then, whether they stand in twos and threes, in hundreds or in thousands, their cause is equally glorious whatever may be the issue. The cause which does not succeed to-day will, if carried on in that spirit and sustained by that energy, succeed to-morrow. I have no personal interest in this election. I care nothing for the issue so far as it can affect myself. I shall have done well if only I can break up the factions that now exist in this colony.

My first object—and I declare it before the world—is to punish traitors, to vindicate our institutions, and to roll back the tide of corruption which has set in upon us. To me it is of no moment whether I go into the Assembly or not; but if by the powers which God has given me I can assist in bringing this struggle to a glorious result, I shall have done a good work. Now, you were told by Mr. Samuel that he did not think that the enemy were strong. Don't undervalue their strength. It is a fatal weakness to underrate the power of your opponents. Fight this battle as if victory depended on every individual, and do not believe you have won it until you see your flag waving over the ramparts of the enemy. You have been told already of some characteristics of the combination which took place thirteen months ago between Sir James Martin and Mr. Robertson, but there is one feature in the character of that combination which I do not recollect having seen noticed. Sir James Martin prides himself on his political standing as a man of ability and political character. He had for twelve years expressed his derision of Mr. Robertson. For twelve years he had indulged in all kinds of condemnation of that gentleman, and yet it appeared twelve months ago that, with all his strength, with all his ability, with all his public standing, he could not form a Government without the assistance of Mr. Robertson. Mr. Robertson—the despised of twelve years—was necessary, logically necessary, to cement his own materials together in that new-fangled Cabinet. So, again, the Ministers have in every conceivable form of language denounced Mr. Buchanan; and that is a service which Mr. Buchanan has also done for them. Yet these Ministers, who four months ago were denounced by Mr. Buchanan, and who regarded Mr. Buchanan as a gentleman who never ought to have a seat in Parliament again, find it necessary to take Mr. Buchanan to cement them together in this election! Thus we see a consciousness of rottenness all through, a consciousness of inherent weakness, a desire to get anybody's strength, be it the strength of the Devil himself, to bind them together.

The combination between Sir James Martin and Mr. Robertson has sometimes been excused by persons of shallow understanding by a reference to other combinations which have taken place. Amongst other cases they have referred to the coalition between Sir James Martin and myself some five, or nearly six, years ago. If you will permit me, I will show you the difference. In the beginning of 1866 Sir James Martin was sitting in Opposition, and had been sitting in Opposition some considerable time—a year or more. I, too, was sitting in Opposition, and had been sitting in Opposition a long time. I had never been in office at that time, and the coalition between him and me was simply a coalition of two members of the Opposition, who disagreed in some particulars, but who agreed in more important matters at that time —on the question of education for example. Coalitions of that kind have often occurred in the mother-country, in this colony, and in the sister colonies. And, indeed, in these small communities, with the limited number of public men who are eligible for office, it is almost impossible to construct a Cabinet without some compromise of that kind. But what was the case between these two gentlemen? One was the accepted leader of a number of men, amongst whom was myself, and the other was the accepted leader of a number of men who had followed him, as I think, with too close a fidelity for many years. They were standing at the head of distinct parties. They had been standing at the head of parties, or struggling to get to the head of parties, for ten or twelve years. They had both been in office. They had both carried Bills into law; and in office and out of office, on the hustings and in public meetings, in the Executive Council and on the Statute-book of the country, they had impressed on the very tissue of their lives their political antipathy to each other. They could not coalesce.

Sir James Martin and Mr. Robertson. 327

They could not combine. They were not in a position to do the one or the other without betraying their friends. And yet the combination was formed, and formed with the avowed object of rendering Parliamentary Opposition impossible in the Legislative Assembly of the country. Now such a combination of men as that is unknown during the present century in the political history of England. I challenge any person to point to any instance in the history of England since the beginning of this century which is in any way analogous; and it is in this the infamy of the combination consists. What was its immediate effect? It was to shock the followers of these gentlemen on both sides. Every man with the slightest pretension to conscientious conviction, every man with the slightest attachment to principle, who believed he was serving under a true chief, felt that he had been deluded and betrayed, and he became shocked and disgusted with public life. The consequence was that the Government gathered round itself the worst men on both sides—the most dangerous men that have entered Parliament, and the Government party is now made up of the waifs and strays of all parties—the shifting, disappointed, and self-seeking men of all sides. The rats came out of all the holes in the old Assembly. By degrees they began to smell the crumbs falling from the Treasury-table, and the result was that they were speedily and palpably seen clustering round the hand that fed them with this corrupt food. That is the state into which the Government of this country had descended.

I dare say there are men in this meeting who have heard my voice before. Possibly there are some who listened to me when responsible Government was first introduced. If there are, they will remember that I said on many occasions that the thing which the electors had to keep in view above all other considerations was to preserve the independence of the Parliament of the country. I used this language sixteen years ago. I have used it at intervals during the intervening period, and I use it most emphatically in almost the same words to-night. Bad men may rise to power; bad laws may be enacted; but you can sooner or later eject the bad men from power, and erase the bad laws from the Statute-book. But once degrade your Parliamentary institutions, and a wrong is done to the country which will not be remedied during your lifetime. Sir James Martin deserves impeachment, if there were any power of impeachment in this country, for degrading and corrupting the Parliament of the country for his own selfish purposes. And yet last night an old colleague of mine—Dr. Wilson, forsooth!—complained that I was opposing my old friends! After such an event as that in December 1870, when these two men consented in the dark to cover up their past differences at whatever cost in the betrayal of their friends—is there any man who will not say I was released at once from all party obligation? Was I the author of this treason? Did I countenance it? Was I in any way associated with it? If persons with whom I might be associated chose to commit an act of treachery, I should be traitorous to myself and false to you if I did not cast off such allegiance for ever.

I for my part am not surprised—not very much surprised—at Mr. Robertson, because I have heard him boast—apparently quite unconscious of how he was exposing himself—that he had served in office with more men than any other person in the country. And I believe he has served in office with about thirty-nine gentlemen. The Assembly consists of seventy-two members, so that at one time or another he has had more than half the members of the Assembly as his colleagues. When I have heard this gentleman boast of it I have looked at him with a sort of curious amazement, as we should do at any newly-found animal—the discovery of a cat with thirty-nine tails, for instance. The idea that his boasting suggested to my mind was that of a young lady priding herself that she had had more lovers than any other girl in the country—that she had brawny men and slight men, tall men and short men, men with dark hair and men with yellow hair, men of an active temperament and men of a slow temperament; in fact that she had had ten times more lovers than any other girl! But I would like to know what honest man would take her for a wife? To me it was astonishing that Mr. Robertson could not see the dangerous inference that would be drawn from those unseemly vauntings. I therefore am not surprised at Mr. Robertson now, and I am not quite sure that he would not take office under that illustrious statesman, Mr. William Cummings, to-morrow! (A voice: " He would under Jack Davies!") I hear some gentleman say he would take office under Mr. John Davies. Why, does not the gentleman know that he has taken office under Mr. John Davies already? Mr. John Davies takes to himself the credit of arranging the whole thing. "We did it!" says Mr. Davies.

Well now, gentlemen, let us come to the fruits of this beautiful combination. When the late Government went out of office, Mr. Wilson was distinguishing himself as the champion of the working-men of this city, and he had a Labour Bill before the Parliament. He presented a petition signed, I think, by ten thousand mechanics in favour of that Bill; and he took great pride to himself when he brought the large roll before us—a roll so large that it nearly concealed his own slight person. He presented another petition from Newcastle, represented by our excellent friend Mr. Lloyd here. He presented petitions from other parts of the country; and he said he should like to see the man who would dare to vote against the Labour Bill. What became of it? I suppose there are mechanics here? What became of that Eight-hour Bill? (Cries: "He shelved it.") Mr. Wilson was prepared to show in the most unanswerable way the philosophy of reducing the hours of labour to eight; and no doubt that is a great social question presenting great interest. Well, Mr. Wilson kept this Bill dangling before the Assembly and the public for three months, I think, at least, after it got to the second reading. I remember distinctly that it often came on in the early part of the day, when he could have proceeded with it, when there was no other business on the paper; but he did not proceed with it, and at last he went into office, and we heard no more about it. Now when Mr. Wilson acceded to office, his mere presence in the Government of the country conferred so many blessings upon the mechanics and labourers of this city and colony that they no longer wanted an Eight-hour Bill. That may be the explanation; but this is certain, from that day to this we never heard another word of this great social question, or of the Labour Bill which this great champion of the working-men of the country was going to carry into law. It is right that things of this kind should be exposed, because it is an unmanly, a mean, and a shameful thing to delude that large body of our fellow-citizens who have not time to attend much to the affairs of the country—and to do it for the mere purpose of making political capital out of them. If Mr. Wilson believed in this Eight-hour Bill, when he got into office he ought to have tried to carry it into law; and I repeat it is a contemptible thing for the mere purpose of securing the favour of the working-classes of this country to pretend to do a thing which either he never believed in, or which he allowed his own personal interests to deter him from doing.

Before I proceed to the measures of the Government I wish to allude to one other matter to show the character for consistency and fair play which distinguish gentlemen. When it was proposed to reduce the wages of the mechanics and labourers a numerously signed petition was presented, I believe, by Mr. Samuel against this reduction. This petition like the other which I have referred to was informal—that is, technically, it was not presentable. But when Mr. Wilson was seeking to please the working-classes he moved that the Standing Orders of the Assembly be suspended for the purpose of presenting that petition on the Labour Bill; but when the petition signed by ten thousand persons was presented by Mr. Samuel against the reduction of wages, and when it was proposed that the Standing Orders should in this case also be suspended to allow the petition to be presented—then the whole of the Ministers either voted against its reception or left the Chamber in order to break up the House. My reason for alluding to these two discreditable incidents is to show the unmanly and mean character of this Government, to show that there is no generosity about them, that there has been no fidelity to their avowed principles, and that they are quite prepared, when it suits their interests, to take advantage of any slight technicality, at one time to defeat that which at another, when it suited their interests, they were quite ready to promote.

When Sir James Martin last appealed to the electors of East Sydney for re-election, after accepting office, he made a very remarkable speech, and many of you will recollect that he gave expression to sentiments of this kind—that the people did not care who were in office, so long as the business of the country was carried on it was nothing to them who carried it on—that the people in fact had no regard to the consistency of public men, no regard to their faithful adherence to their professed principles—that they cared nothing about morality in political matters. We were expected to believe that the people gave up their time to attend public meetings, left their labour to record their votes at elections, not with a view to have the Government of the country carried on by men in whom they believed, but because they did not care what became of the Government of the country! At the time

I thought that this was a very bad omen, and that we should soon see what kind of administration and what kind of legislation a doctrine of such a kind would be made to cover. The first proposal made to the Assembly was one to double the *ad valorem* duties. I am not going to discuss a question of taxation to-night; but I simply refer to facts. For two years before that Mr. Robertson had been constantly promising the repeal of the *ad valorem* duties, and those oft-repeated promises were even put into the mouth of the Governor in the speeches which he read at the opening of Parliament. It certainly was a startling illustration of the doctrine that the people did not care how the affairs of the country were carried on when the same gentleman who had persistently promised the repeal of the *ad valorem* duties, suddenly, and without notice of any change in his opinions, had the barefacedness to propose to double those duties. Then that tariff was submitted which showed no discriminating desire to adjust the burdens of taxation according to the interests of the people; but which did manifest the ruling passion in this Government, and that is to grind down a handful of population and to press out of them the largest amount of revenue. And this revenue was to be expended in fortifying the harbour, in creating in this country a small standing army—a standing army which consists, I believe, of some 250 persons all told, and of these some 53 are officers ! This standing army costs you at once £20,000 a year. The amount for military purposes on the estimates of public expenditure for this year is £20,000 ; and of course, if the military genius of Sir James Martin has full swing, that will soon be £40,000 a year.

In past times we heard a great deal about " cocked-hats" and " swords." The gentleman who used to enliven you with stories of " cocked-hats " and " swords " was Mr. Robertson ; but we have not heard a single word about the " cocked-hats " since he assisted Sir James Martin to create this magnificent standing army. It is said that he lives at a retired bay in our harbour near the Heads ; and stories are told how on every moonlight night a rather emaciated figure, with a long venerable beard, wearing a cocked-hat decorated with a plume, is seen to glide down to the beach, and, with sword dangling at his side, go through his military exercises preparatory to leading his noble army to the banks of the Murray River. So that in reality we have not only got General Martin in the country, but we have got Corporal Robertson too ; and I am told that the wives and daughters of the mechanics and labourers who have been docked three shillings and five shillings a week in their wages—(A voice : " No, twelve")— are not merely satisfied, but delighted at this martial spectacle, and consider it an ample recompense for the deprivation to which they have been subjected, to be allowed to behold Mr. Robertson in his " cocked-hat !" But it is a fact, at all events, that this new appendage to the country, this standing army, which entails upon those very classes of the people these additional burdens, was created at the very time the reductions in the wages of the Government workmen took place.

You have already been told something about the Land Bill. I think I am entitled, whatever view Mr. Samuel may take of it, to regard that Land Bill as it was introduced into the Assembly. The question had been discussed at different periods for the last two years. It had been promised at different periods for the last two or three years. It was not hastily framed, and we have a right to try the intentions and designs of the Ministers by the Bill which they introduced. That Bill I unhesitatingly say is a monstrous class measure. Class legislation is in itself bad, even where it is unavoidable. In some cases, however, laws have to be passed that only affect classes, laws for regulating particular trades for example ; but inherent in all such laws there is a bad principle which nothing but necessity can justify. But no such necessity can be alleged on the land question. This is a question immeasurably above all others, where legislation should be as common as the sunlight of heaven, where whatever you do should be done for all. Whatever principle you enact, whatever provision you frame, should be open to every man who can take advantage of them. I denounce this Land Bill because it is not of this open, this catholic, this general character ; but it is designed exclusively for particular classes of the country. It only professes to deal with the free selectors who are already upon the agricultural lands, and it deals with them in a way from which they pray to be relieved. The other class with which it professes to deal are the pastoral tenants. It extends to the free selectors the power of doubling their present holdings where they now hold the maximum extent which the law allows, and that is 320 acres. So that if they have 320 acres now the Bill will enable them to make it 640 acres, and then it allows them to buy 640

Sir James Martin and Mr. Robertson. 333

acres more of what is called in the Bill back or inferior lands, which they can get at 5s. an acre. Now I believe it is a fact that the great majority—nine out of ten—of the free selectors do not possess so much as 320 acres. Therefore this Bill would be entirely inoperative to nine out of ten of the free selectors. They have not already worked up to the extent which the present law allows them to select; and, therefore, supposing that is a benefit which is offered by the new Bill, it is a benefit which can only be secured by the richer and the more powerful of the free selectors, while the small struggling free selector is left precisely where he is now. While that is the case, it allows the pastoral tenants, if they choose, to buy up the richest parts of their runs, to the extent of 16,000 acres in one block, at an average price of 8s. an acre ; and it does not allow any other person in the country to do the same thing. Suppose our worthy friend, Alderman Macintosh, retired from business to-morrow, and wished to spend £70,000 in locating himself as a land-holder in the interior ; he could not do it. Or if a gentleman arrived in the colony from England with £50,000 to his credit, and wanted to take up land in the same way, he could not do it. This privilege, good or bad, is confined to one class alone, and for that reason it ought to be universally condemned. I say that men who could have such a conception as that of land legislation are utterly unfit to be trusted with disposing of the territory of New South Wales. What does this land question imply amongst us ? What is this soil, this crust of the earth ? It is an element created by the all-wise Creator of the universe for the benefit of man, without which none of us could live for a single day. Everything we use in society, the materials of which this building is composed, of which this table is made, the clothing we have on, the articles of comfort or luxury we have in our homes, the food we eat—everything we enjoy comes out of the land, and without it we could no more live than we could live without the atmosphere. As inhabitants of a new country we have this element of life, from which everything is derived for our comfort, convenience and sustenance, fresh from the God who formed it, and we ought to regard it as one of the most solemn duties—a duty fraught with the most grave and sacred consequences—how we alienate it and dispose of it among the people. There are some philosophers in Europe, numbering amongst them some of the most profound intellects of the age, who believe that land never ought to be held as private property. On account of its connexion with human life in the way I have described, they contend that it ought to be held in trust, and that it ought not to be passed away under the mere seal of any Government. Without going the length of these doctrines, I say unhesitatingly that the work of alienating the land is a work of more sacred and tremendous consequence than anything that can fall to the lot of the statesmen of old countries like England or France. As we perform this work, so will rise the structure of society when we are dead. As we perform this work, so will our descendants be free, independent, and prosperous men, or the reverse. As we perform this work, so this colony will rise to the dignity of a great free country, or become despised and enslaved, and descend amongst the least powerful nations of the world. If therefore this view of mine be at all correct—and I defy any one to prove that it is unsound—it is something like treason to the commonwealth to frame a class measure dealing with the public lands ; and because it is a class measure, without examining its provisions, I say it ought to be condemned.

Coming to the question of the Border duties, if you will permit me I should like to say a few words. I certainly do not wish to weary the attention of the meeting. I have heard views expressed on this question by members of the late Assembly, and by persons professing to deal with public affairs, which have amazed me for their stupidity. I have heard gentlemen engaged in legislating for the country say, " Why should not the people on the River Murray pay duties as well as the people of Sydney ? Why should not the duties be collected on the River Murray when they are collected in the port of Sydney ?" And they seem to be utterly incapable of distinguishing the difference ! These are the people who belong to the class which I once had the honour to describe as gun-barrel philosophers. They are continually looking down a tube, and because they only see a small point of light they do not believe that there is anything else in the universe. " Why should duties not be collected on the Murray when they are collected in Sydney ?" say they ; and they fancy that they have silenced all objections by this astute observation, which they take to be an argument ! I will tell you why. The Murray River is a stream not wider than Pitt-street, except in flood time, where

Sir James Martin and Mr. Robertson. 335

there are persons living in close neighbourhood on both sides of the river. Suppose that whenever the persons living on the west side of Pitt-street went to the east side of Pitt-street to buy a tin pot, six pounds of sugar, a pound of tea, or two or three loaves of bread—suppose they were stopped in the middle of the street by a Custom-house officer, and compelled to go back and get a permit for every article. What a pretty state of harmony Pitt-street would be in! Then there would be work for the standing army, and we should see Alderman Macintosh at the head of the insurgents. Well that is exactly the case of the settlers on the borders of this narrow stream; and yet these wiseacres cannot see the difference between a state of things like that and duties paid on a cargo of goods at the Custom-house in Sydney, where the duty enters into the price of the goods—the merchant charging it to the retailer, and the retailer to the consumer, who may be said to pay the duty without knowing it. Such a state of things as that would be enough to goad on any people to sedition and insurrection; and I say if I was a settler on the River Murray, I would never rest until that state of things was put an end to. Inconvenience is occasioned by the collection of duties here; but on the Murray the collection of them would be a perpetual annoyance, goading on men to desperation and rebellion. It is simply talking nonsense to say that there would be no inconvenience; and persons who fail to see any difference between collecting the duties at Sydney and on the Murray show that they are utterly unable to grasp the large question at issue. I am as desirous of preserving to New South Wales the revenue which belongs to it as any man; but I say if there were no other means of saving our fellow-colonists from a system of annoyance such as this, it would be wise to forego the revenue altogether. But there is no necessity for that, because an arrangement might be made with the other colonies by which substantial justice would be done, and this annoyance to our people be entirely removed. But the gentlemen who govern us prove by their own acts and their own reports to Parliament that they are entirely incompetent to conduct the negotiation necessary to obtain that result. In the first place they proceeded in great state overland to Melbourne. Sir James Martin had heard that negotiators five hundred years ago used to go on their missions in carriages with cocked-hats, swords, and a retinue of young men, who were to be inducted into the science of diplomacy. He imitated this old-fashioned system of diplomacy, and proceeded with his retinue in great form to the borders of the colony. He accepted a little paltry dinner there, and he declared that if his views were not adopted—or, as he put it, if the Victorian people were not reasonably fair—he should not shrink from his duty and re-establish Custom-houses on the Murray. Now, I have put this illustration before at Mudgee; but as you were not at Mudgee you will allow me to state it here. Suppose the Commissioners appointed by the Government of England to proceed to Washington to settle the difference which had arisen between England and America out of the ravages of the pirate ship "Alabama," and out of the Canadian Fisheries question—suppose they had stopped at Liverpool, which will answer to Albury in our colony, and had accepted a dinner; and suppose that at that dinner they had declared that if the Cabinet at Washington would not listen to reason, they would not hesitate to see that the dockyards were put in order and the recruiting-sergeant sent forth. Do you think they would have been received by the Cabinet at Washington? And when they came back to London do you think they would have been listened to with patience by either House of Parliament? Notwithstanding that that Commission was composed of men sprung from illustrious families, distinguished by great services and high talents—notwithstanding all their claims to consideration, do you think they would have been permitted to continue in power in England? (Cries of "No.") I am confident you are right. But that is precisely what our negotiators did before they left this colony, and was it any wonder that they did not succeed? Sir James Martin's own report is that because the Ministers of Victoria said they would not give more than £60,000 per annum, he never pressed his case. By his own report, and by his own explanation before the electors, he admits that he took up the position of an ill-bred, ill-blooded, surly boy, when he virtually said, "Unless you give me what I want I won't have anything more to do with you." Then he put it in another form: "You must give me what I ask, right or wrong; and if after that you can prove that I am entitled to something more, you must give me that too." That is really a fair exposition of the position taken up by Sir James Martin on this question, and I ask you whether it is not dis-

Sir James Martin and Mr. Robertson. 337

creditable to us that we should tolerate any excuse for the bungling of a great question like that? Suppose Mr. Duffy is the person they represent him to be—in place of what he really is, an able and accomplished man—but for the sake of argument we will suppose Mr. Duffy to be what these gentlemen represent him to be—what then are we to think of our own representatives who put it in his power to slap us in the face time after time, while we are bound to admit that these slaps are justly given?

I say the discredit which these persons have brought upon the country is, and ought to be, unpardonable. But then look at the consequences. Is there any man in this city so dead to the federal interests of these young countries as not to know that it is the duty of every public man who can see beyond his own interests, who can rise above the exigency of the day, to promote harmony, peace, and goodwill among the colonies, so that hereafter they may unite in a great Australian empire worthy of the great motherland from which we are descended? But by a course of conduct like this impediments are thrown in the way of harmony, bitterness is promulgated, and if these men are allowed to have their swing, nothing short of disaffection, rebellion, and dismemberment can follow. A Government which is capable of these monstrous proceedings is deserving the support of no man, whether he comes from England, Scotland, or Ireland, or whether he is a native of the soil—is deserving of the support of no man who stands erect in the light of day, who judges of questions for himself, and who is capable of bringing to them a clear and an independent understanding.

My only object here is to support Alderman Macintosh; but it seemed to be necessary to show you the case with which Alderman Macintosh will have to deal. It is because I believe in Alderman Macintosh's conscientiousness, because I believe he will not blink any of these questions, but that he will struggle for the right in the performance of his duty, however unpleasant it may be, that I have come to give him my unqualified support. The time is come when you must suffer no dictation. If any person, be he whom he may, meet you at the corner of the street, take you by the button, begin whispering some story into your ear, and ask you to pledge yourself blindly to some course—tell him you are a free man. The language to address to a person like that is—" Who are you? Who authorised you to interfere with my discharge of my duty?

I am a free subject of a free Government. I am capable of judging of these things for myself. I will have none of your impertinence; but I will do what I believe is for the good of my country by voting as my conscience and my judgment direct me."

THE BORDER CUSTOMS DUTIES.

[MR. PARKES accepted office as Colonial Secretary and Premier May 14th 1872, and immediately a Bill was brought forward in the Legislative Assembly to enable the Government to make conventions with the colonies of Victoria and South Australia for the free passage of the River Murray. In moving that the Bill be read a second time (June 19th) the following speech was delivered by the Minister. The second reading was carried by 37 votes to 17, and the Bill was subsequently passed through all its stages and sent to the Legislative Council. It was, however, defeated in the Upper Chamber. In the next session another Bill for the same purpose was introduced and passed into law; and under the provisions of this Act conventions were made both with Victoria and South Australia for the payment of lump sums in lieu of the collection of Customs duties on goods imported into the three colonies along the River Murray. After some months the Victorian Convention was annulled by the action of the Francis Ministry. The South Australian Convention is still in force.]

SPEECH

Delivered on making the motion that the Border Duties Convention Bill be read a second time in the Legislative Assembly, June 19th 1872.

MR. PARKES said: In moving that this Bill be read a second time, he need not occupy much time in endeavouring to state the question which the Government desired to deal with by the measure in his care. It had been so much under the consideration of Parliament, and had been a subject of such strong opinion out of doors, that it must be pretty well known to all divisions of the public. He approached the question with a full sense of the respect which was due, and which he desired to pay to that portion of the public who thought differently from himself and colleagues. It seemed to him that at all times when there was any question of great public interest, those who took one side were in a special manner required to respect the convictions of those who took the other side. This to a very large extent had been the question—

though he was willing to admit that it was not the only question —upon which the suffrages of the country were taken a very short time ago. It had been debated in the late Assembly on several occasions and under very different circumstances; and it could not be supposed that any single member was not prepared to consider it at the present time. Those who thought with the Government were of opinion that as a matter of policy it was unwise, and would lead to many unpleasant and disastrous consequences, to collect, by actually stationing Custom-house officers on the Murray frontier, the duties which were justly receivable upon goods imported into this colony from the neighbouring colonies or exported from our territory into theirs. Those who took the opposite side maintained the ground that it was in the same manner just and reasonable to collect the Customs duties all along the Murray frontier as it was to collect them in the port of Sydney. He would not attempt to go over the ground which had been gone over so often in order to impress upon the mind of that House the disadvantages and impolitic results that would follow the continued collection of these duties on the Murray River. The Government thought that substantial justice to the colony could be obtained without the necessity for the actual interposition of the Customs authorities—that substantial justice could be obtained for the whole population without placing a portion of that population under circumstances of annoyance, delay, and irritation, to which the rest of their fellow-colonists were not subjected. It was not the case that equal justice was dealt out to them and to the rest of the colonists by enforcing the law alike in the ports of our seaboard and in the river ports along the frontier. Because, as had been frequently pointed out, it was one thing for the Customs duties to be paid upon cargoes or large consignments or whole packages in the port of Sydney, and by a means which in no way came home to the immediate consumer, and it was quite another thing to enforce the same law on a narrow river like that which divided this colony from the colony of Victoria, and where its enforcement was felt in the most irritating manner in close connexion with all the daily transactions of life. And the Government said—not that they desired in any way to favour the remote border settlers—not that they desired in any way to relieve them from the burdens which they ought to bear in common with the rest of the population—but they said that it was sound policy to relieve them from this species of irritation which must, if the law was actually enforced, fall upon them, whilst it did not fall upon the rest of the population. That was the view entertained by some gentlemen of much ability and high standing in this country a very short time ago, who now took an opposite view. The hon. and learned member for East Macquarie (Sir James Martin) was the author of the only agreement which had existed to secure Free-trade across the River Murray. When that agreement was made the subject of legislation—when the honourable and learned member introduced a Bill to make it a part of the law of the country—he delivered a speech full of forcible argument in support of this Free-trade across the intercolonial boundary line. At that time—in the year 1867—the case had not received the large and general discussion which it has since received. Little attention had then been directed to it beyond the districts which were affected by the actual practice in carrying out the law ; and it seemed to the Government that on this account it was now necessary to take a course quite different to the course which was then taken. It seemed to the Government that it was desirable in attempting to deal with this matter at this stage to keep steadily in view the fact that a considerable body of our fellow-colonists had now, as it were, been educated into something like convictions on this question in opposition to the views of the Government. They were a very considerable minority, assuming, as he did assume, and as he thought he was entitled to assume, that those who took the views which he held were the majority in the country. These persons had thought over the question, had formed opinions, and come to conclusions such as had no existence in 1867. And in respect to the persons who had arrived at these conclusions from a process of inquiry and discussion, he thought we were called upon to afford them a fair opportunity of stating their views in opposition, and to fairly enter into a discussion of the question before we came to a settlement of it. And it was for that reason he thought it his duty to give the time—not a very long time he admitted—which was asked for by the honourable gentlemen opposed to this Bill—that was, seven days from the introduction of the Bill to its second reading. Similar considerations induced the Government to seek the authority of Parliament to proceed in this matter rather than enter into an arrangement with the Government of Victoria first, and then seek the ratification of that agreement by the Legislature, as was done five years ago. It seemed to the Government that it would be by far the most desirable way, the most satisfactory to all parties, to bring the matter before the Legislature and get the decision of that House before they attempted to do more than the law authorised them to do. He did not think it could be denied that the Government had done all they could do without the authority of law. Even those who might perhaps think the Government had not taken the most prudent course, that they had made mistakes in judgment, would, he thought, admit that the Government had lost no time in endeavouring to bring the matter at once before the notice of the Governments of the neighbouring colonies, and that they had prepared, as far as they possibly could, the minds of these Governments for legislation on the subject.

Now he wished to explain for himself and for the Government of which he was a member, that whilst they were very anxious to do everything that could be done to relieve the border settlers from the grievances of which they complained, they were at the same time equally anxious to keep in view the interests of the rest of the population of this country. And they did not wish to proceed in doing what they thought the Legislature ought to do in meeting their claims, without at the same time taking every step in view of the interests of other sections of the community. And holding that view, which he did very strongly, and which was in accordance with the expression of his opinions at all times, it seemed to him that it was necessary for the Government to obtain legislative authority in proceeding with this matter, for two or three distinct reasons. In the first place, in consideration of the changed state of public feeling and the altered circumstances to which he had already adverted, it appeared to him necessary to obtain legislative authority to suspend the actual collection of these duties, rather than to take that course by any measure of the Executive Council. But it appeared to him, in a still more forcible manner, necessary to obtain legislative authority in order to ensure correct returns in the accounts upon which a new agreement was to be based. And he said at once that at the present time he should be most unwilling to be a party to taking any account of these duties for a period of twelve months, unless we had the utmost guarantees the law could give us for ensuring the correctness of such account; if there was to be any value attached to the information collected by persons appointed for that purpose, it must be obtained under the authority of law. Persons might be led to give inaccurate information from a variety of motives. And if an agreement was formed between this colony and the colony of Victoria, by which we were to receive a lump sum, in quarterly payments, in lieu of the amount which we should otherwise receive by the actual collection of the duties for a term of years, the revenue would be affected by any inaccurate return, not to the extent of the duty upon that one transaction, but to the extent of such duty for five years. He therefore thought it was incumbent upon the Government not to be a party to the taking of any such account as had been proposed without first ensuring that that account should be thoroughly trustworthy, and fairly represent the commercial traffic across the frontier. In the next place, it seemed to the Government desirable that they should have legislative sanction for inviting the Governments of other colonies to be parties to this account. It appeared to him and his colleagues more satisfactory that that course should be taken with the sanction of Parliament than that they should simply carry out a decision of the Executive Council.

The Bill which the Government had introduced, and which he now asked the House to read a second time, provided in the first section for the suspension of the existing law during twelve months whilst the account was being taken. He was inclined to think that that clause would require to be amended when it got into committee. But he did not think that this would be the first Bill that had been amended in committee. It would not want amending in any way which would affect the principles of the Bill. He thought it would probably require amending in such a way as would give the Governor, with the advice of the Executive Council, power by proclamation to state when the twelve months should commence during which the account was to be taken. The object of the clause was simply to suspend the operation of the existing law during the time the account was being taken. The second section empowered an account to be taken jointly by the officers of the neighbouring colony and officers of this colony. The third section formally gave power to the Government to join with the Governments of the neighbouring colonies in taking an account or accounts, because it was possible that an agreement might be made with Victoria and a separate agreement with South

Australia. By the fourth section it was provided that the money which was shown to be due to New South Wales should be paid into the hands of our Government within thirty days after it had become due. By the Border Duties Agreement which was enacted in 1867, he remembered that notwithstanding that the agreement had the force of law and provided that the sum of £60,000 due to this colony should be paid quarterly, the Victorian Government refused to pay the money for nearly twelve months. He remembered, holding as he did the office of Colonial Secretary at the time, receiving minute after minute from the Treasurer of the day calling his attention to the subject, and he remembered writing letter after letter requiring the money to be paid, and he well remembered receiving letters from Sir James M'Culloch offering reasons for the non-payment of the money when it amounted to nearly £60,000. In fact they declined to pay a single penny, notwithstanding it was the law of our colony that it should be paid every three months, until it had been voted by the Victorian Parliament. Now as it was our revenue, which we should collect through our own Custom-house officers under ordinary circumstances, he denied that there was any constitutional right in the money being voted by a Parliament which had nothing whatever to do with it. And he should require the Government of the neighbouring colony to obtain an enactment, if necessary, authorising them to pay over this money when it was due. Of course our law would have no binding effect upon them. In the former case to which he had alluded, the delay in the payment to us was caused by a dead-lock between the two Houses of the Victorian Legislature. And what, he asked, had we got to do with any dead-lock between those two Houses? The fifth section was framed to enable the Government to make the necessary agreement for suspending the collection of the duties on conditions defined in the other provisions of the Bill. Now he was aware that very possibly objection might be taken to this portion of the measure, and that it might be urged that they were attempting to withhold from Parliament the authority to supervise the terms of the agreement. There was in the House of Commons a party of able men who were insisting that that House ought to be consulted before any international treaties were entered into. But that party in England was at present a very small and powerless one. It was very easy to see how hampered the authority of Government would be in making any arrangements of this kind if they could only be made subject to the consent of Parliament. We had had the views of the Prime Minister of England clearly expressed upon this subject only a few months ago, when a question was asked in the House of Commons by Mr. Horsman as to whether the Government would promise the House not in any way to vary the propositions between the Cabinets of London and Washington without allowing the House of Commons to express its opinion upon any new proposal that might be made. On that occasion the Prime Minister expressed his views upon the existing state of the law and the constitutional course that ought to be pursued under such circumstances; and the leading organs of public opinion—the *Times*, the *Pall Mall Gazette*, and other papers—concurred in applauding the singular soundness of the opinions thus enunciated. He was fully sensible of the great difference between a treaty made between two colonies and one between Great Britain and the United States; yet the only precedents for the guidance of the colonies must be drawn from such cases. The following was the statement to which he referred; he quoted from the *Times*:—

" Mr. Horsman : I will put the question in the form in which it stands on the paper, and I will ask the Prime Minister whether he can give an assurance to the House that, with reference to the Alabama Treaty, no new proposals shall be made or accepted by the British Government as binding on this country until they shall have been made known to Parliament, and an opportunity afforded for an expression of its opinion upon them.

" Mr. Gladstone : Parliament ought to be informed and must be informed of the spirit, aim, and direction of the policy of the Government. Parliament has been informed through the medium of discussion in the two Houses of that spirit, aim, and direction, and of the leading propositions on which the Government has founded its policy."

He thought that one sentence contained a principle that ought to be applied equally to the agreement between this colony and Victoria; and he maintained that the present Government had enabled Parliament to know the spirit, aim, and direction of what they proposed to do more definitely than they could have done had they proceeded on the principle adopted in 1867, because they had confined their course of action within the four corners of a Bill. The report from which he quoted proceeded with Mr. Gladstone's reply :—

" Were there to be any alteration in the spirit, aim, and direction, so far as I go with my right honourable friend it would be the duty of the Government to take care that Parliament was made aware of it. Beyond that, and beyond referring to the declarations that have been already made, I do not think it is possible to meet the demand of my right honourable friend. What is that demand? 'That with reference to the Alabama Treaty' something shall not be done; but I cannot accept that as a limitation, because the principles applicable to the Alabama Treaty would be applicable to every other negotiation of great and critical importance. But, as the question is put, it has reference to the Alabama Treaty, and my right honourable friend asks that no proposals shall be made or accepted by the British Government as binding on this country until they shall have been made known to Parliament, and an opportunity afforded for an expression of its opinion upon them.

"Mr. Horsman: No new proposals.

"Mr. Gladstone: I beg pardon for omitting the word 'new,' but it is immaterial, because any proposals would be new. I have heard my right honourable friend himself, and I have heard other gentlemen, raise questions of very great importance and delicacy and difficulty, by giving an opinion in this House that the treaty-making power of the Crown ought to be limited, and that the Houses of Parliament ought to be made parties to the acceptance of any treaty. Those discussions I have always conceived to be within, not only the competence of the House to entertain, but the competence of any member to raise; and if I have an opinion on one side of the question, I admit there is much to be said on the other side. But the present question of my right honourable friend goes very much indeed beyond this point. It asks that no new proposals shall be made or accepted by the British Government as binding upon this country until Parliament is consulted. Every proposal made by any Government is binding on the country, according to the terms in which it is made; and therefore, in point of fact, the demand is that nothing shall be proposed in the course of these negotiations without the assent of Parliament prior to its promulgation to the world, or at least until the lapse of time sufficient to afford an opportunity for the expression of its opinion. If it were possible, which I do not believe it to be, that such a demand as this could be answered by the House in the affirmative, I should say it would reduce the position of any Government charged with international negotiations to such a state that it would be far better that the Houses of Parliament should place diplomatic negotiations in the hands of committees, or, perhaps, as an improvement upon that, in the hands of a joint committee, for it would render such negotiations entirely impossible; and though errors may be made under the present system, success and the avoidance of error would become absolutely impossible under the system of duality which it appears to me the question points to."

Now supposing the Bill were passed in its present state, it certainly would not give any power to the Government for the time being except to make an agreement in strict accordance with the law as expressed in this Bill, without the possibility of evading the spirit, aim, and direction of the policy embraced by its provisions. The *Times* had a leading article upon Mr. Gladstone's reply to Mr. Horsman, one sentence of which he would read :—

"It is impossible that a person of Mr. Horsman's experience in the management of affairs can have supposed that the Government would hamper themselves in their negotiations with America in the way he suggested, and he could not have expected any other answer than he received."

An authority which stood very high—the *Pall Mall Gazette*—said :—

"The answer which Mr. Gladstone gave to Mr. Horsman yesterday is in many respects far more satisfactory than his answers usually are. Its language and its tone suggested the statesman rather than the word-abounding orator—a rare thing when the Premier speaks. Admitting that it might be wise to adopt here such constitutional rules as give the American Senate a decisive voice in the ratification of treaties, he very properly declared his intention of abiding by the rules in force amongst us till they are changed, and refused to acquiesce in the suggestion (as he put it) that 'no new proposals shall be made or accepted by the British Government as binding upon this country until Parliament is consulted.' But he further declared his opinion that 'Parliament ought not to remain in substantial ignorance of the course of these great affairs while they are in their current state. Parliament ought to be informed, and must be informed, of the spirit, aim, and direction of the policy of the Government.' This appears to us perfectly satisfactory ; nor do Parliament and the country ask for more than that they be kept informed of the spirit and intention of Ministers in their dealings with foreign Powers."

Nothing could be more definite and clear than the aim and object of the Government in the power they asked from the Parliament of this country. It was to make an agreement with the neighbouring colonies, based upon the actual collection of statistics for twelve calendar months, securing to this colony the balance shown to be due upon that account to the uttermost farthing. And there was no other object whatever. This kind of legislation was not new to the colonies. He should be able to show that in the colony of Victoria the law already contained the principle of this Bill. In the Customs Consolidated Act of 1857, an Act passed after the introduction of responsible government into that colony, there was the following clause, which was still in force :—

"236. It shall be lawful for the Governor in Council to make regulations and arrangements with the Governors of New South Wales and South Australia respectively for the importation of goods across the River Murray, and for the imposition of duties, and the amount thereof on such goods, or the exemption of the same from duties, and the recovery of duties on goods so imported into Victoria, and the repayment of such duties, and in other respects so to regulate the trade on the said river as may be from time to time agreed upon by the said Governors or either of them, and also to determine at not less than three months' notice any such arrangements. Provided that no such duties shall exceed the duties of Customs lawfully collected and paid on goods otherwise imported into Victoria."

The Act passed in the year 1862 enacted that the Government of this colony might, with the advice of the Executive Council, enter into a binding treaty with the colony of Queensland. We sought to enable the Government to proceed to make an agreement which we believed could be easily made with each of the neighbouring colonies for relieving our Border settlers from the grievances of which they had so long complained, and which were admitted by a large majority of their fellow-countrymen; and at the same time we hoped to secure what we believed to be justly due to ourselves.

We did not desire to attempt to carry this measure except with a due consideration of all the interests involved. We expected opposition, because we knew that there were gentlemen in this House who had an equal desire to promote the public interests, and who thought that they would best do so by the actual collection of these duties. We knew that they had arrived honestly at these convictions, and we expected a strong, but at the same time a fair opposition from these gentlemen. We, however, thought that the sense of the Parliament and of the country was with us—that equity, sound policy, and good government were also on the side we took in this contest. We believed the Bill was capable of effecting the object at which we aimed, and we thought that an agreement could be made under it which would in a much more certain manner carry out justice than would be the case if we attempted first to make an agreement with the neighbouring colonies, and then came down to the House for an approval of that agreement. We felt that we were pursuing a right course, the more so because we desired if possible to include the three colonies. We saw great chance of delay and mistake if, after an agreement were made between New South Wales and Victoria and South Australia, it had to be referred to the three separate Legislatures.

He desired to speak with the utmost respect of the Governments of the neighbouring colonies, but he thought that those of us who were charged with responsibility in the matter ought to bear in mind that we must expect that each Government would endeavour to make the best terms it could for its own colony. We must be prepared to negotiate with a full knowledge that that was sure to be the case. Our interests would be affected in a much more material way than would the interests of Victoria by the results of this account; and while it might suit Victoria to offer to take this account without any legal guarantee of its correctness as certified by officers appointed for the purpose, it would not suit us to do so. Our revenue to a considerable extent would depend upon the correctness of this account, while that of Victoria would not be materially affected by it. We therefore ought to be extremely careful in accepting this account, while we were prepared to accept in all good faith the offer of the neighbouring colony; and feeling assured that they were acting in good faith, we thought they could not object to our taking the necessary legal guarantees to have the account correctly taken. He could not suppose that the Government of Victoria would object to such a reasonable proposal, and we did not think that we should be safe in entering upon an agreement based on account unless the correctness of that account were secured under the law. It would of course be objected that the taking of that account would be nearly as vexatious as the collection of the duties. That would not be so in fact, because there would be no necessity for the payment of moneys. Information could be given at any point where a person crossing the river met the Customs' officer without any necessity to go back. Admitting however that the practice would be meddlesome, still it seemed the only possible way of doing justice in the settlement of this question; and the trouble which it might cause for twelve months could not, he thought, be considered as against the value of the object to be obtained—a correct basis for an agreement which was to bind this colony for a term of years.

He noticed from the questions put to him by the hon. member for the Tumut that there appeared to be some rumour that a definite proposal had been made to this Government. That was not the case. No proposition had been made to the Government beyond that which was disclosed by the correspondence laid on the table and the telegram which he had had placed in the hands of hon. members. It would be observed that in that telegram Mr. Francis referred to a letter written on the 15th December by the late Government before the House was dissolved, and from some oversight in Victoria which he could not comprehend, he did not allude to the letter of the present Government. He noticed from the telegraphic information in the newspapers, but had no advice of it whatever himself, that a letter was addressed to this Government yesterday by the Government of Victoria. In that case it would probably be in our hands to-morrow or on Friday morning, when probably we should know the views in detail of the Government of Victoria. He had no doubt whatever that the Government of Victoria would enter into the settlement of this difficult and long-pending question. It seemed to him that in any agreement that might be arrived at considerations ought to be entertained beyond the actual balance shown to be due to New South Wales by the twelve months' account at the present time. It would properly be the duty of the Government of this colony to consider what would be the prospective growth of the trade across the Murray, to consider how far the trade might be increased by the completion of their inland railway, and there were other matters which ought to influence negotiations in order to form an agreement upon a basis which should represent the fair average of five years as nearly as it could be calculated. The balance could only be regarded as a basis, not as a thing to be literally followed. We ought to obtain an amount that would represent the fair average of the revenue for five years. It was due to this country that these considerations should have their full weight, and he could not conceive it possible that their equity would not be admitted by Victoria. The Bill, the second reading of which he had now the honour to move, was intended simply to empower the Government to do what Parliament had already declared ought to be done in the interests of the country, what he believed a large majority of the electors who were appealed to declared ought to be done. He had no object whatever, beyond a desire to carry out in a legal and proper manner the policy with which he was identified, in his endeavour to govern this country with an equitable regard to the interests of all classes.

THE CONSTITUTION OF THE UPPER CHAMBER.

[SOME of the earliest efforts of Mr. Parkes as a public speaker were made in opposition to the nominee principle embodied in the Constitution Bill of Mr. Wentworth in 1853. The following speech was delivered twenty years afterwards, when, as Premier, he moved the second reading of the Government Bill to eradicate that principle from the Constitution. The Bill was read a second time by 33 to 12 votes, passed through all its subsequent stages in the Legislative Assembly, and sent to the Council for its concurrence. The Council refused to receive it, on the ground that a measure affecting its constitution ought to have been introduced in that Chamber. In a correspondence with Earl Grey some months afterwards Mr. Parkes explained why the Bill was first considered by the Assmbly. In a letter dated August 8th, 1873, he says :—"If the Bill had been introduced in the Council it would have been defeated on the second reading without any opportunity being afforded for taking the opinion of the representative branch of the Legislature upon its principles. The Bill having now received the approval of the Assembly by large majorities, will be introduced next session in the Council, where I think it is sure to be defeated. Possibly another effort will be made in another session, and then the question of the reconstruction of the Council on a basis of popular election will be remitted to the constituencies." In the next session the Government introduced the Bill in the Legislative Council, where it was a second time got rid of by being referred to a Select Committee, from which it was never reported.]

SPEECH

Delivered in the Legislative Asssmbly on moving that the Bill to Provide for the Representation of the People in the Legislative Council be read a second time, February 13th, 1873.

MR. PARKES said : In making this motion he acknowledged that it was incumbent upon him to show that a necessity existed for the proposed change, and he thought he should be able to satisfy honourable members that the necessity did exist. Before he entered upon that part of his subject however, he would wish to say a few words on the question as to the necessity of a Legislative Council at all. He was fully aware that opinions were entertained that a Legislature consisting of one House only would be quite sufficient for the legislative wants of a country like ours, quite sufficient to meet the needs of our present state of society.

Mr. STEWART: Hear, hear.

Mr. PARKES: He was aware that his honourable friend the member for Kiama held that opinion, and he believed very strongly. He was aware it was entertained by him in common with other gentlemen scarcely less distinguished than his honourable friend; but an opposite opinion was entertained by persons who, at least, had equal claim to be received as authorities on a subject of this kind. He might quote the authority of by far the larger number of eminent persons who had given expression to their views on this question of government; but he should be content with introducing the authority of two very eminent men, and of course he should allude to what these men had said simply as words of authority, because this was a question which to a great extent must be decided by the authority of persons acknowledged as having thought much on the subject, and acted a memorable part in political history. He believed the chief arguments against another Chamber in the colony of New South Wales were based upon the cost, the needless cost as it was contended, of something like £10,000. Well, suppose the cost was five or ten times the amount, the cost was not a matter to be considered in establishing securities for sound legislation. If it could be proved that in reasonable probability we should arrive at sound legislation better by the action of two Houses than by the simple action of one, that result was of such priceless importance to the permanent interests of the country that the question of expenditure was lost in its magnitude. So that he dismissed this consideration as not worthy of a moment's examination by persons who addressed themselves seriously to this large subject of government. He did not think that much importance was to be attached to any of the other objections which he had heard to a second Chamber. One was that it was difficult to find men. Well he held the opinion—and on this question it must be a matter of mere opinion—that it would be very easy to form a Legislative Assembly without the election of any one of the

Constitution of the Upper Chamber. 353

present members, and that that Assembly would in all probability work quite as much to the satisfaction of the country as the one now in existence. The same might be said to a very large extent of the Legislative Council. It was quite true that there were a few gentlemen in the Legislative Council who, from their ripened experience, the services they had rendered to the public, and the individual authority which they had acquired from years of activity in public affairs, could not well be replaced so far as these valuable qualities were concerned. But even in the case of these more eminent members of the Council it could not be for a moment contended that men of equal education, social standing, and ability could not be found within the ranks of our present society. He therefore thought that this could not be held to be a valid objection to a second Chamber. In other words, we had sufficient material for constituting the complex machinery of two Houses quite as good as any other machinery of which the Government of the country was composed.

The authorities in support of two Houses were numerous and eminent. The two he should quote were men who had lived in different countries, under different forms of government, affected by different social circumstances, and who had lived at different times, though not very far removed. One would be Mr. Justice Story, and the other Mr. Mill, the famous political economist. Mr. Justice Story in that great work of his in which he had been recognised as the expounder of the Constitution of the United States, had these words on the wisdom of the dual or double form of Legislature. Speaking of the Constitution of America he said (and of course, so far as principles were concerned, his words applied to these colonies):—

"The Constitution, on the other hand, adopts as a fundamental rule the exercise of the legislative power by two distinct and independent branches. The advantages of this division are, in the first place, that it interposes a great check upon undue, hasty, and oppressive legislation. In the next place it interposes a barrier against the strong propensity of all public bodies to accumulate all power, patronage, and influence in their own hands. In the next place it operates indirectly to retard, if not wholly to prevent, the success of the efforts of a few popular leaders by their combinations and intrigues in a single body, to carry their own personal private or party objects into effect, unconnected with the public good. In the next place it secures a deliberate review of the same measures, by independent minds, in different branches of Government engaged in the same habits of legislation, but organised upon a different system of elections. And in the

Y

last place it affords great securities to public liberty by requiring the co-operation of different bodies, which can scarcely ever, if properly organised, embrace the same sectional or local interests or influences in exactly the same proportion as a single body. The value of such a separate organisation will of course be greatly enhanced the more the elements of which each body is composed differ from each other, in the mode of choice, in the qualifications, and in the duration of office of the members, provided due intelligence and virtue are secured in each body."

Well, he thought the views propounded by Mr. Justice Story might be illustrated and supported by every man's experience in his individual life. In all cases, without coming to the high concerns of legislation, they knew that it was far more likely that they would receive wise and safe conclusions from two persons of equal intelligence and equal virtue than from one. They knew that this had been generally the case—so generally that it might be said of 99 cases out of 100 in the ordinary affairs of life, and the same principle which regulated the actions of individuals applied equally to organised bodies of men. Mr. John Stuart Mill was not a very great stickler for the second legislative Chamber; and of all the men who had an undoubted reputation as profound thinkers, perhaps he offered the least argument in favour of the twofold Legislature. And he quoted his authority in favour of this form of Legislature because it must be considered, if biassed in any direction, biassed against the Upper Chamber. Well, they would hear what Mr. Mill said in this passage from his work on Representative Government :—

"I attach little weight to the argument oftenest urged for having two Chambers—to prevent precipitancy and compel a second deliberation ; for it must be a very ill-constituted representative Assembly in which the established forms of business do not require many more than two deliberations. The consideration which tells most, in my judgment, in favour of two Chambers—and this I do regard as of some moment—is the evil effect produced upon the mind of any holder of power, whether an individual or an assembly, by the consciousness of having only themselves to consult."

This, expressed in compact and perspicuous language, elucidated the principle to which he had endeavoured to direct attention as one which every man might watch and trace in the action of individual lives.

"It is important that no set of persons should be able, even temporarily, to make their *sic volo* prevail, without asking any one else for his consent. A majority in a single assembly, when it has assumed a permanent character, when composed of the same persons habitually acting together, and always assured of victory in their own House, easily becomes despotic

Constitution of the Upper Chamber. 355

and overweening if released from the necessity of considering whether its acts will be concurred in by another constituted authority. The same reason which induced the Romans to have two consuls makes it desirable there should be two Chambers—that neither of them may be exposed to the corrupting influence of undivided power, even for the space of a single year. One of the most indispensable requisites in the practical conduct of politics, especially in the management of free institutions, is conciliation ; a readiness to compromise ; a willingness to concede something to opponents, and to shape good measures so as to be as little offensive as possible to persons of opposite views ; and of this salutary habit the mutual give and take—as it has been called—between two Houses is a perpetual school, useful as such even now, and its utility would probably be even more felt in a more democratic constitution of the Legislature."

Then, the writer was speaking of the Constitution of England ; and while he maintained that this was useful, and calculated to be very beneficial as applied to the Constitution of England, he said its utility would be even more felt in a more democratic constitution.

" But the Houses need not both be of the same composition ; they may be intended as a check on one another. One being supposed democratic, the other will naturally be constituted with a view to its being some restraint upon the democracy. But its efficiency in this respect wholly depends on the social support which it can command outside the House. An Assembly which does not rest on the basis of some great power in the country is ineffectual against one which does. An aristocratic House is only powerful in an aristocratic state of society. The House of Lords was once the strongest power in our Constitution, and the Commons only a checking body ; but this was when the barons were almost the only power out of doors. I cannot believe that in a really democratic state of society the House of Lords would be of any practical value as a moderator of democracy."

Here were the opinions of two men who, he thought, would be accepted everywhere as authorities on questions of this kind.

Mr. STEWART : They are not infallible.

Mr. PARKES : Well, he was fully aware that few persons were infallible except his hon. friend. But they had in Mr. Story perhaps the most finely-balanced judicial mind that ever appeared amongst Englishmen. Probably in the annals of our own country, or in the annals of any other country, they could not find an intellect so admirably constituted to examine profound political questions. They saw that his opinion was deeply and entirely in favour of two Houses of legislature. In Mr. Mill they had a well-known and widely-acknowledged powerful thinker who was not very enthusiastic for two Houses, but who nevertheless gave the strong reasons which he had quoted in support of that form of legislative government. With these authorities, to which he might add almost innumerable others, he might safely leave the question of one or two Chambers of Parliament. He thought it could not be doubted that they would be far better off—that the public interests would be far safer—with two Houses than with one. In the course he was taking he had no sympathy with those gentlemen who were for abolishing the Legislative Council altogether. He had held the view ever since he had been able to think on such subjects that the principle of two Houses was the wisest, the safest, the best.

We then came to the question as to the way in which this second Chamber might be best constituted so as to meet the wants of this country, and to answer all its proper purposes in the most effective and satisfactory manner. And this question, so far as he should give consideration to it, was confined to the two propositions of a nominated and of an elective House. It would be well, just for a moment, to go back and review very cursorily the history of the Upper Chamber which now existed in this country. When the Constitution Act was under consideration in the former Legislature, before the advent of responsible government, the principle of nomination to the second Chamber was very widely discussed by all classes of the people; and he thought he should be borne out by all who heard him when he said that the preponderating majority was entirely against it. Meetings were held in every considerable centre of population, speeches were delivered by some of the ablest men they had ever had amongst them, petitions came in to the old Council—all these exponents of public opinion were arrayed against this provision of Mr. Wentworth's measure. Mr. Wentworth himself was so completely sensible of this fact that he in a manner apologised for its introduction; for he stated distinctly in one of his speeches that he only asked the country to try the experiment, and that he advisedly limited the nominations in the first instance to a period of five years, so that, if the experiment failed, the people could adopt the elective principle. He did not know how more emphatic evidence could be given by Mr. Wentworth of the doubts which he entertained in his inmost mind of the soundness of the principle which he introduced.

It was well known that Mr. 'Wentworth at that time had

Constitution of the Upper Chamber. 357

considerable apprehensions of the inroads of democratic feeling. His speeches showed that he was almost in a state of terror at some supposed invasion of democratic power, and it was undoubtedly with a desire to satisfy his conservative instincts that he introduced this system of nomination. But while he introduced it into his Bill, he in this marked manner expressed his doubts. He recollected distinctly Mr. Wentworth's language—that if in time it was found not to answer the purpose which he believed it would answer, it would then be open to the Legislature to change this principle and to introduce the elective element.

After the first nominations to the Council were made in 1856, and made with considerable care, he thought, by the late Sir Stuart Donaldson, so dissatisfied were many of the more thinking men who up to that time had been in favour of the nominee principle, that they came publicly forward and acknowledged—upon the very threshold of responsible government—that they were wrong; and they declared themselves in favour of the elective principle. Several gentlemen of large experience and undoubted ability, who had taken part in the public affairs of the country, avowed this change on the experience of the first nominations. Well, he ventured to say that those nominations were as unexceptionable as any that had taken place since. He thought that with one or two exceptions they showed that a large amount of solicitude had been shown to appoint men who ought to form the Senate in such a country as this. For several years after the first nominations the popular feeling against the nominee principle so strongly evinced itself that it was almost impossible to find any person avowing himself in favour of it. He could not recollect an instance for several years after the Constitution Act came into force of a gentleman going to the hustings and telling the people he was in favour of the nominee principle. Whatever differences of opinion existed between the candidates on questions of land legislation, of finance, or State-aid to religion, there was a remarkable agreement in their opinions in favour of a change of the constitution of the Upper House. It seemed to him that that circumstance afforded an unanswerable proof that the feeling of the people of this country at the time of the passing of the Constitution Act, and for several years after, and at present, was entirely adverse to the principle of a nominated Upper Chamber. He admitted that there had not been any active opposition for some years past. That could not be denied. The question had been allowed to sleep just as more important questions had, in other countries and in all ages, been allowed to sleep. Any one who had watched the current of thought and opinion in England during the last twenty years would have seen that for a considerable period, ranging over more than ten years, the question of reform so entirely died out that even the most popular men in England could scarcely awaken public attention to it. In the year 1862, so late as ten or eleven years ago, there was a great effort made by Mr. Bright and his associates to awaken public feeling in England in favour of Parliamentary reform; but no large gathering of the people could be obtained, so completely had the question died for the time. There were men who knew then that that apparent apathy did not arise from the indifference of the people of England to the question of Parliamentary reform; and in a very short time the feeling burst out like a live fire, and the consequence was the Reform Act, which had rendered the House of Commons as democratic an assembly almost as the Legislative Assembly of this colony. That the people tired of petitions, tired of meetings in public places, tired of reading newspaper articles, was no proof whatever that any change had taken place in public opinion in this country. We had no marks of public feeling being in favour of the Upper Chamber as at present constituted corresponding to those marks of adverse feeling we saw years ago. We had not had any meetings in favour of it, or declarations on the hustings in favour of it; we had nothing to show that a change had taken place in the public mind.

We had at the present time a nominated Upper Chamber, in which the members held their seats for life. That was a tenure of office so full of serious consequences to the country that, as he had already stated, Mr. Wentworth hesitated to adopt it without giving the principle a trial of five years first. The five years elapsed, and under the existing law since then all nominations to the Upper Chamber had been made for life. He maintained that the principle of making the appointments for life was inconsistent with and did violence to the first principles of representative government. There could be no purely representative government in the country so long as that principle existed. That would not be the case anywhere; but in this country, where the habits of

Constitution of the Upper Chamber. 359

life, the occupations, and generally speaking the education of gentlemen, in no way pointed out any particular class or set of individuals to a distinction of the kind, the principle was utterly and indefensibly inapplicable. And he could not see how we could claim to possess representative institutions in their purity and integrity whilst such a principle was allowed to exist. A man who had performed many marvellous things and sustained a very long and wonderful career in the later years of English history— he meant Lord Brougham—had told us what he conceived to be the essentials of free government. In his book on the British Constitution he had enumerated what he called the canons of representative government; and these were his words :—

"The people's power must be given over for a limited time. This is essential to the system. If the delegation be for ever, allowing the deputy to name or to join with others in naming his successor, or even if he be continued for his life, and the constituent name his successor, the virtue of the system is gone, and the body of representatives becomes an oligarchy, elective indeed, but still an oligarchy, and not a representative body. The power must be given over for a limited period to deputies chosen by the people. This is of all others the most essential requisite. If any authority but the people appoint the deputies, there is an end of representation; the people's power is usurped and taken from them; and instead of having any concern in making the laws that are to govern them, or in administering the affairs of the State, some other power legislates and rules over them, and in spite of them, although it may add insult to injury by the mockery of pretending to govern in their name."

Those conditions of safety could not be found in the nomination of persons for the term of their natural lives to enact laws for the whole people of the country. If there was some power in the country which could take Mr. Smith or Mr. Jones or Mr. Brown, for no conceivable reason under heaven except that the appointing power fancied Mr. Smith or Mr. Jones or Mr. Brown out of a hundred equally qualified and eligible persons, and with no conceivable test of fitness or approval possible to be applied by the people who had to be governed—whilst that power existed, something existed which affected one-half the machinery of legislation, which was quite inconsistent and incompatible with the first principles of representation.

We would now see how this system had worked. It had worked through the prudence and wisdom of the persons temporarily entrusted with power, in placing several of the first men in the country in the Legislative Council. That might be freely admitted without proving anything in favour of the system itself. There were gentlemen in the Legislative Council than whom no fitter persons could be found : gentlemen who had for a number of years devoted themselves to the consideration of large public questions, who had made themselves aquainted with political history, who had shown that they possessed a sound and matured judgment in dealing with critical conjunctures, and who were in every way pre-eminently qualified to fill seats in the Upper Chamber. But how did they get there? They got there because their services were so conspicuously pointed out that they could not be overlooked. They did not get there because of the excellence of the nominee principle. But those men, who were the ornaments of the Legislative Council, were few in number ; and some of them, he lamented to say, were now feeble in health, and not likely to benefit the country by any very long period of service in the future. The number of members had been made up by gentlemen who had no more patent fitness for seats in the Council than any one of a hundred men who might be met any day in a walk down George-street. They were in fact, if he might say so without offence, the fancy men of particular Ministers who had the power of appointing them. He did not desire to mention the names of any members of the other branch of the Legislature. But he might point out one instance to illustrate his argument. The gentleman to whom he alluded was a man so respectable, and possessed so many qualities derived from education and ability, that he could afford to be pointed out. Nevertheless he pointed that gentleman out as a proof of the capricious way in which the power of appointing had been exercised. He alluded to a member of the Bar; a gentleman who by his professional ability and industry had attained a leading position at the Bar, and was still young. He was a gentleman, however, who had never given his time to any public cause that arose in the country, who had never mixed with the people in the promotion of any object for the public good, and had never publicly identified himself with the interests of the colony. That gentleman, without having done any single thing to entitle him to such a distinction—the highest distinction that could be conferred upon any one in this colony— had been appointed one of the senators of the land. He admitted as fully as he possibly could the good qualities of that gentleman ; but we had, he hoped, men all around us possessing similar good qualities, or we should not be the great and prosperous colony

Constitution of the Upper Chamber. 361

which we were acknowledged to be. It was never intended that the power of nomination should be exercised in that way. Mr. Wentworth never contemplated that it would be so exercised. It was intended that the nominee Chamber should consist of men of standing in the country, of men who represented old families and large property interests, of men who had shown some judgment in dealing with public questions, and of men who, if not wealthy nor of lengthened experience, had in some measure devoted their talents and services to the country. For example, who was so eminently fitted to occupy a position in the other Chamber as the late Mr. James Macarthur, on account of the great interest he represented, his historical family connexions, and his proved ability to deal with public affairs? Mr. Macarthur was a citizen of whom we were proud whilst living, and whose death we all lamented.

Mr. ROBERTSON: We cannot fill the House with Macarthurs.

Mr. PARKES: Possibly not with persons as eminent as Mr. James Macarthur, but they might find persons of the same class, though not equally eminent. They might not find twenty-six men of the same high character, representing the same long period of service, and the same high standing, but most assuredly they could find twenty-six men of the several classes to which he had just alluded. They had not done this, and what had been the result? Just in proportion as this life-tenure of power had fallen into the hands of persons who did not understand the nature of legislation, its principles and its responsibilities, it had been misused. They had exhibited in their political lives in a remarkable manner the evil principle pointed out by Mr. Mill—the evil effect produced on the mind of holders of power by the consciousness that they had only themselves to consult. It was that which was doing all the mischief; and it was impossible to shut one's eyes to the fact that there were members of the Upper House who thought so little of the position they occupied apart from their own importance, or of the duties and responsibilities they had undertaken, that they cared less about these than they did about their own amusements. They had no appreciation of the honour which had been done them, and were not guided in their attendance by the importance of the business with which they had to deal, but by such considerations as whether it was or was not convenient for them to attend. They would attend if they had nothing better to do, but they would not forego the most trivial gratification to attend the House, no matter how important the business before it. This arose from a fixed principle in human nature that, if power were placed in the hands of individuals, and all restrictions on them were removed, the result would inevitably be that those persons would habitually regard themselves as the sole depositaries of that power, and abuse, misuse, or forget the importance attaching to its exercise. We had this principle creeping into the heart and soul of the Council—this very day the Council had been unable to get a quorum; whilst this Assembly, despite of all that had been said against it, had for the two last sessions never failed to meet upon any one night for want of a quorum. This was greatly to the credit of the Assembly; whilst these senators, though yesterday they had a large attendance, were to-day obliged to adjourn for want of a quorum. On all occasions it was with the utmost difficulty that eleven gentlemen could be got together to prevent the Council from being broken up, and this arose from the circumstance that these honourable gentlemen had no master to call them to account. If they were appointed even for ten or fifteen years they would have before them a prospect of being called to account at some time; but, being chosen for life, their first act generally was to do something to show their entire independence of those by whom they had been appointed. Thus it happened that gentlemen, selected because they were supposed to be in favour of the views of the Ministers appointing them, marked out a course for themselves when they felt that no one could call them to account, seemingly for no other reason than to show how independent they were of the persons who had appointed them. He would not much complain of this if it were done on principle or from conscientious scruples, but there had been some remarkable instances which went to show that the opposition to Governments had sprung from these gentlemen solely for the purpose of showing that they were under no obligation to the power that made them.

What was worse still, he thought the Upper Chamber had shown a most remarkable want of appreciation of its connexion with Representative Government—a connexion which ought to have been its pride. He was quite aware that it would be said that the members of the Legislative Council were in a certain sense elected, since members of the Assembly were elected by the people Ministers were selected by the Assembly, and members of Council were appointed by the advice of Ministers. If for a moment we entertained this fanciful theory of election, it was a process of double or rather treble election, and he would like to know in what sense it had ever been, or in what manner it had ever shown itself to be answerable to any principle of responsibility attaching to election. If the members of the Council were theoretically elected, he thought they should show some sympathy with the elective principle, but where was the instance in which this had been the case? When had these honourable gentlemen ever sought to find out public opinion? Had they not rather set it at defiance? Let them look at the case of the Border Customs duties—that was a case in point. This question had been referred expressly to the electors of the country at the last general election, and, although he knew that it would be and had been said that other considerations entered into the decision of the constituencies, still the question on which the reference to the electors had been made was the Border Customs duties. Parliament was elected after that reference, and a Bill had been introduced which aimed at carrying out what was supposed to be, and what was, as shown by the results of the elections, the wishes of the constituent bodies. Yet in spite of this the other House had given no consideration to the fact that it was upon this the Assembly had been dissolved, and upon this that the constituencies had spoken out, but had rejected the Bill which had received the assent of members fresh from election. Whatever might have been their object, they thus manifested the unreasoning and irresponsible way in which they performed the duties of legislation entrusted to them. He thought he had now said sufficient to show the unsoundness of the nominee principle in the Parliament of the country. It seemed to him a perfect outrage upon representative institutions that some thirty persons, appointed virtually by the will of the Minister, should be allowed to sit in judgment upon the destinies of the country, and have an equal voice with the people's representatives in making the laws affecting the rights and liberties and lives of the people, without any constituency being asked to give its assent to their appointment.

If the case were as he had stated it—that this principle of appointment was radically wrong and vicious in operation—he came next to consider what was the best mode of remedying the evil which had grown up. In a country like this, where no person had any innate power in himself over his fellow, and where the principle of equality prevailed to as great an extent as in any part of the world, all political power must necessarily flow from the people, and those for whom laws were to be made must have the selection of the law-makers. If the Upper House represented the people it would possess strength to resist this House whenever it was considered necessary; but representing nobody and nothing, how was it to have any power when it came into contact with such a body as this, backed by the power of the people? No legislative body in this country ever could have power unless it had the people at its back to give force to its decisions. Having that end in view it was the object of this Bill to make the members of the other Chamber responsible to the people. The Government had no desire to take any rash or sweeping or inconsiderate step in making this change; they had not desired to overlook—on the contrary they had been extremely anxious to keep in view—the essentials which in their judgment must prevail to make the Upper House what it ought to be—a body to which we might hope to see the best and most experienced of our public men elevated— a body which should have a lively sympathy with the working of the other House, and a lively sense of their responsibility to the people out of doors; and at the same time a sufficient tenure of office and sufficient securities for independence, to act justly and fearlessly, and, if necessary, in direct opposition to the more popular branch of the Legislature. He for one at once disclaimed any desire to see a second Chamber that would simply re-echo on all occasions the sentiments or the opinions of this House, or that would not be in a position to exercise an independent judgment upon all measures submitted to them; that would be deficient in courage and insensible of popular support—that in fact would prove to be unable to resist if a time for resistance should come.

Having considered the question in this spirit, the Government had introduced the Bill, the second reading of which he had just moved, and he would as briefly as possible explain the machinery of the Bill. By the 3rd clause the existing members were continued in their seats for the term for which they had been appointed, and the Government had after much consideration determined to take that course principally for the following reasons:—It was considered that to many minds it would be regarded as a kind of breach of faith if these gentlemen who had

Constitution of the Upper Chamber. 365

been appointed for the term of their natural lives should now be deprived of their seats, and that was an impression it was desirable not to create. It was thought that a vast change would be effected by associating with the present nominee members a larger number of elected members, that the character of the Council would be at once completely changed, and changed for the better. It was thought that the popular element thus introduced would be so influential as to be practically as efficacious as if the seats of the present members were to be summarily abolished. If the Bill passed into law the House would, under the 4th clause of the Bill, be constituted of 67 members—31 of whom would be nominee and 36 elected. That change would be completely radical and thorough, and in all probability as great as if the existing seats were abolished and an equal number of members elected—so much value in the judgment of the Government was to be attached to the increase of numbers in that body. The framers of this Bill did not believe in a close legislative body, and if they were privileged to introduce an Electoral Bill into this Assembly it would be seen that they believed that this Assembly would work much more efficiently and independently if its numbers were largely increased. He therefore thought that the Council consisting of 67 members would be a very much more popular body, calculated to work more independently, wisely, and satisfactorily for the country, than if it consisted simply of 28 or 30 members, even if they were all elected. The 5th clause divided the colony into twelve electoral provinces. We thought over the plan which prevailed in South Australia, where the Legislative Council was elected by the whole colony. We thought over plans by which the Council might be elected by a large number of constituencies, and we came to the conclusion that the better course would be the medium course, and we propose to divide the colony into electoral provinces sufficiently extensive to counteract the effects of any purely local influence, and yet not cumbrously large. We decided upon the expedient of dividing the colony into twelve electoral provinces, each to return three members. We thought that if we had a smaller number of provinces, say four or six, there would be a serious objection to the larger number of members which each electorate would have to return. The verdict of the electors could be got by a smaller number of candidates more satisfactorily than by a larger number of candidates ; and the expedient hit upon appeared to us to be on the whole the best. In the canons of representation laid down by Lord Brougham, that eminent man had something to say upon the constitution of constituencies. He said :—

"The distribution of the representation should be such as to secure representatives of all the great classes in the community, which are sufficiently numerous, in the combined ratio of the importance of the classes and the numbers comprised in them. Population alone cannot safely be taken as the criterion of numbers chosen to represent, and any arrangement is to be reprobated which should give one very large town the choice of too many representatives, by giving it representatives numerous in proportion to its population. Population should not be so far neglected as to give great inequality to the electoral districts, thus enabling a small body of the people, by their representatives, to control those of a much larger body. Districts should be formed for representation so large as to prevent the corruption of the voters by the candidates or their friends."

He thought that our Bill met the requirements there laid down by Lord Brougham as completely as we could meet them by any other expedient within our reach. The 6th clause dealt with the qualification of electors, and if honourable members would give their careful attention to the sections of that clause they would see that the object of the framers of the Bill had been to extend the franchise to the whole of the settled portion of the population of the country. We gave it to householders without any distinction ; we gave it to lodgers under certain conditions ; we gave it to certain classes of professional men ; and the aim had been to give it to the whole of the permanent population as distinguished from the floating population. We did not think that we should be justified in introducing a high property qualification, such as existed in the sister colony of Victoria, or that we should be justified in restricting the suffrage, except in confining it to the permanent residents of the country. The 7th and 8th clauses dealt with disqualifications, the 9th with the qualifications of elected members ; and we had no other qualification than that of age and residence in the country. From the 10th to the 16th clauses the system of registration was dealt with. The framers of the Bill had introduced a system of self-registration which prevailed in some of the other colonies in the election of members to the more popular branch of the Legislature. That system had many advantages to recommend it, and we thought we could not do better than allow it to be fairly tried in this system of election to the Legislative Council. Clauses 17 and

Constitution of the Upper Chamber. 367

18 dealt with the issue of writs, 20 and 21 with the appointment of returning-officers, 22 and 23 with mere matters of consequential detail, 24 and 25 regulated the nomination of candidates, and 26 defined the duration of offices. The framers of the Bill proposed that the term of office should be for six years at first and ultimately for eight years. The first election for the 36 members would take place under these conditions—that 12 members should be elected for two years, or one member for each province ; that 12 members, or one for each province, should be elected for four years ; and that 12 members, or one for each province, should be elected for six years ; but after that all the elections, for a period to be determined by the diminution of the nominees, should take place for six years. It would be seen by this process that there would be a rotary retirement of 12 members every two years. While all would be elected for six years there would be a retirement of one-third every two years. This plan had the great advantage that it preserved the Council always in existence while it was frequently sending a large number of the councillors to their constituencies. This would be the law until the number of nominee members was reduced by resignation, death, or otherwise to 16 ; and when that was the case the number of the elected members would be increased to 48, and thereafter all the elections would take place for eight years, so that while 12 of the whole number retired every two years, the whole body would be elected every eight years. Clause 27 dealt with the filling of vacancies. In the case of a vacancy the newly-elected member would hold his seat only for the remainder of the term for which it was held by the person who had vacated the seat. It would be perceived that by the 29th clause the principle of a dissolution was partially introduced into the organisation of the Council. Notwithstanding the periodical retirement of one-third at first and afterwards one-fourth of the members every two years, as already described, it had been thought desirable to bring a dissolution of Parliament in some way to operate upon this branch of the Legislature. The framers of this Bill were averse to the House being altogether dissolved, because a dissolution of Parliament, which would send both Houses alike to the country, would in their judgment be mischievous ; but they were desirous of bringing the effect of a dissolution to some extent to operate upon the Legislative

Council. It was proposed to enact that one seat in every province should be affected by any dissolution of the Legislative Assembly, and in order that the influence should be brought to bear upon all the elected members alike, it was proposed that the seat should be determined by lot. It was considered that in the first instance the person who polled the smallest number of votes might be singled out for vacating his seat on dissolution, but it was immediately seen that if that was the case the other members would be quite secure, and the dissolution would in no way affect them. It was therefore thought that it would not have the effect which was desired, and it was seen that if none of the elected members knew whose seats would be vacated, it would have an influence upon all alike. So that while it was proposed to have it enacted that one seat in every province should be vacated on dissolution, it was still left to be determined by a process, the result of which could not be in any way foreseen, what seats they would be. It was thought that this would work in a very salutary and satisfactory manner, and would have great influence in tending to bring the Houses into harmony on all questions of magnitude and importance. If the Upper House saw that, if Parliament were dissolved, any member of the House might have to go to his constituents, the effect would be that all the members would be more inclined to think seriously, to inquire dispassionately, and weigh the reasons on both sides deliberately before joining in decisive and irremediable action. They believed this would prove a most valuable feature in the Bill. The remaining clauses of the Bill dealt with mere matters of detail, but he might say it was proposed by the Bill that, although the President would have his seat preserved to him as a member of the Council, he would not have the office of President preserved. If the Bill passed into law, the office of President would be open to election, and it would be open to all the members alike.

These were the principal provisions of the Bill which he now asked the House to read a second time. He might follow the example of Mr. Wentworth, and say that the principle of the Bill was to have an elective Upper House, but he defined the principle of the Bill more definitely and particularly than that. Mr. Wentworth, on moving the second reading of the Constitution Bill, gave himself very great latitude indeed in defining the principle which he asked the House to affirm. These were his words :—

Constitution of the Upper Chamber. 369

" Sir, I shall only say in conclusion that in inviting this House to the second reading of this Bill I have to enunciate distinctly, as I did before, that the sole principle I wish to have affirmed by the second reading is that there shall be two Houses of Parliament, an Upper and a Lower House, and that whether the Upper House was to be elective or nominated is to remain an open question until we shall receive an expression of opinion from the different districts of the country on that subject."

That certainly was giving a very wide latitude in asking the House to affirm the principle of the Bill, and he might, if he followed Mr. Wentworth's example, say that the principle of the Bill was to make the Upper House elective.

Mr. ROBERTSON: Mr. Wentworth was not a responsible Minister.

Mr. PARKES : It was he who laid the foundation of Responsible Government. He defined the principles of the present Bill as the election by the people, and the partial responsibility of the House to the people whenever Parliament was dissolved. There were some other provisions of the Bill which he regarded as matters of principle. He thought the Government had a clear claim to expect the assistance of honourable gentlemen in endeavouring to make the measure as acceptable to the people as it could be made —keeping in view the wise bounds of security, at the same time trying to meet the popular instincts of the country, and above all bearing in mind that in this country no second Chamber could have that position of strength and respect which was not supported by the voice of the whole people.

SELF-REGISTRATION OF VOTERS.

SUBSTANCE OF SPEECH
In the Legislative Assembly when in committee on the Legislative Council
Bill (provisions for self-registration), March 5th, 1873.

MR. PARKES said the honourable member for the Tumut had made a very fair speech upon the clause, and he hoped honourable members would not feel in any way displeased if he said that it was the only speech which appeared to him to have been addressed to the provisions of the Bill. The honourable member had said several very good things; but the best thing he said was that government in this colony was founded upon argumentative reasons—he presumed he referred especially to the present Government. It was because the Government were so constituted that they brought in these provisions. Now he did not regard these provisions of the Bill with anything like the same sense of importance as some honourable members did who had spoken in their support. He did not regard any provisions of legislation which simply aimed at regulating the record of votes as anything more than matters of expediency—means to an end—and he doubted altogether whether there was anything that could be properly defined as a principle in any of the provisions now under consideration. Nothing could be more loose, vague, or devoid of principle than the present Electoral Act, which authorised some collector to go round to the dwellings of the population and take down the names of the persons entitled to vote. There was no principle in that. There was nothing more loose or more opposed to the robust character of independent freemen. That this was a loose way of taking the electoral rolls could not for a moment be denied. It was admitted that since the constabulary had charge of the collection of the rolls they had been more correct—but even in this case some constables were more intelligent and some less intelligent, some more careful, some less so, some more exact and some less exact; but whether the duty was entrusted to the

Self-Registration of Voters.

constabulary, or as was formerly the case to some electioneering agent, what could be more loose than for these men to go round to the dwellings of the people, seldom finding the elector himself, but taking down what a woman or child, assisted by their own knowledge, might give them? Many who had been electors for years and were still qualified were not put down, and men who had never been electors and were not qualified were placed upon the roll. Well, there was something more approaching to principle in this proposition of self-registration, because it required intelligent action from a man's own sense of duty to get upon the roll. He offered these observations in order to show as plainly as he could his view of the machinery adopted for the collection of the electoral roll. He wished to adopt the best means of carrying out the intention of the electoral law, and if that end was attained he should be perfectly satisfied.

He admitted that there were objections to this system of self-registration, and these objections had been stated with a great deal of force by the honourable member for the Tumut. There was an objection in regard to the extent of our own territory and the sparseness of our population ; and there was an objection as to the extent to which the system might be made use of by political and sectarian organisations. He did not think he could agree with the view of the honourable member for Braidwood, that this system alone would destroy political organisations. He admitted the objections, but he said, notwithstanding, that all the balance of argument was in favour of the system of self-registration. What was freedom but a principle out of which the people ought to grow more manly and independent ? It was because the proposed system caused a man to look after his rights intelligently that he thought it was desirable it should be adopted. The arguments urged against this principle were the greatest libel upon the people he had ever heard. It had been said that people only voted for members of the Assembly in view of what they could get, and that the person who paid the shilling for registration would be the most likely to secure the vote. He thought they were the true friends of democracy who stood up for the character of the people and for their sense of self-respect in the due performance of their duties. It had been said that this system of relf-registration would be a restriction upon the franchise, but not one honourable member had used language which was put into their mouths a few minutes ago by the honourable member for Camden (Mr. Garrett) when he said that this provision of the Bill was intended to restrict the franchise. What honourable members had said was that the effect of the clause would be to restrict the franchise, for a time at all events. But it would disfranchise those who were most likely to give their votes against the interest of the country. Persons who would not take a little trouble to secure the enrolment of their names were persons who were not likely to exercise the franchise for the benefit of the country. It was because it was necessary to awaken in the constituencies a spirit of self-respect, and to awaken in each person a patriotic sense of duty, that he and others were in favour of self-registration. Suppose that in its first working the system would tend to contract the electoral rolls—and he did not deny that it might have this effect at first—it was easy to see that before many years passed over, the opposite effect would be produced. Hundreds, he might say thousands, did not take the trouble even now to see that their names were on the electoral rolls. And how could we prevent that, unless we threw upon each individual the duty of obtaining for himself his own rights? This was not an attempt to impair the rights of the people, but to infuse through the constituencies a spirit of self-reliance and self-protection. Men who took the trouble to register themselves were the most likely to take the trouble of ascertaining the character of the men for whom they voted.

He was never more pained than when he listened to some of the arguments against these provisions which went to discredit the constituencies and to show that we had not an intelligent body of electors in the country. A voter for a free Parliament who did not set any value upon his vote was a most dangerous member of society. It was impossible to shut our eyes to the fact that the privilege of the franchise fell upon some who did not value it. But he was happy to think that such persons were few, and if they could be eliminated from the constituent body it would be better for that body. And he thought this system of self-registration was one means of eliminating them.

It was with this view that the Government had thought it right to submit to Parliament these provisions. They looked at them as a means to an end, as the machinery by which this political trust could be most properly performed. No party triumph could be possible in this matter. Not in any spirit of political rancour, but with the most sober knowledge and the most disinterested desire to do what was right did they seek to accomplish the object at which they aimed. He thought that the objections were not so formidable as had been represented. He did not believe that we were in danger of being governed by political organisations. He did not believe that the British people would bend to the power of any organisation for long ; still less did he believe that a sectarian organisation would flourish for any length of time. The free spirit of an English people would assert itself, and it would be assisted by this system of self-registration. He should not hesitate to go before any constituency in the country to vindicate the position he had taken up.

THE
PUBLIC SCHOOL SYSTEM IN 1873.

[ON the 5th of August 1873 Mr. Parkes attended, on invitation, to lay the foundation-stone of the West Maitland Public School. The day was observed as public holiday. A procession of the inhabitants accompanied Mr. Parkes to the ground, and addresses from the Mayor and Aldermen, from the Public School Committee, and from the pupils of the East Maitland and Morpeth public schools, were presented to him. The following is a copy of the Morpeth address :—

" TO THE HONOURABLE HENRY PARKES, M.P., COLONIAL SECRETARY AND PREMIER.

" Sir—We, the pupils of the Morpeth Public School, avail ourselves of your visit to lay the foundation-stone of the public school at West Maitland to express our thanks to you, as the instrument of an All-wise God, for the privilege we now enjoy, and the benefits we derive from the Public School System.

" To your wisdom in forming and establishing a scheme of education we owe a deep debt of gratitude, which we can only repay in some measure by regarding the well-being of those who come after us with that profound interest you have manifested for our advancement.

" We are glad to be present at this important ceremony, the commencement of that which when completed will afford to the pupils of Maitland advantages similar to those we have long possessed.

" In conclusion, sir, we earnestly pray that you may long be spared as a blessing to your family and the country ; and we remain, with deep respect, your most grateful servants,
" PETER SIM,
" ADOLPHUS JONES,
" On behalf of the pupils of the Morpeth Public School."

The assemblage numbered several thousands, including a large number of ladies. After going through the ceremony usual on such occasions, Mr. Parkes delivered the following speech :—]

SPEECH
On laying the foundation-stone of the West Maitland Public School,
August 5th 1873.

MR. PARKES said : It is in no hackneyed terms that I assure you that I feel deeply the honour you have conferred upon me in having invited me here this day. You have shown, by the great demonstration in which you have all concurred, the lively and

The Public School System in 1873. 375

strong interest which you take in the course of public instruction in this country ; and I esteem it a very distinguished honour that you should select me above all other public men to visit West Maitland and lay the foundation-stone of this school. I shall venture to detain you a very short time; but before I enter upon the topic which will be of most interest I should like to say a word or two as to the history of the public school movement in West Maitland. I find from the records of the Council of Education that so far back as 1861—twelve years ago—the people of West Maitland first applied for a school of this character. They applied in that year to the Board of National Education for the establishment of a national school, which, as you are aware, answered in those days to the public school of the present ; but for some cause or other the movement fell through at that time. Again, in 1867, the people of West Maitland applied to the Council of Education for the establishment of a public school. I find, from the records of the Council, that there was then a guarantee of 380 children to attend the school ; but, owing principally to the circumstance that the Council could not approve of the building which your townsmen at that time fixed upon as available, the movement again fell through. Later on, in 1870, another application was made for the establishment of a public school, when I find that 246 children were guaranteed to attend the school ; but as the applicants still desired to appropriate the same building for public school purposes, and the Council could not concur in that proposal, the movement for the third time fell through. You again commenced your efforts in 1872, and we are assembled here to-day to celebrate the crowning success of the fourth attempt. Now I am not for a moment supposing that any want of enthusiasm, any want of earnest effort, existed here which produced these repeated failures, and this non-fulfilment of any effort made throughout the period of twelve years. The result probably is traceable to a variety of causes which it would be difficult, even if it were useful, to point out at the present time. But I think that on account of the failure of these previous efforts you—will you permit me to say we ?—can congratulate ourselves on our success to-day.

Well, you have a school now, the foundation-stone of which is just laid, having a promise at the very commencement of 489 children—nearly 500 children for a beginning. Now I do not know how many persons there may be present who estimate rightly a fact like that. Any schoolroom in any part of the world that takes within its doors nearly 500 children—500 intelligent creatures who are growing up to form the very tissue of society hereafter, is an institution of immense importance to the district where it exists. And to show you how important it is I shall detain you for a short time with some figures bearing upon the constituent parts of our population at present. This school which you are about to erect is intended—I believe I echo the sentiments of those gentlemen who have interested themselves in bringing this result about, and I know I echo the desire of the Council of Education when I say it—is intended to be a model school for this part of the colony. Any one of you who knows anything of the influence of example will know how important it is to keep ever present, not simply to the minds of the population but also to the minds of the teaching class, a high standard of efficiency. You all must have seen the vast influence of some high personal example even in ordinary walks of industry; how it suggests new attempts, new efforts, new thoughts, and new successes to all around it. And just as example operates on individuals so will example operate upon that aggregate of persons of which every school consists. And if you have in this district of the Hunter a number of public schools all founded on the same broad basis of liberality, and presided over by masters trained in the same training-school, there will ever be the danger of some one or other of them falling into arrear through the inefficiency of its local board, or through what I hope is still rarer, the inefficiency of its teachers. Hence it is desirable to establish in the midst of all these schools a model school, where the system will be displayed with as great excellence as possible, and where a high standard of efficiency will be held out before the surrounding schools. By these means your school will diffuse far beyond the range of its pupils the influence of good training and discipline. That is what is meant by a model public school; not that it is to be a school of another character, not that it is to be founded on another system, but that it should be pre-eminent amongst the schools around it; just as some man of commanding influence and weighty character is pre-eminent among his fellow-citizens. I had an extract given to me in Sydney from one of the Council's own reports, containing its views respecting model public schools. The extract is from the report of the Council for the year 1867, and refers to such schools, and the Council's desire to see them established in populous towns. I will read it:—

"The attention of the Council has been forcibly directed to the need which exists in the larger towns of the colony for schools of a somewhat superior class to the ordinary public or certified denominational schools. It is found that schools in which the ordinary course of instruction could be extended by the addition of elementary classics and mathematics would be regarded as a great boon by large numbers of people. The Council has therefore decided to assist in the formation of superior public schools of this description, wherever the people contribute in the usual proportion towards the extra expense which the establishment of such schools would entail."

In accepting this offer of the Council and carrying it out to such success I think the committee formed in West Maitland are well entitled to the thanks and gratitude of their fellow-townsmen.

Now, one word or two as to the system of education to be taught in this school. I am aware that there are those who disapprove of the system. But this large assembly can well afford to allow those gentlemen to entertain a different opinion from ours. The very soul of the free Government of a free country is to allow every man to entertain his own opinion and to act upon it in every legitimate way. But just to the same extent that others are entitled to an opinion we are entitled to ours, and we show our sound sense and genuine liberality by good-humouredly allowing them to do their best against us. We insist upon acting upon our opinion and we interfere with no one else; we make no aggression on any class, or on any individual of any class; but we say that in this great work of primary instruction which so intimately relates to our children and to the country in which our lot is cast —in this great work we ought to carry out such principles as shall place them as men and women on a broad ground of equality. This system of public instruction does not make war upon any creed; it does not make war on any class of opinion or any class of individuals; but it establishes a means by which children shall receive the best primary education that it is possible to obtain, without interference with any opinions their parents may hold, and without subjecting them or their parents to any kind of annoyance whatsoever. Perhaps it is one of the most striking advantages of the system that no person can appear in any school as teacher without having been taught to teach. There was a time in this country not very far back—and there are other countries where the same thing still exists—when any person who had powerful influence could set up as a school teacher. That was the case here some few years back, but that day has gone for ever, and throughout the length and breadth of the land there is no school supported by public money where any person can obtain a footing as a teacher without being properly trained how to teach. This, perhaps, is the most significant feature in the system, and perhaps the most valuable guarantee to parents that their children will be well instructed. It is idle to say that in these public schools religion cannot be taught. There is nothing in the world to prevent the clergyman, or the parents, or any person religiously disposed, from teaching religion; but the system itself, so far as reading, writing, grammar and arithmetic are concerned, is maintained on the assumption that it is far better for these primary objects of instruction to be enforced without mixing them up with any sectarian feeling whatever. Surely teaching a child the alphabet does not affect the salvation of its soul. Surely to teach a child its own name, the name of its parents, and of the town where it lives, cannot in any way trench upon an article of faith; geography can have little to do with the child's religious belief. This system says that all children alike, Protestant or Catholic, or Mormons if there be any, may come up and be instructed in the necessary rudiments of education. And why? Not simply because the child so instructed has a better chance in life than one who has no instruction—although that is a matter of all importance to the child itself—but because the future nation will be composed of men who will be all the better able to exercise the rights of freedom by being properly taught. The system says that the child should be educated, so that the individual child may have a fair field for his exertions; but, looking far beyond and above that consideration, it says that he should be educated in order that the country may take its station amongst the first nations of the world.

These are the principles which the school you are about to erect will enforce. It is very gratifying to me, and I am sure it must be very gratifying to a great many of you, to know that this system of education has made steady progress in this country during the last seven years. In the year 1867, the first year of the operation of the Public Schools Act, there were only 288 public schools in the colony; last year there were 396. In the year 1867, the first

The Public School System in 1873. 379

year of the operation of the Act, the pupils attending public schools numbered only 28,434; last year they numbered 46,458. Under this system of public schools there were two classes of new schools established which never existed in this colony before. One class is known as half-time schools, the other as provisional schools. The provisional school is a school established where there are not 25 children, the number legally required to found a public school. It was thought by the Parliament of the day that there might be places in the remote interior of this colony where there would not be more than 15 or 18 children, and that simply because they were situated in remote places it would be a crime to let them grow up in ignorance; and so the provisional schools pick up these small groups of children until the neighbourhood becomes sufficiently populous for a public school to be established. In 1867 there were only 31 of these schools; last year there were 194 of them. They have dropped down like an angelic agency from heaven in the midst of the wilderness, to give instruction to small groups of children widely separated from all the influences of civilisation. Think what a blessing it must be to the country to have nearly 200 of these schools. The half-time school is founded on the principle that there may be some groups of children altogether too small for a regular school of any kind. There may be only 8 or 10 children, situated 30 miles from another similar small group of children—groups of children living up some gully tenanted by free selectors. These children must if left to themselves grow up into the forms of a white barbarism; and it was determined by the Parliament that in such places, where the children could not go to school, the school should come to them. The half-time school means that the teacher goes to one place where there are 8 or 10 children and teaches them for three days, and then rides on to another place 30 miles distant and teaches another group there for three days. Thus the means has been supplied for these cases of dire necessity where the light of instruction could not have fallen if it had not been for this measure. In 1867, the first year of the operation of the Act, there were only 6 of these schools; now there are 101. I knew one instance—I shall not mention names—where the sons of a farmer in a wild district took to the roads as bushrangers. Two of these unfortunate young men—natives of the soil, who might under other circumstances have been an honour to the country—died on the gallows. The year after, the sisters of these unhappy men were attending one of these schools. I have mentioned this circumstance before, and I mention it again because it is to my mind a most telling illustration of the value which these schools have been to the country at large—how they have brought enlightenment and good influences where without them there would have existed nothing but moral darkness and degradation.

Now just for a moment, if I am not wearying you with these figures, I want to tell you something about the field for the useful operation of schools. I am going to deal with the census returns, but do not be appalled; I will make my figures as tasteful as I can and will not be long about it. The census of this country was taken on the 2nd of April 1871, nearly two years ago. I do not know how many of you have looked at these census tables; they are more interesting than the latest new novel, more suggestive than one of Browning's poems; and if I could only induce you to study them you would find much to instruct and amuse you, and to awaken the most delightful contemplations of the future of the colony. Amongst the returns I find that on the 2nd April 1871 there were in this country 18,000 babies under twelve months of age. Just take in that fact, you unmarried men; 18,000 babies under one year old! All these babies must have been presented to the colony during the preceding year. Very well; two years have elapsed since then, and whatever else may have failed we may rest assured that there has been no failure in the supply of babies. There must have been fully 18,000 babies supplied in each of those years. So that adding these three eighteens we have now altogether not fewer than 54,000 children under three years of age. Just contemplate such a fact as that— an army of 54,000 children under three years of age. In 20 years they will be the real strength of this country, to say nothing of the annual crops of babies during those 20 years rapidly developing into men and women; and is it not worth some little expenditure of money, some little exertion of mind, to provide a system of instruction that shall send forth that vast army of human souls fitted to fulfil the worthy part of men and women in the world? Of course many of these young lives will perish. I am sorry to say that the mortality among the infantile classes is very great. And it might be prevented to a great extent if with the growth of instruction in this country fathers and mothers

The Public School System in 1873. 381

would think more about their homes; if in the building and ordering of their houses they would endeavour to have them well ventilated, that their children may be able to breathe as pure air inside as they can breathe outside their dwellings. If they would pay a little more regard to cleanliness, and to small sanitary arrangements, much of the infantile mortality would cease in the land. I hope that with the advance of education we shall have that result among other results. But though many of these 54,000 children will die, as unhappily they will, a vast number of them will go into the ordinary avenues of society, and one of the most precious things we can give them is the means of sound instruction. But let us trace these figures a little further—I have only dealt with the babies. On the 2nd April, 1871, there were 110,000 children in the colony between the ages of four and twelve. In the ordinary pursuits of society that may be set down as the school age for the children of working people and tradespeople. The children attending school I think numbered 88,000, according to the report of the Council of Education. Take this number from 110,000 and we find 22,000 to be provided for by private schools, or not attending school at all. Here is a field for the useful operation of these new public schools to train these infants, who will come upon the stage of real life in some 20 years, and these 110,000 who will take their places within much shorter periods of time. The total number of men and women in this country between the ages of twenty-one and sixty is only about 221,000. The total number of children under the age of sixteen is 220,000. So that we shall have some of them claiming their places amongst us in two years' time, some in three or four years, a vast crowd in ten years, and that multitude of babies in 20 years; we shall have as many persons coming upon the stage to take their part in the real life of the country as the adult men and women of the present population. They will come, insist upon their right place, elbow some of us aside, settle down in advance of many of us; and are we not performing a beneficent work when we do all that we can to enable them to perform their part virtuously, intelligently, and beneficially for themselves and the country? This is what this system of public instruction is and what it will do. And to apply these general principles to the real business of civilised society, I would ask each of you to consider how much our boasted institutions—this educational system amongst them, and the very political freedom we enjoy—how much all these blessings depend on the right direction of the individual exertions of each member of the population. Depend upon it freedom does not consist merely in manhood suffrage and vote by ballot or in equal electoral districts; it consists in good men and women. And a modern poet, whose thoughts have perhaps been more entwined with the progress of the human family than the thoughts of any of his contemporaries, expresses this in some fine noble lines :—

> " Freedom is re-created year by year
> In hearts wide open on the Godward side—
> In souls calm-cadenced as the whirling sphere,
> In minds that sway the future like a tide.
> No broadest creeds can hold her, and no codes;
> She chooses men for her august abodes."

Depend upon it, if we were to study all the philosophers and all the writers on political science, we should learn no more than is conveyed in these lines of the poet Lowell. It is with men—men of sound heart and aspiring soul—that freedom and good government and all social blessings are built up and held secure. We may have the most perfect laws, the most liberal institutions; but if they fall into the hands of a debased race, who will not know how to use them, the result, gloss it over as you may, will be slavery and degradation. It is only by raising men to be industrious, self-restraining, patriotic, robust citizens, and in raising women to be virtuous, industrious, and careful mothers of families, that you will bring about a condition of healthy freedom, and create a powerful and prosperous state. All your boasted liberal institutions, your platform-talk and your enlightened laws, are as nothing unless you succeed in raising a race that will value the gifts they possess, and who will in their thoughts, words, and deeds continue, in their day and generation, to guard and consolidate the freedom of the country.

I trust that in establishing this school, some of the thoughts to which I have endeavoured to give expression will have weight with those who hear me. And I hope that the whole community will consider that establishing the school is not enough. You must get good teachers, you must put the affairs of the school into the hands of gentlemen forming your school board who will watch it as a mother watches her children. But even more than all this, parents and children must do their duty. However good the school may be, you must remember that the children are only there a few hours, while they are in contact with the vital example of their parents during the greater part of their lives. And however excellent the organisation of the school may be, however well-trained the teachers, however faithfully the local board may perform their part, all these things will be of little avail if the people of this district do not waken up to a sense of the priceless charge they have in their children. They must do their duty, and realise that education commences when the child first looks upon its mother's face, and ceases when the eyelids are closed for ever. Education goes on every day, from the cradle to the grave, under all circumstances, in all societies, at home and abroad. And unless sound influences are brought to bear upon human lives, these lives will not be sound at the core. Therefore with this school system, equalled in no land under the sun; with this school you are about to erect under the supervision of the good men in whom you have shown your confidence—let me impress upon you to do your part to bring about a better training for your children than many of you have had yourselves. I thank you for the patient hearing you have given me, and cannot too fervently express my hope that your most sanguine expectations will be realised in the institution you have this day founded.

THE POLICY OF PROTECTION.

REPEAL OF THE AD VALOREM DUTIES.

[FROM the year 1865 until the close of the year 1873 *ad valorem* duties of 5 per cent. were imposed upon all articles of merchandise imported into New South Wales not subject to a specific duty, and excepting articles included in a limited free list. On the 16th of October 1873, Mr. George A. Lloyd, Treasurer in the Parkes Administration, submitted to the Legislative Assembly, in Committee of Ways and Means, proposals to repeal the whole of the *ad valorem* and a large number of the specific duties, reducing the tariff to 55 articles. These proposals, with slight modifications, were carried into law. Mr. Parkes spoke on the last night of the adjourned debate.]

SPEECH

Delivered in the Legislative Assembly, October 29th 1873.

MR. PARKES said: Before he entered upon the subject under consideration he felt it necessary to say a few words respecting a statement made by the honourable and learned member for East Macquarie (Sir James Martin) the other evening, to the effect that the present Government had received from him and his friends an unusual amount of generosity. The honourable and learned member's words were that other Governments had made the same proposals for railway construction that this Government had made; but that, whilst the present Government and their supporters were in Opposition they prevented these proposals from passing, and now they had come into office and carried them with the assistance of the Opposition.

Mr. ROBERTSON: Hear, hear. That's true.

Mr. PARKES: The fact was, that the only distinctive feature in the proposals of the present Government for railway construction was

The Policy of Protection.

to carry the Southern line further than the Northern or Western. That proposal had been made twice in Parliament (he being Colonial Secretary at both times), and on each occasion it had been opposed by the honourable gentleman (Mr. Robertson) who now sat at the head of the Opposition. The proposal was made in 1867 and was opposed by Mr. Robertson; it was now again made, and was again opposed by the same honourable member. The only difference between the proposals made in 1867 and the proposals of the present Government, was that the Government of which the honourable and learned member and himself were then members, proposed to take the railway a point lower down the Murrumbidgee than the point proposed by the present Government. It must therefore be obvious that the honourable member's observation was inaccurate, because he could not by any possibility have been concerned in opposing this thing, when on the only two occasions of its having been proposed he was a member of the Government. In reply to the honourable and learned member's observation, that the Opposition had assisted the present Government to carry the proposal, he could only say that the honourable and learned member's late colleague opposed the Government as he had done years before, and that the honourable and learned gentleman himself was not on the division amongst the supporters of the present Government. This Government brought down an estimate for an extension of the railway from Goulburn to Wagga Wagga ; and the honourable member moved that the sum necessary to carry the railway from Yass to Wagga Wagga should be omitted, and he divided in a minority of 6 to 41. In that majority of 41, the name of the honourable and learned member for East Macquarie did not appear. Therefore, the honourable gentleman's statement that the present Government carried out a policy which they had opposed when in Opposition was entirely wrong, as was also his statement that he had supported the Government in carrying out this policy. He had taken the trouble to refer to the speech made by the honourable member for West Sydney when, in 1867, he moved an amendment to Sir James Martin's proposal. The honourable member had a most unenviable reputation for trying to cast suspicion upon his opponents whenever they did anything of which he disapproved, and on the occasion referred to he endeavoured to cast suspicion upon the honourable and learned member. These were the honourable member's words :—

"It was a very extraordinary thing, and one that was calculated to excite grave suspicion, that at this particular time the chief engineer, Mr. Whitton, should be smuggled out of the country, and this House thus had no means of knowing what was the opinion of that officer respecting the questions involved in the propositions under discussion. He should like to know why the plans had not been laid on the table, and only the document signed 'John Whitton' had not been circulated in the ordinary manner. He did not appreciate this new dodge of circulating Parliamentary papers. He had now got the paper in his hand, and there was not from Mr. Whitton one word in favour of the line."

Whenever he could not in fairness meet his opponents he was always ingenious—he was always ingenious enough to throw suspicions over the reputations of his opponents.

The honourable member for Camden (Mr. Garrett) was pleased to say that the Government in proposing to abolish the *ad valorem* duties were doing no more than would have been done by any other Minister. The difference between the present and preceding Governments was that the present Government had not said much about it, but were doing it. Other Governments had talked a great deal about doing it, but had never attempted to do it. The honourable member made the statement no doubt in order to take away from the Government the merit of redeeming their promises and acting in accordance with their professions. Then the honourable member stated that he had not done what he proposed to do some thirteen or fourteen years ago—repealed the tea and sugar duties. Thirteen or fourteen years was a period long enough to justify any one in changing his opinion. Nor was it a very discreditable thing for any man to change his opinion if upon further consideration he had arrived at a different conclusion. He did not say whether he had done that or not. But he said that when the Government proposed to remit duties to the amount of nearly £200,000 they might fairly stop. And he should like to know whether honourable gentlemen sitting in that House would have preferred the Government to remit the tea and sugar duties instead of the *ad valorem* duties. The Government could not do both things. In preparing now to abolish the *ad valorem* duties they did not consider themselves justified in interfering with the duties on tea and sugar.

The Government had not submitted to the House any proposal for new taxation. They had been treated with remarks from honourable members, and the question had been dealt with out of doors, as if the Government were proposing to impose new burdens on the country. They were doing nothing of the kind; on the contrary, they stood in the pleasant position of being able to remit taxation without the necessity of imposing new duties. All they proposed to do was to increase the duty upon one article only, whilst the tariff was simplified by the remission of a large number of duties which had had a baneful effect by interfering with the commerce of the country, without having any corresponding beneficial effect upon the revenue. But their proposal, simple as it was, had by some extraordinary means raised the question of Protection ; and as some obser vationshad been made which he very much regretted to hear in an English Legislature, he should say a few words on the question raised.

In dealing with the question the Government found themselves in a very curious position. There were gentlemen opposed to them who entirely dissented from the remission now proposed. The honourable and learned member for East Macquarie entirely dissented from it; the honourable member for Tumut (Mr. Hoskins) and the honourable member for Bathurst (Mr. Combes) also dissented. Then, on the other hand they had a number of gentlemen—including the honourable member, Mr. Robertson, and the honourable member, Mr. Garrett—who declared that they entirely concurred in the course taken by the Government, though they were not disposed to give that Government much credit for it. Honourable members opposite approved of what the Government were doing, and yet the Government had found no friendly intimations of concurrence coming from the other side. What he desired to say on the subject of protection was chiefly in contradiction of the assertions, rather than arguments, that England was falling into a course of ruin by the adoption of her free-trade policy.

Mr. COMBES : I believe it.

Mr. PARKES : He was glad to hear the honourable member's remarks, as it showed that he was not misstating the views of honourable members opposite. The honourable and learned member for East Macquarie, whose contempt for the great free-trade statesmen of England they all knew, had taken occasion, when Mr. Webb was speaking, to interject an observation to the effect that England was now only a third-rate power.

Mr. COMBES : Hear, hear !

Mr. PARKES : By his cheer it seemed that the honourable member for Bathurst concurred in this statement. He was glad to find that such opinions came from members representing Western districts, and were confined to the regions of the setting sun. It was some comfort to know that these honourable gentlemen only represented one portion of the colony, and that where the sun set. But he should take the trouble to show how fallacious were the reasoning and the views of these honourable gentlemen.

Mr. COMBES : I hope you will go back to the Revolution?

Mr. PARKES : He might go back to the time of Edward I., because it was in that reign that Customs duties were first actually collected. The honourable member for Bathurst, however, was quite right, since the collection of Customs duties, to any appreciable extent, dated from the time of the Revolution, or rather from the Restoration. He found on the best authorities he could consult, that from 1660 down to 1784 the Customs accounts of England were in such a complicated state that there were upwards of one hundred separate accounts for the entry of duties ; and yet, notwithstanding all that, the revenue from these duties was very inconsiderable. So numerous were the Customs laws that when a Select Committee of the House of Commons was appointed in 1784 to make inquiry into their number and extent, it was found that the Acts in force filled six large folio volumes. If it were a correct principle that every man should understand the laws under which he was governed, he would ask how it was possible for him to know the state of the Customs laws. Mr. Jickling was employed for twenty-five years in making a digest of these Customs laws. The inferences to be drawn from the facts he was stating would rather surprise honourable gentlemen, and show them the impolicy and the utter absence of wisdom in their efforts to establish a protective policy. In 1787, Mr. Pitt brought in his Customs Laws Consolidation Bill, and at that time it was expressly stated that it was for the purpose of regulating the labour and commerce of the country. Duties were imposed upon 1200 articles, including *ad valorem* duties upon 300 articles of import and 60 of export. Thus the system had lasted for more than 100 years after the introduction of these Customs laws at the Restoration ; nor ought it to be forgotten that the great object of imposing these duties was to protect the industry and trade of England. At the time these laws were imposed the population of England, as shown in a digest of the census now on the table, was 5,466,572. He would wish honourable members to bear in mind that no nation could ever be

The Policy of Protection.

powerful and prosperous unless her people steadily increased in numbers and were well educated to a life of productive industry. What had been the case here? After these duties had been in existence 100 years, and after the brains of succeeding statesmen had been racked to improve them so as to make them protect the commerce and labour of England, the population in 1751 was only.6,335,840. Thus in the 100 years there had been an increase in the population of only 869,268 souls. That was one great fact, and honourable gentlemen would do well to appreciate its significance as going to show how the nation, under this protective legislation, must have struggled on and yet made no progress in population beyond these few hundred thousand souls.

Mr. COMBES : What battles were fought?

Mr. PARKES : He knew there had been wars and civil strife, and, what had been still more fatal, there had been decimating diseases which had run riot through the land; but there was the fact that the nation had shown an utter want of power to make any appreciable advance whatever. In the 17 years from 1798 till the battle of Waterloo in 1815, and after Mr. Pitt had carried his Customs Laws Consolidation Act, Parliament passed 600 new Customs Acts. People in these days would be inclined to regard this statement with incredulity and yet such was the case, that 600 new Acts were required in 17 years in order to give direction to this policy of protection. Previous to the accession of George III. the Acts passed altogether were 800, and during the first 53 years of his reign there were 1300 other Customs Acts passed, these Acts being passed by the constant, irritating, impatient efforts of English statesmen to serve England by protecting her trade and her industries. Still the nation made very little headway in its external commerce, or in the growth of its population, because we found that at the beginning of the century—amazing as it might appear to honourable members who had not looked into these astounding facts—that in the year 1801 the population of England and Wales was only 8,892,536. He could not afford time to trace this matter over the intervening years which brought it to what he recollected himself. He recollected the state of England just prior to the commencement of the beneficent policy which had brought England to her present pitch of prosperity and greatness. The beginning of the great reforms which had taken place in the policy of England was upon the accession to power of Sir Robert Peel in 1841. He was old enough to recollect the state of England then. He recollected that in the year 1838 he was called upon to act upon a coroner's inquest on the death of a mechanic who, from sheer starvation, had tied himself to a nail in the fireplace, and had strangled himself by lying on the floor. The body of that man was reduced to a state of emaciation such as he had never witnessed in any other case, although he had seen many cases of similar suffering from sheer poverty. His family were living without utensils of any kind—without chairs, without beds, and in a state of starvation which scarcely enabled them to walk about. And what he saw himself in that dismal, solitary home was the case all over England. The distress which existed at that time continued, paralysing the trade, paralysing the power of the wealthier classes, and decimating the population, until the accession to power of Sir Robert Peel. Inquiries were made into the causes which produced these results. At Bolton 300 families, comprising 1400 persons, were found whose total income only averaged 15¼d. per head per week; 1000 were found whose income was only 18d. per week, and the remainder, it was stated, were living on incomes of 2s. and 2s. 6d. per week. Sixteen hundred of these unfortunate persons in that one town had only 500 beds amongst them—men, women, and children. The same report showed that at Paisley there were 650 heads of families out of work, and 1200 looms standing idle; and that at Manchester there were 8000 people living on 15d. per week. All this was after 180 years of protective policy. We would see how the state of the country generally was described at that time. A well-known writer on fiscal legislation, Mr. Noble, speaking of this time, said :—

"Every interest in the country was alike depressed; in the manufacturing districts mills and workshops were closed, and property daily depreciated in value; in the seaports shipping was laid up useless in harbour; agricultural labourers were eking out a miserable existence upon starvation wages and parochial relief; the revenue was insufficient to meet the national expenditure; the country was brought to the verge of national and universal bankruptcy. In some of the agricultural districts estates were given up by the owners to the parish authorities because the rates exceeded the rents. The protective system, which was supported with the view of rendering the country independent of foreign sources of supply, and thus, it was hoped, fostering the growth of a home trade, had most effectually destroyed that trade by reducing the entire population to beggary, destitution, and want.

The Policy of Protection. 391

The masses of the population were unable to procure food, and had, consequently, nothing to spend on British manufactures."

After all the gigantic amassing of conflicting laws aiming at a perfect system of protection, which it was impossible for any man to comprehend, that was the result. And while that state of things pervaded the whole nation, the external commerce of the country had dwindled down to an insignificant amount, as it must have done, for that state of things to exist, and the population had remained almost stationary.

Sir Robert Peel came into power and brought Mr. Gladstone with him as President of the Board of Trade. It was well known that, so far back, in association with Sir Robert Peel, Mr. Gladstone was the man who worked at the very core of this question in ameliorating the tariff of England. Sir Robert Peel found, confirmatory of this dismal picture of the state of England at that time, a deficiency staring him in the face of £2,570,000 sterling; and he stated that if no remedial measures were resorted to in a new direction this deficit would go on accumulating until at the end of 1845 it would amount to £10,000,000 sterling. Sir Robert Peel stated that the only remedy was to legislate in a new direction—to diminish the burdens upon the people and upon the commerce of the country ; and by his great measure of that year he reduced the duties on 750 articles, and removed all prohibitions.

Mr. BAKER : And imposed an income-tax.

Mr. PARKES : And imposed an income-tax. But he did not see how that affected his argument : it rather supported it. From that year the population, the prosperity of the people, the fulness of employment, the external commerce of England, had taken as it were electric bounds ; and it was perfectly amazing to see what England had done year by year as the burdens of the people had been removed. As the activity of her people had been relieved from all impediments, the commerce of the people had more and more expanded.

He had already alluded to the stationary character of the population of England during the century which ended in 1751. He had already pointed out to the committee that the increase during that long period was only a little more than three-quarters of a million. Applying the same test, and he knew of no better, to the condition of England, he found that in the century ending

1751 there was an increase in the population of 869,268 ; and at the end of the next hundred years, namely, in 1851, there was an increase of 11,773,570.

Mr. MACINTOSH : Dr. Jenner was the chief cause of one portion of it.

Mr. PARKES readily admitted that the great improvements in surgical science and in medical skill and the more peaceable disposition of the inhabitants had a great deal to do with it. It was very curious to note the increase during the last sixty years up to the present time. In the thirty years ending in 1841 the increase was 5,749,932 ; but during the thirty years ending in 1871—the latest return we had—the increase was 6,798,078. But the elastic power of the country after it was released from the burdens which had crippled its industry and commerce would be seen most remarkably in the exports of the country. We found that within the years 1842-4—the first two or three years after the commencement of the beneficent legislation of Sir Robert Peel—there were remitted duties to the amount of £1,807,597, and the exports from England during that period were £58,534,705. In the period 1845-52, seven years, the remissions of duties amounted to £8,633,216 and the exports mounted up to £78,076,854. In 1853 there were further remissions to the amount of £2,064,091, and the exports measuring the productive power of the country mounted up to £98,933,781. In the year 1854-5 new duties were imposed to the extent of £5,580,483, and the exports immediately receded to £95,933,781—the amount not being much in itself, but being very significant as compared with the increase of about £20,000,000 sterling consequent upon the remissions of Customs duties during the preceding periods. From 1856 to 1857 there were duties remitted to the amount of £3,831,965, and the exports expanded to an average of £122,066,107, or much more than double the exports at the time of Sir Robert Peel's first financial reforms. In the period from 1860-65 the Government of England again remitted duties to the amount of £9,471,420, and the exports increased to £165,835,725. In the year 1871 the exports of Great Britain amounted to £223,066,162 against only £57,000,000 in 1842. But during this time the importations of food rose from the value of £27,911,422 in 1840 to £71,883,930 in 1865 ; and of course a nation must be all the more prosperous the more abundant became its supply of food.

The Policy of Protection. 393

Now he should take the liberty of referring to his own experience for a moment. He returned to England after an absence of 20 years in 1861, and visited all those portions of England with which he was acquainted in his early life—namely, Warwickshire, London, Gloucestershire, and South Wales; and nothing struck him so forcibly, nothing so amazed him, as the improved condition of all classes of the great body of the people. He was prepared for great changes, but there was no change that forced itself upon him as being so remarkable as the improvement in the homes and habits of the people, not even excluding the agricultural labourers. As to the condition of the English farmers, there appeared to be an incredible improvement. He remembered well a farmer going to the exhibition from Berkshire, and entering into conversation with a number of his fellow-farmers in the railway carriage; he remembered one of the expressions he made use of was that nobody was so well off as the farmers. "After we put in our seed," said he, " we have nothing to do— nature does it for us. The grain grows while we sleep, and when our crop is gathered in we have ten customers from whom we can make our choice." The farm-houses, as far as he had an opportunity of contrasting his experience of twenty years before, were in all respects better provided with comforts. In one district where in 1825 he had seen men breast-ploughing the land with a rude instrument a farmers' Agricultural College now existed. Nearly every farmer of any extent had a steam plough, and the improvements which had been brought about and extended by scientific methods were largely introduced on the superior farms. The condition of the class of mechanics was immeasurably improved, and at the present time it was so generally good that there was very little disposition amongst them to leave England.

We might be told, as we had been on other occasions, of the great success of the protective policy in America. He thought of all countries in the world America afforded the most striking example of its failure. He was quite sure he could prove it if he had time, but he had the authority on this subject of a political economist—Mr. Amasa Walker—whose cultivation, deep thought, painstaking investigation, and judicial character caused him to rank as one of the highest authorities on economic science America had produced. Mr. Walker says :—

"It is within our personal knowledge that when the proposal was made to impose the protective tariff of 1816, the leading manufacturers of Rhode Island, amongst whom was the late Mr. Slater, the father of cotton-spinning in this country, met at the counting-room of one of their number, and after deliberate consultation upon the matter, came unanimously to the conclusion that they had 'rather be let alone.' Their business had grown up naturally and succeeded well; and they felt confident of its continued prosperity if uninterfered with by Government. On the other hand they argued that by laying a protective tariff the business would be thrown out of its natural channels and become fluctuating and uncertain. How well founded were these anticipations subsequent events have fully shown. It will doubtless be a matter of profound astonishment to the future historian that a people who had a free and untrammelled industry, with natural advantages for the most productive agriculture in the world, and for the legitimate growth of every kind of manufacture, should ever have asked for restrictions upon trade. But in truth they did not ask for protection at the outset. It was forced upon them by politicians, irrespective of their wishes, for the avowed purpose of securing a home market for cotton. All New England was opposed to the policy and protested against it, yet it was carried. Special forms of manufacturing were brought into existence; and as these were sickly and needed all the help they could obtain from Government, an interested party was formed, which clamoured incessantly for protection. Yet it was not until the third tariff—that of 1824—had gone into operation that the northern and central States became the partisans of protection.

So that according to this authority, the manufacturers themselves held out for eight years before they gave in their adhesion to this policy. He remembered reading, not long ago, a report upon the operation of the protective policy of America, and the example given of its injurious effect was the case of the manufacture of boots and shoes in some town in Massachusetts. The Legislature, in order to protect this particular manufacture, had imposed an import duty upon boots and shoes of foreign make, upon foreign-made leather for boots and shoes, and upon foreign hides which might be tanned into leather. The effect of protecting the industry was to destroy these manufactures entirely. It kept out the foreign-made boots and shoes, but it kept out the leather, and the hides which were made into leather, and as the domestic-grown hides were not one-hundredth part of the supply, the manufacture of boots and shoes was for the most part destroyed. That was a singular, and perhaps extreme instance of the infelicitous and blind way in which the Legislature endeavoured to effect an object which it could not effect. They found that it did not bring in revenue. By the tariff which was brought into existence in 1840, and continued without change until 1846, the average imposed duty of 33 per cent. on imports brought in revenue amounting to 26,000,000 dollars. In 1848 another tariff was brought in with the duties considerably reduced, and that continued until 1857, the average during that period being 24½ per cent., and the tariff bringing in revenue to the amount of 46,000,000 dollars.

The state of things in America would be best shown by glancing for a moment at the course of her shipping. Her protective policy was virtually destroying her shipping. In the years 1860-61 the registered tonnage was 5,539,813 tons, but in the years 1869-70 it was only 4,246,507 tons. The tonnage engaged in the coasting trade in 1860-61 was 2,657,292, and in 1869-70 it was only 2,595,328. The tonnage engaged in the cod fishery in 1860-61 was 127,310, and in 1869-70 it had dwindled down to 82,612. Then let them examine for a moment the foreign trade of the United States during these periods. Between the United States and the Brazils in 1860 there were 346 American and only 118 foreign ships employed, and in 1869 there were 114 American ships and 359 foreign ships employed in the trade between the two places. If they came to the direct trade between the United States and Great Britain, in 1860 there were 924 American and 613 foreign ships employed, while in 1869 the American vessels had dwindled down to 365, and foreign vessels had risen to 1391. Again, if they looked to the relations of British Possessions in America, it would be seen that for a long time the United States had a considerable trade with Canada. Very recently a gentleman (Mr. J. R. Larned) was appointed to report upon the commercial relations of the United States with the British Possessions in America, and in his report, addressed to the Treasurer of the United States in February, 1871, he spoke in the following terms:

". . . . The balance of trade in our favour was 39,410,899 dollars; but in 1863 the balance shifted to the other side, and ever since the preponderance against us has steadily and rapidly increased, until now we are exchanging commodities for little more than one-half that we buy from the British provinces. Indeed, the exchange of our own productions covers less than one-half of the amount that we are importing from the provinces."

The same authority—and let them remember that this was a Commissioner appointed by the United States Government—said in another place :—

" The range of the Canadian market for American productions appears to be lamentably limited, and almost confined to the rawest products of agriculture, with hardly an appreciable opening for the benefit of our skilled labour in any department, and this, too, in the case of the nearest neighbours we have upon the globe."

One of the effects of this protective policy had been to extinguish the United States trade with Canada, which in former years was very considerable. And then Mr. Wells, who was formerly Commissioner of Revenue for the United States, commented thus upon this report of the officers appointed to report upon the state of the relations of the United States with Canada :—

"It thus admits of demonstration that the highly protective policy which has characterised the fiscal legislation of the United States since 1860, conjoined with the use of an irredeemable and fluctuating paper currency, has been productive of effects directly opposite and antagonistic to what its authors prophesied and anticipated ; and that the country thereby, so far from having been made commercially and industrially independent, has been really rendered more dependent than at any former period—the flag of its commercial marine having been almost swept from the ocean ; the power to sell in foreign markets the products of its manufacturing industries having greatly diminished, while the importation of the products of foreign competitive industries has continually and most remarkably augmented."

He thought that these facts and authorities showed that protection had not done what its advocates proclaimed it to have done for England or the United States of America ; and many persons who might be considered to a large extent impartial, and who treated the question more from an historical point of observation than any other, firmly believed that America would before long revert to a commercial policy similar to that of Great Britain. But there could be no doubt whatever of the gigantic growth of Great Britain under its free-trade policy. That was beyond all question ; and as they had no light for their guidance so safe as the light of experience, they could not believe that England would have progressed at the same rapid pace under protection.

He had dwelt thus long on this subject because he did not think it right that opinions should go forth that Great Britain had lost power, prestige, or position among the nations by the free-trade policy which she had now acted upon so persistently for some thirty years. But the question of protection, in his judgment, was not properly raised in this colony by what the Ministry at the present time proposed. He had already pointed out that they were imposing no new duty of any kind. They were simply remitting burdens. Nor could they lay any great claim to making a large step in the direction of free-trade. Their course was a course that might be more correctly described as an attempt to simplify the existing tariff—to relieve the operations of persons engaged in commerce from all unnecessary and vexatious interference. They remitted a very large number of duties. Altogether they removed duties imposed upon nearly 200 articles, 147 of which were embraced under the *ad valorem* duties. They did not by the removal of the specific duties do much injury to the revenue, because to a large extent these duties produced a very limited amount, and it could scarcely be said that any one of these duties could be considered in its effects a protective duty. If the advocates of protection were sincere and in earnest—if the honourable and learned member for East Macquarie, who last session said he would try this question of protection in Parliament, was in earnest—what he should do would be to simplify the tariff in the direction in which they were now simplifying it, and at the same time impose duties on those articles which could be made in the colony, say to the extent of 25 per cent., which, though they would not possibly be quite prohibitory, would be substantially protective. But it was the idlest pretence to say that *ad valorem* duties of 5 per cent. upon furniture could be regarded as any appreciable benefit to the colonial cabinet-maker. Why, there was upon this class of articles in the great cost of transit from the country of manufacture to the country of consumption a duty amounting at least to one-third of the first cost, and in many instances to more.

Mr. BOOTH : We had to compete with articles made in penitentiaries.

Mr. PARKES : Experience told us that articles made in penitentiaries were not the cheapest articles in the world ; and in most instances they could not be made even so cheaply as they could be made by other labour. The probability was that, though the sentiment awakened in connexion with these manufactured articles fixed upon them a kind of varnish of cheapness, they were not one bit cheaper for being manufactured in penitentiaries, even supposing that articles so manufactured found their way in any quantity here. But he did not think that fact could be very well established. It was idle to say that an *ad valorem* duty of 5 per cent. could be any appreciable encouragement to the local manufacturer. But supposing it to be admitted that it was an encouragement, it would still be preposterous that for the sake of a 5-per-cent. bonus on five or six industries we should harass and cripple trade by imposing duties upon some 140 articles. Persons in favour of free-trade said human labour was the source of all value and power, and that the purchasing power of labour in all its manifold forms ought not to be limited by any legislative restrictions for the benefit of any particular class—that the person who gave his labour in the creation of wealth, whether as a labourer, an artist, a clerk, or a merchant, should have the widest and most unrestricted purchasing power as the result of this labour; or in other words that he should buy as freely as possible from all the markets of the world where he could get the most immediate or the most substantial return for the labour he had given. Could that be doubted for a moment? It did not appear to him to admit of any possible argument in opposition. You say, on the other side of the question, that by imposing some duty which would restrict the importation and currency of some manufacture made in Great Britain, you would thereby enable half a dozen or half a score of persons who made a similar article here to get a better price for it. In plain language this means that you would compel the whole population to pay a higher price for it. That was essentially an unjust and a wicked thing. He could conceive of no just reason for imposing taxation except to provide the revenue necessary to maintain the services of the State; and when taxes were imposed for any other object—to regulate trade, to root industries where they would not otherwise take root, they only encouraged a sickly growth, subject to artificial fluctuations, and which sooner or later must perish, and inflict serious consequential or collateral injuries upon the country. Persons therefore who supported a free-trade policy stood upon this clear and broad ground—their policy gave to all alike the unrestricted purchasing power of labour—whether that labour was in the exercise of talent or muscle, or of the two combined, in the direction of capital; and any legislation enacted for the purpose of building up some industry which could not otherwise take root was an unjust interference with this freedom of labour, both in its exercise and its reward.

All the merit to which the Government could lay claim in this direction was that they proposed to make the tariff more simple—to release our commerce from impediments and inconveniences to which it ought never to have been subjected. They had prepared

The Policy of Protection. 399

the field for this battle, if they were to have the conflict—whether the policy of this country should be assimilated to the policy of modern England, or whether it should be restrictive, such as the policy of England was in that dreary century to which he had at some length alluded. The Government were redeeming the distinct promise they had made to Parliament to abolish the *ad valorem* duties, and he ventured to say they were doing great good by removing in addition those specific duties which did not bring in any appreciable amount of revenue, and confining the tariff of the country to some 56 or 57 articles.

By the abolition of the postal charge upon newspapers they had given up a net amount of £10,000; and by the abolition of the Newcastle tonnage dues they had given up a net amount of £7000; by the abolition of the *ad valorem* duties, and the 57 specific duties which they intended to include with them, they now gave up an amount of something like £172,000, making altogether a sum of about £190,000 in round figures. They thought that was rather too large an amount of revenue to give up at one time notwithstanding the flourishing state of the revenue; and in looking round for some assistance to the revenue to enable them to do what the public interest required, and what they considered it was their duty to endeavour to do, they thought that the least objectionable course would be to impose an additional duty upon the article tobacco. He did not believe that any article within the whole range of consumption could be pointed out more eligible for taxation. It conformed to nearly every condition that had been laid down by persons of authority on the subject of taxation. It was essentially an article of luxury.

An HONOURABLE MEMBER: Not to the working man.

Mr. PARKES: He denied that assertion altogether. He had not been without experience among working men, as much perhaps as the honourable member who had just interrupted him, and he knew there was a large number of them who never consumed tobacco at all.

An HONOURABLE MEMBER: A greater number do use it; more use it than do not.

Mr. PARKES: If tobacco was largely consumed by working men and if he was reminded of that fact with any view to drawing down upon him unpopularity with the working classes, honourable gentlemen greatly misunderstood him if they thought he feared any penalty of that kind. But tobacco was essentially a luxury, and there could be no article selected, consumed by anyone whatever, that was more completely a luxury than tobacco. Again, it was an article the tax upon which any person could decline to pay. They were told that it made an article a legitimate subject for taxation when it was of a nature that rendered a person who consumed it the free choice of consuming it or not. Now any person declining to consume tobacco could escape from paying the tax. This was not the case with many other articles—with bread for instance. But tobacco was an article, and eminently so, in which the consumer had the free choice to pay this tax or not. Economists told them further that any article was a fair subject for taxation if in case the tax diminished the consumption of the article no harm was done to society. Tobacco conformed as eminently to that test as any article that could be selected, because if the consumption decreased no man would be hardy enough to say that any harm was thereby done to society. It just came to the question whether the tax was excessive, and he did not think that any person who reasoned upon the subject would think that this tax of 3s. and 2s.—3s. upon manufactured tobacco, and 2s. upon unmanufactured tobacco—was excessive. Indeed a very extensive manufacturer of tobacco told him only yesterday that he considered the article would bear the tax just as well as it bears the tax at present in existence. Independently of this opinion altogether, he maintained that this article would fairly bear the tax that the Government proposed, and that it would be much more suitable to place this tax upon tobacco than upon the people's tea and sugar. Then came the question arising out of the Border relations with the other colonies. It was useless to disguise the fact that those relations rendered the proposals of the Government more embarrassing than they would be if no Border treaty existed. There were objections arising from our relations with the sister colony of Victoria on our Border question. He admitted that this introduced an element of considerable embarrassment. But he did not admit all that had been said on the Opposition side. There were at the present time the same difference in the duties levied in South Australia and New South Wales as there would be in the duties of Victoria and New South Wales if this increased duty were assented to; if not quite to the same amount, to an amount that should have been attractive according to the arguments that had been used. Yet they did not hear that there had been any attempt to take advantage of the Convention which existed between this colony and South Australia. There had been a premium all along to the amount of 50 per cent., and that, according to the reasonings he had heard, would form a very large profit after paying the cost of carriage; yet it had not induced a single package of tobacco to come up the River Murray from South Australia during the four or five months that this Convention had been in operation. Then it should be borne in mind, that by the 10th clause of the Convention between this colony and Victoria we were at liberty, on a notice of three months, to remove the article of tobacco from the operation of the Convention, and only allow it to pass duty paid or in bond. Up to this period, if he was correctly informed, the largest quantity of tobacco had gone from this colony into Victoria. He had a private letter from the Commissioner of Customs in Victoria informing him that, in consequence of the large quantity of tobacco going from this colony into Victoria overland, the Victorian Government were very likely to put in force that 10th clause, and except tobacco from the operation of the Convention. He thought it best that the Committee should know that the complaints were not all on one side. But he did not anticipate anything like the results which honourable gentlemen had pointed out as likely to follow this increased duty on tobacco. He should, however, be very unwilling for any movement of his to call into active force that provision of the Convention, after the labours which had been expended in efforts to establish free intercourse across the Border.

The Government shared with honourable members considerable feelings of annoyance that persons engaged in trade in Sydney should have evaded the operation of the measure proposed by taking tobacco out of bond in large quantities. They felt a great deal of annoyance that this had taken place, but it was not the first time that persons, anticipating an increase in the Custom duties, had speculated in paying duties upon articles that they thought would be affected by the changes about to be made. On all occasions mercantile men were remarkable for shrewd penetration in the anticipation of probabilities. They watched the course of events, picking up information of what was likely to happen, drawing their own inferences from supposed facts, often from mere suppositions in which they were entirely mistaken; and, in paying a few thousand pounds upon an article which in the course of their business was likely to be consumed in a few months, wealthy firms were put to but little inconvenience, while if their speculations proved right they would make a large sum of money at the expense of the revenue. The same thing had been done before, and to a greater extent than was now the case. But the Government was much annoyed that this should have been done at all, and they were not insensible of the difficulties which beset them on the border; although as he stated before, they did not believe those difficulties approached to anything like the extent represented by honourable gentlemen. But in order to punish these speculators, and in order that the Government should not run any risk of unsettling the Border Customs treaty, his honourable colleague the Treasurer would inform the committee that he would not submit the increased duty on tobacco.

Mr. ROBERTSON: Caved in.

Mr. PARKES: He heard the shrill musical voice of the honourable gentleman across the table, who was always so exultant when the Ministry was making progress; and he was delighted that the honourable gentleman was so pleased with the course proposed to be taken by the Government. They were influenced in the step they were now taking by these considerations:—that as a portion of the revenue had been anticipated, they would lose that proportion of the increased duty, and the Government thought it was better for them to take the course they now proposed than to give persons who had anticipated the increased duty their hoped-for advantage. And they were influenced from this other consideration, that if even they succeeded in carrying their proposal (and they knew that there was a chance of their not succeeding) they would have, according to their present view, to call into operation that provision of the Border treaty which would remove tobacco from its operation; and they confessed that they did shrink from creating that difficulty. They confessed that, having restored feelings of contentment and satisfaction upon the Border, they would not like to be the first to tamper with the arrangement that had been made. They did not think, if they got the amount of revenue they calculated upon from the increased duty, that it would compensate them for any mischief that might arise from altering the Customs treaty. He had stated the reasons which induced the Government to propose the increased duty, and the considerations which now induced them to take the present course.

They had substantially done what the public required of them. From their expressions of opinion and from the indications of their course of policy, it was fairly and properly expected that the Government should lose no time in repealing the *ad valorem* duties. They had in their proposals now before the committee done that, and they had gone further in the same direction—as far as prudence justified them in going. They had not yet carried their proposals into law ; but he believed they had done what was in accordance with the wish of that House and the wish of the country, and was, therefore, certain to become law. Their tariff, which would reduce the taxation of the country, would be more clear, more simple, and more in the direction of a definite and sound policy than any that had existed for many years in the country.

THE CASE OF THE PRISONER GARDINER.

THE PREROGATIVE OF PARDON.

[A NOTORIOUS prisoner, known as Frank Gardiner, was conditionally pardoned by the Governor of New South Wales in 1874. This case was seized upon by the Parliamentary Opposition, and agitated by every kind of misrepresentation, in which the Governor himself was not spared, until it led to a change of Ministry. The principal circumstances of this case which may be considered of permanent interest, as showing the means resorted to for political ends in the colony, are explained in a memorandum by Mr. Parkes, published as an appendix. The first substantial motion made in the Legislative Assembly on the subject was submitted by Mr. Edward Combes on the 3rd of June, on which occasion the following speech was delivered :—]

SPEECH

Delivered in the Legislative Assembly, June 3rd, 1874.

MR. PARKES said : The honourable member for Bathurst had made a speech which he took the liberty of saying was in tone hardly befitting the large subject the honourable member had taken in hand. He scarcely thought it was becoming, on an occasion like that, to present to the House sensational pictures of some particular phase of crime. Crime in all its phases was repulsive, and a thing of which we might draw the most vivid and deterrent pictures; but the question with which we now had to deal was one that ought to be approached in a calm, patient, and thoughtful manner. The honourable member had given himself a very wide range, and had brought under review the whole question of prison management, and the system of carrying out the sentences of the courts of law. The honourable member had said some things

The Case of the Prisoner Gardiner. 405

which he thought would have been better left unsaid. He did not think that the honourable member had any fair ground for accusing him of disingenuousness in these proceedings. He thought that honourable members on both sides of the House must admit that he had offered every information in his power.

Mr. FORSTER: Oh, oh.

Mr. PARKES: The honourable member was a single exception.

Mr. J. ROBERTSON: Oh, oh.

Mr. PARKES: Then there were two honourable members, both of whom had a special interest in any question which might be supposed to embarrass the present Government, and who, unlike leaders of opposite sides in the House of Commons, eagerly took advantage of any occasion which would bring about what they most desired. He was disposed to deal with this question without saying a single word to which any one could take exception, if he was allowed to proceed without interruption. The honourable member told them that it was his fixed determination to do all he could to prevent what he called a "great wrong." He need not have told them that, for although he had manifested no great determination on any other question, he had certainly given evidence of a determination to do something now. The honourable member told them that they might suppose they were still living under prerogative government. Well, so far as this question—the exercise of the Royal prerogative of pardon—was concerned, he would simply say that, whatever form of government they lived under, that power hitherto in this colony had been exercised independently of the Minister. He was prepared to prove this part of his case by the evidence of successive Governors, and, what was of more importance, from the action of different Ministers. The honourable member quoted from *Broom's Commentaries*, and said that in Sir Erskine May's book they were told that the House of Commons had the right to advise the Crown, and that Mr. Canning described the House of Commons as a council of control, and that Mr. Pitt, so far back as nearly a hundred years ago, spoke of the House of Commons as having a Constitutional right of inquiry. The honourable member quoted from a number of similar authorities to the same effect. Not a single person had denied these powers of the House of Commons, or similar powers on the part of the Legislative Assembly. Then the honourable gentleman said that it was admitted that the House had a right to advise and control the exercise of the Royal prerogative, and he quoted again from a number of text books, and from the utterances of distinguished men who had given general opinions on questions of Constitutional principle; but he had failed to produce one solitary instance where the House of Commons had attempted *to control* the exercise of the Royal prerogative in the manner now attempted here. One solitary case would be more to the purpose than fifty authorities in these general terms on matters of abstract principle. They knew that the House of Commons had power to do anything. It was shown that it once had power to behead a king. But in the practical business of governing England the Imperial Parliament had learned to impose upon itself wise and accepted restraints, which were now a part of Constitutional practice; and it would be much more to the purpose to show them where it had ever endeavoured to control the Royal prerogative of mercy. It certainly had interfered by asking questions, but scarcely ever to the extent of calling for papers; and in most cases it had interfered in the cause of mercy, when it was thought that the prerogative had been or was in danger of being precipitately or harshly exercised. The honourable member spoke of Lord Brougham's resolutions; but he could not understand any application that the carrying of those resolutions could have to the present case. The Assembly carried a resolution the other night which was directly in the teeth of the Constitution Act. But would that override the provisions of the Constitution? It was one thing to carry a resolution expressing opinions as to how things should be done, and it was quite another to control the doing of these things, especially in the exercise of the Royal prerogative. The honourable member occupied some little time in telling them what were the powers of the Secretary of State. No one doubted the powers of the Secretary of State, nor did the honourable gentleman's observations in that regard touch the question they had to deal with in any of its branches. Then the honourable member alluded to what he called the direct instructions to the Governor by Lord Kimberley's circular dispatch, and, as far as he could judge—and he said it with great deference—the honourable member entirely misunderstood the drift of that dispatch. In the first place, he ought to have been aware that the whole of these dispatches together formed correspondence which,

The Case of the Prisoner Gardiner. 407

instead of proving that the practice of England existed here, as the honourable member put it, incontestably proved that the matter was in a state of doubt, and required instructions. The dispatch of Lord Belmore in 1869 was written for no other purpose than to obtain instructions. It was written for no other reason than because things here were in a state of doubt, and that neither the Governor nor his Minister knew exactly how to act. The very dispatch which originated this correspondence proved that the matter was in an unsettled and unsatisfactory state. The effect of these dispatches was not to leave the question in the state in which the honourable gentleman appeared to think it always ought to have been left, but to remove it from the ordinary category of the business transactions of the Government. There was no other possible reading of these dispatches than that the Governor was in a marked and special manner to exercise his own power and to act upon his own judgment in his intercourse with his Ministers on this subject, and to regard the advice he was instructed to seek from them in a special and an exceptional sense. And, moreover, there was certainly no reason to suppose that the Governor was instructed to ask advice of his Ministers, except when he thought of granting a pardon. The honourable member had failed to read the dispatches, or if he had read them he had failed to understand them. Then the honourable member complained in detail of the answers given by the Government to his questions. He did not see how the answers he gave to the honourable gentleman were justly open to complaint. He answered him as fully and as explicitly as it was possible for him to do; but the honourable member took special exception to his saying in answer to his fifth question, "The date for the case to be re-submitted to His Excellency is the 8th July." That was strictly the case. His Excellency's decision was that the case might be submitted at the end of ten years, and the Colonial Secretary's office was so guarded and scrupulous in communicating this decision of His Excellency that it was given in precisely the same terms in the communication made to the gaol authorities, and the only communication therefore made to this prisoner was this:—" I am directed by the Colonial Secretary to state, for your information and guidance, that His Excellency the Governor has been pleased to approve of your bringing the prisoner's case forward for consideration when he shall have served ten years of his sentence." That was precisely the decision arrived at by His Excellency. It was very true that His Excellency, on some subsequent petition, appeared to have written a minute which was never acted upon, because the office had acted upon the decision when it was first given. Under some impression apparently that he had done more than he really had done, his Excellency wrote the following minute :—" I have already decided to grant a conditional pardon at the termination of ten years' imprisonment.—H.R., 7/12/72." But the communication to the gaol authorities in the ordinary course of business was by the letter he had already read, which adopted the precise language of His Excellency's first minute. The honourable gentleman stated, also, that he firmly believed that pressure had been used with His Excellency, and he supposed the honourable member meant that the Ministry had in some way urged this decision.

Mr. COMBES: No.

Mr. PARKES: He was very glad to hear the honourable member say it was not so. That was all he had to say on the speech the honourable member had made, and he now came to the case upon which the House was asked to pronounce an opinion.

He desired to bring the minds of honourable gentlemen to as undisturbed and calm an examination of the whole matter as was possible. In the first place, what was it that had been done in the cases of those prisoners who now formed the subject of the honourable gentleman's motion ? He made no complaint whatever of his moving a resolution other than the one of which gave notice. He thought the honourable member did all that could be expected, in giving notice that he intended to bring this subject before the House. They must bear in mind that he was not now raising the question whether it was right or whether it was wrong —whether the House might deem it expedient or inexpedient, wise or unwise, to grant these remissions of sentence—but he maintained that what had been done was directly in accordance with the prison policy of the British nation. There had been no extreme act of mercy in these cases—there had been no extraordinary release from punishment which was not in accord with the principles and policy of the mother-country in the treatment of prisoners ; and he thought, if he established that, he should establish a great deal in justification of the course taken by His Excellency the Governor. And he should in the course of his

The Case of the Prisoner Gardiner. 409

observations show—and he thought he should show to the satisfaction of every honourable member whose mind was open to conviction—that in this colony, up to the present time, the Governor had exercised the prerogative of mercy as a rule without reference to his Ministers. He did not mean that His Excellency had not referred occasionally to Ministers for further information, or to the Attorney-General for his view of the law ; but he should be able to show that the prerogative of mercy had been exercised by the Governor on his independent judgment, and that Ministers had not practically interfered. He should be able to show that the release of prisoners by the mitigation of punishment had been going on under all Governors and under all Administrations.

In the year 1870, when the honourable member for West Sydney was in office with Sir Charles Cowper, there were fifty prisoners released in a shorter time than the regulations would admit. One was Vane, the bushranger, who, under a sentence of fifteen years, was released in five years. In the year ending on the 30th April, 1872—the year when the honourable gentleman was in office with Sir James Martin—fifty-two prisoners were released in the same manner. It would thus be seen that what had been done in this case was in accord with the practice prevailing here, and that prisoners had been continually released before the expiration of the terms of their sentences under all Administrations.

The petition in Gardiner's case must have been got up two and a-half years ago, because it was two and a-half years ago at the very least since he saw that petition when it was brought to him for signature. This petition was written on uniform sheets of paper, which was not always the case with documents of this kind. The petition itself was from the two sisters of the prisoner Gardiner —Mrs. Griffiths and Mrs. Cale—and all the other sheets attached to it had this heading—there was no signature signed to any one of the sheets which had not this heading : —

"We, the undersigned, beg most respectfully to recommend the foregoing petition to your Excellency's merciful consideration, and more especially from the desire to reform evidenced by the prisoner before capture, and his conduct since his incarceration, and trust that your Excellency may be pleased, under all the circumstances of the case, *to deem the period of the sentence already expired sufficient for the ends of justice.*"

That was pretty clear. It would not be denied that the persons who signed their names to those words were of opinion that the prisoner Gardiner ought to be released at the end of seven and a-half years. That could not be explained away. Every signature was written upon sheets which had this heading. If the honourable member for Bathurst (Mr. Combes) or the honourable member for West Macquarie (Mr. Webb) had been asked to sign a petition of this character, and they had thought it their duty to state any facts they were aware of in the prisoner's favour, while at the same time they could not agree with the recommendation of the petition, they would have taken care to say that they could not join in the recommendation. He was sure that those honourable members would admit that if they had known some favourable facts which they thought they ought to state, though they could not join in the petition, they would have guarded themselves from being supposed to concur in this heading. They would have done what he had often seen done in similar petitions—they would have taken objection to the recommendation, and then stated what they wished to state. Mr. Forster's name was written to his minute on one of these sheets, and it was written without any exception to the recommendation of the petition which preceded it. That was the fact—he did not wish to place any forced construction upon it. Was not the minute itself equally as strong as the preceding recommendation? There were only two signatures to the original heading recommending the instant release of the prisoner Gardiner, and the third signature was that of the honourable member (Mr. Forster), preceded by his own minute, which he looked upon as an additional recommendation. Mr. Forster's memorandum was in these words:—

"Having been referred to in a petition for the mitigation of the sentence of Francis Christie* as holding the office of Colonial Secretary when an outbreak occurred in Darlinghurst Gaol, I have much pleasure in testifying to the fact of Christie's good conduct on that occasion, as well as to his general conduct during the entire period of his incarceration, so far as it came under my notice in either case. I am glad to record this opinion, so that it may operate as it ought in the prisoner's favour. And so far as these and other circumstances mentioned in the petition entitle his case to the favourable consideration of the Government, I am willing to add my testimony and recommendation.

"December 29th, 1871. "WILLIAM FORSTER."

The petition was for the prisoner's instant release. What was meant by an ex-Premier writing that he states certain facts with a view that they may operate in the prisoner's favour, without

---

*The prisoner Gardiner's *alias* was Francis Christie.

The Case of the Prisoner Gardiner. 411

any qualifying words in reference to the prayer of the petition—without saying a single word that he did not agree with the recommendation? "So far as these and other circumstances mentioned in the petition entitle his case to the favourable consideration of the Government, I am willing to add my testimony and recommendation." If you "added" a written "recommendation" in such a case, was it not added to the recommendation of the petition? That was the meaning he put upon it, and the meaning that he thought would be put upon it by the country. There was a gentleman of wealth and education, who had held the office of Solicitor-General, who signed this recommendation that "We trust your Excellency may be pleased, under all the circumstances of the case, to deem the period of the sentence already expired sufficient for the ends of justice." That was when the prisoner had served seven and a-half years. This petition was signed by a number of persons of undoubted reputation; by several members of Parliament; by a gentleman who had filled the position of Solicitor-General of the colony, and had therefore been answerable for the due administration of criminal justice. It was signed by another gentleman who had been twice Colonial Secretary and once Premier. Was it not likely, then, that this petition would receive every consideration at the hands of His Excellency? And was it not intended to be viewed with consideration? Did any one put his name to that paper without intending that the weight of his name, and of his standing in the country, should attach to the recommendation? He did not think that any one who signed that petition could be justified in any way trying to explain away the fact. To his mind it had always appeared that men ought to pause before giving the weight of their names and of the position they occupy to a document of this kind. And, although he was neither in office nor in Parliament at the time, and because he had filled the office of Colonial Secretary, he refused to attach the weight of the office he had been permitted to hold to the recommendation of this petition when it was brought to him.

Some observations had been made upon a minute that he had thought it his duty to write on sending these papers to His Excellency the Governor. That minute simply pointed out the names and the standing of the most conspicuous persons who had signed the petition. It seemed to him that he was bound in justice to the prisoner to point out to the Governor, who was then a stranger in the country, the positions which those gentlemen occupied—that it was his duty to point out any circumstances he knew which appeared to be in the prisoner's favour, at the same time stating the crime he had committed, the reputation he held, and all the circumstances of the case as well as he knew them. He had before described in a speech he had occasion to make on a previous evening that he did make it his business to see the Governor in reference to this case, and enter into a conversation with him, not for the purpose of giving advice but to place His Excellency in possession of all the information he could affecting this case. He told His Excellency that this man was the most remarkable prisoner in the history of this country, and was reputed to have been the ringleader of a series of gangs of bush-rangers which infested the country some years ago, and that he was reputed to be the organiser and leader of the band of men who robbed the gold escort in the year 1862. He explained to His Excellency that this man had been tried for offences of a very heinous character, and had received the sentences which the papers showed. He explained at the same time that the prisoner appeared to be connected with a family of good character as far as he could learn. He explained that there was a number of persons of standing and high reputation who appeared to take an interest in this case; and he also explained that the prisoner's conduct had been uniformly good since he had been in gaol. That was the substance of his conversation with His Excellency. He explained all he knew on both sides, and he conceived that it was his duty so to do. It was only right for him to say that since these discussions had taken place His Excellency had told him that he was under the impression that he was not unfavourable to a merciful consideration of this case. But it was right also to say that His Excellency admitted, in the most direct terms, that he never offered any advice, and that His Excellency never asked any advice from him, in reference to this matter. His Excellency might have formed such an impression as he had alluded to, for they often found that, after explaining a matter in the simplest manner possible to their own minds, an impression was left upon other minds which very much surprised them. All he could say was that what he wished to do, and what he thought he did, was to explain both sides of this case —to give the gaol history of the prisoner, the nature of his crime,

The Case of the Prisoner Gardiner. 413

and the sentences he had received ; and, on the other side, his good conduct in prison, the real character and standing of the persons who seemed to be in his favour, some of whom had undoubtedly signed this petition for his release at the end of seven and a-half years, and the character, as far as he knew, of his relatives, who had petitioned for his release.

With regard to the prisoner Gardiner, he felt it necessary to say that he, perhaps, of all men in this country occupying a similar public position, knew least of him. When the gold escort robbery took place he was 13,000 miles away. It took place in June, 1862; and he did not leave England on his return to the colony until the October following. He did not arrive in Sydney until the end of January, 1863. He then remained in private life for a considerable time, paying little attention to public affairs. He believed that he never read the report of the trials of the escort robbers. To account for that, he might explain that as a rule he never read the reports of trials of this character. But there were other reasons. He was immersed in transactions of his own, which occupied his attention entirely for a considerable time after his arrival, and he paid little attention to the case of Gardiner. He well remembered feeling surprise on returning from England that this man, whose name he had never heard of prior to his leaving the colony, had become a kind of criminal hero. Well, things went on, and he never thought of Gardiner until he took office in 1866, because he had no occasion to think of him. While on his first visit to Darlinghurst Gaol, Mr. Read, the principal gaoler, pointed out a prisoner to him, and told him that that was Frank Gardiner. He looked at the prisoner, but from that day, though he had visited the gaol probably forty times, he had never exchanged a single word with him, and for this reason—that he had imposed upon himself as a rule of his life, never while Colonial Secretary to enter into conversation with prisoners, even though he had known them before their imprisonment. It appeared to him that this was a right rule ; but he found that this rule was not observed by others. The late Chief Justice who tried this case, on visiting the prison entered into a long conversation with him. He found that others, including members of Parliament, often did the same thing. He had felt it right to offer this explanation to the House. It was only recently that he had given himself the trouble to go beyond the gaol authorities to try and get information respecting this prisoner. As far as he could understand, there did not appear to be legal evidence that he was engaged in the escort robbery. The Attorney-General of the time (Sir James Martin) declined to put him on his trial because, as he said in a minute, the evidence was insufficient. The evidence against Gardiner appeared to have been that of the approver Charters, uncorroborated by a single circumstance except that the sergeant of police thought he could swear to Gardiner's voice. The honourable member for Illawarra (Mr. Forster) must know a great deal more about this case than he did, because the honourable gentleman was Colonial Secretary in 1859, when the prisoner was released after five years' imprisonment, from two cumulative sentences of seven years each.

Mr. FORSTER : That was his first offence.

Mr. PARKES : He admitted that Gardiner had not then acquired his criminal notoriety, and that the honourable gentleman's attention might not have been specially called to the case. Nevertheless, it was a remarkable release of a prisoner convicted of two offences of enormity, for which he received two cumulative sentences of seven years each, to be let out of gaol after five years' imprisonment. From a report of proceedings in the Assembly some years ago, to which he had occasion to refer that day, he noticed that the honourable member (Mr. Forster) said, in reference to this question of pardoning, that no act of the kind was done when he was in office without his advice and consent. If that was so, he must have advised and consented to the liberation of Gardiner in 1859, though the papers did not say so much. The honourable gentleman probably acted in the same way as every one else had done. The honourable gentleman was Colonial Secretary again, some four years afterwards, when the Government refused to put Gardiner upon his trial for the escort robbery, and the honourable gentleman was also Colonial Secretary for some considerable time after Gardiner's imprisonment commenced. Now, recently it had come to the knowledge of the Government that there was reason to suppose, though it did not appear to be proved, that this prisoner was identical with a person who, in 1850, committed a robbery in Geelong, Port Phillip at that time being a part of this colony, for which he was convicted and sentenced to seven years' imprisonment, subsequently escaping from Pentridge. This was unknown to the Government, and unknown to the

The Case of the Prisoner Gardiner.

Comptroller of Prisons, until about eight or nine days ago. This knowledge appeared to have been in the possession of the police for some time past, but honourable gentlemen who knew anything about police operations knew that it was one principle of effective police action to keep anything secret unless there was some necessity for making it known. This was necessary for the promotion of efficiency in the Police Department, and it was necessary also that prisoners, when they were let out of gaol, might have an opportunity of getting an honest livelihood. This explanation was due to the police. He found that when the honourable member was in office, and immediately after Gardiner's conviction, Mr. John Thomas Smith, then Mayor of Melbourne, applied to him for permission to see the prisoner, to ascertain whether he could identify him as the person who had been confined in Pentridge, and escaped. The honourable gentleman granted the following order to Mr. Smith :—

"To the Gaoler, Darlinghurst.
"Dear Sir—Mr. J. T. Smith, Mayor of Melbourne, is desirous of seeing the prisoner Gardiner, with the view of ascertaining his possible identity with a person of his description some time ago confined in Pentridge Stockade, Victoria. You will, therefore, be good enough to afford Mr. Smith such facilities as may be consistent with your convenience and duty.
"I am, &c.,
" WILLIAM FORSTER."

He could easily understand that the honourable gentleman might not have attached much importance to this at the time, and that he might never have had a conversation with Mr. Smith after his visit to the gaol. And what he should like to know—and if time had permitted he should have communicated with Mr. Smith on the subject—was whether Mr. Smith, after this visit to the prisoner, in 1864, informed the honourable member for Illawarra that Gardiner was the same person who had escaped from Pentridge ?

Mr. FORSTER : It will be upon record in the office.
Mr. PARKES : It is not on record.
Mr. FORSTER : Surely the result is known in the gaol.
Mr. PARKES : It was very improbable that the result would be known there. Mr. Smith would not be likely to tell the gaoler that Gardiner was the man who had broken out of Pentridge. He would be more likely to go back to the Colonial Secretary and tell him.

Mr. FORSTER : He certainly told me nothing that I recollect.

Mr. PARKES : He should consider it his duty to communicate with Mr. Smith, to see what was the result of this interview. The case of Gardiner came before His Excellency the Governor in the way he had explained. His Excellency decided, not that the prisoner should be liberated at the end of seven and a-half years, but that, if the prisoner's conduct continued good for ten years, the case might then be brought before His Excellency again. That was the decision arrived at upon the case submitted.

This decision had been spoken of as if it was an unconditional release—a release under some extraordinary circumstances. The punishment actually carried out by this decision was an imprisonment of ten years, in the face of uniformly good conduct, accompanied by banishment for twenty-two years afterwards. Now, he ventured to say that that was a severer punishment than any sentence short of death in the former days of darkness in England, when sentences of transportation were inflicted upon persons found guilty of crimes of equal magnitude. The punishment of persons in England in the last century, and in the early years of this, was transportation for life for offences of equal magnitude; but that was nothing to be compared to the punishment of ten years' close imprisonment, with twenty-two years' banishment afterwards. And he learned, on the highest authority that could be obtained, that, a few years ago, there was not a single prisoner out of all the many thousands in the gaols of England who had been in close detention ten years. To show that he was not making this statement recklessly, he would produce his authority. That authority was Sir Walter Crofton, an Imperial officer, who stood second to none in his knowledge of prison management and penal discipline, and as a witness of experience on a subject of this kind. And how was that evidence given? It was given before a Royal Commission, with the Duke of Richmond at its head, and comprising Mr. Gathorne Hardy, Sir John Taylor Coleridge, Dr. Lushington, Mr. Bright, Mr. George Ward Hunt, and other gentlemen of equal standing and eminence. Sir Walter Crofton, in giving his evidence, in answer to the chairman, the Duke of Richmond, said :—

"The convict system in this country, and in Ireland, was devised without any regard whatever to the possibility of keeping men for their lives, or for any very long period, in confinement, in England particularly ; they were

The Case of the Prisoner Gardiner. 417

always sent to the colonies after certain periods of detention, and I do not believe that at this moment you have men who have been ten years under detention in the convict establishments of this country. In Ireland we have had them for periods ranging from ten to fifteen years under our notice. I have known men, and have particularly observed them, who have been fourteen and fifteen years under imprisonment. I obtained within the last few days from Captain Whitty, who is now at the head of the convict establishment in Ireland, a return of the number of men who are at present under detention in the Irish convict prisons, and have been so for a period exceeding ten years. . . . There are now in the Irish convict prisons 70 male convicts under life sentences and 9 female convicts. Exceeding 10 years under detention there are 28 males and 7 females ; exceeding 12 years there are 18 males and 1 female ; exceeding 13 years there are 13 males and 1 female ; exceeding 14 years there are 3 males and 1 female ; exceeding 15 years there are 2 males. There is one man, I understand, who has been 15 years and 8 months."

That was the only instance in Ireland of a man having been more than fifteen years in confinement. On the cessation of transportation a statute was passed to punish criminals within the United Kingdom, and the highest sentences that could be imposed under that statute, in lieu of the old sentences of fifteen years or any longer period of transportation, was imprisonment for not less than six years nor more than ten. What was it that the prison reformers, from Howard down to our own day, had been contending for? and the rank of prison reformers of the present century had included men of the highest and purest character, the most profound learning, and the most distinguished position. What had been their object? Their object had been to ensure the punishment of offenders being carried out in accordance with the dictates of humanity—that, for example, the health of the prisoners should not suffer from unhealthy conditions of prison life. Whilst the law was considerate in protecting society, it was held to be the duty of the State, in the highest interests of society, to hold out hope of redemption to every prisoner who came under the sentence of the law. Statesmen, philanthropists, jurists, and all who had given the subject practical consideration, had unanimously held the opinion that hope should be held out to every prisoner. And so much was that practice recognised in other countries, that in Belgium, where capital punishment had been abolished, and where imprisonment for life had taken the place of capital punishment for such crimes as murder, imprisonment for life was frequently reduced to imprisonment for twelve years. That was the evidence given before the Royal Commission. Well, on the testimony of the authorities he had quoted, it was clear that the spirit of revenge had passed away from the laws of civilised countries; such a spirit as he had seen in these discussions had no part in the consideration of these questions by enlightened men. Society had no interest in immuring men in prison for their lives. Better by far put them to death than imprison them indiscriminately for life. The opinions of persons who had thought upon the subject were unanimous in this view—that offenders against the laws of the country in which they lived ought to be divided into two distinct classes. He did not know any person whose opinion was entitled to weight who dissented from that view—that offenders ought to be divided into two separate classes, habitual offenders and casual or accidental offenders.

There was a class of persons in the mother-country—he hoped there were none answering to the same class here—who were born to habits of thieving, trained to it as regularly as children in purer circumstances were trained to habits of industry. They lived by depredations upon property throughout their lives, and died thieves. Undoubtedly there was a large class of such persons in the mother-country; and honourable gentlemen would be astonished to hear, upon the authority of Mr. W. R. Greg, that no less than 100,000 prisoners were released unconditionally in England every year. In addition to those releases, there were not fewer than 2000 released under tickets-of-leave every year, whose crimes ranged up to those of the highest enormity. The police took cognisance of their proceedings, but did not inform people who they were, in order that the liberated persons might have a chance of self-redemption. He had alluded to the enormous criminal class in England in order to draw a comparison highly favourable to this country. Mr. Matthew Davenport Hill, a very high authority, stated that amongst the habitual criminals detection was so seldom that it was supposed that not more than one conviction took place in some 60 depredations. Mr. Hill gave the police returns on the proportion of convictions for forging Bank of England notes, and, according to that return, during a period of 32 years the convictions for forging Bank of England notes had been only as one to 164 cases of forged notes presented to the bank for payment. But what he desired to call attention to was that in this country there was good reason to suppose that comparatively few offences took place where detection did not follow, and

The Case of the Prisoner Gardiner. 419

that arose not from the superiority of the police force—which, however, was quite equal to that of England—but from the circumstances of the country rendering detection much more easy than it was in a dense population of 30,000,000.

He now came to the list of the 24 cases which had attracted so much attention. The great majority of the men in that list answer strictly to the category of criminals who were other than habitual criminals. It could not be doubted that the greater number of those young men, natives of the country, had, until they were inveigled into the crime of bushranging, lived industrious and reputable lives. He was somewhat amused at the honourable and learned member for the Western Gold-fields (Mr. Buchanan), who was continually interrupting him, and by his interruptions expressing his opposition to the statements he was making. The honourable and learned gentleman, nine years ago—a few months after the conviction of two of the men in this list—moved a resolution in favour of the release of those two men at that time. The honourable and learned member, on the 7th March, 1865, moved the following resolution :—

"That an address be presented to the Governor, praying that His Excellency will be pleased to cause the instant release of the prisoners Bow and Fordyce, found guilty of robbing the gold escort from Forbes, and sentenced to death, but reprieved by His Excellency, against the advice of his Ministers, on the ground that it was contrary to the practice of the English tribunals to accept the unsupported testimony of an approver, and stating that the release of those prisoners is also desired in consideration of the irregular and improper, if not illegal, nature of their trial and conviction."

He now came to what had been done in regard to the proposed release of these persons ; and then he should proceed to show what had been the course taken in this country in the exercise of the prerogative of mercy under other Governments. The cases of these persons had been considered mainly on the ground that for the most part the offenders belonged to an exceptional class. It was beyond doubt that in most cases these young men had never come under the observation of the police, or been known to offend against the law, before they had taken to bushranging. And what had been done ? With respect to the proposed release of these twenty-four men, the remissions of sentence by the express exercise of the prerogative of pardon did not, in the majority of the cases, greatly abridge the period of sentence below what might have been obtained under the legal regulations. The difference was this : by the gaol regulations, a man who was sentenced to ten years was entitled to his release at the end of eight years; but under the exercise of the prerogative in this instance, he was released at the end of seven years and six months, or only six months short of the legal term. The man who was sentenced to fifteen years' penal servitude would be entitled by the regulations to be released at the end of eleven years and three months; by the exercise of the prerogative he was released at the end of eight years and nine months. A man who received a sentence of 30 years could claim his release with good conduct at the end of 22 years and 6 months; but under the special mode of treatment these men had received he would be able to claim it at the end of 17 years and 6 months. Of the 24 men whom it was proposed to release 10 only would be liberated in the colony, leaving 14 to be exiled; and this exile meant not merely banishment from the colony, but banishment from all the Australian colonies and from New Zealand, whilst if they returned they were liable to be arrested and made to serve out the remainder of their sentences. On inquiry he had found that there was scarcely a case known of an exile returning to the colony. Now let them see what had been done by other Governors before the arrival of Sir Hercules Robinson. In the year commencing June 20th, 1864, and ending June 20th, 1865, there were 80 persons released in the same manner. Within one year no less than 190 applications for remission were submitted, of which 110 were refused and 80 were granted. In the year 1870, in Mr. Cowper's last Administration, no less than 44 prisoners were released unconditionally, and 5 exiled, making altogether 49; and amongst these was Vane, the bushranger, who had been sentenced to 15 years' imprisonment, and was released at the end of 5 years. In the years 1871-2, 49 prisoners received unconditional pardons, and 3 were exiled, making a total of 52; and this system of release had been going on year by year unmarked by the House until the present moment. He was speaking now solely of persons in whose favour the prerogative of mercy had been exercised. In the year 1862 Mr. Cowper, who had held office as Colonial Secretary longer than any other person in the colony, and whose great administrative ability was universally acknowledged, had a letter read to the prisoners at Cockatoo, Darlinghurst, and Parramatta, pointing out to them that the door of hope was not shut against them; but by good

The Case of the Prisoner Gardiner.

conduct they might open it at any time through the exercise by His Excellency of the prerogative of mercy. He should himself have objected to the adoption of so unusual a course as this—of having a letter written specially to be read to the prisoners, making the official announcement that the prerogative of mercy was open to them. On one occasion Mr. Cowper—at a time when the honourable member for Sydney West (Mr. Robertson) was his colleague—actually released 9 persons in order to celebrate the Prince of Wales' birthday. On another occasion he released 29 prisoners, or rather the Minister submitted their cases for the consideration of His Excellency, who assented to their release. [An Honourable Member—" What were their crimes ?"] It had been asked what were their offences ? One of them was a sentence of fifteen years for rape. He did not know what importance honourable members attached to it, but he knew that most persons regarded it as a serious crime ; and yet this man who was convicted in 1862 and was sentenced to fifteen years, was one of the prisoners released in 1870 by the Ministry of which Mr. Robertson was a member—thus serving eight years instead of fifteen years, through the exercise of the prerogative of mercy. Another of the men was sentenced to ten years for robbery under arms, and was released at the end of five years, being relatively a much shorter term of imprisonment than any of the prisoners in this list had undergone. These were two of the cases, and there was a long list of similar cases.

The honourable member who made this motion had contended that Ministers in this country occupied the same position as the Home Secretary in England; and this assertion had been cheered by the honourable member for Sydney West (Mr. Robertson), but that honourable gentleman when in office had never occupied any such position, as the honourable gentleman very well knew. The question was not whether it ought to be so, but whether it really had been so. He was prepared to show conclusively that no Minister had been clothed with similar authority in this colony. In the dispatches on the table they had the statement of Sir Alfred Stephen, who, having been Chief Justice during the term of office of every succeeding Administration, ought to be in a position to know the practice that had prevailed. They had also the statement of Sir Hercules Robinson, who had now been two years in the colony, and who had had every opportunity of consulting persons of authority on the matter. On this testimony the state of things in this colony was that the Colonial Secretary had been solely the instrument of placing before the Governor all the facts of the several cases, and that His Excellency exercised the prerogative of mercy without advice. He had himself filled the office of Colonial Secretary close upon five years, and he could say that such had been the course of practice during the whole time he had held office. He had adopted that course because he had always understood that it was that which had been adopted by his predecessors in office; and he could readily understand how in a country like ours, which was a dependent country in its relation to the British Empire, there must necessarily be defects in our Parliamentary government. We had no treaty rights, there were very many things we had not the power of doing, and it was not in the nature of things that we should have complete independent powers so long as we remained the mere colony of a nation. That being so he was content to leave this sacred power of the exercise of the prerogative of mercy—the power of abridging sentences which had been arrived at upon sworn testimony in the courts of law—entirely with the representative of the Crown; and as far as his opinion went he believed it would be best so to leave it. As a member of this community who had taken an active part in public affairs—as one who was more anxious for the character and permanent good of the country than for any other thing in life—he declared that in his opinion this power of pardon would be more safely and more beneficially exercised by the Governor than by any one else. That was his individual opinion, and he would come to the constitutional part of the question just now. He need not go beyond what Sir Alfred Stephen and Sir Hercules Robinson said to show that this hitherto had been the practice. Sir Alfred Stephen, at the time he was writing, was the Acting-Governor of the colony, and he said:—

"The Colonial Secretary, in whose department all correspondence on the subject of crime, after conviction, is carried on, does not in the first instance express any opinion on a petition for pardon or mitigation. He may have done so in a few cases, but as a general rule he certainly does not. The mode of dealing with the petition is determined, and in effect all references concerning it are directed by the Governor, a very considerable portion of whose time is occupied (I may say in every week) in the investigation of and deliberation upon such cases. Neither does the Governor, in general, confer with any Minister on them."

The Case of the Prisoner Gardiner. 423

Who was the person who gave this evidence? For over 30 years he was the Chief Justice, and at the time he spoke he was the Acting-Governor of the colony. If this learned gentleman did not know what the custom was, who was to know? Well, His Excellency the present Governor said this :—

"Hitherto the practice here has been for all applications for mitigation of sentences to be submitted to the Governor for his independent decision thereon. Some are sent to him direct through the post by the petitioners, others are presented personally by influential persons interested, whilst the remainder reach him through the Colonial Secretary's office, without any expression of opinion from the Minister. Taken altogether these applications are numerous. I have not kept any count of them, but I should think that a weekly average of 12 would certainly be below the number. All are carefully perused by the Governor. Some—in which the grounds stated, even if proved, would be insufficient to justify remission—are summarily rejected ; others, upon which inquiry may seem desirable, are referred for the report of the sheriff and the sentencing official, and sometimes the opinion of the Crown law officer is asked for. Previous petitions and papers in each case, if any, are carefully perused, and eventually the Governor gives his decision according to his own independent judgment."

Honourable members opposite perhaps questioned the authority of Sir Alfred Stephen ; perhaps they questioned the authority of the Governor. But if so, let us see what Mr. Cowper said on the subject—Mr. Cowper who was so long the chief of the honourable gentleman who had cheered the very opposite doctrine. In the year 1865—nine years ago, and when Mr. Cowper had passed through his most powerful Administrations—he delivered his opinion on this subject in his place in this House, no doubt amidst the cheers of the honourable member for Camden (Mr. Garrett). A motion was brought forward about the case of two men named Levey and Shoveller by the honourable member for the Western Gold-fields (Mr. Buchanan). It was seconded by the Honourable John Bowie Wilson, who was no longer a member of this House, but who had previously held office as Secretary for Lands. Mr. Cowper in his speech on that occasion said that he was not surprised at anything the honourable member for the Western Gold-fields might say, but he was astonished that a motion like that should be seconded by a gentleman who had held office as a Minister of the Crown. Mr. Cowper on that occasion, as reported in the *Sydney Morning Herald*, said :—

"He was not surprised at the motion from the quarter it emanated; he was surprised that a gentleman who had occupied the position of a Minister of the Crown, and ought to know better, should have seconded the motion,

The honourable member must know that Ministers very rarely interfere with matters of this kind; and when the House is asked to pass a censure against the Government for exercising the prerogative of mercy, it is more particularly levelled against an individual who was not there to defend himself. There were hundreds of prisoners whose petitions were received by him, but he never looked at them, because he thought this was one of those matters with which the political Ministers should interfere as little as possible. These papers came before him every day, and he simply initialled them and sent them on to the judge who tried the case, and then they came before His Excellency, who decided the matter on his own responsibility. He thought the charges that had been made so recklessly this afternoon might have some foundation; therefore he said that the honourable member (Mr. Wilson) knew well that these papers were seldom seen by the Colonial Secretary, therefore the Act was one almost entirely in the province of one individual. But he was not going to shelter himself with that argument, because the House might say he was responsible, and that these were matters which he ought to interfere with and ought to be held responsible for. In this particular case, so far as he recollected, His Excellency did ask his opinion, and he found that in February a petition for the remission of sentence was refused. He thought he understood the honourable member to say it was refused by the Government who preceded him, and whom he had so lauded; but that was not the fact, because the petition was dealt with soon after he came into office, and the letter written soon after the death of Mr. Elyard proved this; therefore it must have been his (Mr. Cowper's) act, and not that of the honourable member for the Lachlan. The honourable member wished to know why the petition was refused in February and was granted in April. He understood the Jewish Rabbi had been to His Excellency in this particular case, because, when the gentlemen composing the deputation came to him, he assured them he had no power, and they then went and saw His Excellency personally; and he believed the Jewish Rabbi was one of those who interested himself in this case. His Excellency had, however, conversed with him on this case. And Mr. Darvall, who was Attorney-General at that time, also stated his opinion; and the decision of His Excellency came after that discussion. But the honourable member seemed to think this case was one of extraordinary atrocity, and that no interest had been made sufficient to justify the Executive Government in the course they took. Here was a petition, signed by 250 persons—including a clergyman of the Church of England, the Church of Rome, and other respectable persons—and this went to the judge, who made his report, and it then went to His Excellency. He used no influence with His Excellency, and never spoke to him on the subject until he asked him. He took no interest in the matter. He had interfered on one or two occasions, but he had made no impression. He did so in the case of Spicer, although it was publicly stated that he did all he could to keep him in gaol. He complained of Spicer being kept in gaol; but His Excellency refused to abate his sentence, and it was only after repeated remonstrances that he pardoned Spicer; and yet he had been accused of having kept him in gaol. He thought that it was hardly fair that he should be accused of tyranny in

The Case of the Prisoner Gardiner. 425

one case and corruption in the other. He believed this discussion would be most injurious, and that this interference with the prerogative was injurious. It would not affect the individual aimed at, nor would it affect him. He cared not whether the House passed this vote of censure or not, because he had never taken any interest in the matter. It was possible that some persons might have spoken to him about it, but he distinctly asserted that His Excellency asked him about it after the petition was sent in February, and that in April the Governor gave way and exercised the prerogative. In the case of Shoveller a longer term of imprisonment elapsed. The petitions were signed by respectable persons who had known the prisoners for some time."

He had, he thought, shown that the system in this colony under all Administrations had been for the Minister to inform the Governor of all the facts of the case, and to leave the exercise of the prerogative of mercy entirely to his independent judgment. In some cases, as had been stated by His Excellency, and as he had stated the other night, and as he stated now, the Minister might point out new features or new facts; and in some few cases—and they were very few—the Governor might ask for the advice of his Minister. The Minister never advised unless he were asked for an opinion. He had proved on the authority of Sir Alfred Stephen, of His Excellency the Governor, and of Mr. Cowper who had held office as Prime Minister longer than any one else, that in this country the prerogative of mercy had been withdrawn from the range of ordinary Ministerial functions. The Minister had supplied the facts, had obtained the reports, and submitted them; and if at any time he had been asked for his opinion, the Minister gave that opinion; but that in nearly all cases when an opinion had been sought, it was that of the Attorney-General on some point of law. He interfered very recently in one case in this list, and that was the case of the boy Brookman, the circumstances of which had been already explained to the House. The boy was inveigled into a gang of bushrangers when he was only fourteen years of age; he was apprehended and tried for a capital offence. His conduct in gaol had been very exemplary. He was now twenty years of age. On account of his mother, who was undoubtedly a reputable woman, and who had pleaded very hard that the boy should be released in the colony, he being her only son, he had expressed the opinion to His Excellency that he thought it would be better to release this young man in the colony rather than that he should be exiled. He thought this youth would be much more likely to commence a new course of life under the influence of his mother, his home, and his friends, than he would be if he were thrown adrift upon the world. He simply expressed that opinion, and that was the extent of his interference. In another case, where a man was imprisoned for cattle-stealing, a number of new features had been brought before the Government which made the case somewhat peculiar. One was that this person had been informed that he would be tried at a given date, and that in place of that he was tried several weeks earlier, and at another place, where he could not obtain his witnesses nor engage counsel for his defence. In that case the opinion of the late Attorney-General was taken, and on that opinion His Excellency released the prisoner. Except in cases of this kind, where something peculiar presented itself, no advice had been offered by any Minister. All the papers he had looked at showed simply that the cases were referred to the Governor without advice.

Now he came to the dispatches which had been laid before the House. In July, 1869, a dispatch was written by Lord Belmore to the Secretary of State for the Colonies, which showed that the matter was in a state of so much perplexity and doubt that both the Minister (Mr. John Robertson) and the Governor desired explicit instructions. Lord Belmore desired to know what weight the recommendation of the Colonial Secretary ought to have with the Governor—whether, in fact, the latter was bound by his instructions to act upon his own independent judgment or not. He need not go through the replies of Earl Granville and Lord Kimberley of a later date, or the dispatch which reached the colony about twelve months ago from Lord Kimberley in answer to Sir Alfred Stephen. It was sufficient that these dispatches, to any one who would patiently read them, showed that what was contemplated by the Secretary of State was that the Governor should continue to decide these cases upon his independent judgment, but that before pardoning he should consult his Ministers. But did not that place the case entirely out of the ordinary range of Ministerial advice? The Minister was not to be called upon to advise in the case unless the Governor proposed to pardon. What position would the Minister be in in such a case as that? If he dissented from the Governor's advice he would be placed in the most objectionable light of objecting to mercy being extended. What position would he occupy as a responsible Minister, called in when the matter had been considered by some independent authority that was not responsible to Parliament?

The Case of the Prisoner Gardiner. 427

Mr. HOSKINS : The Governor is responsible.

Mr. PARKES : What, the Governor ?

Mr. HOSKINS : Yes.

Mr. PARKES: The honourable gentleman had to read up another chapter upon constitutional law. The Governor was responsible to his masters, and was not responsible to that House. The Minister would go in to the consultation, when he would simply be employed to confirm and support the decision of the Governor, but he had no voice in the consideration of cases where a pardon was refused in the first instance. He, for one, would not take that position; and all the Parliaments in the world would not compel him to take it. There was one thing—he was master of his own course of action; and neither the fear of Parliament nor the edict of the Secretary of State would induce him to take the position of giving advice for which he would be responsible without possessing any adequate authority in the matter. The case, as raised by these dispatches, came before him in this perplexed state; and, on account of the pressure of parliamentary business throughout this long session, he certainly would have deferred it until the recess in order to give a more calm and undisturbed consideration to the whole matter; but under the heat of these discussions he became very sensible of the awkward part of the situation as affecting the Governor—a gentleman of distinguished ability who had filled every position he had occupied as a servant of the Crown with honour, and who as Governor of this colony had, he believed, the liveliest sense of his obligations as a constitutional Governor.

Here was this distinguished man, the Governor of the country, exercising the Queen's prerogative in accordance with the principles of the criminal treatment in the mother-country and other parts of the empire; and he had been ruthlessly attacked in that House where he had no power of defending himself and could not explain his conduct. He was recklessly attacked, and his Ministers were comparatively helpless in keeping his name out of these intemperate parliamentary conflicts. He had one way of doing it by taking upon the Government the whole responsibility, and he met the question so. He declined to accept this divided responsibility, he declined to exercise this inferior kind of advice, but he was willing to meet the thing fairly in the light of the Constitution, and to be answerable for his decision in every case, accepting as a consequence that if in any case their advice was not accepted, Ministers would resign office. But the question had never been in that position before. The Government had placed it in that position now. The case in this country had been exactly as he had described it, and until now a Ministry had never stepped into the position of being directly responsible to Parliament in cases of pardon as in all other cases. Even now the difference between the Minister in this country and the Home Secretary would be very material. The Home Secretary virtually decided the question; but here the Governor, as an Imperial officer, would have to examine each case himself; and the advice of the Minister might at any time be refused—the Governor of course taking the consequences. This was not the case in England. There was no instance of the advice of the Home Secretary being refused. The Crown had practically delegated the prerogative to the English Minister. The absolute power which the Secretary of State exercised had been made a matter of complaint by a number of eminent lawyers and jurists, and all kinds of expedients had been suggested to take what was considered a dangerous power out of his hands. Many persons of considerable eminence had proposed a Court of Revision, or a body of assessors composed of retired Judges, to consider these cases, instead of the Home Secretary, on account of what had been supposed to be abuses in the Home Office. The Royal Commission which sat to consider the question of capital punishment in 1868 examined Mr. Walpole, who had presided over the Home Office; and they examined Sir George Grey, who at that time had at different periods filled the office of the Home Secretary for twelve years. The following were passages from the examination of Mr. Walpole:—

* * * * * * *

"483. DUKE OF RICHMOND: Will you be kind enough to state what is the general practice at the Home Office? The practice at the Home Office may be stated very shortly. Wherever there was a case of a man found guilty of murder, or of any other offence for which capital punishment was inflicted, before murder was the only offence for which it was inflicted, the practice was, when the matter was brought before the Home Office, to examine the memorial which was sent with reference to that case; to consult the Judge who had tried the case; to have a report from the Judge of the evidence; to lay before the Judge any new facts or any facts which had been brought under the notice of the Secretary of State, and to request from the Judge a report as to his opinion upon that new evidence, or upon the matter. Upon all those materials being brought before the Secretary of State, he was then in a position, not in the least degree to rehear the case, but simply to advise the Crown whether there were any circumstances which would justify the exercise of mercy either in an absolute or in a qualified sense; that is to say, either pardon or a commutation of punishment.

"484. That brings me to the point of the possibility or the advisability of establishing what is called a court of appeal, or a new trial. Has that subject occupied your attention at all? It has very much occupied my attention.

"485. First of all, I understand you to think strongly that there must be, as is generally admitted, a final appeal to the Sovereign in all cases? I expressed that opinion very strongly indeed, and I do not see how you can possibly avoid it. I think that there must be that prerogative vested somewhere, that is to say, in the Sovereign; and I cannot conceive how it would be so well exercised, so well as by and through the Secretary of State acting, of course, upon his responsibility in making a recommendation. I am very glad that your Grace has mentioned that point, because one of the circumstances which induces me to think that you ought not to have a court of appeal in cases of murder or in any criminal cases, as a matter of right, would be this—that when you have had your appeal, you will leave the parties still as free as they are now to go on pressing upon the Home Office, that is to say, upon the Crown through the Home Office, to alter the punishment; and all the objections which are urged against the exercise of that prerogative by the Home Office now (such objections as that the Home Secretary is rehearing alone, which is not accurate, what has been determined by the Judge and jury) would be ten times aggravated, because he would then be rehearing also what had been determined by the court of appeal and by all the judges who had decided the case in the court above. That is one reason why I think that a court of appeal would be most objectionable. The other reason given by Lord Wensleydale I entirely concur in, namely, that it would be really an appeal for the rich and not for the poor. Another reason is, that I cannot conceive, if you once admit an appeal on the part of the criminal, how you can refuse to grant an appeal on the part of the prosecutor; it would be the most one-sided justice in the world, and society, in my opinion, could not be secure if you were to say that an additional chance of escape should be given to the criminal when you did not give to society an equal power of saying, "You have escaped improperly, and now we will have you brought to trial again."

* * * * * * *

"501. Mr. GATHORNE HARDY: In fact, a great deal of matter comes before the Home Office which is not calculated to come before a court at all? It could not be done.

"502. Matter which is very proper for inquiry before the tribunal of mercy, but which would be very unfit to be brought before a Court of justice? Yes. If the public would only bear in mind that the Home Office is not a court of appeal, but a court of mercy, and that its function is merely to ascertain whether circumstances justify an alteration or mitigation in the punishment, I think that their opinion with reference to the practice of the Home Office would be very materially changed.

"503. Dr. LUSHINGTON: But sometimes it operates as a court of appeal; take Smethurst's case? It may operate as a court of appeal.

"504. Mr. WADDINGTON: In a few cases where the question is one of guilt or innocence it must act as a court of appeal? Yes.

"505. Not judicially, but of necessity, it must advise the Crown whether the case is sufficiently clear to justify the sentence being carried out? Quite so.

"506. Not only in capital cases, but in all other cases? Quite so.

"507. Mr. GATHORNE HARDY: And in effect it must continue to exist whatever intermediate court you may have? I am confident it must.

"508. Mr. NEATE: In your experience is it not very unusual for the Home Secretary to act at variance with the recommendation of the Judge who tried the case? I do not think that it is usual to do so in one sense, because I really believe, from my experience at the Home Office, that there is no necessity to differ from the Judge who tried the case. Now and then there is such a necessity, and then the Secretary of State does take upon himself the responsibility of differing.

"509. There is no settled rule at the Home Office that you will not act at variance with the recommendation of the Judge after you have put the case before him? Certainly not.

"510. DUKE OF RICHMOND: The judgment of the Secretary of State is entirely unfettered? Absolutely unfettered.

"511. He decides according to his own judgment and conscience? I think you may take it that everything which is done by the Secretary of State in revising the punishment is done entirely upon his own responsibility, but with all the aid which he can get."

* * * * * * *

He had had a purpose in reading the views of Mr. Walpole, because they seemed to indicate the course that should be taken, and the rules that should be applied in examinations of the kind in this country. The evidence seemed to prove also that, whatever scheme might be devised for the consideration of these cases, you could not get rid of the necessity for a final appeal to the Crown. He had another extract from Sir George Grey.

* * * * * * *

"1502. DUKE OF RICHMOND: I apprehend that each case which comes before you for the exercise of mercy must stand upon its own merits? Certainly.

"1503. It is very difficult to define what ground would actuate you in recommending the Crown to exercise the prerogative of mercy? Certainly; but I may say, generally, that there are a number of cases so clear that although there are very few in which there is not some petition, yet they admit of no doubt whatever, and the petition is not entertained.

"1505. In these cases, has the Secretary of State invariably a communi-

The Case of the Prisoner Gardiner.

cation with the Judge? No; but when the memorial states facts or circumstances, or considerations which, upon the face of them, might be regarded as having an important bearing upon the case, that memorial is invariably sent to the Judge, and he always answers it in writing; but if any doubt remains, or if his answer is not a very decided one, he either offers to come to the Secretary of State, or the Secretary of State requests to see him, and then the subject is very fully discussed; and I should add, with the assistance of the Under Secretary, Mr. Waddington, although the undivided responsibility of the decision exclusively rests in all cases with the Secretary of State.

"1507. Mr. EWART: Do you think that the Home Office should state their reasons when they grant a reprieve? I have done so occasionally, where it has been possible to do it. In the Worcester case, I gave my reasons to the Mayor of Worcester; but, generally speaking, they are not given.

"1508. You would not recommend that it should be done? No, not in all cases."

* * * * * * *

That seemed to be the position of the Secretary of State, and the practice which obtained in England; upon the authority of two men of eminence, who had held the office of Home Secretary, one of them for a period of 12 years.

He now came to another part of the subject, which was rather a delicate one—the extent to which the House of Commons has interfered in cases of this kind. That interference did not in any way correspond with the representations made of it by the honourable gentleman who moved this resolution. The House of Commons occasionally asked questions, but he had not found a case where the House went the length of pressing for the production of papers. A question might be asked, and the Secretary of State might answer it, and motions had been made for the production of papers, but he had not found a case where the motion had been passed. He would give four quotations, not from textbooks or from writers on government, where the object was to lay down general principles, but in the words of distinguished members of both Houses of Parliament, engaged in the practical business of government. The first opinion was from the Marquis of Normanby, in the House of Lords, who said :—

"I think it would be inconvenient and unusual, as a general principle, to lay before the House the grounds on which that discretion proceeds which dictates leniency or severity on the part of the responsible advisers of the Crown."

The Marquis of Westmeath asked :—

"I again ask whether this commutation has taken place under the sanction of the Judge who tried the prisoner?"

The Marquis of Normanby replied :—

"I must decline answering the question, because I could not do so without discussing the whole subject."

The Duke of Newcastle, on another occasion, said :—

"It was a most delicate matter for either House of Parliament to interfere in any matter connected with the administration of justice, and still more with regard to the exercise of the prerogative of mercy, which belonged to the Crown. He thought it would be most improper of him to give any other answer to an inquiry that ought not to have been made, than that in this case the usual course would be followed by the Government in respect of any representation which might be laid before them."

Sir George Grey, in the House of Commons, speaking upon a motion for the production of papers, which was not pressed, said :—

"It is a solemn responsibility—a most painful duty; but at the same time, I cannot accept the doctrine of the honourable member that the Secretary of State is bound to consider the verdict of a jury in a capital case as absolutely final, and to refuse to investigate any alleged facts which may be stated to him tending to alter the view of the case submitted to the Judge and jury. The duty of a Secretary of State would be easy if in all cases he refused to receive any appeal for mercy founded upon facts not stated at the trial. But he cannot shrink from the performance of the duty which is now imposed upon him, however painful it may be. If he did, his conduct would meet with universal condemnation. In the present instance I could not, consistently with the discharge of my duty, have taken any other course. The case was most extraordinary, and the honourable member has only partially stated the circumstances; but I am not going into the evidence, because this House is not competent to sit as a court of appeal."

On another occasion Lord Macaulay used these words in the House of Commons, speaking to a motion respecting the conduct of the Secretary of State in the exercise of the prerogative of pardon :—

"I have no hesitation in saying with regard to this power—the prerogative of mercy—that I would rather entrust it in the hands of the very worst Ministry that ever held office than allow it to be exercised under the direction of the very best House of Commons."

What then became of the House of Commons being a Council of Control over the exercise of the prerogative of mercy? Lord Macaulay went on to say that he did not know a case where the House of Commons would be justified in interfering; if any such case could be conceived it would be some case of monstrous oppression. Lord Macaulay's words were these :—

" I do not know a case in which, as a member of the House of Commons, I should be disposed to interfere with the Ministry in advising the Crown on this matter. If I could contemplate such a case, it would be some case of most momentous necessity—some flagitious and monstrous case of oppression—something like the severity that had been exercised in the reign of King James the Second against those who had taken up arms against him in the Monmouth rebellion—some case the mere mention of which would be enough to make the blood boil—to make the hair of one's head stand on end."

That was the only case—some extreme case of oppression—in which he could conceive of the possibility of the House of Commons interfering with the exercise of the prerogative. In this country, where he supposed Ministers in future would be held directly responsible for advice in every case, the number of petitions for mitigation was perfectly startling. He did not know what the exact number might be, but the Governor, who had dealt with all these cases hitherto, said they must average quite twelve a-week. And in every instance the personal influence brought to bear had a tendency to regard each case as an exceptional one. In other words, there was very little disposition on the part of any one to consider the cases upon any general principle, but solely in the light of special circumstances known only to the individuals interesting themselves in the particular case. Every set of petitioners or single individual who interfered considered that at all events the present case was one that ought to be complied with, and used every influence they could command to obtain compliance. He had stated before, and he stated now, that looking through the papers in these cases, sending them to the Judges or to the benches of magistrates, getting other facts in order that the fullest information should be placed before the Crown, and seeing persons who interested themselves in the cases—even in this mode of treatment fully one-fourth of his available time for office work, apart from the business of Parliament and purely political duties, was taken up. If this system of petitioning were to be kept up it would be almost enough to fill up the whole of one Minister's time.

He mentioned these things because he trusted that members of Parliament would impose some little restraint upon themselves in pressing Ministers, whether he was in office or out of office. One thing he thought the change was likely to lead to was a harsher treatment of prisoners. He was speaking now not for himself or for his colleagues, but for the Ministers who might succeed them. When they had to exercise virtually the whole power they ought·

to be left free and unfettered to act upon their own judgment and sense of duty. All men were liable to influence, often unconsciously; but it would be necessary for the Minister for his own sake to be as cautious as possible, and to resist all importunities for the mitigation of sentences. He did not say that he should refuse all applications; but he should resist until he could resist no longer from the force of the facts. He thought he had shown that the particular cases which had led to this discussion were not very unusual, according to the practice in this country, except that there had been twenty-four cases grouped together for consideration. These discussions, considering the extent to which they had gone, without definite aim or careful thought, must produce harm. It must injure the reputation of the country if it went forth that there was an immunity for criminals here which was inconsistent with the treatment of prisoners in other parts of the Empire, and which, if it went forth, would not be the fact. It must do harm so far as it stirred up discussions among persons who sympathised with prisoners; and it must do harm where, as in one case he had noticed, resolutions were submitted to a public meeting by persons who had inconsiderately busied themselves, which were negatived by the meeting. It must do harm to awaken any manifestation of feeling which would seem to be unfavourable to the repression of crime; and loose and intemperate conduct upon all matters of this kind must result in mischief to the community. With regard to this resolution, it appeared to him, to say the least of it, a most ill-considered and injudicious resolution, which could produce no good result whatever, and which affirmed in part what very few persons would desire to affirm. It affirmed, for instance, that the House disapproved of the release of Bow and Fordyce, notwithstanding that a number of honourable members said that they ought to have been released seven years ago. Then the resolution affirmed that this boy Brookman should not be released. He did not believe that there were many persons who understood that case who would not be in favour of the release, and he unhesitatingly said that it was as proper a case for the exercise of the prerogative of mercy as was ever submitted to the Crown. This return included other cases which would be favourably considered by nearly every one in the community, and that would be treated leniently in any part of the British dominions. If it was right to release a bushranger after serving five years, how could it be wrong to release these young men, who stood in the same position, after they had served double that period? It seemed proper for him to state that, so far as he could learn from the police authorities and from the authorities in charge of the prisons, that comparatively few persons released after long imprisonment returned to a course of crime in this country. He did not say that none did. There was every reason to believe that of all those who had been exiled, as far as any knowledge had been obtained of them, the majority had adopted a reputable course of life under new circumstances. He had seen papers within the last day or two from several of these men, showing that they had adopted an entirely new course of life, and in many instances were now living as respectable members of society. They knew that such was the case in former days under transportation from the mother-country.

Some honourable gentlemen appeared to be under the impression that sentences imposed in England were carried out according to the letter of those sentences. He had heard the question asked—"What was the use of sentencing men to thirty years' imprisonment, if it was not intended that they were to serve thirty years?" Nothing of this kind was ever contemplated in the criminal jurisprudence of the British Empire. If it were the case, it would lead to the most calamitous results, for there would be no distinction made between the well-conducted and the ill-conducted. It would remit them to the old times of darkness and rude justice, which happily had passed away from the face of England, and from the whole civilised world. He had already shown that by the Statute law of England, passed on the cessation of transportation, the period of imprisonment in a gaol in England was not less than six nor more than ten years in substitution of the longest sentence of transportation, and for shorter sentences the imprisonment substituted was correspondingly short. He had already shown that in all the gaols of England, with the multitudes of prisoners passing through them, there was not supposed to be one single person imprisoned over ten years. He had shown that in the enlightened country of Belgium, where constitutional government prevailed more perfectly than in any other continental nation, imprisonment for life, which took the place of the punishment of death, was very frequently commuted to twelve years. The very object, the very essence of the modern system of treating prisoners was to recognise good conduct—to hold out a hope to the prisoner that would lead to his reformation. What would be the state of things if this merciful and enlightened principle did not prevail? Suppose all their prisoners were immured in dungeons for the terms to which they were sentenced, without reference to conduct in prison: their gaols would be twice as large as they were, their prison population would be doubled. It was only by this merciful and wise exercise of authority in consideration of good conduct that the penal establishments of the country were kept within reasonable bounds; while at the same time there was a second and sometimes a third chance held out to a prisoner to abandon the pursuit of crime and take to an honest life. But the effect would not stop there. Besides doubling the expenditure of public money, the prisoners, being without hope, would be driven to despair. They would be savages within iron cages. The slaughter of their keepers would be of frequent occurrence, and they would produce in this land—lighted up with the living principles of Christianity—something of the pandemonium that existed in Norfolk Island and in Tasmania in the old convict days now happily passed away. Was it come to this, that they were to fan the flame of revenge in the execution of their laws, and drive the criminal population to desperation by the severity of their punishments, for their prisoners were men and women after all? While he was and always had been in favour of severely dealing with the prison population of the country—while he was and always had been in favour of the Government devising every safeguard for the protection of life and property, he did not believe that the best interests of the country would be answered by carrying out any such harsh and unenlightened views as he had heard propounded in the House since these discussions commenced. He believed that it was a duty in dealing with these sentences under the law to respect the opinions of the Judges. It was a duty also to place the prisoners under the healthiest state of prison management, to employ them so as to compel them to contribute as largely as possible to their maintenance, to instruct them as far as was practicable, and, if their conduct proved that they were deserving of consideration, to enable them—before they were overtaken by old age and became helpless—to start on a new career and live honestly. That was the view taken by the first statesmen in England—that was the view taken by the first statesmen in

The Case of the Prisoner Gardiner.

America—and that was the view taken by the first statesmen among continental nations. And he at all events, whatever others might think, was content to follow humbly in the footsteps of those enlightened men.

APPENDIX A.

THE PREROGATIVE OF PARDON.—THE CASE OF THE PRISONER GARDINER.

A CHAPTER OF HISTORY.

IN the year 1862 the crime of bushranging broke out with much violence in New South Wales, and in particular the name of Frank Gardiner became notorious as that of the reputed leader of a gang who stopped and robbed the gold escort at Eugowra. Several young men, arrested on the charge of being engaged in the escort robbery, were tried before Sir Alfred Stephen, Chief Justice, and capitally convicted of the crime, one of them suffering death. Gardiner, however, was not apprehended until February 1864, when he was discovered keeping a store at Apis Creek, in Queensland, under the name of Christie. He was brought up for trial before Sir Alfred Stephen in July following, not for the escort robbery, but on two charges not capital, of which he was convicted, receiving three cumulative sentences amounting to thirty-two years' imprisonment, the first two years in irons. Mr. Martin, then Attorney-General (now Sir James Martin, Chief Justice), stated, in a minute :—" The only capital case against Gardiner appears to be the case of the escort robbery, and as to that it seems to me that a conviction could not be reasonably expected," adding his reasons for this opinion.

In 1871—a little more than seven years after Gardiner's conviction—two sisters of the prisoner got up a petition for his release; and they succeeded in obtaining in support of their petition the signatures of many respectable persons, including some who had held high offices in the colony. Mr. William Bede Dalley, who had held office as Solicitor-General, and who is now Attorney-General of the colony, signed his name to the following recommendation :—
" We the undersigned beg most respectfully to recommend the foregoing petition to your Excellency's merciful consideration, the

more especially from the desire to reform evidenced by the prisoner before capture, and his conduct since his incarceration ; and trust that your Excellency may be pleased, under all the circumstances of the case, *to deem the period of the sentence already expired sufficient for the ends of justice.*" Mr. Dalley must have signed this recommendation before the end of 1871, as the next minute on the same sheet is dated December 29th of that year. Among others who signed recommendations in the above form were Richard Driver, Esq., M.P.; Richard Hill, Esq., M.P.; Joseph Eckford, Esq., M.P., and a number of magistrates and well-known merchants and traders. Mr. William Forster, M.P., who had filled the office of Colonial Secretary at the time of Gardiner's conviction, was specially referred to in the body of the petition. It stated that, on the occasion of an outbreak of prisoners in the gaol, Gardiner's conduct was "so noticed by the Inspector-General of Police that he assured the prisoner that he would see the Colonial-Secretary (Mr. Forster), and have a record of it made for the future benefit of the prisoner." The petition, with this special reference to himself, was taken to Mr. Forster (then out of office) for his signature ; and, with his attention thus challenged, he wrote, and subscribed his name under, the following words :—" Having been referred to in a petition for the mitigation of the sentence of Francis Christie, as holding the office of Colonial Secretary when an outbreak occurred in Darlinghurst Gaol, I have much pleasure in testifying to the fact of Christie's good conduct on that occasion, as well as to his general conduct during the entire period of his incarceration, so far as it came under my notice in either case. I am glad to record this opinion, so that it may operate as it ought in the prisoner's favour. And, so far as these and other circumstances mentioned in the petition entitle his case to the favourable consideration of the Government, I am willing to add my testimony and recommendation." The "recommendation" of Mr. Forster was dated December 29th 1871— about seven years and six months after Gardiner's conviction— and it was written immediately below Mr. Dalley's " recommendation," which expressed the hope that the Governor would be pleased, " under all the circumstance of the case, *to deem the period of the sentence already expired sufficient for the ends of justice.*"

I entered upon the duties of the Colonial Secretary's Office on the 14th May 1872, and the petition for the mitigation of

Gardiner's sentence came to me in due course to be dealt with. As the prayer for the mitigation principally rested on the ground of Gardiner's good conduct in prison, I sent the petition in the first instance to the Inspector of Prisons for his report. As reports from this officer are not called for in all cases, my calling for a report from him in Gardiner's case was subsequently attempted to be tortured into evidence that I had some design to favour the prisoner. But it must be obvious to every intelligent and unprejudiced mind that, in a case of so much importance, where the question was one mainly of the prisoner's good conduct, if I had not obtained the report of the only officer whose business it was to be well acquainted with his prison-life, I should have greatly failed in my duty, and laid myself open to well-merited blame. With this report, and reports from the officers of the gaol, and all other papers connected with the case, the petition was sent for the report of the Chief Justice, who had tried and sentenced Gardiner. So far from seeing any impropriety in the report from the Inspector of Prisons, the Chief Justice in his own report characterised that officer's remarks as "very judicious."

Having thus brought together all the facts of the case, the opinions and testimony of the principal officers who had had charge of the prisoner, and the views of the judge by whom he had been tried, I submitted the petition to the Governor with a written minute of my own explaining the standing of the principal persons whose names were appended to it. This I did more fully in conversation with His Excellency about the same time, but I certainly had no desire, and never intended at any time, to do more than fairly explain both sides of the case. I took this course of explanation because His Excellency, having but recently arrived in the colony, could not be supposed to know either the special features of the prisoner's case or the positions of the persons who were seeking to exercise their influence in his favour, two of whom were ex-members of the Executive Council. Up to this time I had regarded the prerogative of pardon as vested absolutely in the Representative of the Crown, and I was aware of my own knowledge that two Governors at least—Sir John Young and the Earl of Belmore—had exercised it, as a rule, without the advice of Ministers.

On receiving this petition, in December 1872, what did the Governor himself do? He did not grant the prayer of the

The Prerogative of Pardon. 441

petitioners. He did not concur in the recommendation of Mr. Attorney-General Dalley in December 1871—that the ends of justice would be answered by the seven years and six months of his sentence which the prisoner had then suffered, and that he might be released instantly and unconditionally. He did not yield to the specious " recommendation" of Mr. Forster, who had recorded his opinion in December 1871 also, " that it might operate as it ought in the prisoner's favour." Sir Hercules Robinson judged the case on its merits, possibly attaching some weight to the opinions of the two ex-members of the Executive Council, but really mastering for himself the perplexities which surround the abnormal condition of our prison population. He knew that good-conduct prisoners are immured for unlimited years within the four dead walls of the same gaol in few Christian countries. His decision, I believe, while merciful to the prisoner, was just to society, and thoroughly sound in the interests of criminal treatment. He decided that, if the prisoner's conduct continued good for the term of ten years, he might then be allowed to exile himself. In arriving at this decision Sir Hercules Robinson took care to state that he " did not concur with the petitioners that the sentence which the prisoner had undergone was sufficient for the ends of justice."

Several months after this decision in favour of Gardiner's exile—namely, in the early part of 1874—another petition was got up by one of the prisoner's sisters, praying that he might be released in the colony ; and I find the name of Mr. Attorney-General Dalley appended to this second petition. The case was again referred to the Inspector of Prisons for his report, and was then submitted to the Governor with the following words covered by my initials :—
" The Sheriff* strongly deprecates a compliance with the prayer of the petition." The Governor minuted the petition simply " Refused."

This, then, was the case, as favoured by the powerful influence of Mr. Forster in 1871, as dealt with ministerially by me and as decided by Her Majesty's representative in 1872, which in 1874 was inflamed by political passion and distracted by misrepresentations in order to overthrow a Government whose measures and policy were generally approved and which was now vigilantly seized upon for that purpose by Mr. Forster himself amongst

---

* The Sheriff at this time also held the office of Inspector of Prisons.

Appendix A.

others. The atmosphere is now somewhat clearer and calmer, and it may be well to follow the course of events through the turmoil which was created out of this prisoner's case.

In April 1874, I was questioned by a member of the Assembly whether the Government intended to release the prisoner Gardiner before the expiration of the sentences passed upon him. As my reply was not considered satisfactory, this gentleman moved the adjournment of the House, to enable him to express his views on the subject. A somewhat heated discussion was raised, in the course of which I offered some fuller explanation to the House of what had been done. Speaking of the difference between the exercise of the prerogative of pardon in England and in the colonies, I am reported to have said:—

" Here that power was vested in the representative of the Crown alone; and though most probably His Excellency would not disregard any representation that might be made to him by his responsible advisers, yet it was entirely removed from the province of their duties; not only need the Governor not seek the advice of his Ministers, but he might even act in opposition to their advice if tendered. Now, what had he done? When this petition came before him, he went out of his way to place all possible information before His Excellency. Of course the matter was referred to Sir Alfred Stephen, who tried the case, for his report; and, besides this, he had taken the unusual course of calling upon the Sheriff to send in a special report upon this prisoner, so that the Governor, who had not been long in the colony, might have the best information possible to guide him in his duty; and when he referred the petition to His Excellency, he did so with some remarks upon the position of the different gentlemen who had signed the petition. It had never occurred to him that these names were nothing more than a delusion. He presumed that they all expressed what was intended, and that the intention would not afterwards be repudiated. The Governor then had the fullest information that the judge could give him, that the head officer placed over the prison population could give him, and His Excellency also had such information as he (Mr. Parkes) could give him as to the standing of the gentlemen who signed the petition; and on these facts His Excellency was pleased to say that the prisoner should be liberated after the expiration of ten years' imprisonment. He had never intruded his advice upon his Excellency in cases of this kind; for, if he shrunk from anything, it was from putting himself forward to do what he was not entitled to do. As he had no power in the matter, he had given no advice upon it; though, had he possessed the power, he should not probably have incurred the responsibility of liberating this prisoner at so early a date as ten years. He did not say this by way of inferring in any way that a wrong act had been done, because it was an exceedingly difficult thing to decide upon the proper mode of dealing with that class of prisoners."

Some of the speakers charged me with seeking to shelter myself

The Prerogative of Pardon. 443

from my just responsibility by improperly bringing forward the Governor's name. Charges of similar character were in later discussions dealt out in every conceivable form. On this occasion, however, I claimed my privilege to explain at the close of the discussion what I had really said, and I find myself reported to have used the following words :—

"So far from explaining, or saying anything that could be construed into bringing the Governor's name forward as a cloak to his proceedings, he simply stated that he informed His Excellency of all the facts of the case, and did so in the light of not interfering in any way further. He stated that if he had been asked for advice, it was doubtful whether he should have taken the responsibility of recommending the man's release at this early period ; and there was nothing inconsistent with that in the remark that he was willing to bear any responsibility that might devolve upon the Government in this matter. He should have committed a very doubtful act, considering that he had no real power in the matter, by interfering between the Governor and a prisoner in the exercise of the prerogative of mercy."

Some expressions of mine (included, I believe, in the above quotations), as they appeared in the reports of this first discussion of the subject in the Assembly, were displeasing to the Governor, who told me next day that he had dealt with the prisoner's case under the impression that I was not unfavourable to a merciful consideration of it, and that he thought it was improper for me to express my doubts whether, if I had been asked for my advice, I should have dealt with it as mercifully myself, which seemed to imply disapproval of what he had done, when I had expressed no disapproval at the time of his decision. I think, however, that the force of His Excellency's objections applied more to his reading of what I had said than to the meaning I had endeavoured to convey to the Assembly. What I meant was, not that any wrong decision had been given, but that the Minister in such case, acting under his sense of responsibility to Parliament, would have acted, though perhaps unconsciously, in view of hostile criticisms from his political adversaries, and therefore was not in a position of equal independence with the Governor. This was in accord with opinions I have frequently expressed on the exercise of the prerogative. With the exception of this misunderstanding in the first instance, the Governor, so far as I am aware, was perfectly satisfied with my course throughout; and the existence of this misunderstanding I explained in my speech on June 3rd in the Assembly.

Appendix A.

The case of Gardiner now became the subject of frequent questioning and reference in the House, and Mr. Edward Combes, then member for Bathurst, gave notice of a condemnatory motion, which, as the case had been considered in connexion with twenty-three others, finally took the following form :—" That this House disapproves of the release of the long-sentenced prisoners whose names are set forth in the returns laid upon the table of this House by the Honourable the Colonial Secretary on the 22nd May 1874, including the name of the notorious prisoner Gardiner." Mr. Combes made his motion on June 3rd, as an amendment on going into Supply, and the debate was continued over several nights, closing on June 11th with a division of 26 to 26. The motion was negatived by the Speaker's casting vote.

In the meantime I and my colleagues had addressed ourselves to the consideration of the position in which the prerogative of pardon was actually exercised, and what ought to be the responsibility of Ministers in relation to its exercise. It appeared to me, and I believe to my colleagues also, that the questions we had to consider were perplexed rather than cleared of perplexities by recent despatches from the Imperial Government on the subject. The result of our deliberations was embodied in the following paper :—

"MINUTE FOR HIS EXCELLENCY THE GOVERNOR.

"I have given much consideration to the expediency of changing the system of treatment in the cases of petitions presented for the absolute or conditional pardon of convicted offenders, and have carefully read the correspondence on the subject, commencing with Lord Belmore's dispatch of July 14 1869, and closing with Lord Kimberley's despatch of February 17 1873.

"The minute of Mr. Robertson, which gave rise to this correspondence, does not appear to me to deal with the real question which the dispatches of the Secretary of State present for determination in the colony. That question, in any view, is the extent to which the Minister is to have an active voice in the decision of these cases ; but in my view it is much more —it is whether the Minister is virtually to decide in every case upon his own direct responsibility, subject of course to the refusal of the Crown to accept his advice, which refusal at any time should be held to be, as in all other cases, tantamount to dispensing with his services. The seventh paragraph of the minute alone touches the question of the Minister's relation to the Crown, and it seems to prescribe a position for the Minister in which, on submitting petitions to the Governor, he is to express an opinion on each case, to be "viewed as embodying no more than a recommendation," after which he is to have no further concern in the matter. I cannot subscribe to this principle of Ministerial conduct, if this be what was intended by Mr. Robertson.

"There can be no question, I believe, that from the beginning of the present reign the Home Secretary in England decides absolutely in all matters of this kind in the name of the Crown, and that the Crown does not in practice interfere. At no former time when the Crown took an active part in such decisions could the Crown, in the nature of things, be subject to a superior or an instructing authority. The wide difference between the position of the Minister and his relations to the Crown and to Parliament in the colony and in England is at once apparent on reading the dispatches from the Secretary of State. The Governor is invested with the prerogative of the Crown to grant pardons, and, by the letter of the instructions conveyed to him by Lord Kimberley's circular of November 1, 1871, he 'is bound to examine personally each case in which he is called upon to exercise the power entrusted to him.' By the instructions previously conveyed to the Governor of this colony by Lord Granville, in reply to Lord Belmore's despatch of July 14, 1869, he is told that 'the responsibility of deciding upon such applications rests with the Governor,' and, in reference obviously to advice that may be tendered, it is expressly added that the Governor 'has undoubtedly a right to act upon his own independent judgment.' And finally, after the question has been re-opened by Sir Alfred Stephen, it is repeated by Lord Kimberley's dispatch of February 17 1873, that 'in granting pardons' the Governor 'has strictly a right to exercise an independent judgment.'

"It seems to be clear that the 'portion of the Queen's prerogative' entrusted to the Governor of a colony, unlike the prerogative in England, is intended to be a reality in its exercise. It is undeniably the case that the representative of the Crown in a colony, unlike the Crown itself, is subject to a superior or instructing authority. What then is the position of the Minister, and what is intended to be the nature of the advice he may be called upon to give, and under what circumstances is that advice to be given?

"In no sense of responsibility in this respect has the Minister in this colony hitherto been in the same position as the Home Secretary in England. He has neither exercised the function of pardon, nor as a rule been asked for advice. Except in rare cases, and then only in a limited degree, when special features or new facts have presented themselves, he has never actively interfered. What would be his position if ·he entered upon a system of partial advice, and accepted in matters of the gravest moment a secondary or limited authority, irreconcilable with the nature of his duties and responsibilities a a Minister under Parliamentary Government?

"Lord Granville says, 'The Governor would be bound to allow great weight to the recommendation of his Ministry.' The circular of November 1, 1871, says, 'He will of course pay due regard to the advice of his Ministers.' Lord Kimberley, in his dispatch of February 17 1873, repeats the words of Lord Granville.

"It cannot be doubted that the advice here intended is wholly distinct in its nature from the advice given in the general conduct of affairs. In the general case the advice is uniformly accepted, as the first condition of the adviser continuing to hold office. In all his acts the Minister's responsibility to Parliament is simple, undivided, and direct. But in pardoning convicted offenders, the Governor, although he is to 'pay due regard to the advice of his Ministers,' is at the same time informed by the Secretary of State that he ' is bound to examine personally each case in which he is called upon to exercise the power entrusted to him,' and that with him rests the responsibility. The exceptional advice implied seems to be of the nature of opinions or suggestions to which weight may be attached as coming from persons 'responsible to the colony for the proper administration of justice and the prevention of crime,' but which in any case, or in every case, may be partially or wholly disregarded.

"It does not appear to be clear that the Governor is required by the Secretary of State to seek even this secondary class of advice in all cases. It would rather seem that the instruction does not necessarily extend beyond cases in which pardons are proposed to be granted, in which cases the Minister would simply have to concur in a decision already formed, or be placed in the somewhat invidious position of objecting to the extension of mercy. This view would shut out from the Minister's limited power of advice the numerous cases in which much concern is frequently felt by portions of the public, where a merciful consideration is prayed for and is refused.

"I entertain grave doubts whether any change at present from the system which has hitherto prevailed will be beneficial to the colony. In a community so small as ours the distinctions between classes are very slight. The persons entrusted with authority and the relatives and friends of prisoners move closely together. The means of political pressure are easily accessible. A larger share by the Minister in the exercise of the prerogative of pardon would not, in my judgment, be more satisfactory to the public. But if a change is to take place, and the cases of prisoners are to be decided on the advice of Ministers, I can see no sufficient reason for making a distinction between this class of business and the ordinary business of Government. The Minister ought to inquire into and examine each case, and each case ought to be decided on his advice. The refusal of the Governor to accept his advice in any case of this kind ought to have the same significance and effect as a similar refusal in any other case. In no other way can the Minister be fairly responsible to Parliament for what is done. Either ' the responsibility of deciding upon such applications ' must still 'rest with the Governor,' as Lord Granville expresses it, or it must rest with the Minister in the only way in which it would be just to hold him responsible.

"HENRY PARKES.

"Colonial Secretary's Office, Sydney, 30th May 1874."

The change proposed—namely, that the prerogative of pardon should in future be exercised on the advice of Ministers—met with the approval of the Governor, who signified his concurrence, with a full explanation of his own views, in the minute which I now subjoin :—

The Prerogative of Pardon. 447

"MINUTE BY THE GOVERNOR FOR THE EXECUTIVE COUNCIL.

"I have read the minute of the honourable the Colonial Secretary upon the subject of pardons, and it has occurred to me that the difficulty of dividing the responsibility in this matter, in the manner suggested by the late Secretary of State, can perhaps best be illustrated by showing how such a system would work in the practical transaction of business.

"Hitherto the practice here has been for all applications for mitigation of sentences to be submitted to the Governor for his independent decision thereon. Some are sent to him direct through the post by the petitioners, others are presented personally by influential persons interested, whilst the remainder reach him through the Colonial Secretary's office, without any expression of opinion from the Minister. Taken altogether these applications are numerous. I have not kept any count of them, but I should think that a weekly average of twelve would certainly be below the number. All are carefully perused by the Governor. Some—in which the grounds stated, even if proved, would be insufficient to justify remission—are summarily rejected ; others, upon which inquiry may seem desirable, are referred for the report of the Sheriff and the sentencing official, and sometimes the opinion of the Crown Law Officer is asked for. Previous petitions and papers in each case (if any) are carefully perused, and eventually the Governor gives his decision according to his own independent judgment. The papers are then sent to the Colonial Secretary's office, where the necessary official steps are taken to carry the decision into effect, without, I believe, in ordinary cases, the matter being even brought under the notice of the Minister.

"If a change such as has been suggested were to be carried out, the first question to be decided would be by whom should all petitions and applications for mitigation of sentences be considered in the first instance—by the Governor or by the Minister ?

"If, as at present, by the Governor, what would be the consequence under the instructions contained in the Secretary of State's circular dispatch of the 1st November 1871? The words of that dispatch are as follows :—

"'The Governor, as invested with a portion of the Queen's prerogative, is bound to examine personally each case in which he is called upon to exercise the power entrusted to him, although, in a colony under Responsible Government, he will of course pay due regard to the advice of his Ministers, who are responsible to the colony for the proper administration of justice and prevention of crime, *and will not grant and pardon without receiving their advice thereupon.*'

"The last few words which I have underlined are not quoted by the Colonial Secretary in his minute, but they are important as showing the precise view taken by the Secretary of State. The Governor apparently may, after personally examining any petition for mitigation, and after giving due weight to the advice of his Ministers, exercise an independent judgment, and reject the application. He may say 'No' on his own authority, but he can only say 'Yes' on the advice of a Minister. The idea would seem to be to make the Governor and the Ministers mutually act as checks on each other. Either can negative a prayer for pardon, but both must concur before any such application can be granted. If, therefore, the petitions were considered in the first instance by the Governor, all cases rejected by him would at once be withdrawn from the cognizance or control of the Minister—a proceeding of which the latter might justly complain if any responsibility at all were to be imposed on him in this matter. In all cases in which the Governor proposed to mitigate the sentence, his decision would have to be approved and confirmed by the Minister, who might, if he saw fit, veto the merciful intentions of the Governor. It appears to me the Governor and the Minister would occupy somewhat anomalous positions in such cases. Under a constitutional form of Government the Crown is supposed to accept or reject the advice of responsible Ministers : in this matter the Minister would adopt or reject as he pleased the advice of the Representative of the Crown !

" But suppose, on the other hand, that all petitions were considered and reported on in the first instance by the Minister, what would then be the result ? Why, all cases rejected by the Minister need never be sent on at all to the Governor, to whom they would be addressed. For, as the Governor could not pardon without the advice of the Minister, there would be no object in troubling him with applications which he could not comply with. In cases in which the Minister advised a mitigation, the Governor could of course, if he saw proper, in the exercise of his 'undoubted right,' reject such advice—upon being prepared to accept the consequences. But practically he would never do so, except in cases which in his view involved such a gross abuse of the prerogative that both the Secretary of State and local public opinion would be likely to support him in the adoption of extreme measures. In all ordinary cases, in which neither Imperial interests nor policy were involved, the Governor, whatever his own private opinion might be, ' would be bound to allow great weight to the recommendation of his Ministry, who are responsible to the colony for the proper administration of justice and prevention of crime.' Practically under such a system the prerogative of mercy would be transferred from the Governor to the Minister charged with such duties.

" It was perhaps the recognition of some such difficulties which led to the suggestion of a compromise between these two systems, thrown out in Lord Kimberley's last dispatch on the subject. In effect, his Lordship appears to suggest that the Governor might continue, as at present, to examine into and deal with all petitions for pardon ; but that he should, before granting a mitigation of sentence in any case, ascertain by means of informal consultation that the Minister concurred in such a step. I fear that such a plan would not work well, and that its effect would simply be to fritter away any real or clearly-defined responsibility in such matters. In the first place, who would be responsible for the appeals rejected upon which charges of sectarian partiality or official corruption might possibly be based ? Is the Governor to remain responsible for refusals, and the Minister to become responsible for pardons ? Again, if the Minister is to be responsible for pardons, he would have, unless his concurrence were a mere matter of form, to go through all the reports and papers in each case in which a pardon was proposed by the Governor ; and, as I have before shown, he would

The Prerogative of Pardon. 449

have to place upon the papers in writing his final acceptance or rejection of the Governor's advice. If such grave matters were disposed of in informal conversations, such a loose mode of transacting business would inevitably result in mistakes and misapprehensions. The Governor might decide a case under the full impression that the Minister concurred in his view, and yet he might find subsequently that there was some misunderstanding, and that his decision was repudiated and condemned.

"For these reasons I entirely concur in the conclusion arrived at by the honourable the Colonial Secretary in his minute—that the responsibility for the exercise here of the Queen's prerogative of pardon must either, as heretofore, rest solely with the Governor, or it must be transferred to a Minister who will be subject in this as in the discharge of other administrative functions only to those checks which the Constitution imposes on every servant of the Crown who is at the same time responsible to Parliament. The real question at issue is thus brought within narrow limits.

"The Colonial Secretary expresses 'grave doubts whether any change at present from the system which has hitherto prevailed here will be beneficial to the colony,' and he thinks that under the circumstances existing here the prerogative of pardon will be better exercised by the Governor than by the Minister. If the validity of such an argument were once admitted, it might perhaps be held to extend to other branches of administrative business. But the very essence of the Constitution is responsibility to Parliament for the administration of local affairs; and possessing, as the system does within itself, a prompt and effectual means of correcting any abuse of power, there can be little doubt that political training and official experience will soon impose restraints upon those impulses which sometimes mar the earlier attempts at self-government.

"I have felt ever since my first arrival in the colony that the practice which has hitherto prevailed here, of entrusting an important branch of local administration solely to an officer who is not responsible to Parliament, is highly objectionable; and as I fail to see that any plan of divided responsibility in such a matter can be devised, I can only repeat here what I have on several occasions since the receipt of Lord Kimberley's last dispatch stated to the Colonial Secretary in conversation—namely, that I am quite prepared to adopt a change of system; and I think for the future all applications for mitigation of sentences should be submitted to me through the intervention of a responsible Minister, whose opinion and advice as regards each case should be specified in writing upon the papers. "HERCULES ROBINSON.

"Government-house, 1st June 1874."

The Executive Council, on 2nd June, approved of the change, which was at once acted upon in all new cases. This step was not taken by me without serious misgivings, which I still feel, as to the entire wisdom of the change. But it seemed that the Ministers of the day had forced upon them by an unscrupulous party movement the choice between responsibility without authority and the authority of an active judgment coupled with a just responsibility. The new practice has now been substantially approved by the Secretary of State.*

After the defeat of Mr. Combes' motion on June 11th, Sir Hercules Robinson sought, as most persons will consider he had a right to seek, a consultation with the Chief Justice—Sir James Martin—(Sir Alfred Stephen having resigned in November, 1873)—to enable him the better to decide on a reconsideration of Gardiner's case. This consultation took place at Government-house on June 14th, the third day after the division in the Assembly. I and my colleagues, having regard to the exceptional state of the prerogative question up to that time, did not look upon Mr. Combes' motion as one entitled to political significance; and, as we were then over-burdened with public business, no communication in reference to it was made to the Governor for some days afterwards. On June 18th the Assembly sat all night, not rising until ten minutes past eight o'clock on the following morning. On that morning I received a letter from His Excellency, informing me that he had been anxiously reconsidering the whole case; that he had a long conversation with the Chief Justice on the subject; and that he had been led to the conclusion, in which Sir James Martin entirely concurred, that his only course was to let Gardiner have the conditional pardon promised to him, taking all practicable securities to prevent his returning to Australasia. The Governor further informed me in this letter that Sir James Martin said that if the reasons which had led to this conclusion, as explained by His Excellency to him, could be made known, public opinion would turn round and approve of the course taken; and His Excellency asked whether I thought it desirable to give publicity in some shape or other to his views. My first thought on reading Sir Hercules Robinson's letter was that if Gardiner's case could be reconsidered under the new practice of direct advice from Ministers, I might at once relieve His Excellency from all further embarrassment; and I wrote the following reply, which I am permitted to publish:—

"Colonial Secretary's Office,
"Sydney, June 19th 1874.

"MY DEAR SIR HERCULES—I did not leave the Assembly until after eight o'clock this morning, and then had to go out to Ashfield; in consequence, I have only just reached the office—twenty minutes past one p.m.

"I take up your note of yesterday respecting the prisoner Gardiner.

---

* See Lord Carnarvon's dispatch of October 7th 1874, No. 54.

The Prerogative of Pardon. 451

"Do I rightly understand that you desire me to tender to you my opinion or advice on the case as it stands? and I do not think Gardiner's case can be separated from the other twenty-three.

"I may say at once (though only as a private person) that my advice as Minister would be that you should strictly adhere to whatever you consider has been a positive or implied promise; and I am of course quite prepared to stand between you and Parliament, and take all the responsibility of such advice.

"I should be glad to learn, however, whether you wish that my opinion should cover the proposal you explained in a previous letter to send the prisoner to England, to be kept there under the observation of the police.

"Very truly yours,
"HENRY PARKES."

I received an immediate answer to the effect that the Governor's sole object in writing to me was to ascertain whether I thought it desirable for him to place before the public the reasons which had led him to the conclusion that he was bound in honour to carry out the implied promise of the Crown to Gardiner, no reference being made to my offer of advice. I have His Excellency's permission to publish my reply to this second letter.

"Colonial Secretary's Office,
"Sydney, June 19th 1874.

"MY DEAR SIR HERCULES—I do not see very clearly how you are to place before the public (except at a future time when your dispatches may be published) the reasons which have led you to your conclusion in the Gardiner case. Already statements and comments in variously tortured form are made to fix upon your advisers—and myself especially—charges of unworthy conduct in seeking to shelter ourselves by your interposition between us and Parliament. These unscrupulous references, often in a shape which it is not easy to notice, cannot be other than unpleasant to you, and they are extremely annoying to us. Any paper of the kind you suggest of which I can form a conception would be seized upon and used for this purpose. So I think.

"I believe your course throughout has been quite right with the single exception of a difference in point of time in Gardiner's case (two to four years only), in which my view may not be correct after all. And I should indeed be glad if anything could be done to make this appear more clear to the public. But the principal persons who are making this commotion do not want it to be made clear.

"As to the general public, the feeling will soon work itself to a sober and sound state.

"Yours faithfully,
"HENRY PARKES."

One of the many charges levelled at me in 1874, intensified by endless repetition, was that I endeavoured to shield myself from the displeasure of the Assembly by the interposition of the name

Appendix A.

and authority of the Governor. This charge in one of the daily papers assumed the odiously specific form that I, as a sworn adviser of the Crown, had led the Governor into a difficulty and then shrunk from my responsibility and sought to cast the blame upon innocent persons. The explanation now made will surely convince all honest minds of the injustice of those charges. My letters of June 19th will also show that, so far from counselling the minute of June 23rd, my unbiassed judgment was unfavourable to any publication at that time; and that I clearly foretold the use that would be made of any document of the kind. My judgment, however, was overruled; and I eventually consented to the now famous minute of His Excellency, and became responsible for laying it before Parliament. From that responsibility, once incurred, I never for a moment shrank.

I will not here attempt to defend the minute of June 23rd* from

---

* The following is a copy of the minute of Sir Hercules Robinson :—
"MINUTE BY THE GOVERNOR FOR THE EXECUTIVE COUNCIL.

"I have to lay before the Executive Council six petitions and memorials which have been addressed to me with regard to the proposed mitigation of Gardiner's sentence. These representations, viewed in connexion with the public discussions which have recently taken place on the same subject, have led me very carefully to consider whether any fresh facts have been brought to light which would justify me in disappointing now the expectations which I raised when this prisoner's case was first submitted to me—about eighteen months ago.

"It is true that no positive compact was then made with the prisoner, or any decision given in the nature of an absolute remission, which would of course have been irrevocable; but it is beyond question that a hope was held out to him by my minute of the 5th December 1872 that, if he continued to conduct himself well, he would in all probability be allowed a pardon, conditional on his leaving the country, so soon as he had served ten years of his sentence.

"I think that this may fairly be held to have been tantamount to a promise, contingent alone on the prisoner's good conduct in gaol; and that it was so viewed by myself at the time, and by the honourable the Colonial Secretary subsequently, is apparent from my minute of the 7th December 1872, in which I stated—'I have already decided to grant a conditional pardon at the termination of ten years' imprisonment;' and from the Colonial Secretary's minute of the 24th April last, in which, when submitting to me a petition for Gardiner's unconditional release, he observes —'The prisoner has been authorised a conditional pardon, the condition being exile.' The Sheriff, too, obviously viewed the matter in precisely the same light, and referred in his letter of the 21st January 1873, and in his minute of the 20th April 1874, to Gardiner's case as one that had been practically decided and disposed of.

the attacks made upon it by gentlemen like Mr. Alexander Stuart. It has been defended with conclusive argument by the Governor himself in his despatches to the Secretary of State. But it is

"I may mention that it has been the practice here for many years for the Governor, when dealing with applications for mitigation which have appeared premature, to fix a date at which the case might again be brought under his consideration. Hopes so held out have always been regarded by the prison authorities, and by the prisoners themselves, as equivalent to promises of pardon, conditional on good conduct; and in every such case the expectation so raised has been, I believe, scrupulously fulfilled. I remember one case in which Sir Alfred Stephen, as Administrator of the Government, intimated to one of the most prominent and daring of the bushrangers that his case might again be brought forward for consideration as soon as he had served seven out of the nineteen years to which he had been sentenced. The papers came before me at the time specified, and, as the case appeared to me a bad one, I declined to sanction any greater remission than that contemplated under the general regulations for bushranging cases, unless Sir Alfred Stephen's intimation was held to be a promise. I was informed by the Sheriff that this was unquestionably the view in which the decision had been looked on in the gaol, and I accordingly authorised the prisoner's discharge on a conditional pardon four years before the date at which he would have been eligible for exile under the special mitigation regulations laid down for such cases.

"Of course I am aware that, under certain circumstances, it might be wise and proper to withhold the fulfilment of such promises, whether positive or implied. For example, a promise given under false representations would not be binding; and a promise to release a prisoner which it was subsequently found would, if carried out, imperil the public safety, should be cancelled. The practical question for consideration in the present case is, therefore, simply this—Are there any such grounds that would justify me in now withholding the conditional pardon which nearly two years ago I led Gardiner and his friends to expect that he might receive about this time?

"I have seen it urged that Gardiner's case was decided upon false representations—it being alleged that some of the signatures attached to the petition were forgeries, and that there was a previous conviction against Gardiner in Victoria which had been concealed. But I think these grounds, even if they were facts—which they have not been proved to be—would be quite insufficient to release me from my implied promise. In a petition so numerously and influentially signed, a few signatures more or less of persons of whom I had no knowledge would have been immaterial; and I cannot say that my decision would have been different if it had been stated on the papers that, before Gardiner commenced his criminal career in New South Wales, he had been convicted in Victoria of horse-stealing in 1850—nearly a quarter of a century ago. In view of the grave character of his crimes in New South Wales such a comparatively minor offence would have appeared insignificant. I must, therefore, as I have said, dismiss these pleas as insufficient.

quite clear that even Mr. Robertson, with all his lynx-eyed watchfulness for favourable points of attack, saw nothing very objectionable in this minute until he became aware of its effect upon

"The question remains—Would the public safety be in any way jeopardised if the expectation held out to Gardiner of being allowed to exile after ten years were now fulfilled? I think not. Sir Alfred Stephen observes, in his letter on Gardiner's case, that 'the end and object of all punishment are—first, the preventing of the individual, and secondly, the deterring of other individuals, from the committing of similar crimes.' Have these ends been attained in the present case? I think they have. The sentence of thirty-two years passed upon Gardiner was imposed at a time of great excitement, and his punishment would seem to have been measured more in view of the crimes with which he was supposed to have been connected than with reference solely to those of which he was actually convicted. It was probably never intended that such a sentence should be served in full; and, looking dispassionately at all the circumstances of the case, I consider that ten years of rigorous penal discipline within the walls of a gaol—the first two years in irons—followed by expatriation for a further period of twenty-two years, is a punishment amply sufficient to satisfy the ends of justice and to deter others from following Gardiner's bad example.

"Whether Gardiner's apparent reformation is sincere is a point which time alone can determine. I am myself disposed to think that, after the experience he has gained, and under the altered circumstances of the colony, he might be released even in Sydney without any substantial danger; but there are many persons who apparently think differently, and who believe that if Gardiner had an opportunity he would revert to bushranging; and these fears, which are entitled to consideration, have been aggravated by a few isolated robberies which have occurred just at the time when this case was attracting public attention. Assuming, however, that these apprehensions are reasonable and well-founded, it appears to me that they are fully met by the condition of exile, which the Government will of course take effectual means to enforce. A legislative enactment authorises and empowers the Government to take the necessary steps for this purpose, and none of the old and settled counties will offer opportunities for the peculiar crime of bushranging, even if Gardiner were disposed to revert to it. I do not think that sufficient weight has been allowed throughout the community to this condition of exile which it is intended to attach to Gardiner's pardon, and which supplies, in my opinion, effectual security for 'preventing the individual from the committing of similar crimes.'

"The end and object of all punishment would therefore seem to have been secured by the course which it is proposed to adopt in the present case. The prisoner has, I hold, been sufficiently punished, and he can, I conceive, with safety be set free upon condition of his leaving the country. If, while entertaining as I do these opinions, I were to break faith with the prisoner, and retain him in gaol beyond the time specified for his liberation, I should be doing so, not because I think such a course necessary, but simply in

The Prerogative of Pardon. 455

the heated feelings of less intelligent persons. The minute was laid on the table on the last day of the session†, June 25th. The next session commenced November 3rd, when the minute had been before the public more than four months. Mr. Robertson did not fail to attack the Government the moment the House met, but the Governor's minute on the Gardiner case did not form one of his grounds of attack. He submitted an amendment on the address, censuring the Government for not calling Parliament together at an earlier date, for its conduct in the matter of the Pacific Mail Service, and for other matters; but his motion contained no word of censure on the Governor's minute. On this motion of censure Mr. Robertson was beaten by 37 to 13, showing with sufficient clearness the feeling of the Assembly on the general policy of the Government. On November 25th Mr. Combes brought forward a resolution condemning the Governor's minute, which was substantially copied by Mr. Robertson as his amendment on the address in January following. The House divided, with 28 to 28, Mr. Combes' motion being again negatived

---

response to clamour which I believe to be unreasonable and unjust. It is indispensable for the maintenance of prison discipline that every hope held out to prisoners should be scrupulously fulfilled; that every promise made or implied should be held sacred, or broken only on grounds the sufficiency of which would be apparent even to prisoners' minds. I can see no such grounds in the present case, and I am convinced that the moral bad effect upon the whole body of prisoners throughout the colony, as well as upon the community generally, which would result from disappointing without sufficient reason an expectation raised by Her Majesty's Representative, would be infinitely greater than any practical inconvenience which would be likely to result from keeping faith with the prisoner, and allowing him to leave the country.

"For these reasons I think that Gardiner should receive a conditional pardon at the time when he was led to expect one; and that the Government should at the same time take steps to secure, as far as practicable, the continued absence of the prisoner from the Australasian colonies during the unexpired term of his sentence. I am sorry to think that such an exercise of the Royal prerogative of pardon is unfavourably regarded at the present moment by certain sections of the public, but it appears to me that the course which I suggest is the only course now open to the Government consistent with honour and justice, and I confidently anticipate that the fairness of this view will eventually be acknowledged by all impartial and reflecting members of the community.

"HERCULES ROBINSON.

" Government-house, 23rd June 1874."

† The dates will show that it could not have been produced earlier.

by the Speaker's casting vote. Ministers could not regard this decision by the vote of the Speaker as they regarded the decision of June 11th. The terms of the motion, and the course of action virtually marked by disapproval, were wholly different, and assumed more distinctly a political complexion. We could not hope after this vote to conduct business in the Assembly with satisfaction, and we therefore advised the Crown to dissolve the House, which in any case was approaching, under the new Triennial Act, the end of its existence.

The general election that followed resulted in the return of a large majority of members who either openly approved, or abstained from expressing disapproval, of the general policy of the Government. The new Parliament met on January 27th 1875, and Mr. Robertson, having learned a lesson from Mr. Combes, abstained from attacking the Government on general grounds, but moved an amendment on the address in the following words :—

"We would desire, with reference to the important matter which led to the dissolution of the late Parliament, most respectfully to express our regret that your Excellency's responsible Ministers should have advised you to communicate to the Legislative Assembly your minute to the Executive Council, dated the 23rd June last, with reference to the release of the prisoner Gardiner, because it is indefensible in certain of its allegations, and because, if it is considered to be an answer to the respectful and earnest petitions of the people, it is highly undesirable to convert the records of this House into a means of conveying censure or reproof to our constituents ; and if it refer to the discussions in this Chamber, then it is in spirit and effect a breach of the constitutional privileges of Parliament."

Thus, the Governor's minute, which had been entirely overlooked by Mr. Robertson in the beginning of November, was in January made Mr. Robertson's battle-ground. It was decided by my colleagues, contrary to my wish and advice, that I should follow Mr. Robertson in the debate. No other Minister spoke, nor was any motion for adjournment proposed. The division was taken before midnight on the 28th, and in a House of 62 members the Government was defeated by a majority of four.

The defeated Ministers did not wait for any further expression of the feeling of Parliament, but on the next day our resignations were tendered to the Governor, who, however, declined for several days to accept them. His Excellency very naturally felt aggrieved by the words in the amendment which declared that his minute was "indefensible in certain of its allegations." The address as amended was presented by the Speaker, no motion having been

The Prerogative of Pardon. 457

made for its presentation by the House. On February 2nd His Excellency sent down by his *aide-de-camp* the following message in reply :—

" 1. The Governor, having been precluded by the mode of presentation of the address of the Legislative Assembly in reply to his opening speech from giving his answer in the usual manner, deems it respectful to the Assembly to do so by message.

" 2. He acknowledges with satisfaction their expressions of loyalty to Her Most Gracious Majesty.

" 3. He cannot, consistently with his duty, acquiesce in the statement that a minute laid by him before the Executive Council was indefensible in certain of its allegations. As ultimately responsible for the exercise of the prerogative of mercy, the Governor claims for himself unreserved freedom of communication with the Executive Council while seeking its advice, and he cannot admit that the minute, viewed in that light, was not entirely justifiable.

"4. While thus asserting the constitutional rights of the office which he has the honour to hold, the Governor trusts he will ever pay the fullest respect to those of the representatives of the people, and he therefore, with this qualification, is prepared to accept the decision of the Assembly.

" Government-house, Sydney, 2nd February 1875."

The Governor in the first instance entrusted the formation of a new Administration to Sir William Manning, and it was not until Sir William returned his commission, on February 5th, that Mr. Robertson's services were sought by His Excellency. When Mr. Robertson attended at Government-house, in obedience to the Governor's summons, the following memorandum was handed to him at the same time that he was asked by His Excellency to undertake the task of forming a Ministry:—

" MEMORANDUM BY HIS EXCELLENCY THE GOVERNOR FOR MR. ROBERTSON.

" I desire to point out that for any delay or difficulty connected with the formation of a new Administration I am not responsible.

" If the amendment to the address had stopped, as I think it should have done, at the end of the first sentence—expressing regret that I had been advised to lay my Executive Council minute upon the table of the House— all difficulty would have been obviated. I should, in such case, have accepted the resignation of Ministers, and probably at once have sent for Mr. Robertson to form a new Administration.˙ I should not myself have concurred with the House as to the impropriety of the step censured, or as to the importance attached to it; but my own views on these points would have been immaterial. I should have recognised the fact that the matter was one upon which it was competent for the House to hold and express its own opinion, and I should at once have proceeded to give to that opinion its intended constitutional significance.

"But the amendment went further, and proceeded to give reasons for the regret entertained by the House, which it was quite unnecessary to communicate to me. The first reason advanced was that my minute to the Executive Council was indefensible in certain of its allegations. It appeared to me that this was not only a personal imputation upon myself, but an invasion of the constitutional rights of my office; and that the Legislative Assembly were not justified in presenting to me an address couched in such terms.

"My difficulty was increased by the unusual mode adopted by the Assembly as regards the presentation of the address. It has been the almost invariable practice for the Legislative Assembly to attend at Government-house with the address in answer to the Governor's speech on opening Parliament, to which the Governor has been in the habit of giving a verbal reply. On this occasion the course adopted left me no alternatives but silence or a message; and I had no opportunity for the latter subsequent to the resignation of Ministers, which took place late on Friday, 29th January, before the following Tuesday, the 2nd February—the next day appointed for the meeting of Parliament.

"When, therefore, the Cabinet tendered their resignations, I felt placed in a position of unprecedented difficulty; for, whilst I was prepared to give effect to the implied wish of the Assembly as regards a change of Ministry, I was not prepared to pass over in silence an encroachment upon the prerogative of the Crown. But I could not accept the resignation of Ministers until I had placed the formation of an Administration in other hands. If I had sent down my protest against what I conceived to be the unconstitutional part of the Assembly's amendment before accepting the resignation of Ministers, my readiness to acquiesce in the decision of the Assembly upon that part which was clearly within their constitutional rights might possibly have been called in question. If, on the other hand, I had sent for Mr. Robertson, and entrusted to him the formation of a Government, and then sent down my protest to the House, Mr. Robertson, and probably the leading Members of the Opposition who had carried the amendment, would have been absent from their seats. It appeared to me indispensable that the leaders of the party who had carried the amendment should be present in their places and free to take what action they pleased when my message in reference to the amendment was read to the House.

"A fair escape from these several difficulties presented itself in the selection of Sir William Manning, a distinguished member of the Upper House, to form a Government. Sir William Manning's ability and character, and the high respect in which he is held throughout the entire community, appeared to fit him especially for such a position. He had been associated with Mr. Robertson in former Administrations, and he had been designated by public rumour as one of the leading members of a new Government, in the event of Mr. Robertson being entrusted with its formation.

"Besides, apart from the special reasons which led me to ask Sir William Manning to undertake the responsibility of forming an Administration, the plan seemed to me to offer the best possible chance of forming a strong Government. It appeared to me that, supported as I thought he would

The Prerogative of Pardon. 459

have been by the leading members of the Opposition, it would have been possible for Sir William Manning to have united under his leadership a party able to carry on the Government of the country with vigour for a lengthened period. I have been disappointed in the experiment; but, looking to the state of parties in the Assembly, the narrowness of the late majority, and the exceptional character of the question which resulted in the present crisis, I fail to see that there was any arrangement which held out a better prospect of success—viewed solely in the light of the public good. I do not regret, therefore, having made the attempt.

"With these observations, which are, I think, called for from me under the peculiar circumstances of this case, I am prepared to give effect to Sir William Manning's recommendation, which is that, as he has failed in obtaining the help he anticipated, I should now send for Mr. Robertson.

"HERCULES ROBINSON.

"Government-house, Sydney, 5th February 1875."

Under these circumstances Mr. Robertson came back to office in February 1875, having succeeded in converting the Gardiner case into a lever to displace a Government, respecting whose general management of affairs there was no evidence up to the last that the country disapproved. With him, and by the same means also, came back—one as Attorney-General and the other as Colonial Treasurer—Mr. Dalley and Mr. Forster, who had been the most active influential agents in obtaining the mitigation of Gardiner's sentence. The change is unique, and it is to be hoped will not soon be paralleled in the progress of responsible government in the Australian colonies. Yet it cannot be denied that Mr. Robertson and his friends are in one sense deserving of the prize which, after so many desperate efforts, they have at length grasped. No men ever strove more laboriously, or hesitated less, in their sacrifices to obtain their object.*

It may be doubted still whether this noble struggle for office will prove an unmixed good to our political institutions. Precedents may possibly be drawn from it hereafter to justify unlooked-for courses of action. It is difficult indeed to foresee what resistance to majorities, what abuse of Parliamentary forms, what desperate use of favouring chances, what bold repudiation of one's own inconvenient words or actions, what reckless misrepresentation of others, what wholesale traffic in calumny, what systematic waste of public time, could not be supported by the examples afforded by Mr.

---

* In a marked manner the tactics of the Opposition to the Parkes Administration in the session of 1873-4 was to occupy time so as to render the progress of public business next to impossible. Four of the present Ministers during that session made no fewer than 1800 speeches.

Robertson and some of his present colleagues when lately in Opposition.

One word as to the predicted consequences of Sir Hercules Robinson's decision in Gardiner's case. Have any of the evil prognostics been fulfilled? Has bushranging been encouraged into fresh life? Has crime erected a more defiant crest? On the other hand, has any clearer or safer rule of criminal treatment been established by the intemperate agitations which Mr. Robertson did his utmost to keep alive till his end was answered? Has he in any way contributed one jot of wisdom towards the settlement of the difficult question of prison management? Is it not a fact that Mr. Robertson's Government, during the eleven months of its existence, has released prisoners whose cases are worse than the case of the prisoner Gardiner? On the whole, the result proves that the Governor's decision to allow Gardiner to exile himself, in consideration of his ten years of good conduct in a close gaol, was well-judged, sound, and wise.

HENRY PARKES.
Sydney, January 4th, 1876.

APPENDIX B.

APPOINTMENTS TO THE MAGISTRACY.

[As the Donaldson Ministry of 1856 now belongs to history, there can be no objection to the publication of the following correspondence :—]

Private and confidential.]

Colonial Secretary's Office,
Sydney, June 1856.

SIR—As a new Commission of the Peace is about to be issued, it is desirable to make it as complete as possible by appointing only the very *best men* as magistrates, and such gentlemen only as are *fit, proper,* and of *undoubted honour* and *respectability*. In this I am quite sure you will agree with me, and as you must have an intimate knowledge of the resident gentlemen in the district you represent in Parliament, may I beg that you will be so good as to favour me with the names of the persons whom you would recommend to be appointed magistrates?

Appointments to the Magistracy. 461

All the present justices whose characters and conduct are unimpeached, and who have manifested a disposition to give a reasonable amount of time and attention to the discharge of the duties of their offices, will probably be included in the new commission; but all unfit and improper persons will be silently left out, and will thenceforth cease to be qualified as magistrates.

Any communication you may make will be considered by the Government as strictly confidential.

I have the honour to be, sir,
Your most obedient servant,
STUART A. DONALDSON.

Henry Parkes, Esq., M.P., Sydney.

Private.] Ryde, June 30th 1856.

SIR—I beg to acknowledge the receipt of your communication marked "private and confidential," informing me that a new commission of the peace is about to be issued, and requesting that I will favour you with the names of the persons I " would recommend to be appointed magistrates ;" and, further, intimating to me the considerations that will guide the Government in re-constructing the commission.

In reply, I have the honour to state that I do not feel at liberty to make any recommendation in a matter of such grave concern to the public welfare, wherein, it appears to me, the Government should act without being influenced by parties who cannot share their responsibility. I have always held the opinion that great mischief resulted from recommendations of this kind being made by members of the Legislature. In some instances I have witnessed the pernicious effects where members of the former Council recommended their friends for the commission of the peace in order to secure certain interests in their constituencies, and not on account of any visible merit in the persons so recommended; and I have heard the late Attorney-General, Mr. Plunket, openly and repeatedly declare that the worst magistrates were those who had been recommended for appointment by members of Council. I do not see how it could be otherwise; for I am sure it will not be denied that some members of the present Parliament are qualified for the performance of any duty rather than that of selecting men to administer justice in our inferior courts, where the utter friendlessness in some cases, and the

Appendix B.

deep villany in others, require a painstaking and penetrative intelligence not less than a calm integrity of purpose in the magistrate.

I assure you I most cordially agree with you that the "very best men" should be appointed to the new commission. This is demanded equally by the interests of justice and the honour of the country. But were the Government to employ the means within their power for obtaining a correct knowledge of the character of gentlemen in the various districts where magistrates are required, without reference avowedly to any appointment or affording any clue as to the purpose for which the information was sought, I honestly think they would be enabled of their own exclusive action to make the "very best" selection that could be made under the circumstances of the colony. The course now proposed to be pursued will probably lead to this result—that while the better and more independent members decline to interfere, those who have their little private ends to answer will freely avail themselves of the opportunity held out to them; and thus the public will get the ascendancy of a very undesirable kind of counsel.

These remarks I fear will be deemed gratuitous on my part; but the suggestions I have ventured upon will at least show that I am not actuated by any political feeling, nor desirous of throwing any impediment in the way of the present Government.

I am, sir,
Your most obedient servant,
HENRY PARKES.

The Honourable Stuart A. Donaldson, M.P.,
Colonial Secretary.

APPENDIX C.

APPOINTMENTS TO THE CIVIL SERVICE.

[THE following letter was addressed to a gentleman occupying an elevated station, in reply to a note transmitting to Mr. Parkes a testimonial in favour of the promotion of a member of the Civil Service :—]

Appointments to the Civil Service. 463

Colonial Secretary's Office,
30th May 1868.

My Dear * * * * * *—I have your note respecting Mr. * * * * * * *, and have read the paper in his favour signed by gentlemen resident at * * * * * * *. My experience tells me that testimonials of this kind can be obtained by any public officer whose personal qualities are even negatively good, and that persons in authority cannot be guided by less safe evidence of fitness for duty. No constable is dismissed who does not produce a number of gentlemen who will testify to his good character.

If the public service is to be raised in efficiency and economy, the considerations *that ought to be forced on men in office*, whoever they may be, are :—

1. What does the public require in the situation for which this salary is paid?
2. Who is the best man to do what the public requires?

So long as we consider the interests of the applicant before the interests of the public in filling situations, so long will the public who pays be served badly and at unnecessary cost. For myself, the longer I remain in office the more I am determined to act on some such principles as I have indicated. I have no friends of my own whom I wish to serve. Why should I disregard my own judgment in serving the friends of others?

In the present case these gentlemen would act more to the purpose if they could show in what way the transference of Mr. * * * * * * * to some other situation would increase his usefulness. Not one of them, I apprehend, would take him into his own service at a higher salary and with lighter duties.

In England an order has been issued by the Lords of the Treasury against persons in the public service seeking to use this kind of influence on their own behalf. It is pointed out very justly that either they are not prepared to rest their claims upon their merits, or they suppose that the heads of departments will be open to considerations apart from the public interests.

You have frequently yourself made observations reflecting on the manner in which appointments have been made in this colony. But I think you would find great difficulty in pointing out any situation for which Mr. * * * * * * * is specially fitted in the sense of best serving the public. Say the Customs : the public ought to have young, vigorous, active men in every branch of that service. In my judgment the time is come when the public service of this colony ought to assume the character of a profession, and only young men ought to be received into it, who should all have a "fair field" to work themselves up through the varying ranks of official employment.

I hope I shall not be misunderstood in what I have said. I certainly have no feeling adverse to Mr. * * * * * * *, and shall be glad to see him receive any appointment for which his capabilities really qualify him.

Yours very truly,
HENRY PARKES.

www.ingramcontent.com/pod-product-compliance
Lightning Source LLC
Chambersburg PA
CBHW051843300426
44117CB00006B/256